MSU LIBRARIES
3 2109 00094 5114

WITHDRAWN
D1365264

POPULAR MUSIC

Other Books by Nat Shapiro

Hear Me Talkin' to Ya (Co-Editor)
The Jazz Makers (Co-Editor)

VOLUME 1

1950 - 1959

POPULAR MUSIC

An Annotated Index of American Popular Songs

Edited by

NAT SHAPIRO

ADRIAN PRESS

First Edition

Library of Congress Catalog Card Number 64-23761

Jacket designed by Robert Cato

Printed in the United States of America
by the Lerman Printing Co., New York, N. Y.

 426

POPULAR MUSIC

An Annotated Index of American Popular Songs
Volume 1
1950 - 1959

Additional Information and Corrections

p. 15. **Just Say I Love Her,** also known as **Dicitencello Vuie**
Adapted from an Italian song by R. Falvo. An earlier version by Jack Val and Jimmy Dale, entitled "That Night in Napoli," originally published in 1939.

p. 31. **Cherry Pink and Apple Blossom White**
Revived in 1961 with best-selling record by Jerry Murad and his Harmonicats (Columbia).

p. 38. **It's All in the Game**
Best-selling records in 1951 and 1958 by Tommy Edwards (M-G-M).

p. 56. **Full Time Job**
Correct spelling of writer's name, Gerry Teifer.

p. 62. **Just a Little Lovin' Will Go a Long Way**
Original copyright date, 1948. Introduced by Eddy Arnold. Best-selling record in 1952 by Eddie Fisher (RCA Victor).

p. 97. **Song from Moulin Rouge, The,** also known as **Where Is Your Heart**
Correct title as listed above.

p. 120. **Midnight Sun**
Words by Johnny Mercer, music by Sonny Burke and Lionel Hampton.

p. 128. **Till Then**
Original copyright date, 1944. Best-selling record in 1944 by The Mills Brothers (Decca).

p. 143. **I Wish You Love**
Lee Wilson is a pseudonym for Albert A. Beach.

p. 204. **Freight Train**
Original version attributed to, but never copyrighted by, Elizabeth Cotten. Introduced in England by Peggy Seeger.

Acknowledgments

The Editor is particularly indebted to Betty Martone, Miles Kreuger, Bill Randle, Felice Faust, Hal B. Cook, Tom Noonan, Russell Sanjek, Saul Weinbaum, Elias Feilich, Mark Sikelianos, Amy L. Shapiro, the Index Department of the American Society of Composers, Authors and Publishers (ASCAP), the Index Department of Broadcast Music, Inc. (BMI), and the scores of authors, composers, and performers who patiently, and sometimes painfully, took the time to remember, confirm, and correct.

Special credit belongs to Dr. Vera Miller (Mrs. Nat Shapiro), whose research training, editorial meticulousness, and determined energy helped to bring the masses of material collected over the years to organized and usable form.

Table of Contents

About the Book and How To Use It

Galloping chaos has been a classic and chronic symptom of the artistic as well as the commercial state of American popular music throughout its entire untidy history. The very special, inbred community of music publishers, song writers, and performers of popular music is peopled by a remarkable collection of artists and hacks, craftsmen and hoodlums, geniuses and mountebanks, aesthetes and vulgarians, poets and pedants, and philosophers and fools. Considering this marvelous motley, it is no wonder that a reliable record of the accomplishments —and follies—of these colorful souls is virtually non-existent.

This volume is the first of a series, the aim of which is to set down in permanent and practical form a selective, annotated list of the significant popular songs of our times. Previous indexes of popular music have either dealt with special areas, such as jazz or theatre and film music, or been concerned chiefly with songs which achieved a degree of popularity as measured by the variably reliable music business trade indicators.

There is no single source of comprehensive information about popular songs, and those sources which do exist do not publish complete material about even the musical works with which they are directly concerned. Two of the major proprietors of basic information about our popular music are the performing rights societies—the American Society of Composers, Authors and Publishers (ASCAP) and Broadcast Music, Inc. (BMI). Although each of these organizations has considerable information about the songs of its own writer and publisher members and has also issued indexes of its own songs, their files and published indexes are designed primarily for clearance identification by the commercial users of music. Their publications of annual or periodic lists of their "hits" necessarily include only a small fraction of their songs, and the facts given about these are also limited. Both ASCAP and BMI are, however, invaluable and indispensable sources of data about popular music. It is just that their data and special knowledge are not readily accessible to the researcher.

Another basic source of information about musical compositions and their creators and publishers is the *Catalog of Copyright Entries* issued by the Copyright Office of The Library of Congress. Each year, two massive volumes are published by the Copyright Office listing each published, unpublished, republished, and renewed copyright of songs registered with the Office. While these volumes are helpful in determining the precise date of the declaration of the original ownership of musical works, they contain no other information, are unwieldy, and, lacking a unified index, difficult to use. To complicate matters further, some authors, composers, and publishers have been known to employ rather makeshift methods of protecting their works legally, and there are several songs listed in *Popular Music* which are not to be found in The Library of Congress files.

In preparing this series, the Editor was faced with a number of separate problems. The first and most important of these was the basic one of selection. In this regard, the solution was determined by adherence to the stated aim of the project itself—to offer the user of the Index as comprehensive and accurate a listing of significant popular songs as possible. Significance was decided objectively and without any editorial prejudice for or against any type of popular music. It was not the Editor's intention to evaluate the importance or quality of rock and roll, show tunes, Blue Grass music, movie themes, or nonsense songs. Rather, it was the purpose of *Popular Music* to document those musical works which (1) achieved a substantial degree of popular acceptance, (2) were exposed to the public in especially notable circumstances, or (3) were accepted and given important performances by influential musical and dramatic artists.

Another problem was whether or not to classify the songs as to type. The 1950's were characterized by an integration of several divergent streams of creative musical activity in the United States. Country and western songs, rhythm and blues, authentic folk music, and jazz found enormous new audiences as the result of a number of economic, social, and cultural factors. A growing population, with an increase in the number of young people; general economic prosperity; a phenomenally expanded phonograph record industry; television; the rise of Nashville, Tennessee as a center of musical creativity and productivity; and the intensified struggle for civil rights and equal opportunity for Negroes—all these elements, and others as well, were related to the integration of several formerly restricted types of songs into the mainstream of American popular music. This integration was, perhaps, the outstanding development of the 1950's.

Under these circumstances, it seemed arbitrary and misleading to label a given song as "rhythm and blues," "country and western," "folk," or "jazz." Most works of music are subject to any number of interpretations and, although it is possible to describe a particular performance, it is more difficult to give a musical composition a label applicable not only to its origin but to its subsequent musical history. In fact, the most significant versions of some songs are often quite at variance with their origins. It is believed, however, that the information in *Popular Music* for such songs indicates the important facts about not only their origins but also their subsequent lives.

The principal sources of information for the titles, authors, composers, publishers, and dates of copyright of the songs in this volume were the Copyright Office of The Library of Congress, ASCAP, BMI, and individual writers and publishers. Data about best-selling recordings were obtained principally from the three leading music business trade journals—*Billboard, Cash Box,* and *Variety.* For the historical notes; anecdotes; information about foreign, folk, public domain, and classical origins; and identification of theatrical, film, and television introducers of songs, the Editor relied on his own and the New York Public Library's collections of record album notes, theatre programs, sheet music, newspaper and magazine articles, and other material.

The information for each song in Volume 1, published in the 1950's, is listed under the year of its original copyright. The reader is, therefore, advised to consult the List of Titles to determine the year of the song's original copyright.

The primary listing for a song published in the 1950's includes, first of all, the full title and alternate title or titles, exactly as they appear on The Library of Congress copyright card or, in some cases, the sheet music. Since even a casual perusal of the List of Titles indicates considerable variation in spelling and punctuation, it should be noted that these are neither editorial nor typographical errors but the colloquialisms of the music trade. The title of a given song as it appears in this volume is the one under which it is legally registered.

In all cases, the primary listing reports the author or authors and the composer and composers. Here, too, the reader will find variations in the spelling of a song writer's name. Again, the form of the name of a writer used in connection with any particular song is the form under which that copyright was registered.

The publisher listed is the current publisher. Since *Popular Music* is designed as a practical reference work rather than an academic study, and since copyrights more than occasionally change hands, the current publisher is given instead of the original holder of the copyright.

If the song is of foreign origin, the primary listing indicates the country of origin after the title. Additional information about the original title, copyright date, writers, publisher, and other facts about the adaptation are noted.

The primary listing also includes first or best-selling records, indicating the performer and the record company; the production in which the song was introduced and, where important, by whom it was introduced in the case of theatre, film, and television songs; any other performers identified with the song; and other relevant data.

In all cases, if any fact about a song relates to a year other than the year of the original copyright, the year of such fact is noted in the primary listing. Cross-references to such songs appear under the other years in which there are significant facts for them. The one exception is that there are no cross-references to best-selling records appearing in the year immediately following the copyright year. Since many songs become popular in the year following the copyright year, such cross-references would have cluttered the book to the point of distracting the reader. The year of any annotation, including those of best-selling records, subsequent to the copyright year is, of course, noted in the primary listing. Cross-references for all important alternate titles of songs are also listed.

The List of Publishers, which is alphabetically arranged, includes the performing rights affiliation (ASCAP or BMI) and current address of each publisher of a song appearing in Volume 1.

A word of apology for a minor, temporary inconvenience to the reader: Volume 1 includes some songs which were copyrighted in years before 1950. Such songs are listed under the years in the 1950's in which they achieved note, with only a reference to the year of the original copyright. The primary listing for such songs will appear in the appropriate forthcoming volumes of *Popular Music,* covering the decades before 1950. Repeating full listings for earlier songs in each of the later volumes would be inconsistent and cumbersome. The reader's inconvenience will be diminished substantially with the publication of each of the forthcoming volumes of *Popular Music,* and it is hoped that, before very long, he will have available to him the comprehensive, selective documentation of American popular songs of the twentieth century which *Popular Music* will be.

1950-1959

1950

Accidents Will Happen
Words by Johnny Burke, music by James Van Heusen.
Burke-Van Heusen & Associates Music Corp.
Introduced by Bing Crosby and Dorothy Kirsten in *Mr. Music* (film).

Adelaide's Lament
Words and music by Frank Loesser.
Frank Music Corp.
Introduced by Vivian Blaine in *Guys and Dolls* (musical).

All My Love (French)
English words by Mitchell Parish, French words by Henri Contet, music by Paul Durand.
Éditions Continental, Paris, France, 1948/Mills Music, Inc.
Introduced in France as "Bolero" by Jacqueline Francois. Best-selling record by Patti Page (Mercury).

American Beauty Rose
Words and music by Hal David, Redd Evans, and Arthur Altman.
Jefferson Music Co., Inc.
Best-selling record by Frank Sinatra (Columbia).

And You'll Be Home
Words by Johnny Burke, music by James Van Heusen.
Burke-Van Heusen & Associates Music Corp.
Introduced by Bing Crosby in *Mr. Music* (film).

Andiamo
Words by Dorothy Fields, music by Harold Arlen.
Harwin Music Corp.
Introduced by Ezio Pinza in *Mr. Imperium* (film).

Anticipation Blues
Words and music by Tennessee Ernie Ford and Cliffie Stone.
Century Songs, Inc.
Best-selling record by Tennessee Ernie Ford (Capitol).

A-Razz-A-Ma-Tazz
Words by Irving Taylor, music by Dave Coleman.
Consolidated Music Publishers, Inc.
Introduced by Teresa Brewer.

A-round the Corner (Beneath the Berry Tree) (South African)
Words and music by Josef Marais.
Frank Music Corp.
From the South African folk song repertoire of Josef Marais. Best-selling record in 1952 by Jo Stafford (Columbia).

Autumn Leaves (French)
English words by Johnny Mercer, French words by Jacques Prévert, music by Joseph Kosma.
Enoch & Cie, Paris, France, 1947/Ardmore Music Corp.
From the Prévert poem, "Les Feuilles Mortes." Popularized in France by Juliette Greco. Featured in *Les Portes de la Nuit* (French film). Best-selling record in the United States, instrumental, in 1955 by pianist Roger Williams (Kapp).

Baby, Baby, Baby
Words by Mack David, music by Jerry Livingston.
Famous Music Corp.
Introduced by Teresa Brewer in *Those Redheads from Seattle* (film).

Bad, Bad Whiskey
Words and music by Thomas Maxwell Davis.
American Academy of Music, Inc.
Best-selling record in 1950 and 1951 by Amos Milburn (Aladdin).

Bamboo
Words by Buddy Bernier, music by Nat Simon.
Shapiro, Bernstein & Co., Inc.
Best-selling record by Vaughn Monroe (RCA Victor).

Be Mine
Words by Jack Elliott, music by Harold Spina.
Edwin H. Morris & Co., Inc.
Best-selling record by Mindy Carson (RCA Victor).

Be My Love
Words by Sammy Cahn, music by Nicholas Brodszky.
Robbins Music Corp.
Introduced by Mario Lanza in *The Toast of New Orleans* (film). Nominated for Academy Award, 1950. Best-selling record by Mario Lanza (RCA Victor).

Beloved, Be Faithful
Words and music by Ervin Drake and Jimmy Shirl.
Pickwick Music Corp.
Best-selling record by Russ Morgan and his Orchestra (Decca).

Best Thing for You, The
Words and music by Irving Berlin.
Irving Berlin Music Corp.
Introduced by Ethel Merman and Paul Lukas in *Call Me Madam* (musical).

Bewitched, see 1941.

Birmingham Bounce
Words and music by Sid "Hardrock" Gunter.
Prince Music.
Best-selling record by Red Foley (Decca).

Bloodshot Eyes
Words and music by Hank Penny and Ruth Hall.
Lois Publishing Co.
Best-selling records in 1950 by Hank Penny (King) and in 1951 by Wynonie Harris (King).

Blue Light Boogie
Words and music by Jessie Mae Robinson and Louis Jordan.
Cherio Music Publishers, Inc.
Best-selling record by Louis Jordan (Decca).

Blue Shadows
Words and music by Lloyd C. Glenn.
Arc Music Corp./High Society Music Publishers.
Best-selling record by Lowell Fulson (Swingtime).

Boutonniere
Words by Bob Hilliard, music by Dave Mann.
Joy Music, Inc.
Best-selling record in 1951 by Mindy Carson (Columbia).

Bring Back the Thrill
Words by Ruth Poll, music by Pete Rugolo.
Alamo Music, Inc./Maypole Music, Inc.
Adapted from the Italian song, "Carmela." Best-selling record by Eddie Fisher (RCA Victor).

Broken Down Merry-Go-Round
Words and music by Arthur Herbert and Fred Stryker.
Travis Music Co.
Best-selling record by Margaret Whiting and Jimmy Wakely (Capitol).

Bushel and a Peck, A
Words and music by Frank Loesser.
Frank Music Corp.
Introduced by Vivian Blaine in *Guys and Dolls* (musical). Best-selling single record by Betty Hutton and Perry Como (RCA Victor).

Calypso Blues
Words by Don George, music by Nat "King" Cole.
Crestview Music Corp.
Best-selling record by Nat "King" Cole (Capitol).

Can Anyone Explain (No! No! No!)
Words and music by Bennie Benjamin and George Weiss.
Valando Music Corp.
Best-selling record by The Ames Brothers (Coral).

Candy and Cake
Words and music by Bob Merrill.
Joy Music, Inc.
Best-selling record by Arthur Godfrey (Columbia).

C'est Si Bon (French)
English words by Jerry Seelen, French words and music by Henri Betti.
Éditions Arpège, Paris, France, 1947/Leeds Music Corp.
Best-selling record by Johnny Desmond (M-G-M). Revived in 1953 with best-selling record by Eartha Kitt (RCA Victor).

Chattanoogie Shoe Shine Boy
Words and music by Harry Stone and Jack Stapp.
Fred Rose Music, Inc.
First recorded by Red Foley (Decca). Best-selling record by Bing Crosby (Decca).

Cherry Pies Ought To Be You
Words and music by Cole Porter.
Buxton Hill Music Corp.
Introduced by William Redfield, Barbara Ashley, Charlotte Greenwood, and David Burns in *Out of This World* (musical).

Choo'n Gum
Words by Mann Curtis, music by Vic Mizzy.
Bregman, Vocco & Conn, Inc.
Best-selling record in 1952 by Teresa Brewer (Coral).

Christmas in Killarney
Words and music by John Redmond, James Cavanaugh, and Frank Weldon.
Remick Music Corp.
Best-selling record in 1951 by Dennis Day (RCA Victor).

Cincinnat-ti Dancing Pig
Words by Al Lewis, music by Guy Wood.
Avon Music, Inc.
Best-selling record by Red Foley (Decca).

Come On-a My House
Words and music by Ross Bagdasarian and William Saroyan.
Duchess Music Corp.
Written by playwright Saroyan and his cousin, Bagdasarian, while on an automobile trip across New Mexico in 1939. Interpolated in an off-Broadway production of the Saroyan short play, *Son,* in 1950. First recorded by Kay Armen. Best-selling record in 1951 by Rosemary Clooney (Columbia).

Count Every Star
Words by Sammy Gallop, music by Bruno Coquatrix.
Paxton Music, Inc.
Best-selling record, instrumental, by Hugo Winterhalter and his Orchestra (RCA Victor).

Cry, Cry Baby
Words and music by Robert Ellen and Mack Ellen.
Rockland Music Corp.
Best-selling record by Ed Wiley (Sittin' In).

Cry of the Wild Goose, The, see 1949.

Cuban Mambo
Words by Jack Wiseman, music by Xavier Cugat and Rafael Angulo.
Pemora Music Co., Inc.
Best-selling record by The Irving Fields Trio (Fiesta).

Cuddle Buggin' Baby
Words and music by Red Rowe.
Hill and Range Songs, Inc.
Best-selling record by Eddy Arnold (RCA Victor).

Cupid's Boogie
Words and music by Johnny Otis.
Savoy Music Co.
Best-selling record by Little Esther, Johnny Otis, and Mel Walker (Savoy).

Daddy's Little Boy
Words and music by Billy Collins.
Cherio Music Publishers, Inc.
Best-selling record by The Mills Brothers (Decca).

Dark Is the Night
Words by Sammy Cahn, music by Nicholas Brodszky.
Leo Feist, Inc.
Introduced by Jane Powell in *Rich, Young and Pretty* (film).

Darn It Baby, That's Love
Words and music by Joan Edwards and Lyn Duddy.
Chappell & Co., Inc.
Introduced by Bill Norvas and Phyllis Cameron in *Tickets Please* (revue).

Dear Hearts and Gentle People, see 1949.

Dearie
Words and music by Bob Hilliard and Dave Mann.
Laurel Music Corp.
Best-selling record by Ray Bolger and Ethel Merman (Decca).

Deceivin' Blues
Words and music by Johnny Otis.
Savoy Music Co.
Best-selling record by Little Esther (Savoy).

Did Anyone Ever Tell You Mrs. Murphy, see 1949.

Do Something for Me
Words and music by William E. Ward and Rose Marks.
Lois Publishing Co.
Best-selling record in 1951 by The Dominoes (Federal).

Domino (French)
English words by Don Raye, French words by Jacques Plante, music by Louis Ferrari.
Arpège Éditions Musicales, Paris, France/Pickwick Music Corp.
Best-selling record in 1951 by Tony Martin (RCA Victor).

Don'cha Go 'way Mad
Words by Al Stillman, music by Jimmy Mundy and Illinois Jacquet.
Advanced Music Corp.
Adapted from the instrumental composition, "Black Velvet." Best-selling record by Ella Fitzgerald (Decca).

Don't Rock the Boat, Dear
Words by Ralph Blane and Harold Arlen, music by Harold Arlen.
Harwin Music Corp.
Introduced by Betty Grable and Dan Dailey in *My Blue Heaven* (film).

Double Crossing Blues
Words and music by Johnny Otis.
Savoy Music Co./Hill and Range Songs, Inc.
Best-selling record by Johnny Otis, Little Esther, and Mel Walker (Savoy).

Down the Lane
Words and music by George Howe and Bobby Burns.
Screen Gems-Columbia Music, Inc.
Best-selling record by Russ Morgan (Decca).

Earth and the Sky
Words and music by John Rox.
Frank Music Corp.
Introduced by Polly Bergen in 1953 in *John Murray Anderson's Almanac* (revue).

Enclosed, One Broken Heart
Words and music by Sadie Nordin Sallis and Eddy Arnold.
Hill and Range Songs, Inc.
Best-selling record by Eddy Arnold (RCA Victor).

End of a Love Affair, The
Words and music by Edward C. Redding.
Duchess Music Corp.
Introduced by Mabel Mercer. First recording by Dinah Shore (RCA Victor).

Enjoy Yourself (It's Later Than You Think), see 1948.

Every Day I Have the Blues, **see 1952.**

Fancy Free
Words by Johnny Mercer, music by Harold Arlen.
Harwin Music Corp.
Introduced in *The Petty Girl* (film).

Fat Man, The
Words by Antoine "Fats" Domino, music by Dave Bartholomew.
Travis Music Co.
Best-selling record by Fats Domino (Imperial).

Follow the Fold
Words and music by Frank Loesser.
Frank Music Corp.
Introduced by Isabel Bigley and Pat Rooney, Sr. in *Guys and Dolls* (musical).

For You My Love, **see 1949.**

Friendly Islands, The
Words by Ralph Blane and Harold Arlen, music by Harold Arlen.
Harwin Music Corp.
Introduced in *My Blue Heaven* (film).

Friendly Star
Words by Mack Gordon, music by Harry Warren.
Leo Feist, Inc.
Introduced by Judy Garland in *Summer Stock* (film).

From This Moment On
Words and music by Cole Porter.
Buxton Hill Music Corp.
Dropped from the New York production of *Out of This World* (musical) and introduced in the film version of *Kiss Me Kate.*

Frosty the Snow Man
Words and music by Steve Nelson and Jack Rollins.
Hill and Range Songs, Inc.
Best-selling record in 1951 by Gene Autry (Columbia).

Fugue for Tinhorns, also known as **Three Cornered Tune**
Words and music by Frank Loesser.
Frank Music Corp.
Introduced by Stubby Kaye, Johnny Silver, and Douglas Deane in *Guys and Dolls* (musical).

Get Out Those Old Records
Words and music by Carmen Lombardo and John Loeb.
Lombardo Music, Inc.
Introduced by Guy Lombardo and his Royal Canadians.

Go to Sleep, Go to Sleep, Go to Sleep
Words by Sammy Cahn, music by Fred Spielman.
Walt Disney Music Co.
Best-selling record by Arthur Godfrey and Mary Martin (Columbia).

God's Country
Words by Haven Gillespie, music by Beasley Smith.
Robbins Music Corp.

Golden Rocket
Words and music by Hank Snow.
Hill and Range Songs, Inc.
Best-selling record in 1951 by Hank Snow (RCA Victor).

Gone Fishin'
Words and music by Nick Kenny and Charles Kenny.
Leo Feist, Inc.
Best-selling record by Arthur Godfrey (Columbia).

Goodbye, John
Words by Edward Eager, music by Alec Wilder.
Robert Music Corp.
Introduced by Peggy Lee (Capitol).

Goodnight Irene
Words and music by Huddie Ledbetter and John Lomax.
Ludlow Music, Inc.
First recorded for the Library of Congress archives by Leadbelly (Huddie Ledbetter) while he was a prisoner at the Angola, Louisiana State Prison. Included in *Negro Folk Songs As Sung by Lead Belly,* edited by John and Alan Lomax and published by The MacMillan Co. in 1936. Best-selling records by The Weavers with Gordon Jenkins and his Orchestra (Decca) and Ernest Tubb and Red Foley (Decca).

Hallowe'en
Words by Ralph Blane and Harold Arlen, music by Harold Arlen.
Harwin Music Corp.
Introduced by Jane Wyatt, Betty Grable, Dan Dailey, and David Wayne in *My Blue Heaven* (film).

Happy Feet
Words by Al Stillman, music by Roy Ross.
Cromwell Music, Inc.
Based on the advertising jingle, *Miles Ahead,* written by Ted Cott and Roy Ross for Miles Shoes, Inc. Best-selling record by Dean Martin (Capitol).

Harbor Lights, see 1937.

Hard Luck Blues
Words and music by Roy Brown.
Blue Ridge Publishing Co.
Best-selling record by Roy Brown (De Luxe).

Harry Lime Theme, The, see **The Third Man Theme,** 1949.

Hillbilly Fever
Words and music by George Vaughn.
Cherio Music Publishers, Inc.
Best-selling record by Little Jimmy Dickens (Columbia).

Hold My Hand
Words and music by Jack Lawrence and Richard Myers.
World Music, Inc.
Featured in 1954 in *Susan Slept Here* (film). Nominated for Academy Award, 1954. Best-selling record in 1954 by Don Cornell (Coral).

Home Cookin'
Words and music by Jay Livingston and Ray Evans.
Famous Music Corp.
Introduced by Bob Hope and Lucille Ball in *Fancy Pants* (film).

Hoop-Dee-Do
Words by Frank Loesser, music by Milton De Lugg.
Frank Music Corp.
Best-selling record by Perry Como (RCA Victor).

Horse Told Me, The
Words by Johnny Burke, music by James Van Heusen.
Burke-Van Heusen & Associates Music Corp.
Introduced by Bing Crosby in *Riding High* (film).

Hostess with the Mostes' on the Ball, The
Words and music by Irving Berlin.
Irving Berlin Music Corp.
Introduced by Ethel Merman in *Call Me Madam* (musical).

Hot Rod Race
Words and music by George Wilson.
Four Star Sales Co.
Best-selling record by Tiny Hill (Mercury).

How Could You Believe Me When I Said I Love You When You Know I've Been a Liar All My Life
Words by Alan Jay Lerner, music by Burton Lane.
Leo Feist, Inc.
Introduced by Jane Powell and Fred Astaire in *Royal Wedding* (film).

I Almost Lost My Mind
Words and music by Ivory Joe Hunter.
Hill and Range Songs, Inc.
Introduced by Ivory Joe Hunter. Best-selling records in 1950 by Ivory Joe Hunter (M-G-M) and in 1956 by Pat Boone (Dot).

I Am Loved
Words and music by Cole Porter.
Buxton Hill Music Corp.
Introduced by Patricia Gillette in *Out of This World* (musical).

I Can Dream Can't I, see 1937.

I Can See You
Words by Sammy Fain, music by Nicholas Brodszky.
Leo Feist, Inc.
Introduced by Jane Powell in *Rich, Young and Pretty* (film).

I Cross My Fingers
Words and music by Walter Kent and Walter Farrar.
United Music Corp.
Best-selling record by Percy Faith and his Orchestra (Columbia).

I Didn't Slip, I Wasn't Pushed, I Fell
Words and music by Eddie Pola and George Wyle.
Remick Music Corp.
Best-selling record by Doris Day (Columbia).

I Love a New Yorker
Words by Ralph Blane and Harold Arlen, music by Harold Arlen.
Harwin Music Corp.
Introduced by Betty Grable and Dan Dailey in *My Blue Heaven* (film).

I Love the Girl, see **I Love the Guy.**

I Love the Guy, also known as **I Love the Girl**
Words and music by Cy Coben.
Shapiro, Bernstein & Co., Inc.
Best-selling record by Sarah Vaughan (Columbia).

I Love You Because, see 1949.

I Need You So
Words and music by Ivory Joe Hunter.
Hill and Range Songs, Inc.
Best-selling record by Ivory Joe Hunter (M-G-M).

I Never Had a Worry in the World
Words and music by Jim Morehead and Sandra Kent.
Screen Gems-Columbia Music, Inc.
Best-selling record by Dinah Shore (Columbia).

I Quit My Pretty Mama
Words and music by Ivory Joe Hunter and Lois Mann.
Lois Publishing Co.
Best-selling record by Ivory Joe Hunter (King).

I Said My Pajamas, and Put On My Pray'rs
Words and music by Eddie Pola and George Wyle.
Leeds Music Corp.
Best-selling record by Fran Warren and Tony Martin and Henri René and his Orchestra (RCA Victor).

I Still Feel the Same about You
Words and music by Don Reid and Dick Manning.
Odette Music Corp.
Best-selling record in 1951 by Georgia Gibbs (Coral).

I Taut I Taw a Puddy Tat, also known as **I Thought I Saw a Pussy Cat**
Words and music by Alan Livingston, Billy May, and Warren Foster.
Remick Music Corp.
Best-selling record by Mel Blanc (Capitol).

I Thought I Saw a Pussy Cat, see **I Taut I Taw a Puddy Tat.**

I Wanna Be Loved, see 1933.

I Will Wait
Words and music by Mildred Colclough.
Savoy Music Co.
Best-selling record in 1951 by The Four Buddies (Savoy).

If, see 1934.

If I Knew You Were Comin' I'd've Baked a Cake
Words and music by Al Hoffman, Bob Merrill, and Clem Watts.
Robert Music Corp./Orten Music Co.
Best-selling record by Eileen Barton (National and Mercury).

If I Were a Bell
Words and music by Frank Loesser.
Frank Music Corp.
Introduced by Isabel Bigley in *Guys and Dolls* (musical).

If You Feel Like Singing, Sing
Words by Mack Gordon, music by Harry Warren.
Four Jays Music Co.
Introduced in *Summer Stock* (film).

If You've Got the Money (I've Got the Time)
Words and music by Lefty Frizzell and Jim Beck.
Peer International Corp.
Best-selling record in 1951 by Lefty Frizzell (Columbia).

(Day after Day) I'll Always Love You, also known as **Querida Mia**
Words and music by Jay Livingston and Ray Evans.
Famous Music Corp.
Introduced by Dean Martin and The Guadalajara Trio in *My Friend Irma Goes West* (film).

I'll Know
Words and music by Frank Loesser.
Frank Music Corp.
Introduced by Isabel Bigley and Robert Alda in *Guys and Dolls* (musical).

I'll Never Be Free
Words and music by Bennie Benjamin and George Weiss.
Laurel Music Corp.
Best-selling records by Kay Starr and Tennessee Ernie Ford (Capitol) and Paul Gayten and Annie Laurie (Regal).

I'll Sail My Ship Alone
Words and music by Lois Mann, Morry Burns, Henry Bernard, and Henry Thurston.
Lois Publishing Co.
Best-selling record by Moon Mullican (King).

I'm Bashful
Words by Bob Merrill, music by Al Schofield.
Joy Music, Inc.
Best-selling record by Mindy Carson (RCA Victor).

I'm Gonna Live Till I Die
Words and music by Al Hoffman, Walter Kent, and Mann Curtis.
Barton Music Corp.
Original version written in 1939 but not published. First recorded by Danny Scholl (National). Best-selling record by Frankie Laine (Mercury).

I'm Movin' On
Words and music by Hank Snow.
Hill and Range Songs, Inc.
Best-selling record in 1950 and 1951 by Hank Snow (RCA Victor).

(Remember Me) I'm the One Who Loves You
Words and music by Stuart Hamblen.
Hamblen Music Co., Inc./Hill and Range Songs, Inc.
Best-selling records by Stuart Hamblen (Columbia) and Ernest Tubb (Decca).

It Isn't Fair, see 1933.

It's a Lovely Day Today
Words and music by Irving Berlin.
Irving Berlin Music Corp.
Introduced by Russell Nype and Galina Talva in *Call Me Madam* (musical).

It's So Nice To Have a Man around the House
Words by Jack Elliott, music by Harold Spina.
Edwin H. Morris & Co., Inc.
Best-selling record by Dinah Shore (Columbia).

I've Got Five Dollars and It's Saturday Night
Words and music by Ted Daffan.
Peer International Corp.
Best-selling record in 1956 by Faron Young (Capitol).

I've Never Been in Love Before
Words and music by Frank Loesser.
Frank Music Corp.
Introduced by Robert Alda and Isabel Bigley in *Guys and Dolls* (musical).

Jing-A-Ling, Jing-A-Ling
Words by Don Raye, music by Paul J. Smith.
Walt Disney Music Co.
Based on a theme from *Beaver Valley* (film).

Just Say I Love Her
Words by Martin Kalmanoff and Sam Ward, music by Jack Val and Jimmy Dale.
Larry Spier, Inc.
Best-selling record by Vic Damone (Mercury).

La Vie en Rose (French)
English words by Mack David, French words by Edith Piaf, music by Louiguy.
Éditions Arpège, Paris, France, 1946/Harms, Inc.
Introduced in France and the United States by Edith Piaf. Best-selling record in English by Tony Martin (RCA Victor).

Let's Go to Church (Next Sunday Morning)
Words and music by Steve Allen.
Beechwood Music Corp.
Best-selling record by Jimmy Wakely and Margaret Whiting (Capitol).

Letters Have No Arms
Words and music by Arbie Gibson and Ernest Tubb.
Hill and Range Songs, Inc.
Best-selling record by Ernest Tubb (Decca).

Life Is So Peculiar
Words by Johnny Burke, music by Jimmy Van Heusen.
Burke-Van Heusen & Associates Music Corp.
Introduced by Bing Crosby, Peggy Lee, The Merry Macs, and Groucho Marx in *Mr. Music* (film).

Little Angel with a Dirty Face, **see 1948.**

London by Night
Words and music by Carroll Coates.
Barton Music Corp.
Introduced by Frank Sinatra.

Lonely Wine
Words and music by Roy Wells.
Rosarita Music, Inc.
Best-selling record by Les Baxter and his Orchestra (Capitol).

Long Gone Lonesome Blues
Words and music by Hank Williams.
Fred Rose Music, Inc.
Best-selling record by Hank Williams (M-G-M).

Love Don't Love Nobody
Words and music by Roy Brown.
Blue Ridge Publishing Co.
Best-selling record by Roy Brown (De Luxe).

Lovebug Itch, The
Words and music by Jenny Lou Carson and Roy Botkin.
Hill and Range Songs, Inc.
Best-selling record by Eddy Arnold (RCA Victor).

Loveliest Night of the Year, The
Words by Paul Francis Webster, music adapted by Irving Aaronson.
Robbins Music Corp.
Adapted from the Juventino Rosas waltz, "Sobre los Olas." Introduced by Ann Blyth in *The Great Caruso* (film). Best-selling record by Mario Lanza (RCA Victor).

Luck Be a Lady
Words and music by Frank Loesser.
Frank Music Corp.
Introduced by Robert Alda in *Guys and Dolls* (musical).

Mambo Jambo (Mexican)
Words by Raymond Karl and Charlie Towne, music by Perez Prado.
Editorial Mexicana de Musica Internacional, S.A., Mexico, D. F./ Peer International Corp.
Mexican title, "Que Rico el Mambo." Introduced in the United States by Sonny Burke and his Orchestra (Decca).

Marrying for Love
Words and music by Irving Berlin.
Irving Berlin Music Corp.
Introduced by Paul Lukas and Ethel Merman in *Call Me Madam* (musical).

May the Good Lord Bless and Keep You
Words and music by Meredith Willson.
Pickwick Music Corp.
Sign-off theme of Tallulah Bankhead's radio show. Best-selling record by Frankie Laine (Mercury).

Melancholy Rhapsody
Words by Sammy Cahn, music by Ray Heindorf.
M. Witmark & Sons.
Introduced by Harry James on the soundtrack of *Young Man with a Horn* (film).

Merry-Go-Round, see **La Ronde.**

M-i-s-s-i-s-s-i-p-p-i
Words and music by Curley Williams and Billy Simmons.
Fred Rose Music, Inc.
Best-selling record by Red Foley (Decca).

Mr. Touchdown U.S.A.
Words and music by Ruth Roberts, Gene Piller, and William Katz.
Paxton Music, Inc.
Best-selling record by Hugo Winterhalter and his Orchestra (RCA Victor).

Mistrustin' Blues
Words and music by Johnny Otis.
Savoy Music Co.
Best-selling record by Johnny Otis, Little Esther, and Mel Walker (Savoy).

Moanin' the Blues
Words and music by Hank Williams.
Fred Rose Music, Inc.
Best-selling record by Hank Williams (M-G-M).

Mona Lisa, see 1949.

More I Cannot Wish You
Words and music by Frank Loesser.
Frank Music Corp.
Introduced by Pat Rooney, Sr. in *Guys and Dolls* (musical).

Mule Train, see 1949.

Music! Music! Music! (Put Another Nickel In)
Words and music by Stephen Weiss and Bernie Baum.
Cromwell Music, Inc.
Best-selling record by Teresa Brewer (Coral).

My Destiny
Words by Mack David, music by Jerry Livingston.
Walt Disney Music Co.
Best-selling record by Billy Eckstine (M-G-M).

My Foolish Heart, see 1949.

My Heart Cries for You
Words and music by Carl Sigman and Percy Faith.
Massey Music Co., Inc.
Adapted from the French folk song, "Chanson de Marie Antoinette." Best-selling record by Guy Mitchell and Mitch Miller (Columbia).

My Time of Day
Words and music by Frank Loesser.
Frank Music Corp.
Introduced by Robert Alda in *Guys and Dolls* (musical).

Nevertheless, see 1931.

No Man Is an Island
Words and music by Joan Whitney and Alex Kramer.
Bourne, Inc.

No Other Love
Words and music by Bob Russell and Paul Weston.
Walt Disney Music Co.
Adapted from Chopin's "Etude in E Major." Best-selling record by Jo Stafford (Capitol).

Nobody's Chasing Me
Words and music by Cole Porter.
Buxton Hill Music Corp.
Introduced by Charlotte Greenwood in *Out of This World* (musical).

(Dance to the Music of) Ocarina, The
Words and music by Irving Berlin.
Irving Berlin Music Corp.
Introduced by Galina Talva in *Call Me Madam* (musical).

Oh Babe!
Words and music by Louis Prima and Milton Kabak.
Alamo Music, Inc.
Introduced by Louis Prima and his Orchestra.

Old Master Painter, The, see 1949.

Old Piano Roll Blues, see 1949.

Oldest Established, The
Words and music by Frank Loesser.
Frank Music Corp.
Introduced by Sam Levene, Stubby Kaye, Johnny Silver, and ensemble in *Guys and Dolls* (musical).

On the Outgoing Tide
Words by Lew Brown, music by Mabel Wayne.
Shapiro, Bernstein & Co., Inc.
Best-selling record by Perry Como (RCA Victor).

Once upon a Time Today
Words and music by Irving Berlin.
Irving Berlin Music Corp.
Introduced by Ethel Merman in *Call Me Madam* (musical).

One Finger Melody
Words and music by Al Hoffman, Kermit Goell, and Fred Spielman.
Barton Music Corp.
Best-selling record by Frank Sinatra (Columbia).

Orange Colored Sky
Words and music by Milton De Lugg and Willie Stein.
Frank Music Corp.
Introduced by Milton De Lugg and his Orchestra on the Jerry Lester television show. Best-selling record by Nat "King" Cole with Stan Kenton and his Orchestra (Capitol).

Our Lady of Fatima
Words and music by Gladys Gollahon.
Robbins Music Corp.
Best-selling record by Kitty Kallen (Mercury).

Patricia
Words and music by Benny Davis.
Bregman, Vocco & Conn, Inc.
Best-selling record by Perry Como (RCA Victor).

Penny a Kiss, a Penny a Hug, A
Words and music by Buddy Kaye and Ralph Care.
Shapiro, Bernstein & Co., Inc.
Best-selling record by Dinah Shore and Tony Martin (RCA Victor).

Peter Cottontail
Words and music by Steve Nelson and Jack Rollins.
Hill and Range Songs, Inc.
Easter song. Best-selling record by Gene Autry (Columbia).

Petite Waltz, The (Belgian)
Words by E. A. Ellington and Phyllis Claire, music by Joe Heyne.
World Music Co. and Éditions Pletincks, Brussels, Belgium/Duchess Music Corp.
First recording by The Three Suns (RCA Victor).

Picnic Song, The
Words and music by Carmen Dello and Theresa Dello.
Chappell & Co., Inc.
Best-selling record by Johnny Desmond (M-G-M).

Pink Champagne
Words and music by Joe Liggins.
Venice Music, Inc.
Best-selling record by Joe Liggins (Specialty).

Play a Simple Melody, see 1914.

Poison Love
Words and music by Elmer Laird.
Hill and Range Songs, Inc.
Best-selling record in 1951 by Johnnie and Jack (RCA Victor).

Quicksilver, see 1949.

Rag Mop
Words and music by Johnnie Lee Wells and Deacon Anderson.
Hill and Range Songs, Inc.
Best-selling record by The Ames Brothers (Coral).

Rainy Day Refrain (Dadim, Dadom) (German)
English words by Eric Maschwitz, German words and music by Heino Gaze.
Peter Schaeffers Musikverlag, Berlin, Germany, 1949/Leeds Music Corp.
Original German title, "Schnurlregen." Best-selling record by Mindy Carson (RCA Victor).

Red Top
Words and music by Gene Ammons.
Cherio Music Publishers, Inc.
Best-selling record by Gene Ammons (Mercury).

Rockin' Blues
Words and music by Johnny Otis.
Savoy Music Co.
Best-selling record in 1951 by Johnny Otis and Mel Walker (Savoy).

Roses
Words and music by Tim Spencer and Glenn Spencer.
Hill and Range Songs, Inc.
Introduced by The Sons of the Pioneers. Best-selling record by Sammy Kaye and his Orchestra (RCA Victor).

Roving Kind, The
Words and music by Jessie Cavanaugh and Arnold Stanton.
Hollis Music, Inc.
Adapted from the English folk song, "The Pirate Ship." Also known among folk singers as "The Rakish Kind." Best-selling record in 1951 by Guy Mitchell and Mitch Miller (Columbia).

Sail Away
Words and music by Noël Coward.
Chappell & Co., Inc.
Introduced by Graham Payn in London in *Ace of Clubs* (musical). Re-introduced by James Hurst in 1961 in Coward's *Sail Away* (musical).

Sam's Song (The Happy Tune)
Words by Jack Elliott, music by Lew Quadling.
Sam Weiss Music, Inc.
Best-selling records by Joe "Fingers" Carr (Lou Busch) (Capitol) and Bing and Gary Crosby (Decca).

Sea of the Moon, The
Words by Arthur Freed, music by Harry Warren.
Robbins Music Corp.
Introduced in *Pagan Love Song* (film). Best-selling record by Tony Martin (RCA Victor).

Sentimental Me, see 1949.

Sentimental Music
Words and music by Bernie Wayne and Ralph Care.
Town and Country Music, Inc.
Best-selling record in 1951 by Bing Crosby (Decca).

Shifting, Whispering Sands, The
Words by V. C. Gilbert, music by Mary M. Hadler.
Gallatin Music Corp.
Best-selling records in 1955 by Rusty Draper (Mercury) and Billy Vaughn (Dot).

Shot-Gun Boogie
Words and music by Tennessee Ernie Ford.
Century Songs, Inc.
Best-selling record in 1951 by Tennessee Ernie Ford (Capitol).

Show Me the Way To Get Out of This World ('cause That's Where Everything Is)
Words by Les Clark, music by Matt Dennis.
Oriole Music Corp.
Introduced by Matt Dennis.

Silver Bells
Words and music by Ray Evans and Jay Livingston.
Paramount Music Corp.
Introduced in *The Lemon Drop Kid* (film).

Sinner's Prayer
Words by Lowell Fulson, music by Lloyd C. Glenn.
Progressive Music Publishing Co., Inc.
Identified with Ray Charles.

Sit Down, You're Rockin' the Boat
Words and music by Frank Loesser.
Frank Music Corp.
Introduced by Stubby Kaye in *Guys and Dolls* (musical).

Sittin' on It All the Time
Words and music by Lois Mann and Henry Bernard.
Lois Publishing Co.
Best-selling record by Wynonie Harris (King).

Sleigh Ride
Words by Mitchell Parish, music by Leroy Anderson.
Mills Music, Inc.
Best-selling record by Leroy Anderson and his Orchestra (Decca).

Slipping Around, see 1949.

Smooth Sailing
Words and music by Arnett Cobb.
Wayne Music Publishing Co.
Best-selling record in 1951 by Ella Fitzgerald (Decca).

So Long (It's Been Good To Know Yuh)
Words and music by Woody Guthrie.
Folkways Music Publishers, Inc.
Originally written in 1939 about a dust storm in Texas during the depression years. Adapted and best-selling record by The Weavers and Gordon Jenkins (Decca).

Song of Delilah
Words by Jay Livingston and Ray Evans, music by Victor Young.
Famous Music Corp.
Promotional song for *Samson and Delilah* (film).

Stay with the Happy People
Words by Bob Hilliard, music by Jule Styne.
Edwin H. Morris & Co., Inc.
Introduced by Lina Romay in *Michael Todd's Peep Show* (revue).

Sue Me
Words and music by Frank Loesser.
Frank Music Corp.
Introduced by Sam Levene and Vivian Blaine in *Guys and Dolls* (musical).

Sugarfoot Rag
Words by George Vaughn, music by Hank Garland.
Valley Publishers, Inc.
Best-selling record by Red Foley (Decca).

Sunshine Cake
Words by Johnny Burke, music by Jimmy Van Heusen.
Burke-Van Heusen & Associates Music Corp.
Introduced by Bing Crosby, with Coleen Gray and Clarence Muse, in *Riding High* (film).

(We've Got) Sure Thing, A
Words by Johnny Burke, music by James Van Heusen.
Burke-Van Heusen & Associates Music Corp.
Introduced by Bing Crosby in *Riding High* (film).

Swamp Girl, The, see 1949.

Syncopated Clock, The
Words by Mitchell Parish, music by Leroy Anderson.
Mills Music, Inc.
Best-selling record, instrumental, by Leroy Anderson and his Orchestra (Decca).

Take Back Your Mink
Words and music by Frank Loesser.
Frank Music Corp.
Introduced by Vivian Blaine in *Guys and Dolls* (musical).

Take Me in Your Arms and Hold Me, see 1949.

Teardrops from My Eyes
Words and music by Rudolph Toombs.
Simon House, Inc.
Best-selling record in 1950 and 1951 by Ruth Brown (Atlantic).

Teasin'
Words by Richard Adler, music by Philip Springer.
Pickwick Music Corp.
Best-selling record by Connie Haines (M-G-M).

Tennessee Waltz, see 1948.

There Must Be Something Better Than Love
Words by Dorothy Fields, music by Morton Gould.
Chappell & Co., Inc.
Introduced by Pearl Bailey in *Arms and the Girl* (musical).

There's No Tomorrow, see 1949.

Thing, The
Words and music by Charles R. Grean.
Hollis Music, Inc.
Best-selling record by Phil Harris (RCA Victor).

Thinking of You, see 1927.

Third Man Theme, The, also known as **The Harry Lime Theme,** see 1949.

Three Cornered Tune, see **Fugue for Tinhorns.**

Throw Your Love My Way
Words and music by Ernest Tubb and Loys Southerland.
Ernest Tubb Music, Inc.
Best-selling record by Ernest Tubb (Decca).

To Think You've Chosen Me
Words and music by Bennie Benjamin and George Weiss.
Valando Music Corp.
Best-selling record by Eddy Howard (Mercury).

Too Late Now
Words by Alan Jay Lerner, music by Burton Lane.
Leo Feist, Inc.
Introduced by Jane Powell in *Royal Wedding* (film). Nominated for Academy Award, 1951.

Tzena, Tzena, Tzena (Israeli)
Authorized version: English words by Mitchell Parish, music by Julius Grossman (Michrovsky) and Issachar Miron.
Mills Music, Inc.
Originally written by a Palestinian, Issachar Miron, in 1941. Rewritten by Julius Grossman (Michrovsky) in 1947 and published in the book, *Songs of Israel.* First English-language version with words by Gordon Jenkins and music arranged by Spencer Ross, published by Cromwell Music, Inc. This version voided by legal action. Best-selling record by The Weavers and Gordon Jenkins and his Orchestra (Decca).

Unwanted Sign upon Your Heart
Words and music by Hank Snow.
Hill and Range Songs, Inc.
Best-selling record in 1951 by Hank Snow (RCA Victor).

Use Your Imagination
Words and music by Cole Porter.
Buxton Hill Music Corp.
Introduced by William Redfield and Patricia Gillette in *Out of This World* (musical).

Valentino Tango, The, also known as **Noche de Amor**
Words by Jack Lawrence, music by Heinz Roemheld.
Leeds Music Corp.
From *Valentino* (film).

Violins from Nowhere
Words by Herb Magidson, music by Sammy Fain.
Bregman, Vocco & Conn, Inc.
Introduced by Art Carroll in *Michael Todd's Peep Show* (revue).

Wanderin'
Words and music by Sammy Kaye.
Republic Music Corp.
Based on an American folk song discovered in Minnesota by Carl Sandburg. Best-selling record by Sammy Kaye and his Orchestra (Columbia).

We Never Talk Much
Words by Sammy Cahn, music by Nicholas Brodszky.
Robbins Music Corp.
Introduced by Fernando Lamas and Jane Powell in *Rich, Young and Pretty* (film).

Well, Oh, Well
Words and music by Tiny Bradshaw, Lois Mann, and Henry Bernard.
Lois Publishing Co.
Best-selling record by Tiny Bradshaw (King).

(Ah, the Apple Trees) When the World Was Young (French)
English words by Johnny Mercer, French words by Angela Vannier, music by M. Philippe-Gérard.
Enoch & Cie, Paris, France/Criterion Music Corp.
Original French title "Le Chevalier de Paris (Les Pommiers Doux)." Introduced in the United States by Peggy Lee.

Where, Oh Where?
Words and music by Cole Porter.
Buxton Hill Music Corp.
Introduced by Barbara Ashley in *Out of This World* (musical).

Why Do Things Happen to Me
Words and music by Roy Hawkins.
Modern Music Publishing Co.
Best-selling record by Roy Hawkins (Modern).

Why Don't You Love Me
Words and music by Hank Williams.
Fred Rose Music, Inc.
Best-selling record by Hank Williams (M-G-M).

Why Fight the Feeling
Words and music by Frank Loesser.
Paramount Music Corp.
Introduced by Betty Hutton in *Let's Dance* (film).

Why Should I Cry
Words and music by Zeke Clements.
Hill and Range Songs, Inc.
Best-selling record by Eddy Arnold (RCA Victor).

Why Should We Try Anymore
Words and music by Hank Williams.
Fred Rose Music, Inc.
Best-selling record by Hank Williams (M-G-M).

Wilhelmina
Words by Mack Gordon, music by Josef Myrow.
Leo Feist, Inc.
Introduced in *Wabash Avenue* (film). Nominated for Academy Award, 1950.

Winter Waltz, The
Words and music adaptation by Larry Neill.
Gale & Gayles, Inc.
Adapted from Waldteufel's "Skater's Waltz." Best-selling record by Mitch Miller and his Orchestra (Columbia).

With These Hands
Words by Benny Davis, music by Abner Silver.
Ben Bloom Music Corp.
Introduced by Nelson Eddy and Jo Stafford in 1951. Best-selling record in 1953 by Eddie Fisher (RCA Victor).

Wonder Why
Words by Sammy Cahn, music by Nicholas Brodszky.
Robbins Music Corp.
Introduced by Jane Powell in *Rich, Young and Pretty* (film). Nominated for Academy Award, 1951.

You and Your Beautiful Eyes
Words by Mack David, music by Jerry Livingston.
Paramount Music Corp.
Introduced by Dean Martin in *At War with the Army* (film).

You Don't Remind Me
Words and music by Cole Porter.
Buxton Hill Music Corp.
Introduced by George Jongeyans in *Out of This World* (musical).

You Wonderful You
Words by Jack Brooks and Saul Chaplin, music by Harry Warren.
Four Jays Music Co., Inc.
Introduced by Gene Kelly and Judy Garland in *Summer Stock* (film).

You're All I Want for Christmas, see 1948.

You're Just in Love
Words and music by Irving Berlin.
Irving Berlin Music Corp.
Introduced by Ethel Merman and Russell Nype in *Call Me Madam* (musical). Best-selling record by Perry Como (RCA Victor).

Zing Zing — Zoom Zoom
Words by Charles Tobias, music by Sigmund Romberg.
Robbins Music Corp.
Best-selling record by Perry Como (RCA Victor).

1951

Aba Daba Honeymoon, see 1914.

Alice in Wonderland
Words by Bob Hilliard, music by Sammy Fain.
Walt Disney Music Co.
Introduced in *Alice in Wonderland* (film).

All Night Long
Words and music by Johnny Otis.
Savoy Music Co.
Best-selling record by Johnny Otis (Savoy).

Almost
Words and music by Vic McAlpin and Jack Toombs.
Acuff-Rose Publications.
Best-selling record in 1952 by George Morgan (Columbia).

Always, Always (Italian)
English words by Jessie Cavanaugh, music by P. G. Redi.
Edizioni Musicali, Milan, Italy, 1949/Hollis Music, Inc.
Best-selling record by Percy Faith and his Orchestra (Columbia).

Always Late (With Your Kisses)
Words and music by Lefty Frizzell and Blackie Crawford.
Hill and Range Songs, Inc.
Best-selling record in 1951 and 1952 by Lefty Frizzell (Columbia).

And So to Sleep Again
Words and music by Joe Marsala and Sunny Skylar.
George Paxton, Inc.
Best-selling record by Patti Page (Mercury).

Another Autumn
Words by Alan Jay Lerner, music by Frederick Loewe.
Chappell & Co., Inc.
Introduced by Tony Bavar in *Paint Your Wagon* (musical).

Any Time, see 1921.

Asia Minor
Music by Roger King Mozian.
Consolidated Music Publishers, Inc.
Introduced by Machito and his Orchestra (Mercury). Revived in 1961 with best-selling record by Kokomo (Felsted).

At Last! At Last! (French)
English words by Florence Miles, French words and music by Charles Trenet.
France Music Co./Leeds Music Corp.
Original title, "L'Âme des Poetes." Introduced in the United States by Tony Martin. A subsequent, more literal adaptation, "The Poet's Dream," with English words by Mal Peters, published in 1959.

Baby, Let Me Hold Your Hand
Words and music by Ray Charles.
Golden State Songs.
Best-selling record by Ray Charles (Swingtime).

Baby We're Really in Love
Words and music by Hank Williams.
Fred Rose Music, Inc.
Best-selling record in 1952 by Hank Williams (M-G-M).

Be Mine Tonight, also known as **Noche de Ronda** (Mexican)
English words by Sunny Skylar, Spanish words and music by Maria Teresa Lara.
Asociacion Mexicana de Autores y Compositores, S.A., Mexico City, D. F., 1935/Peer International Corp.
Original title, "Noche de Ronda." Introduced in Mexico by Augustine Lara.

Be My Life's Companion
Words and music by Bob Hilliard and Milton De Lugg.
Edwin H. Morris & Co., Inc.
Best-selling records by The Mills Brothers (Decca) and Rosemary Clooney (Columbia).

Beautiful Brown Eyes
Words and music by Arthur Smith and Alton Delmore.
American Music, Inc.
Adapted from a traditional "country" song. Best-selling record by Jimmy Wakely (Capitol).

Because of You, see 1940.

Because You're Mine
Words by Sammy Cahn, music by Nicholas Brodszky.
Leo Feist, Inc.
Introduced by Mario Lanza in *Because You're Mine* (film). Nominated for Academy Award, 1952.

Belle, Belle (My Liberty Belle)
Words and music by Bob Merrill.
Joy Music, Inc.
Best-selling record by Guy Mitchell (Columbia).

Bermuda
Words and music by Cynthia Strother and Eugene R. Strother.
Suffolk Music, Inc.
Best-selling record in 1952 by The Bell Sisters with Henri René and his Orchestra (RCA Victor).

Best Wishes
Words and music by Roy B. Milton.
The Bar Music Publishing Co., Ltd.
Best-selling record in 1952 by Roy Milton (Specialty).

Black Night
Words and music by Jessie Mae Robinson.
Travis Music Co.
Best-selling record by Charles Brown (Aladdin).

Blue Tango
Music by Leroy Anderson.
Mills Music, Inc.
Words by Mitchell Parish added in 1952. Best-selling record in 1951 and 1952 by Leroy Anderson and his Orchestra (Decca).

Blue Velvet
Words and music by Bernie Wayne and Lee Morris.
Vogue Music, Inc.
Initially popularized by Tony Bennett. Best-selling record in 1963 by Bobby Vinton (Epic).

Blue Violins
Music by Ray Martin.
Pickwick Music Corp.
Best-selling record, instrumental, by Hugo Winterhalter and his Orchestra (RCA Victor).

Bluebird Island
Words and music by Hank Snow.
Hill and Range Songs, Inc.
Best-selling record by Hank Snow (RCA Victor).

Bonne Nuit—Goodnight
Words and music by Jay Livingston and Ray Evans.
Burke-Van Heusen & Associates Music Corp.
Introduced by Bing Crosby in *Here Comes the Groom* (film).

Booted
Words and music by Roscoe Gordon.
Modern Music Publishing Co.
Best-selling record in 1952 by Roscoe Gordon (Chess and RPM).

Bundle of Southern Sunshine, A
Words and music by Sunny Clapp.
Milene Music.
Best-selling record in 1952 by Eddy Arnold (RCA Victor).

Calla Calla
Words by Lenny Adelson and Margarite Almeda, music by Eddie Samuels.
Peer International Corp.
Best-selling record by Vic Damone (Mercury).

Castle Rock
Words by Ervin Drake and Jimmy Shirl, music by Al Sears.
Wemar Music Corp./Arc Music Corp.
First instrumental record by Johnny Hodges and his Orchestra (Mercury). First vocal record by Frank Sinatra (Columbia).

Chains of Love
Words by Ahmet Ertegun, music by Van Walls.
Progressive Music Publishing Co., Inc.
Best-selling record by Joe Turner (Atlantic).

Cherokee Boogie
Words and music by William Chief Redbird and Moon Mullican.
Lois Publishing Co.
Best-selling record by Moon Mullican (King).

Cherry Pink and Apple Blossom White (French)
English words by Mack David, French words by Jacques Larue, music by Louiguy.
Hortensia-Music, Paris, France, 1950/Chappell & Co., Inc.
Love theme from *Underwater* (film). Best-selling records in 1955 by Perez Prado and his Orchestra (RCA Victor) and, in a vocal version, by Alan Dale (Coral).

Chica Boo
Words and music by Lloyd C. Glenn.
Golden State Songs.
Best-selling record by Lloyd Glenn (Swingtime).

Cold, Cold Heart
Words and music by Hank Williams.
Fred Rose Music, Inc.
Introduced by Hank Williams. Best-selling records by Tony Bennett (Columbia) and Hank Williams (M-G-M).

Crazy Heart
Words and music by Fred Rose and Maurice Murray.
Milene Music.
Best-selling records in 1951 by Guy Lombardo and his Royal Canadians (Decca) and in 1951 and 1952 by Hank Williams (M-G-M).

Cry
Words and music by Churchill Kohlman.
Mellow Music Publishing Co.
Best-selling record in 1951 and 1952 by Johnnie Ray (Columbia).

Cryin' Heart Blues
Words and music by J. Brown.
Aberbach, Inc.
Best-selling record by Johnnie and Jack (RCA Victor).

Dance Me Loose
Words by Mel Howard, music by Lee Erwin.
Erwin-Howard Music Corp.
Best-selling record by Arthur Godfrey and The Chordettes (Columbia).

Dear John
Words and music by Aubrey A. Gass and Tex Ritter.
Tex Ritter Music Publications, Inc.
Best-selling record by Hank Williams (M-G-M).

Dear Old Stockholm
Music by Stan Getz.
Rockaway Music Corp.
Jazz instrumental.

Destination Moon
Words by Roy Alfred, music by Marvin Fisher.
Fred Fisher Music Co., Inc.
Best-selling record by Nat "King" Cole (Capitol).

Detour, see 1945.

Didja Ever?
Words by Mann Curtis, music by Vic Mizzy.
Miller Music Corp.
Introduced by Tony Martin in *Easy To Love* (film).

Don't You Know I Love You
Words and music by Ahmet Ertegun.
Progressive Music Publishing Co., Inc.
Best-selling record by The Clovers (Atlantic).

Down the Trail of Achin' Hearts
Words and music by Jimmy Kennedy and Nat Simon.
Temple Music, Inc.
Best-selling records by Patti Page (Mercury) and Hank Snow (RCA Victor).

Down Yonder, see 1921.

Fool, Fool, Fool
Words and music by Ahmet Ertegun.
Progressive Music Publishing Co., Inc.
Best-selling records by The Clovers (Atlantic) and Kay Starr (Capitol).

Gee, Baby
Words and music by Johnny Otis.
Savoy Music Co.
Best-selling record by Johnny Otis and Mel Walker (Savoy).

Getting To Know You
Words by Oscar Hammerstein II, music by Richard Rodgers.
Williamson Music, Inc.
Introduced by Gertrude Lawrence in *The King and I* (musical).

Girl in the Wood
Words and music by Terry Gilkyson, Neal Gilkyson, and Stewart Gilkyson.
American Music, Inc.
Introduced by Frankie Laine in *Rainbow 'round My Shoulder* (film).

Give Me More, More, More of Your Kisses
Words and music by Lefty Frizzell and Ray Price.
Hill and Range Songs, Inc.
Best-selling record in 1952 by Lefty Frizzell (Columbia).

Gonna Get Along without You Now
Words and music by Milton Kellem.
Reliance Music Corp.
Introduced by Teresa Brewer. Best-selling records in 1956 by Patience and Prudence (Liberty) and in 1964 by Skeeter Davis (RCA Victor).

Got Her off My Hands but Can't Get Her off My Mind
Words by Sam Lewis and Joe Young, music by Fred Phillips.
Remick Music Corp.
Best-selling record by The Mills Brothers (Decca).

Got You on My Mind
Words and music by Joe Thomas and Howard Biggs.
Raleigh Music, Inc.
Best-selling record in 1952 by John Greer (RCA Victor).

Guy Is a Guy, A
Words and music by Oscar Brand.
Ludlow Music, Inc.
Adapted by Brand from a bawdy song of ancient origin, of which a World War II version was called "A Gob Is a Slob." Best-selling record in 1952 by Doris Day (Columbia).

Half As Much
Words and music by Curley Williams.
Fred Rose Music, Inc.
Best-selling records in 1952 by Rosemary Clooney (Columbia) and Hank Williams (M-G-M).

Heart Strings
Words and music by Merle Moore.
Hill and Range Songs, Inc.
Best-selling record by Eddy Arnold (RCA Victor).

Hello, Young Lovers
Words by Oscar Hammerstein II, music by Richard Rodgers.
Williamson Music, Inc.
Introduced by Gertrude Lawrence in *The King and I* (musical).

Here's to My Lady
Words by Johnny Mercer, music by Rube Bloom.
Mayfair Music Corp.
Best-selling record by Nat "King" Cole (Capitol).

Hey Good Lookin'
Words and music by Hank Williams.
Fred Rose Music, Inc.
Best-selling record by Hank Williams (M-G-M).

Hold Me—Hold Me—Hold Me
Words by Betty Comden and Adolph Green, music by Jule Styne.
Edwin H. Morris & Co., Inc.
Introduced by Dolores Gray in *Two on the Aisle* (revue).

House Is a Home, A
Words by Hal David, music by Leon Carr.
Hubert Music Corp.

How D'ye Do and Shake Hands
Words and music by Oliver Wallace and Cy Coben.
Walt Disney Music Co.
Introduced in *Alice in Wonderland* (cartoon film).

How High the Moon, see 1940.

Howlin' at the Moon
Words and music by Hank Williams.
Fred Rose Music, Inc.
Best-selling record by Hank Williams (M-G-M).

I Apologize, see 1931.

I Can't Help It (If I'm Still in Love with You)
Words and music by Hank Williams.
Fred Rose Music, Inc.
Best-selling record by Hank Williams (M-G-M).

(When I Dance with You) I Get Ideas (Argentine)
English words by Dorcas Cochran, music by Sanders.
Hill and Range Songs, Inc.
Adapted from the Argentine tango, "Adios Muchachos." Best-selling record by Tony Martin (RCA Victor).

I Got Loaded
Words and music by Harrison Nelson.
Travis Music Co.
Best-selling record by "Peppermint" Harris (Aladdin).

I Have Dreamed
Words by Oscar Hammerstein II, music by Richard Rodgers.
Williamson Music, Inc.
Introduced by Doretta Morrow and Larry Douglas in *The King and I* (musical).

I Like It, I Like It
Words by Mann Curtis, music by Vic Mizzy.
Frank Music Corp.
Best-selling record by Jane Turzy (M-G-M).

I Love the Sunshine of Your Smile
Words by Jack Hoffman, music by Jimmy MacDonald.
Johnstone-Montei, Inc.

I Love the Way You Say Goodnight
Words and music by Eddie Pola and George Wyle.
Remick Music Corp.
Introduced by Doris Day and Gene Nelson in *Lullaby of Broadway* (film).

I Love You a Thousand Ways
Words and music by Lefty Frizzell and Jim Beck.
Peer International Corp.
Best-selling record by Lefty Frizzell (Columbia).

I Ran All the Way Home
Words and music by Bennie Benjamin and George Weiss.
Laurel Music Corp.
Best-selling record by Eddy Howard (Mercury).

I Still See Elisa
Words by Alan Jay Lerner, music by Frederick Loewe.
Chappell & Co., Inc.
Introduced by James Barton in *Paint Your Wagon* (musical).

I Talk to the Trees
Words by Alan Jay Lerner, music by Frederick Loewe.
Chappell & Co., Inc.
Introduced by Tony Bavar and Olga San Juan in *Paint Your Wagon* (musical).

I Waited a Little Too Long
Words and music by Sidney Miller and Donald O'Connor.
Bishop Music Co.
Best-selling record by Kay Starr (Capitol).

I Wanna Play House with You
Words and music by Cy Coben.
Alamo Music, Inc.
Best-selling record by Eddy Arnold (RCA Victor).

I Want To Be with You Always
Words and music by Lefty Frizzell and Jim Beck.
Hill and Range Songs, Inc.
Best-selling record by Lefty Frizzell (Columbia).

I Whistle a Happy Tune
Words by Oscar Hammerstein II, music by Richard Rodgers.
Williamson Music, Inc.
Introduced by Gertrude Lawrence in *The King and I* (musical).

I Wish I Wuz (Hi Ho, Fiddle Dee Dee)
Words and music by Sid Kuller and Lyn Murray.
United Music Corp.
Introduced in *Slaughter Trail* (film).

I Won't Cry Anymore
Words by Fred Wise, music by Al Frisch.
United Music Corp.
Best-selling record by Tony Bennett (Columbia).

I'd Like To Baby You
Words and music by Jay Livingston and Ray Evans.
Famous Music Corp.
From *Aaron Slick from Punkin Crick* (film).

If Teardrops Were Pennies
Words and music by Carl Butler.
Peer International Corp.
Best-selling record by Carl Smith (Columbia).

If You Go (French)
English words by Geoffrey Parsons, French words and music by Michel Emer.
Éditions Masspacher, Paris, France, 1947/Peter Maurice Co., Ltd./Pickwick Music Corp.
Original title, "Si Tu Partais." Introduced in English by Vera Lynn.

If You Turn Me Down (Dee-Own-Down-Down)
Words by Carl Sigman, music by Peter De Rose.
Jefferson Music Co., Inc.
Best-selling record by Dinah Shore (RCA Victor).

I'll Buy You a Star
Words by Dorothy Fields, music by Arthur Schwartz.
Putnam Music, Inc.
Introduced by Johnny Johnston in *A Tree Grows in Brooklyn* (musical).

I'm a Fool To Want You
Words and music by Jack Wolf, Joel Herron, and Frank Sinatra.
Barton Music Corp.
Introduced by Frank Sinatra.

I'm Gonna Play the Honky Tonks
Words and music by Marie Adams and Don D. Robey.
Lois Publishing Co.
Best-selling record in 1952 by Maxie Adams (Peacock).

I'm Hans Christian Andersen
Words and music by Frank Loesser.
Frank Music Corp.
Introduced by Danny Kaye in *Hans Christian Andersen* (film).

I'm in Love Again, see 1925.

I'm in the Mood
Words and music by Jules Taub and John Lee Hooker.
Modern Music Publishing Co.
Best-selling record by John Lee Hooker (Modern).

I'm Late, see 1949.

I'm Like a New Broom
Words by Dorothy Fields, music by Arthur Schwartz.
Putnam Music, Inc.
Introduced by Johnny Johnston in *A Tree Grows in Brooklyn* (musical).

I'm on My Way
Words by Alan Jay Lerner, music by Frederick Loewe.
Chappell & Co., Inc.
Introduced by members of the cast and chorus in *Paint Your Wagon* (musical).

I'm Waiting Just for You
Words and music by Carolyn Leigh, Henry Glover, and Lucky Millinder.
Lois Publishing Co.
First recorded by Lucky Millinder (King). Revived in 1957 with best-selling record by Pat Boone (Dot).

I'm Yours To Command
Words and music by Russ Columbo.
Algonquin Music, Inc.
Previously unpublished song by the popular crooner of the early 1930's, Russ Columbo.

In the Cool, Cool, Cool of the Evening
Words by Johnny Mercer, music by Hoagy Carmichael.
Famous Music Corp.
Introduced by Bing Crosby and Jane Wyman in *Here Comes the Groom* (film). Academy Award-winning song, 1951.

Inch Worm, The
Words and music by Frank Loesser.
Frank Music Corp.
Introduced by Danny Kaye in *Hans Christian Andersen* (film).

Invitation to a Broken Heart
Words and music by Phil Baker, Paul Mann, and Al Lewis.
Famous Music Corp.

It Is No Secret What God Can Do
Words and music by Stuart Hamblen.
Duchess Music Corp.
Introduced and best-selling record by Stuart Hamblen (Columbia).

It's All in the Game
Words by Carl Sigman, music by General Charles Gates Dawes.
Remick Music Corp.
From "Melody," an instrumental composition written and published in 1912 by General Dawes, who was Vice-President of the United States from 1925 to 1929. Best-selling records in 1958 by Tommy Edwards (M-G-M) and in 1963 and 1964 by Cliff Richard (Epic).

It's Beginning To Look Like Christmas
Words and music by Meredith Willson.
Plymouth Music Co., Inc.

Jalousie, see 1927.

Jet
Words by Bennie Benjamin and George Weiss, music by Harry Revel.
Laurel Music Corp.
Introduced instrumentally by Les Baxter and his Orchestra in 1949 as part of Revel's *Perfume Set to Music* album (RCA Victor). Best-selling vocal record by Nat "King" Cole (Capitol).

Jezebel
Words and music by Wayne Shanklin.
Hill and Range Songs, Inc.
Best-selling record by Frankie Laine (Columbia).

Just When We're Falling in Love
Words by Bob Russell, music by "Sir" Charles Thompson and Illinois Jacquet.
Atlantic Music Corp.
Version without lyrics, entitled "Robbins' Nest," dedicated to disc jockey Fred Robbins, copyrighted in 1948.

Kentucky Waltz, see 1948.

Kiss To Build a Dream On, A, see 1935.

Kisses Sweeter Than Wine
Words by Paul Campbell (pseudonym for The Weavers—Pete Seeger, Lee Hays, Fred Hellerman, and Ronnie Gilbert), music by Joel Newman (pseudonym for Huddie Ledbetter).
Folkways Music Publishers, Inc.
Adapted from an old Irish folk song entitled "Drimmer's Cow." Introduced by The Weavers (Decca). Best-selling record in 1957 by Jimmie Rodgers (Roulette).

Kissin' Bug Boogie
Words by Allan Roberts, music by Robert Allen.
Laurel Music Corp.
Best-selling record by Jo Stafford (Columbia).

Lady Drinks Champagne, The
Words and music by Jack Wilson and Alan Jeffreys.
Sunbeam Music Corp.
Introduced by Johnnie Ray.

Lean Baby
Words by William May, music by Roy Alfred.
Ardmore Music Corp.
Best-selling record by Billy May and his Orchestra (Capitol).

Let Me In
Words and music by Bob Merrill.
Joy Music, Inc.
Best-selling record by The Fontane Sisters (RCA Victor).

Let Old Mother Nature Have Her Way
Words and music by Loys Southerland and Louie Clark.
Peer International Corp.
Best-selling record in 1951 and 1952 by Carl Smith (Columbia).

Let's Live a Little
Words and music by Ruth E. Coletharp.
Peer International Corp.
Best-selling record by Carl Smith (Columbia).

Life Is a Beautiful Thing
Words and music by Jay Livingston and Ray Evans.
Famous Music Corp.
Introduced by Dinah Shore in *Aaron Slick from Punkin Crick* (film).

Little White Cloud That Cried, The
Words and music by Johnnie Ray.
Carlyle Music Publishing Corp.
Introduced and best-selling record in 1951 and 1952 by Johnnie Ray (Okeh).

Lonely Little Robin
Words and music by Cy Coben.
Joy Music, Inc.
Best-selling record by Mindy Carson (Columbia).

Longing for You (English)
Words by Bernard Jansen, music by Walter Dana.
Chappell & Co., Ltd. and J. B. Cramer & Co., Ltd., London, England/Ludlow Music, Inc.
Based on Oscar Straus' "Waltz Dream." Best-selling record by Sammy Kaye and his Orchestra (Columbia).

Look What Thoughts Will Do
Words and music by Lefty Frizzell, Dub Dickerson, and Jim Beck.
Peer International Corp.
Best-selling record by Lefty Frizzell (Columbia).

Look Who's Dancing
Words by Dorothy Fields, music by Arthur Schwartz.
Putnam Music, Inc.
Introduced by Marcia Van Dyke and Shirley Booth in *A Tree Grows in Brooklyn* (musical).

Lost Love
Words and music by Percy Mayfield.
Venice Music, Inc.
Best-selling record by Percy Mayfield (Specialty).

Love Is the Reason
Words by Dorothy Fields, music by Arthur Schwartz.
Putnam Music, Inc.
Introduced by Shirley Booth in *A Tree Grows in Brooklyn* (musical).

Love Makes the World Go 'round, see La Ronde, 1954.

Love Ya
Words by Charles Tobias, music by Peter De Rose.
Harms, Inc.
Introduced by Doris Day in *On Moonlight Bay* (film).

Lygia
Words by Paul Francis Webster, music by Miklos Rozsa.
Robbins Music Corp.
Love theme from *Quo Vadis* (film).

Make the Man Love Me
Words by Dorothy Fields, music by Arthur Schwartz.
Putnam Music, Inc.
Introduced by Marcia Van Dyke and Johnny Johnston in *A Tree Grows in Brooklyn* (musical).

March of the Siamese Children, The
Music by Richard Rodgers.
Williamson Music, Inc.
Introduced in *The King and I* (musical).

Marshmallow Moon
Words and music by Jay Livingston and Ray Evans.
Famous Music Corp.
Introduced in *Aaron Slick from Punkin Crick* (film).

Metro Polka
Words and music by Willie Evans and George Vaughn (pseudonym for Vaughn Horton).
Valley Publishers, Inc.
Best-selling record by Frankie Laine (Mercury).

Midnight
Words and music by Boudleaux Bryant and Chet Atkins.
Acuff-Rose Publications.
Best-selling record in 1952 and 1953 by Red Foley (Decca).

Mister and Mississippi
Words and music by Irving Gordon.
Shapiro, Bernstein & Co., Inc.
Best-selling records by Patti Page (Mercury) and Tennessee Ernie Ford (Capitol).

Mister Moon
Words and music by Carl Smith, Autry Inman, and Shirly Lyn.
Peer International Corp.
Best-selling record by Carl Smith (Columbia).

Misto Cristofo Columbo
Words and music by Jay Livingston and Ray Evans.
Burke-Van Heusen & Associates Music Corp.
Introduced by Bing Crosby, assisted by guest artists Dorothy Lamour, Cass Daley, Louis Armstrong, and Phil Harris, in *Here Comes the Groom* (film).

Mixed Emotions
Words and music by Stuart F. Louchheim.
Roger Music, Inc.
Best-selling record by Rosemary Clooney (Columbia).

Mockin' Bird Hill, see 1949.

Mom and Dad's Waltz
Words and music by Lefty Frizzell.
Hill and Range Songs, Inc.
Best-selling record in 1951 and 1952 by Lefty Frizzell (Columbia).

Morningside of the Mountain, The
Words and music by Dick Manning and Larry Stock.
Remick Music Corp.
Best-selling record by Tommy Edwards (M-G-M).

Music Makin' Mama from Memphis
Words and music by Hank Snow.
Hill and Range Songs, Inc.
Best-selling record in 1952 by Hank Snow (RCA Victor).

My Beloved
Words and music by Jay Livingston and Ray Evans.
Famous Music Corp.
Introduced by Robert Merrill in *Aaron Slick from Punkin Crick* (film).

My First and Last Love
Words and music adapted by Remus Harris and Marvin Fisher.
Fred Fisher Music Co., Inc.
Music adapted from the "Prince" theme from Rimsky-Korsakov's "Scheherezade." Best-selling record by Nat "King" Cole (Capitol).

My Love and Devotion (English)
Words and music by Milton Carson.
John Fields Music Co., Ltd., London, England/Shapiro, Bernstein & Co., Inc.
Best-selling record by Perry Como (RCA Victor).

My Resistance Is Low
Words by Harold Adamson, music by Hoagy Carmichael.
Carmichael Music Publications, Inc.
Introduced by Hoagy Carmichael in *The Las Vegas Story* (film).

My Truly, Truly Fair
Words and music by Bob Merrill.
Joy Music, Inc.
Best-selling record by Guy Mitchell and Mitch Miller (Columbia).

Never
Words by Eliot Daniel, music by Lionel Newman.
Robbins Music Corp.
Introduced by Dennis Day in *Golden Girl* (film). Nominated for Academy Award, 1951.

No Two People
Words and music by Frank Loesser.
Frank Music Corp.
Introduced by Danny Kaye and Jane Wyman in *Hans Christian Andersen* (film).

Noche de Ronda, see **Be Mine Tonight.**

Old Soldiers Never Die
Words and music by Tom Glazer.
Warock Music, Inc.
Best-selling record by Vaughn Monroe (RCA Victor).

On Top of Old Smoky
New words and arrangement by Pete Seeger.
Folkways Music Publishers, Inc.
Adaptation of an American Southern Highlands folk song popularized by The Weavers and Gordon Jenkins (Decca).

Once
Words by Bob Russell, music by Harold Spina.
Walt Disney Music Co.
Best-selling record by Billy Eckstine (M-G-M).

One Little Candle
Words by Jay Maloy Roach, music by George Mysels.
Shawnee Press, Inc.
Best-selling record in 1952 by Perry Como (RCA Victor).

Place in the Sun, A
Words by Jay Livingston and Ray Evans, music by Franz Waxman.
Paramount Music Corp.
Theme from *A Place in the Sun* (film). Academy Award-winning score.

Please Mr. Sun
Words by Sid Frank, music by Ray Getzov.
Weiss & Barry, Inc.
Best-selling records in 1951 and 1952 by Johnnie Ray (Columbia) and in 1951 by Tommy Edwards (M-G-M).

Please Send Me Someone To Love
Words and music by Percy Mayfield.
Venice Music, Inc./Hill and Range Songs, Inc.
Best-selling record in 1950 and 1951 by Percy Mayfield (Specialty).

Pretty-Eyed Baby, see 1947.

Puzzlement, A
Words by Oscar Hammerstein II, music by Richard Rodgers.
Williamson Music, Inc.
Introduced by Yul Brynner in *The King and I* (musical).

Quiet Village
Music by Les Baxter.
Granson Music Co.
Introduced by Les Baxter and his Orchestra as part of an album of original music entitled *Le Sacre du Sauvage* (Capitol). Best-selling record in 1959 by Martin Denny (Liberty).

Ramblin' Man
Words and music by Hank Williams.
Fred Rose Music, Inc.
Best-selling record in 1953 by Hank Williams (M-G-M).

Red's Boogie
Music by Willie Perryman.
Hill and Range Songs, Inc.
Best-selling record, instrumental, by Piano Red (RCA Victor).

Rhumba Boogie, The
Words and music by Hank Snow.
Hill and Range Songs, Inc.
Best-selling record by Hank Snow (RCA Victor).

Robbins' Nest, see **Just When We're Falling in Love.**

Rocket 88
Words and music by Jackie Brenston.
Hill and Range Songs, Inc.
Best-selling record by Jackie Brenston (Chess).

Rose, Rose, I Love You (Chinese)
Words by Wilfred Thomas, music adapted from a traditional Chinese melody.
Chappell & Co., Inc.
Best-selling records by Frankie Laine (Columbia) and Gordon Jenkins (Decca).

Satisfied
Words and music by Martha Carson.
Acuff-Rose Publications.
Introduced by Martha Carson (RCA Victor).

Seven Long Days
Words and music by Jessie Mae Robinson.
Travis Music Co.
Best-selling record by Charles Brown (Aladdin).

Seven Wonders of the World, The
Words and music by Cy Coben.
George Paxton, Inc.
Best-selling record by Skip Farrell (M-G-M).

Shall We Dance?
Words by Oscar Hammerstein II, music by Richard Rodgers.
Williamson Music, Inc.
Introduced by Gertrude Lawrence and Yul Brynner in *The King and I* (musical).

(Why Did I Tell You I Was Going to) Shanghai
Words and music by Bob Hilliard and Milton De Lugg.
Advanced Music Corp.
Best-selling record by Doris Day (Columbia).

Shrimp Boats
Words and music by Paul Mason Howard and Paul Weston.
Walt Disney Music Co.
Best-selling record in 1951 and 1952 by Jo Stafford (Columbia).

Sick, Sober and Sorry
Words and music by Tex Atchinson and Eddie Hazelwood.
Red River Songs, Inc.
Best-selling record by Johnny Bond (Columbia).

Silver and Gold
Words by Henry Prichard, music by Del Sharbutt and Bob Crosby.
Blue River Music, Inc.
Best-selling record in 1952 by Pee Wee King (RCA Victor).

(It's No) Sin
Words by Chester R. Shull, music by George Haven.
Algonquin Music, Inc.
First record made by The Four Aces, produced in Chester, Pennsylvania for Victoria Records. Best-selling records by The Four Aces (Decca) and Eddy Howard (Mercury).

Sixty Minute Man
Words and music by William Ward and Rose Marks.
Armo Music Corp.
Best-selling record by Billy Ward and The Dominoes (Federal).

Slow Poke
Words and music by Pee Wee King, Redd Stewart, and Chilton Price.
Ridgeway Music.
Best-selling record in 1951 and 1952 by Pee Wee King (RCA Victor).

Snowflakes
Words and music by Marjorie Kurtz.
Lombardo Music, Inc.
Winner of the *Songs for Sale* television show competition when the composer was nine years old. Best-selling record by Evelyn Knight with Guy Lombardo and his Royal Canadians (Decca). Sung by Judy Garland in 1963 in *A Child Is Waiting* (film).

Solitaire
Words by Renée Borek and Carl Nutter, music by King Guion.
Screen Gems-Columbia Music, Inc.
Best-selling record by Tony Bennett (Columbia).

Somebody Bigger Than You and I
Words and music by Johnny Lange, Hy Heath, and Sonny Burke.
Bulls-Eye Music, Inc.
Introduced by Gene Autry in *The Old West* (film).

Somebody's Been Beatin' My Time
Words and music by Zeke Clements.
Hill and Range Songs, Inc.
Best-selling record by Eddy Arnold (RCA Victor).

Somebody's Stolen My Honey
Words and music by Boudleaux Bryant.
Acuff-Rose Publications.
Best-selling record by Ernest Tubb (Decca).

Something Old, Something New (Something Borrowed and Blue)
Words and music by Cy Coben and Charles Grean.
Alamo Music, Inc.
Best-selling record by Eddy Arnold (RCA Victor).

Something Wonderful
Words by Oscar Hammerstein II, music by Richard Rodgers.
Williamson Music, Inc.
Introduced by Dorothy Sarnoff in *The King and I* (musical).

Song Angels Sing, The
Words by Paul Francis Webster, music adapted by Irving Aaronson.
Leo Feist, Inc.
Music based on the Third Movement of Brahm's "Third Symphony." Introduced by Mario Lanza in *Because You're Mine* (film).

Sound Off
Words and music by Willie Lee Duckworth.
Shapiro, Bernstein & Co., Inc.
Song originally used for close order drill training by units of the United States armed forces and originally published in *The Cadence System of Teaching Close Order Drill,* by Colonel Bernard Lentz. Best-selling popular record by Vaughn Monroe (RCA Victor).

Sparrow in the Treetop
Words and music by Bob Merrill.
Joy Music, Inc.
Best-selling record by Guy Mitchell and Mitch Miller (Columbia).

Straight, No Chaser
Music by Thelonious Monk.
Thelonious Music.
Introduced on records by Thelonious Monk (Blue Note).

Strange Little Girl, The
Words and music by Jerry Ross and Richard Adler.
Frank Music Corp.
Best-selling record by Eddy Howard (Mercury).

Suzy Snowflake
Words and music by Sid Tepper and Roy Brodsky.
Alamo Music, Inc.
Best-selling record by Rosemary Clooney (Columbia).

Sweet Violets
Words and music adapted by Cy Coben and Charles Grean.
Edwin H. Morris & Co., Inc.
Adapted from a traditional folk song. Best-selling record by Dinah Shore (RCA Victor).

"T" 99 Blues
Words and music by Jules Taub and Jimmy Nelson.
Modern Music Publishing Co.
Best-selling record by Jimmy Nelson (RPM).

Tell Me Why
Words by Al Alberts, music by Marty Gold.
Signet Music Co.
Best-selling records in 1951 and 1952 by The Four Aces (Decca) and Eddie Fisher (RCA Victor).

Tell Me You Love Me
Words and music by Sammy Kaye.
Republic Music Corp.
Adapted from the aria, "Vesti la Giubba," from R. Leoncavallo's opera, *Pagliacci*. Best-selling record by Vic Damone (Mercury).

Tell the Lady I Said Goodbye
Words and music by Johnnie Ray.
Carlyle Music Publishing Corp.
First recording, coupled with "Whiskey and Gin," made by Johnnie Ray (Okeh).

Tend To Your Business, see 1954.

That's What You're Doing to Me
Words and music by Rose Marks and William Ward.
Lois Publishing Co.
Best-selling record in 1952 by The Dominoes (Federal).

There Stands the Glass
Words and music by Mary Jean Shurtz and Russ Hull.
Hill and Range Songs, Inc.
Best-selling record in 1953 and 1954 by Webb Pierce (Decca).

There's Been a Change in Me
Words and music by Cy Coben.
Alamo Music, Inc.
Best-selling record by Eddy Arnold (RCA Victor).

These Things I Offer You (For a Lifetime)
Words and music by Morty Nevins, Bennie Benjamin, and George Weiss.
Valando Music Corp.
Best-selling record by Sarah Vaughan (Columbia).

They Call the Wind Maria
Words by Alan Jay Lerner, music by Frederick Loewe.
Chappell & Co., Inc.
Introduced by Rufus Smith in *Paint Your Wagon* (musical).

Too Old To Cut the Mustard
Words and music by Bill Carlisle.
Acuff-Rose Publications.
Best-selling record in 1952 by Red Foley and Ernest Tubb (Decca). Also recorded by Marlene Dietrich in duet with Rosemary Clooney (Columbia).

Too Young
Words by Sylvia Dee, music by Sid Lippman.
Jefferson Music Co., Inc.
Introduced by Johnny Desmond. Best-selling record by Nat "King" Cole (Capitol).

Travelin' Blues, see 1931.

Tulips and Heather
Words and music by Milton Carson.
Shapiro, Bernstein & Co., Inc.
Best-selling record by Perry Como (RCA Victor).

Turn Back the Hands of Time
Words and music by Jimmy Eaton, Larry Wagner, and Con Hammond.
Choice Music, Inc.
Best-selling record by Eddie Fisher (RCA Victor).

Two Brothers
Words and music by Irving Gordon.
Shapiro, Bernstein & Co., Inc.
Introduced by Kay Starr.

Unbirthday Song, The, see 1948.

Uncle Pen
Words and music by Bill Monroe.
Kentucky Music, Inc.
Best-selling record in 1956 by Porter Wagoner (RCA Victor).

Undecided, see 1939.

Under Paris Skies (French)
English words by Kim Gannon, French words by Jean Drejac, music by Hubert Giraud.
Éditions Choudens, Paris, France/Leeds Music Corp.
Original French title, "Sous le Ciel de Paris."

Unforgettable
Words and music by Irving Gordon.
Bourne, Inc.
Best-selling records by Nat "King" Cole (Capitol) and in 1959 by Dinah Washington (Mercury).

Unless, see 1934.

Vanity
Words by Jack Manus and Bernard Bierman, music by Guy Wood.
Jefferson Music Co., Inc.
Best-selling record by Don Cherry (Decca).

Wand'rin Star
Words by Alan Jay Lerner, music by Frederick Loewe.
Chappell & Co., Inc.
Introduced by Rufus Smith, Robert Penn, and Jared Reed in *Paint Your Wagon* (musical).

We Kiss in a Shadow
Words by Oscar Hammerstein II, music by Richard Rodgers.
Williamson Music, Inc.
Introduced by Doretta Morrow and Larry Douglas in *The King and I* (musical).

Weary Blues from Waitin'
Words and music by Hank Williams.
Fred Rose Music, Inc.
Best-selling record in 1953 by Hank Williams (M-G-M).

Weaver of Dreams
Words by Jack Elliott, music by Victor Young.
Edward Kassner Music Co., Inc.
Best-selling record by Nat "King" Cole (Capitol).

Weepin' and Cryin'
Words and music by Tommy Brown.
T. Brown & Sons.
Best-selling record in 1952 by The Griffin Brothers (Dot).

When You and I Were Young Maggie Blues, see 1922.

While You Danced, Danced, Danced
Words and music by Stephan Weiss.
Cromwell Music, Inc.
Best-selling record by Georgia Gibbs (Mercury).

Whiskey and Gin
Words and music by Johnnie Ray.
Carlyle Music Publishing Corp.
First recording, coupled with "Tell the Lady I Said Goodbye," made by Johnnie Ray (Okeh).

Whispering, see 1920.

Willie the Whistling Giraffe
Words by Rube Goldberg, music by Ruth Cleary Patterson.
Ben Bloom Music Corp.

Wimoweh (South African)
Words and music adapted and arranged by Paul Campbell (collective pseudonym for The Weavers—Pete Seeger, Fred Hellerman, Lee Hays, and Ronnie Gilbert). New lyrics by Roy Ilene added in 1952.
Folkways Music Publishers, Inc.
Adapted from the South African (Zulu) song, "Mbube," first recorded in South Africa in the 1930's by Solomon Linda. Best-selling record by The Weavers and Gordon Jenkins (Decca). Adapted in 1961 as "The Lion Sleeps Tonight," with new words and music by Hugo Peretti, Luigi Creatore, George Weiss, and Albert Stanton. Best-selling record in 1961 by The Tokens (RCA Victor).

Wonderful Copenhagen
Words and music by Frank Loesser.
Frank Music Corp.
Introduced by Danny Kaye in *Hans Christian Andersen* (film).

World Is Waiting for the Sunrise, The, see 1919.

Would I Love You (Love You, Love You)
Words by Bob Russell, music by Harold Spina.
Walt Disney Music Co.
Best-selling record by Patti Page (Mercury).

You Can Fly! You Can Fly! You Can Fly!
Words by Sammy Cahn, music by Sammy Fain.
Walt Disney Music Co.
Introduced in *Peter Pan* (cartoon film).

1952

Alabama Jubilee, see 1915.

Alone at Last
Words by Bob Hilliard, music by Victor Young.
Paramount Music Corp.
Introduced in *Something To Live For* (film).

Am I in Love
Words and music by Jack Brooks.
Famous Music Corp.
Introduced by Bob Hope and Jane Russell in *Son of Paleface* (film). Nominated for Academy Award, 1952.

Anywhere I Wander
Words and music by Frank Loesser.
Frank Music Corp.
Introduced by Danny Kaye in *Hans Christian Andersen* (film). Best-selling record in 1953 by Julius La Rosa (Cadence).

Are You Teasing Me?
Words and music by Ira Louvin and Charles Louvin.
Acuff-Rose Publications.
Best-selling record by Carl Smith (Columbia).

A-round the Corner (Beneath the Berry Tree), see 1950.

Auf Wiederseh'n, Sweetheart (German)
Words by John Sexton and John Turner, music by Eberhard Storch.
Editions Corso GmbH, Berlin, Germany, 1949/Peter Maurice Music Co., Ltd., London, England/Hill and Range Songs, Inc.
Best-selling record by Vera Lynn (produced in England) (London).

Baby, Don't Do It
Words and music by Lowman Pauling.
Bess Music Co.
Best-selling record in 1953 by The Five Royales (Apollo).

Back Street Affair
Words and music by Billy Wallace.
Copar-Forrest Music Corp.
Best-selling record in 1952 and 1953 by Webb Pierce (Decca).

Be Anything (But Be Mine)
Words and music by Irving Gordon.
Shapiro, Bernstein & Co., Inc.
Best-selling record by Eddy Howard (Mercury).

Bells
Words and music by Billy Ward.
Billy Ward Music Co.
Best-selling record in 1953 by The Dominoes (Federal).

Beloved
Words by Paul Francis Webster, music by Nicholas Brodszky.
Harms, Inc.
Introduced by Mario Lanza in *The Student Prince* (film).

Bemsha Swing
Music by Thelonious Monk and Denzil Best.
Bayes Music Corp.
Introduced by Thelonious Monk (Blue Note).

Bigger the Figure, The
Words and music by Marshall Barer and Alec Wilder.
Dartmouth Music, Inc.
Melody based on "Largo al Factotum" from Rossini's *Barber of Seville*. Best-selling record by Louis Prima (Columbia).

Bim Bam Baby
Words and music by Sammy Mysels.
Case Music Corp.
Best-selling record by Frank Sinatra (Columbia).

Blackberry Boogie
Words and music by Ernie J. Ford.
Central Songs, Inc.
Best-selling record by Tennessee Ernie Ford (Capitol).

Blacksmith Blues, The
Words and music by Jack Holmes.
Hill and Range Songs, Inc.
Copyrighted in 1950 under the title "Happy Payoff Day." Best-selling record by Ella Mae Morse (Capitol).

Blow Out the Candle
Words and music by Phil Moore.
Chappell & Co., Inc.
Best-selling record by Jane Wyman (Decca).

Blues in Advance
Words and music by Nell Drummond.
Hollis Music, Inc.
Introduced by Dinah Shore.

Boston Beguine
Words and music by Sheldon M. Harnick.
Joy Music, Inc.
A satire on tropical love songs introduced by Alice Ghostley in *New Faces of 1952* (revue).

Botch-a-Me (Italian)
English words and music adaptation by Eddie Y. Stanley, Italian words and music by R. Morbelli and L. Astore.
Fono Enic S.A., Milan, Italy, 1941/Hollis Music, Inc.
Original title, "Ba-Ba Baciami Piccina." Introduced in *Una Famiglia Impossibile* (Italian film). Best-selling record by Rosemary Clooney (Columbia).

Bourbon Street Parade
Music by Paul Barbarin.
Travis Music Co.
First recorded by Paul Barbarin and his New Orleans Band (Atlantic).

Bunny Hop, The
Words and music by Ray Anthony and Leonard Auletti.
Moonlight Music, Inc.
Best-selling record by Ray Anthony and his Orchestra (Capitol).

Call Operator 210
Words and music by Floyd Dixon.
Travis Music Co.
Best-selling record by Floyd Dixon (Aladdin).

Charmaine, see 1926.

Chelsea Bridge
Music by Billy Strayhorn.
Tempo Music, Inc.
Introduced instrumentally by Duke Ellington and his Orchestra.

Chicago Style
Words by Johnny Burke, music by James Van Heusen.
Famous Music Corp.
Introduced by Bob Hope and Bing Crosby in *Road to Bali* (film).

Choo'n Gum, see 1950.

Comes A-long A-Love
Words and music by Al Sherman.
Shapiro, Bernstein & Co., Inc.
Best-selling record by Kay Starr (Capitol).

Count Your Blessings Instead of Sheep
Words and music by Irving Berlin.
Irving Berlin Music Corp.
Introduced by Bing Crosby in *White Christmas* (film, 1954). Nominated for Academy Award, 1954. Best-selling record by Eddie Fisher (RCA Victor).

Daddy, Daddy
Words and music by Rudolph Toombs.
Progressive Music Publishing Co., Inc.
Best-selling record by Ruth Brown (Atlantic).

Day of Jubilo, The
Words and music by Terry Gilkyson.
Montclare Music Corp.
Best-selling record by Guy Mitchell (Columbia).

Delia's Gone
Words and music by Blake Alphonso Higgs (Blind Blake).
Hollis Music, Inc.
From a West Indian folk song. Best-selling record by Harry Belafonte (RCA Victor).

Delicado (Brazilian)
Words by Jack Lawrence, music by Waldyr Azevedo.
Remick Music Corp.
Best-selling record by Percy Faith and his Orchestra (Columbia).

Dennis the Menace
Words by Dick Manning, music by Al Hoffman.
Joy Music, Inc.
Based on the comic strip, *Dennis the Menace,* by Hank Ketcham. Best-selling record by Rosemary Clooney and Jimmy Boyd (Columbia).

Doggie in the Window, see That Doggie in the Window.

Don't Ever Be Afraid To Go Home
Words by Bob Hilliard, music by Carl Sigman.
Remick Music Corp.
Best-selling record by Bing Crosby (Decca).

Don't Just Stand There (When You Feel Like You're in Love)
Words and music by Ernest Tubb and Cherokee Jack Henley.
Ernest Tubb Music, Inc.
Best-selling record by Carl Smith (Columbia).

Don't Stay Away ('Till Love Grows Cold)
Words and music by Lefty Frizzell and Loys Southerland.
Hill and Range Songs, Inc.
Best-selling record by Lefty Frizzell (Columbia).

Dream Girl
Words and music by Marvin Phillips and Jesse Belvin.
Venice Music, Inc.
Best-selling record in 1953 by Jesse and Marvin (Specialty).

Easy, Easy Baby
Words and music by Rudolph Toombs.
Savoy Music Co.
Best-selling record by Varetta Dillard (Savoy).

Easy on the Eyes
Words and music by Cy Coben and Eddy Arnold.
Alamo Music, Inc.
Best-selling record by Eddy Arnold (RCA Victor).

Ecstasy Tango
Music by José Belmonte.
Sidney Bron, London, England/Jefferson Music Co., Inc.
Best-selling record, instrumental, by The Three Suns (RCA Victor).

Eggbert, the Easter Egg
Words and music by Sid Tepper and Roy Brodsky.
Alamo Music, Inc.

Eight Days in a Week
Words and music by Warren Weidler, Walter Weidler, and George Weidler.
Daywin Music, Inc.
Introduced by Doris Day (Columbia).

Every Day, see **Every Day I Have the Blues.**

Every Day I Have the Blues, also known as **Every Day**
Words and music by Peter Chatman.
Arc Music Corp./Golden State Songs.
Originally copyrighted under the title, "Nobody Loves Me." Introduced in 1950 by Lowell Fulson (Swingtime). Best-selling record by Joe Williams with Count Basie and his Orchestra.

Ev'ry Street's a Boulevard in Old New York
Words by Bob Hilliard, music by Jule Styne.
Chappell & Co., Inc.
Introduced by Jack Whiting in 1953 in *Hazel Flagg* (musical). Featured in 1954 in *Living It Up* (film).

Faith Can Move Mountains
Words by Ben Raleigh, music by Guy Wood.
Hill and Range Songs, Inc.
Best-selling record by Johnnie Ray (Columbia).

Fandango
Words by Johnny Bradford, music by Frank Perkins.
Mills Music, Inc.
Best-selling record, instrumental, by Hugo Winterhalter and his Orchestra (RCA Victor).

Feet Up (Pat Him on the Po-Po)
Words and music by Bob Merrill.
Joy Music, Inc.
Best-selling record by Guy Mitchell and Mitch Miller (Columbia).

Five Long Years
Words and music by Eddie Boyd.
Frederick Music Co.
Best-selling record by Eddie Boyd (Job).

5-10-15 Hours
Words and music by Rudolph Toombs.
Progressive Music Publishing Co., Inc.
Best-selling record by Ruth Brown (Atlantic).

Fool Such As I, A
Words and music by Bill Trader.
Leeds Music Corp.
Best-selling record in 1953 by Jo Stafford (Columbia). Revived in 1959 by Elvis Presley (RCA Victor).

For the Very First Time
Words and music by Irving Berlin.
Irving Berlin Music Corp.

Forever and Always
Words and music by Lefty Frizzell and Lessie Lyle.
Hill and Range Songs, Inc.
Best-selling record by Lefty Frizzell (Columbia).

Full Time Job
Words and music by Gerry Tiefer.
Acuff-Rose Publications.
Best-selling record by Eddy Arnold (RCA Victor).

Funny (Not Much)
Words and music by Hughie Prince, Marcia Neil, and Philip Broughton.
Shapiro, Bernstein & Co., Inc.
Best-selling record by Nat "King" Cole (Capitol).

Gal Who Invented Kissin', The
Words and music by Charles Orr and Earl Griswold.
Hill and Range Songs, Inc.
Best-selling record in 1952 and 1953 by Hank Snow (RCA Victor).

Gandy Dancers' Ball, The
Words and music by Paul Weston and Paul Mason Howard.
Walt Disney Music Co.
Best-selling record by Frankie Laine (Columbia).

Glow-Worm, The (German)
Revised English words by Johnny Mercer, first English version by Lilla Cayley Robinson, original German words and music by Paul Lincke.
Apollo Verlag, Berlin, Germany, 1902/Edward B. Marks Music Corp., 1907, 1952.
Original German title, "Glühwürmchen." First introduced in the United States by May Naudain in Lew Fields' production of *The Girl behind the Counter* (musical). Best-selling record of the new version in 1952 and 1953 by The Mills Brothers (Decca).

Goin' Home
Words and music by Antoine "Fats" Domino and Alvin E. Young.
Travis Music Co.
Best-selling record by Fats Domino (Imperial).

Goin' Steady
Words and music by Faron Young.
Central Songs, Inc.
Best-selling record by Faron Young (Capitol).

Gold Rush Is Over, The
Words and music by Cindy Walker.
Hill and Range Songs, Inc.
Best-selling record by Hank Snow (RCA Victor).

Gone
Words and music by Smokey Rogers.
Elvis Presley Music, Inc./Dallas Music Co., Inc.
Best-selling record in 1957 by Ferlin Husky (Capitol).

Greatest Show on Earth, The
Words by Ned Washington, music by Victor Young.
Famous Music Corp.
Introduced in *The Greatest Show on Earth* (film).

Guess Who I Saw Today
Words and music by Elisse Boyd and Murray Grand.
Joy Music, Inc.
Introduced by June Carroll in *New Faces of 1952* (revue).

Hambone
Words and music by Red Saunders and Leon Washington.
Rush Music Corp.
Adapted from a traditional children's play song. Best-selling records by Red Saunders and his Orchestra with Dolores Hawkins (Okeh) and Jo Stafford and Frankie Laine (Columbia).

Have a Good Time
Words and music by Felice Bryant and Boudleaux Bryant.
Acuff-Rose Publications.
Best-selling record by Tony Bennett (Columbia).

Have Mercy, Baby
Words and music by Billy Ward.
Vogue Music, Inc.
Best-selling record by The Dominoes (Federal).

Have You Heard
Words and music by Lew Douglas, Frank Lavere, and Roy Rodde.
Brandom Music Co.
Best-selling record in 1953 by Joni James (M-G-M).

Heavenly Father
Words and music by Edna McGriff.
Garrawak Music Co.
Best-selling record by Edna McGriff (Jubilee).

Here in My Heart
Words and music by Pat Genaro, Lou Levinson, and Bill Borrelli.
Mellin Music, Inc.
Best-selling record by Al Martino (BBS).

He's a Tramp
Words and music by Peggy Lee and Sonny Burke.
Walt Disney Music Co.
Introduced by Peggy Lee in 1955 on the soundtrack of *The Lady and the Tramp* (cartoon film).

Hey, Miss Fannie
Words and music by Ahmet Ertegun.
Progressive Music Publishing Co., Inc.
Best-selling record by The Clovers (Atlantic).

High Noon, also known as **Do Not Forsake Me**
Words by Ned Washington, music by Dimitri Tiomkin.
Leo Feist, Inc.
Introduced by Tex Ritter in *High Noon* (film). Academy Award-winning song, 1952. Best-selling record by Frankie Laine (Columbia).

Hi-Lili, Hi-Lo
Words by Helen Deutsch, music by Bronislau Kaper.
Robbins Music Corp.
Introduced by Leslie Caron and Mel Ferrer in *Lili* (film).

Hold Me, Thrill Me, Kiss Me
Words and music by Harry Noble.
Mills Music, Inc.
Best-selling record in 1953 by Karen Chandler (Coral).

Honky Tonk Blues, see 1948.

Hot Toddy
Words by Herb Hendler, music by Ralph Flanagan.
Valley Entertainment Enterprises, Inc.
Introduced and best-selling record by Ralph Flanagan and his Orchestra (RCA Victor).

How Do You Speak to an Angel?
Words by Bob Hilliard, music by Jule Styne.
Chappell & Co., Inc.
Introduced by John Howard in 1953 in *Hazel Flagg* (musical). Sung by Dean Martin in 1954 in *Living It Up* (film).

"I"
Words and music by Milton Berle, Buddy Arnold, and Robert Mellin.
Sherwin Music, Inc.
Best-selling record by Don Cornell (Coral).

I Believe
Words and music by Ervin Drake, Jimmy Shirl, Al Stillman, and Irvin Graham.
Cromwell Music, Inc.
Introduced by Jane Froman on her television show, *USA Canteen.* Best-selling record in 1953 by Frankie Laine (Columbia).

I Don't Know
Words and music by Willie Mabon, with additional lyrics by Joe Thomas.
Republic Music Corp.
Best-selling records in 1953 by Willie Mabon (Chess) and Buddy Morrow (RCA Victor).

I Feel Like I'm Gonna Live Forever
Words by Bob Hilliard, music by Jule Styne.
Chappell & Co., Inc.
Introduced by Helen Gallagher in 1953 in *Hazel Flagg* (musical).

I Hear a Rhapsody, see 1940.

I Heard the Bluebirds Sing
Words and music by Hod Pharis.
Peer International Corp.
Best-selling record in 1957 by Jim Edward and Maxine and Bonnie Brown (RCA Victor).

I Laughed at Love
Words by Benny Davis, music by Abner Silver.
Redd Evans Music Co.
Best-selling record by Sunny Gale (RCA Victor).

I Let the Stars Get in My Eyes
Words and music by Slim Willet.
Four Star Sales Co.
Best-selling record in 1953 by Goldie Hill (Decca).

I Remember When (French)
Music by Sidney Bechet.
S.A.R.L. Vogue Records, Paris, France/Regent Music Corp.
Original title, "Si Tu Vois Ma Mère." Bechet's instrumental recording released in the United States in 1956 (Coral).

I Saw Mommy Kissing Santa Claus
Words and music by Tommie Connor.
Harman Music, Inc.
Best-selling record by Jimmy Boyd (Columbia).

I Want To Be Evil
Words and music by Raymond Taylor and Lester Judson.
Duchess Music Corp.
Best-selling record by Eartha Kitt (RCA Victor).

I Went to Your Wedding
Words and music by Jessie Mae Robinson.
St. Louis Music Corp.
Best-selling records by Patti Page (Mercury) and Hank Snow (RCA Victor).

I Won't Be Home No More
Words and music by Hank Williams.
Fred Rose Music, Inc.
Best-selling record by Hank Williams (M-G-M).

I'll Drown in My Tears
Words and music by Henry Glover.
Lois Publishing Co.
Best-selling record by Sonny Thompson (King).

I'll Never Get Out of This World Alive
Words and music by Hank Williams and Fred Rose.
Milene Music.
Best-selling record in 1952 and 1953 by Hank Williams (M-G-M).

I'll Walk with God
Words by Paul Francis Webster, music by Nicholas Brodszky.
Harms, Inc.
Introduced by Mario Lanza in *The Student Prince* (film).

I'm an Old Old Man (Tryin' To Live While I Can)
Words and music by Lefty Frizzell.
Hill and Range Songs, Inc.
Best-selling record by Lefty Frizzell (Columbia).

I'm Gone
Words and music by Leonard Lee and Dave Bartholomew.
Travis Music Co.
Best-selling record in 1953 by Shirley and Lee (Aladdin).

I'm Gonna Walk and Talk with My Lord
Words and music by Martha Carson.
Acuff-Rose Publications.

I'm in Love with Miss Logan
Words and music by Ronnie Graham.
Joy Music, Inc.
Introduced by Robert Clary in *New Faces of 1952* (revue).

I'm Never Satisfied
Words and music by Herb Perry.
Simon House, Inc.
Best-selling record by Nat "King" Cole (Capitol).

I'm Yours
Words and music by Robert Mellin.
Algonquin Music, Inc.
Best-selling records by Eddie Fisher (RCA Victor) and Don Cornell (Coral).

Indian Love Call, see 1924.

Invitation
Music by Bronislau Kaper.
Robbins Music Corp.
Theme from *Invitation* (film). Words by Paul Francis Webster added in 1956.

It Isn't Right
Words and music by Robert Mellin.
Mellin Music, Inc.
Best-selling record in 1955 by The Platters (Mercury).

It Wasn't God Who Made Honky Tonk Angels
Words and music by J. D. Miller.
Peer International Corp.
Best-selling record by Kitty Wells (Decca).

It's a Lovely, Lovely World
Words and music by Boudleaux Bryant.
Acuff-Rose Publications.
Best-selling record by Carl Smith (Columbia).

It's in the Book
Words and music by Johnny Standley and Art Thorsen.
Magnolia Publishing Co.
Best-selling record by Johnny Standley (Capitol).

Jambalaya (On the Bayou)
Words and music by Hank Williams.
Fred Rose Music, Inc.
Introduced by Hank Williams. Best-selling records by Hank Williams (M-G-M) and Jo Stafford (Columbia).

Juke
Words and music by Walter Jacobs.
Arc Music Corp.
Best-selling record by Little Walter (Checker).

Jump Back Honey
Words and music by Hadda Brooks.
Rush Music Corp.
Introduced by Hadda Brooks.

Junco Partner
Words and music by Ellen Shad.
Frederick Music Co.
Best-selling record by Richard Hayes (Mercury).

Just a Little Lovin' Will Go a Long Way
Words and music by Eddy Arnold and Zeke Clements.
Hill and Range Songs, Inc.

Just Because You're You
Words by Carolyn Leigh, music by Nacio Porter Brown.
Sunbeam Music Corp.
Best-selling record by Jo Stafford (Columbia).

Just Like a Man
Words by Ogden Nash, music by Vernon Duke.
Remick Music Corp.
Introduced by Bette Davis in *Two's Company* (revue).

K. C. Loving, see **Kansas City,** 1959.

Kansas City, see 1959.

Kaw-Liga
Words and music by Fred Rose and Hank Williams.
Milene Music.
Best-selling record in 1953 by Hank Williams (M-G-M).

Keep It a Secret
Words and music by Jessie Mae Robinson.
Shapiro, Bernstein & Co., Inc.
Best-selling records in 1952 and 1953 by Slim Whitman (Imperial) and Jo Stafford (Columbia).

Kiss of Fire (Argentine)
Words and adaptation of music by Lester Allen and Robert Hill, original music by A. G. Villoldo.
Duchess Music Corp.
Adapted from the Argentine tango, "El Choclo," first published in the United States in 1913. Best-selling record by Georgia Gibbs (Mercury).

Lady Love
Words and music by Lester Lee and Bob Russell.
Cromwell Music, Inc.
Introduced in *Sound Off* (film). Best-selling record by Vaughn Monroe (RCA Victor).

Lady Loves, A
Words by Mack Gordon, music by Josef Myrow.
Leo Feist, Inc.
Introduced by Debbie Reynolds in *I Love Melvin* (film).

Lady of Spain, see 1931.

Lady's Man
Words and music by Cy Coben.
Alamo Music, Inc.
Best-selling record by Hank Snow (RCA Victor).

Last Waltz, The
Words and music by Webb Pierce and Myrna Freeman.
Ark-La-Tex Publishing Co.
Best-selling record by Webb Pierce (Decca).

Lawdy Miss Clawdy
Words and music by Lloyd Price.
Venice Music, Inc.
Best-selling record by Lloyd Price (Specialty).

Let Me Go Home Whiskey, also known as **Let's Go Home Whiskey**
Words and music by Shifte Henri.
Travis Music Co.
Best-selling record in 1953 by Amos Milburn (Aladdin).

Let's Go Home Whiskey, see **Let Me Go Home Whiskey.**

Lizzie Borden
Words and music by Michael Brown.
Hill and Range Songs, Inc.
Introduced in *New Faces of 1952* (revue).

Love Is a Simple Thing
Words by June Carroll, music by Arthur Siegel.
Joy Music, Inc.
Introduced by Rosemary O'Reilly, Robert Clary, Eartha Kitt, and June Carroll in *New Faces of 1952* (revue).

Lover, see 1933.

Lullaby of Birdland
Words by B. Y. Forster, music by George Shearing.
Patricia Music Publishing Corp.
Entitled after the New York jazz club, Birdland. Introduced by George Shearing. Best-selling version (in French) by The Blue Stars (Mercury).

Luna Rossa, also known as **Blushing Moon** (Italian)
English words by Kermit Goell, Italian words by V. De Crescenzo, music by A. Vian.
Edizioni Abici, Naples, Italy, 1951/Bregman, Vocco & Conn, Inc.
Best-selling record by Tony Martin (RCA Victor).

Ma Says, Pa Says (South African)
Words and music by Josef Marais.
Artists Music, Inc.
From the South African repertoire of Josef Marais. Best-selling record by Doris Day and Johnnie Ray (Columbia).

Married by the Bible, Divorced by the Law
Words and music by Johnny Rector, Pee Wee Truehitt, and Neva Starns.
Hill and Range Songs, Inc.
Best-selling record by Hank Snow (RCA Victor).

Meet Mister Callaghan (English)
Music by Eric Spear.
David Toff Music Publishing Co., London, England/Leeds Music Corp.
Best-selling record, instrumental, by Les Paul and Mary Ford (Capitol).

Middle of the Night
Words and music by Ahmet Ertegun.
Progressive Music Publishing Co., Inc.
Best-selling record by The Clovers (Atlantic).

Midnight Hour, The
Words and music by Sam Sweet.
Progressive Music Publishing Co., Inc.
Identified with Ray Charles.

Missing in Action
Words and music by Helen Kaye and Arthur Q. Smith.
Peer International Corp.
Best-selling record by Ernest Tubb (Decca).

Mister Tap Toe
Words and music by Terry Gilkyson, Richard Dehr, and Frank Miller.
Montclare Music Corp.
Best-selling record by Doris Day (Columbia).

Monotonous
Words by June Carroll, music by Arthur Siegel, with additional lyrics by Ronnie Graham.
Joy Music, Inc.
Introduced by Eartha Kitt in *New Faces of 1952* (revue).

My Baby's Coming Home
Words and music by William G. Leavitt, John C. Grady, and Sherm Feller.
Roxbury Music Co.
Best-selling record by Les Paul and Mary Ford (Capitol).

My Flaming Heart
Words by Leo Robin, music by Nicholas Brodszky.
Robbins Music Corp.
From *Small Town Girl* (film). Nominated for Academy Award, 1953.

My Heart Belongs to Only You
Words and music by Frank Daniels and Dorothy Daniels.
Merrimac Music Corp.
Best-selling record by Betty McLaurin (Derby). Revived in 1964 with best-selling record by Bobby Vinton (Epic).

My Lady Loves To Dance
Words and music by Sammy Gallop and Milton De Lugg.
United Music Corp.
Best-selling record by Julius La Rosa (Cadence).

My Love Is a Wanderer
Words and music by Bart Howard.
Cromwell Music, Inc.
Introduced by Portia Nelson. Sung by Polly Bergen in 1953 in *John Murray Anderson's Almanac* (revue).

My Love, My Love
Words by Bob Haymes, music by Nick Acquaviva.
Travis Music Co.
Best-selling record in 1953 by Joni James (M-G-M).

Never Let Her Go
Words and music by Kay Twomey, Fred Wise, and Ben Weisman.
Joy Music, Inc.
Best-selling record by Ray Bloch and his Orchestra (Coral).

Night Train
Words by Oscar Washington and Lewis C. Simpkins, music by Jimmy Forrest.
Frederick Music Co.
Best-selling record, instrumental, by Jimmy Forrest (United).

Nina Never Knew
Words by Milton Drake, music by Louis Alter.
Jefferson Music Co., Inc.
Best-selling record, instrumental, by The Sauter-Finegan Orchestra, vocal by Joe Mooney (RCA Victor).

No Help Wanted
Words and music by Bill Carlisle.
Acuff-Rose Publications.
Best-selling records by The Carlisles (Mercury), Hank Thompson (Capitol), and Red Foley and Ernest Tubb (Decca).

No More Doggin'
Words and music by Roscoe Gordon.
Modern Music Publishing Co.
Best-selling record by Roscoe Gordon (RPM).

No Other Arms, No Other Lips
Words and music by Joan Whitney, Alex Kramer, and Hy Zaret.
Whitney-Kramer-Zaret Music Co.
Best-selling record in 1959 by The Chordettes (Cadence).

Noodlin' Rag
Words by Allan Roberts, music by Robert Allen.
Bregman, Vocco & Conn, Inc.
Best-selling record by Perry Como (RCA Victor).

Oh, Happy Day
Words and music by Don Howard Koplow and Nancy Binns Reed.
Bregman, Vocco & Conn, Inc.
Best-selling record in 1952 and 1953 by Don Howard (Essex-Triple A).

Older and Bolder
Words and music by Cy Coben.
Alamo Music, Inc.
Best-selling record by Eddy Arnold (RCA Victor).

On the First Warm Day
Words and music by Bart Howard.
Lion Music Corp.
Introduced by Mabel Mercer.

One Mint Julep
Words and music by Rudolph Toombs.
Progressive Music Publishing Co., Inc./Regent Music Corp.
Best-selling records by The Clovers (Atlantic) and Louis Prima (Columbia). Revived in 1961 with best-selling record by Ray Charles (ABC Paramount).

Oooh, Oooh, Oooh
Words and music by Lloyd Price.
Venice Music, Inc.
Best-selling record by Lloyd Price (Specialty).

Out of the Clear Blue Sky
Words by Ogden Nash, music by Vernon Duke.
Remick Music Corp.
Introduced by Peter Kelly and Sue Hight in *Two's Company* (revue).

Outside of Heaven
Words by Sammy Gallop, music by Chester Conn.
Bregman, Vocco & Conn, Inc.
Best-selling record by Eddie Fisher (RCA Victor).

Padam . . . Padam . . . (How It Echoes the Beat of My Heart) (French)
English words by Mann Holiner and Alberta Nichols, French words by Henri Contet, music by Norbert Glanzberg.
Éditions Salabert, Paris, France, 1951/Leeds Music Corp.
Best-selling record by Tony Martin (RCA Victor).

Penny Candy
Words by June Carroll, music by Arthur Siegel.
Joy Music, Inc.
Introduced by June Carroll and Carol Lawrence in *New Faces of 1952* (revue).

Petite Fleur (French-American)
Music by Sidney Bechet.
Vogue Records, Paris, France/Hill and Range Songs, Inc.
Introduced in France by expatriate New Orleans jazzman, Sidney Bechet. Revived and best-selling record in 1959 and 1960 by British jazz musician Chris Barber (Laurie).

Piel Canela (Tú, y Tú, y Tú) (Cuban)
Spanish words and music by Bobby Capo.
Edward B. Marks Music Corp.
Best-selling record by Bobby Capo and his Orchestra (Seeco).

Pittsburgh, Pennsylvania
Words and music by Bob Merrill.
Joy Music, Inc.
Best-selling record by Guy Mitchell and Mitch Miller (Columbia).

Port of Rico
Music by Illinois Jacquet.
Jatap Publishing Co., Inc.
Best-selling record by Illinois Jacquet (Mercury).

Pretend
Words and music by Lew Douglas, Cliff Parman, and Frank Lavere.
Brandom Music Co.
Best-selling record in 1952 and 1953 by Nat "King" Cole (Capitol) and, as an instrumental, by Ralph Marterie (Mercury).

Rock Me All Night Long
Words and music by Jimmy Ricks and Bill Sanford.
Moonlight Music, Inc.
Best-selling record by The Ravens (Mercury).

Rock of Gibraltar
Words and music by Terry Gilkyson.
Montclare Music Corp.
Best-selling record by Frankie Laine (Columbia).

Rosanne
Words by Dick Manning, music by Glenn Osser and Edna Osser.
ABC Music Corp.
Best-selling record by Vic Damone (Mercury).

Round About, see 1946.

Rub-a-Dub-Dub
Words and music by Hank Thompson.
Brazos Valley Music, Inc.
Best-selling record in 1953 by Hank Thompson (Capitol).

Ruby and the Pearl, The
Words and music by Jay Livingston and Ray Evans.
Famous Music Corp.
Introduced in *Thunder in the East* (film).

Sad Hours
Music by Walter Jacobs.
Arc Music Corp.
Best-selling record in 1952 and 1953 by Little Walter (Checker).

Say You're Mine Again
Words and music by Charles Nathan and Dave Heisler.
Blue River Music, Inc.
Original version by The Three Dons and Ginny Greer (Allied). Best-selling record in 1953 by Perry Como (RCA Victor).

Settin' the Woods on Fire
Words and music by Fred Rose and Edward G. Nelson.
Milene Music.
Best-selling record by Hank Williams (M-G-M).

Sinner or Saint
Words and music by Irving Gordon.
M. Witmark & Sons.
Best-selling record by Sarah Vaughan (Columbia).

Smokey the Bear
Words and music by Steve Nelson and Jack Rollins.
Hill and Range Songs, Inc.
Anti-forest fire song promoted by the United States Forestry Service.

So Madly in Love
Words and music by Kim Gannon and Mabel Wayne.
Shapiro, Bernstein & Co., Inc.
Best-selling record by Georgia Gibbs (Mercury).

Soft
Words and music by Tiny Bradshaw.
Lois Publishing Co.
Best-selling records in 1953 by Tiny Bradshaw (King) and Bill Doggett (King).

Somewhere along the Way
Words by Sammy Gallop, music by Kurt Adams.
United Music Corp.
Best-selling record by Nat "King" Cole (Capitol).

Spring Has Sprung
Words by Charles Tobias, music by Peter De Rose.
M. Witmark & Sons.
Introduced in *About Face* (film).

String Along
Words and music by Dave Coleman.
Regent Music Corp.
Best-selling record by The Ames Brothers (Coral).

Sugarbush (South African)
Words and music by Josef Marais.
G. Schirmer, Inc.
Original version first published in the 1942 collection, *Songs from the Veld.* With additional words and music, best-selling record by Doris Day and Frankie Laine (Columbia).

Summer Is A-Comin' In
Words by Marshall Barer, music by Alec Wilder.
Essex Music, Inc.
Introduced by Nat "King" Cole.

Suzanne (Ev'ry Night When the Sun Goes Down)
Words and music by Harry Belafonte and Millard Thomas.
Leo Feist, Inc.
Adapted from an American folk song. Introduced by Harry Belafonte in *Bright Road* (film).

Sweet Sixteen
Words and music by Ahmet Ertegun.
Progressive Music Publishing Co., Inc.
Best-selling record by Joe Turner (Atlantic).

Take Me in Your Arms and Hold Me, see 1949.

Take These Chains from My Heart
Words and music by Fred Rose and Hy Heath.
Milene Music.
Best-selling record in 1953 by Hank Williams (M-G-M).

Takes Two To Tango
Words and music by Al Hoffman and Dick Manning.
Harman Music, Inc.
Best-selling record by Pearl Bailey (Coral).

Talk to Your Heart
Words and music by Louise Ulrich and C. M. Bradley.
Peer International Corp.
Best-selling record by Ray Price (Columbia).

Tennessee Tango
Words and music by Redd Stewart and Pee Wee King.
Ridgeway Music.
Best-selling record by Pee Wee King (RCA Victor).

Tennessee Wig-Walk, The
Words by Norman Gimbel, music by Larry Coleman.
Vogue Music, Inc.
Best-selling record by Bonnie Lou (King).

That Doggie in the Window
Words and music by Bob Merrill.
Joy Music, Inc.
Best-selling record in 1953 by Patti Page (Mercury).

That Heart Belongs to Me
Words and music by Webb Pierce.
Ark-La-Tex Publishing Co.
Best-selling record by Webb Pierce (Decca).

That's All
Words by Alan Brandt, music by Bob Haymes.
Travis Music Co.
Introduced instrumentally, under the title, "C'est Tout," by Acquaviva and his Orchestra (M-G-M). Best-selling record by Nat "King" Cole (Capitol).

('Cause I Love Ya) That's A-Why
Words and music by Bob Merrill.
Joy Music, Inc.
Best-selling record by Guy Mitchell and Mindy Carson (Columbia).

That's Me without You
Words and music by J. D. Miller and Bennett Wyatt.
Valley Publishers, Inc.
Best-selling record in 1952 and 1953 by Webb Pierce (Decca).

That's the Chance You Take
Words by Sylvia Dee, music by Sid Lippman.
George Paxton, Inc.
Best-selling record by Eddie Fisher (RCA Victor).

This Is My Song
Words and music by Dick Charles.
Lear Music, Inc.
Theme song of Patti Page's television show.

Three O'Clock Blues
Words by Jules Taub, music by Riley King.
Modern Music Publishing Co.
Best-selling record by B. B. King (RPM).

Thumbelina
Words and music by Frank Loesser.
Frank Music Corp.
Introduced by Danny Kaye in *Hans Christian Andersen* (film). Nominated for Academy Award, 1952.

Till I Waltz Again with You
Words and music by Sidney Prosen.
Hill and Range Songs, Inc./Village Music Co.
Best-selling record in 1952 and 1953 by Teresa Brewer (Coral).

Ting A Ling
Words and music by Ahmet Ertegun.
Progressive Music Publishing Co., Inc.
Best-selling record by The Clovers (Atlantic).

To Know You Is To Love You
Words by Allan Roberts, music by Robert Allen.
Roncom Music Co.
Best-selling record by Perry Como (RCA Victor).

Trying
Words and music by Billy Vaughn.
Randy-Smith Music Corp.
Best-selling record by The Hilltoppers (Dot).

Vanessa
Music by Bernie Wayne.
Vogue Music, Inc.
Dedicated to film and television actress Vanessa Brown. Best-selling record, instrumental, by Hugo Winterhalter and his Orchestra (RCA Victor).

Waiting in the Lobby of Your Heart
Words and music by Hank Thompson and Billy Gray.
Brenner Music, Inc.
Best-selling record by Hank Thompson (Capitol).

Walkin' My Baby Back Home, see 1930.

Walkin' to Missouri
Words and music by Bob Merrill.
Joy Music, Inc.
Best-selling record by Sammy Kaye and his Orchestra (Columbia).

Watermelon Weather
Words by Paul Francis Webster, music by Hoagy Carmichael.
Edwin H. Morris & Co., Inc.
Best-selling record by Perry Como and Eddie Fisher (RCA Victor).

What Would You Do (If You Were in My Place)
Words and music by Richard Adler and Jerry Ross.
Frank Music Corp.
Best-selling record by Rosemary Clooney (Columbia).

Wheel of Fortune
Words and music by Bennie Benjamin and George Weiss.
Laurel Music Corp.
Best-selling records by Kay Starr (Capitol) and Sunny Gale (Derby).

When I Fall in Love
Words by Edward Heyman, music by Victor Young.
Victor Young Publications, Inc./Northern Music Corp.
Introduced in *One Minute to Zero* (film). Best-selling record by Nat "King" Cole (Capitol). Revived in 1962 with best-selling record by The Lettermen (Capitol).

Where Can I Go without You
Words by Peggy Lee, music by Victor Young.
Ivan Mogull Music Corp.
Introduced by Nat "King" Cole.

Where Did the Night Go?
Words and music by Harold Rome.
Chappell & Co., Inc.
Introduced by Patricia Marand and Jack Cassidy in *Wish You Were Here* (musical).

Whispering Winds
Words and music by Corky Robbins.
Lear Music, Inc.
Best-selling record by Patti Page (Mercury).

Why Don't You Believe Me
Words and music by Lew Douglas, King Laney, and Roy Rodde.
Brandom Music Co.
Best-selling record in 1952 and 1953 by Joni James (M-G-M).

Why Try To Change Me Now
Words and music by Cy Coleman and Joseph A. McCarthy.
Consolidated Music Publishers, Inc.
Introduced by Frank Sinatra.

Wild Side of Life, The
Words and music by W. Warren and A. A. Carter.
Travis Music Co.
Best-selling record by Hank Thompson (Capitol).

Wish You Were Here
Words and music by Harold Rome.
Chappell & Co., Inc.
Introduced by Jack Cassidy in *Wish You Were Here* (musical).
Best-selling record by Eddie Fisher (RCA Victor).

Wishing Ring
Words and music by Al Britt and Pete Maddux.
Acuff-Rose Publications.
Best-selling record in 1953 by Joni James (M-G-M).

Wondering
Words and music by Joe Werner.
Aberbach, Inc./Hill and Range Songs, Inc.
Best-selling record by Webb Pierce (Decca).

Yesterday's Girl
Words and music by Hank Thompson and Billy Gray.
Brazos Valley Music, Inc.
Best-selling record in 1953 by Hank Thompson (Capitol).

You
Words by Sunny Skylar, music adapted by Morton Frank.
Republic Music Corp.
Adapted from "Musetta's Waltz" from Puccini's *La Boheme*. Best-selling record by Sammy Kaye and his Orchestra (Columbia).

You Belong to Me
Words and music by Pee Wee King, Redd Stewart, and Chilton Price.
Ridgeway Music.
First recording by, and recording debut of, Joni James (Smash). Best-selling records by Jo Stafford (Columbia) and Patti Page (Mercury). Revived in 1962 with best-selling record by The Duprees (Coed).

You Know I Love You
Words by Riley King, music by Jules Taub.
Modern Music Publishing Co.
Best-selling record by B. B. King (RPM).

You'll Never Get Away
Words and music by Joan Whitney, Alex Kramer, and Hy Zaret.
Bourne, Inc.
Introduced by The Paulette Sisters. Best-selling record by Teresa Brewer and Don Cornell (Coral).

Your Cheatin' Heart
Words and music by Hank Williams.
Fred Rose Music, Inc.
Best-selling records in 1953 by Hank Williams (M-G-M) and Joni James (M-G-M).

Yours, see 1931.

You've Changed
Words and music by Edward Heyman, Tony Martin, and Victor Young.
Victor Young Publications, Inc.
Introduced in *The Fabulous Senorita* (film).

Zing a Little Zong
Words by Leo Robin, music by Harry Warren.
Famous Music Corp.
Introduced by Bing Crosby and Jane Wyman in *Just for You* (film). Nominated for Academy Award, 1952.

1953

Acorn in the Meadow
Words and music by Richard Adler and Jerry Ross.
Frank Music Corp.
Introduced by Harry Belafonte in *John Murray Anderson's Almanac* (revue).

Allez-Vous-En, Go Away
Words and music by Cole Porter.
Buxton Hill Music Corp.
Introduced by Lilo in *Can-Can* (musical).

Almost Always
Words and music by Katherine Lichty, Lew Douglas, and Frank Lavere.
Brandom Music Co.
Best-selling record by Joni James (M-G-M).

And This Is My Beloved
Words and music by Robert Wright and George Forrest.
Frank Music Corp.
Adapted from the Third Movement of Borodin's "String Quartet in D Major." Introduced by Doretta Morrow, Richard Kiley, Alfred Drake, and Henry Calvin in *Kismet* (musical).

Angel Eyes
Words by Earl Brent, music by Matt Dennis.
Bradshaw Music, Inc.
Introduced by Matt Dennis in *Jennifer* (film).

Angelina
Words and music by Tommie Connor and Edward Lisbona.
Frank Music Corp.
Best-selling record by Lou Monte (RCA Victor).

Anna, also known as **El Negro Zambon (Italian)**
English words by William Engvick, Italian words by F. Giordano, music by R. Vatro.
Redi-Ponti-De Laurentiis, Milan, Italy, 1952/Hollis Music, Inc.
Introduced by Silvana Mangano, using the dubbed voice of Flo Sandons, in *Anna* (Italian film). Best-selling record by Silvano Mangano (M-G-M).

Answer Me, My Love (German)
English words by Carl Sigman, German words and music by Gerhard Winkler and Fred Rauch.
Papagena Verlag Hans Sikorski, Hamburg, Germany, 1952/Bourne, Inc.
Best-selling record in 1954 by Nat "King" Cole (Capitol).

April in Portugal (Portuguese)
English words by Jimmy Kennedy, Portuguese words by José Galhardo, music by Paul Ferrão.
Chappell & Co., Inc.
Published in 1947 as "Coimbra" and in 1949 as "Avril in Portugal." English lyrics written in 1953. Best-selling record, instrumental, by Les Baxter and his Orchestra (Capitol).

Bad and the Beautiful, The, also known as **Love Is for the Very Young**
Music by David Raksin.
Robbins Music Corp.
Theme from *The Bad and the Beautiful* (film). Lyrics written in 1960 by Dory Langdon. Version with lyrics copyrighted in 1960.

Baión, The
Words by Ben Raleigh, music by Paulo Alencar.
Simon House, Inc.
Introduced by Paulo Alencar and his Orchestra (Coral).

Baubles, Bangles, and Beads
Words and music by Robert Wright and George Forrest.
Frank Music Corp.
Based on a theme of Borodin's. Introduced by Doretta Morrow in *Kismet* (musical). Best-selling records in 1953 by Peggy Lee (Decca) and in 1958 by The Kirby Stone Four (Columbia).

Bell Bottom Blues
Words by Hal David, music by Leon Carr.
Shapiro, Bernstein & Co., Inc.
Best-selling record by Teresa Brewer (Coral).

Belle of the Ball
Words by Mitchell Parish, music by Leroy Anderson.
Mills Music, Inc.
Music originally published in 1951. Best-selling record, instrumental, by Leroy Anderson and his Orchestra (Decca).

Bernie's Tune
Words and music by Bernie Miller, Mike Stoller, and Jerry Leiber.
Atlantic Music Corp./Sky View Music Corp.
Introduced by Gerry Mulligan as a jazz instrumental. First vocal version in 1955 by The Cheers (Capitol).

Best Things Happen While You're Dancing, The
Words and music by Irving Berlin.
Irving Berlin Music Corp.
Introduced by Danny Kaye in *White Christmas* (film, 1954).

Big Black Giant, The
Words by Oscar Hammerstein II, music by Richard Rodgers.
Williamson Music, Inc.
Introduced by Bill Hayes in *Me and Juliet* (musical).

Big Mamou
Words and music by Link Davis.
Peer International Corp.
Best-selling record by Pete Hanley (Okeh).

Bimbo
Words and music by Rodney Morris.
Travis Music Co.
Best-selling record in 1953 and 1954 by Jim Reeves (Abbott).

Blowing Wild, also known as **The Ballad of Black Gold**
Words by Paul Francis Webster, music by Dimitri Tiomkin.
M. Witmark & Sons.
Introduced in *Blowing Wild* (film).

Blue Canary
Words and music by Vincent Fiorino.
Valando Music Corp.
Best-selling record by Dinah Shore (RCA Victor).

Blue Gardenia
Words and music by Bob Russell and Lester Lee.
Harms, Inc.
Introduced by Nat "King" Cole. From *Blue Gardenia* (film).

Blue Pacific Blues, The, see **Sadie Thompson's Song.**

Boogie Woogie Maxixe
Words and music by Sammy Gallop, Gil Rodin, and Bob Crosby.
Bregman, Vocco & Conn, Inc.
Recorded instrumentally by Bob Crosby and his Orchestra in 1939. Vocal version introduced by The Ames Brothers.

Breakin' the Rules
Words and music by Hank Thompson, Billy Gray, and Al Blasingame.
Hill and Range Songs, Inc./Texoma Music Corp.
Best-selling record in 1954 by Hank Thompson (Capitol).

Bumming Around
Words and music by Pete Graves.
Four Star Sales Co.
Best-selling record by Jimmy Dean (Four Star) and T. Texas Tyler (Decca).

Butterflies
Words and music by Bob Merrill.
Joy Music, Inc.
Best-selling record by Patti Page (Mercury).

Call of the Far-Away Hills, The, also known as **Shane**
Words by Mack David, music by Victor Young.
Paramount Music Corp.
Theme from *Shane* (film).

Can-Can
Words and music by Cole Porter.
Buxton Hill Music Corp.
Introduced by Lilo and Gwen Verdon in *Can-Can* (musical).

Can't I
Words and music by Leroy Lovett.
Harvard Music, Inc./Wemar Music Corp.
Best-selling record by Nat "King" Cole (Capitol).

Caravan, see 1937.

Caribbean
Words and music by Mitchell Torok.
American Music, Inc.
Best-selling record by Mitchell Torok (Abbott).

C'est Magnifique
Words and music by Cole Porter.
Buxton Hill Music Corp.
Introduced by Lilo and Peter Cookson in *Can-Can* (musical).

C'est Si Bon, see 1950.

Changing Partners
Words by Joe Darion, music by Larry Coleman.
Porgie Music Corp.
Best-selling record in 1953 and 1954 by Patti Page (Mercury).

Choo Choo Train (French)
English words by Jack Lawrence, French words and music by Marc Fontenoy.
Walt Disney Music Co.
French title, "Le Petit Train." Best-selling record by Doris Day (Columbia).

Clock, The
Words and music by David J. Mattis.
Lion Publishing Co., Inc.
Best-selling record by Johnny Ace (Duke).

Come Along with Me
Words and music by Cole Porter.
Buxton Hill Music Corp.
Introduced by Erik Rhodes and Hans Conried in *Can-Can* (musical).

Come What May
Words by Allen Schiller, music by Al Sanchez.
Joy Music, Inc.
Best-selling record by Patti Page (Mercury).

Comment Allez-Vous? (How Are Things with You?)
Words by Ralph Blane and Robert Wells, music by Josef Myrow.
Mills Music, Inc.
Introduced by Gilbert Roland in *The French Line* (film).

Confirmation
Music by Charlie Parker.
Atlantic Music Corp.
Introduced by Charlie Parker (Clef).

Congratulations to Someone
Words by Roy Alfred, music by Al Frisch.
United Music Corp.
Best-selling record by Tony Bennett (Columbia).

Crawlin'
Words and music by Rudolph Toombs.
Progressive Music Publishing Co., Inc.
Best-selling record by The Clovers (Atlantic).

Crazy Man, Crazy
Words and music by Bill Haley.
Eastwick Music Co.
Introduced by Bill Haley and The Comets (Essex).

Creep, The (English)
Words by Carl Sigman, music by Andy Barton.
Miller Music Corp.
Introduced by Ted Heath and his Orchestra in England (London).

Cry Me a River
Words and music by Arthur Hamilton.
Saunders Publications, Inc.
Best-selling record by Julie London (Liberty).

Crying in the Chapel
Words and music by Artie Glenn.
Valley Publishers, Inc.
Introduced by Darrell Glenn, son of the composer. Best-selling records by June Valli (RCA Victor), Rex Allen (Decca), and The Orioles (Jubilee).

Dancin' with Someone (Longin' for You)
Words and music by Bennie Benjamin, George Weiss, and Alex Alstone.
Valando Music Corp.
Best-selling record by Teresa Brewer (Coral).

Dansero
Words by Sol Parker, music by Richard Hayman and Lee Daniels.
B & F Music Co., Inc.
Best-selling record by Richard Hayman (Mercury).

Dear John Letter, A
Words and music by Billy Barton, Billy Liebert, and Charles "Fuzzy" Owen.
American Music, Inc.
Best-selling record by Jean Shepard and Ferlin Husky (Capitol).

Death of Hank Williams
Words and music by Jack Cardwell.
Lois Publishing Co.
Best-selling record by Jack Cardwell (King).

Doggone It, Baby, I'm in Love
Words and music by Arrett Keefer and Jack Amway.
Hill and Range Songs, Inc.
Best-selling record by Carl Smith (Columbia).

Don't Call My Name
Words and music by Bennie Benjamin and George Weiss.
Laurel Music Corp.
Best-selling record by Helene Dixon (Okeh).

Don't Deceive Me (Please Don't Go)
Words and music by Chuck Willis.
Tideland Music Publishing Corp.
Best-selling record by Chuck Willis (Okeh).

Don't Forget, see **Non Dimenticar.**

Don't Let the Stars Get in Your Eyes
Words and music by Slim Willet, Cactus Pryor, and Barbara Trammel.
Four Star Sales Co.
Introduced by Slim Willet. Best-selling records by Perry Como (RCA Victor), Skeets McDonald (Capitol), and Slim Willet (Four Star).

Downhearted
Words by Bob Hilliard, music by Dave Mann.
George Paxton, Inc.
Best-selling record by Eddie Fisher (RCA Victor).

Dragnet
Music by Walter Schumann.
Alamo Music, Inc.
Theme from *Dragnet* (television series). Also known as "Dragnet March" and "Danger Ahead." Best-selling record by Ray Anthony and his Orchestra (Capitol).

Earth and the Sky, see **1950.**

Ebb Tide
Words by Carl Sigman, music by Robert Maxwell.
Robbins Music Corp.
Best-selling record, instrumental, in 1953 by Frank Chacksfield and his Orchestra (recorded in England) (London). First recording with lyrics by Vic Damone (Mercury). Best-selling record, vocal, in 1954 by Roy Hamilton (Epic). Revived in 1964 with best-selling record by Lenny Welch (Cadence).

Eddy's Song
Words and music by Charles Grean and Cy Coben.
Delmore Music Co.
Best-selling record by Eddy Arnold (RCA Victor).

Eh, Cumpari! (Italian)
Words and music by Julius La Rosa and Archie Bleyer.
Crescent Music Publishing Co.
Adapted from a traditional Italian folk song. Best-selling record by Julius La Rosa (Cadence).

Embrasse, also known as **Hold Me Close** (French)
English words by Richard Driscoll, French words by Henri Contet, music by Paul Durand.
Societé Intercontinentale d'Éditions Musicales, Paris, France, 1952/ Walt Disney Music Co.
French title, "Embrasse Moi Bien." Introduced in *Bedeviled* (film). Best-selling record by Felicia Sanders (Columbia).

Eternally, also known as **Limelight** or **The Terry Theme**
Words by Geoffrey Parsons, music by Charles Chaplin.
Bourne, Inc.
Theme from Charles Chaplin's *Limelight* (film). Best-selling record, instrumental, by Frank Chacksfield (recorded in England) (London).

Even Now
Words and music by Richard Adler, Jerry Ross, and Dan Howell (pseudonym for Dave Kapp).
Pickwick Music Corp.
Best-selling record by Eddie Fisher (RCA Victor).

Face to Face
Words by Sammy Cahn, music by Sammy Fain.
M. Witmark & Sons.
Introduced by Jane Powell and Gordon MacRae in *Three Sailors and a Girl* (film).

Fate
Words and music by Robert Wright and George Forrest.
Frank Music Corp.
Adapted from Borodin's "Symphony No. 2 in B Minor." Introduced by Alfred Drake and Doretta Morrow in *Kismet* (musical).

Fini
Words and music by Richard Adler and Jerry Ross.
Frank Music Corp.
Introduced by Polly Bergen in *John Murray Anderson's Almanac* (revue).

Fool Was I, A
Words by Roy Alfred, music by Kurt Adams.
Gale & Gayles, Inc.
Best-selling record by Nat "King" Cole (Capitol).

Forty Cups of Coffee
Words and music by Danny Overbea.
Arc Music Corp.
Best-selling record by Bill Haley and The Comets (Decca).

Free Home Demonstration
Words and music by Charles Grean and Cy Coben.
Joy Music, Inc.
Best-selling record by Eddy Arnold (RCA Victor).

From Here to Eternity
Words by Bob Wells, music by Fred Karger.
Barton Music Corp.
"Inspired by" *From Here to Eternity* (film). Best-selling record by Frank Sinatra (Capitol).

Gambler's Guitar
Words and music by Jim Lowe.
Frederick Music Co.
Best-selling record by Rusty Draper (Mercury).

Gee!
Words and music by Viola Watkins, Daniel Norton, and William Davis.
Patricia Music Publishing Corp.
Best-selling record in 1954 by The Crows (Rama).

Gigi (French)
Words by Harold Adamson, music by Florence Veran.
Éditions Musicales Paris-Melodies, Paris, France, 1950/Alamo Music, Inc.
Best-selling record by Les Baxter and his Orchestra (Capitol).

Go, Boy, Go
Words and music by Floyd F. Wilson.
Valley Publishers, Inc.
Best-selling record in 1954 by Carl Smith (Columbia).

God Bless Us All
Words by Tom Murray, music by Tony Burello.
Brewster Music Publishers, Inc.
Best-selling record by Brucie Weil (Barbour).

Going to the River, see 1957.

Gomen-Nasai (Forgive Me)
Words by Benedict Myers, music by Raymond Hattori.
Walt Disney Music Co.
Introduced by United States soldier Richard Bowers, with the Columbia Tokyo Orchestra, in Japan. Record released in the United States by Columbia.

Good Lovin'
Words and music by Leroy Kirkland, Danny Taylor, Ahmet Ertegun, and Jesse Stone.
Raleigh Music, Inc.
Best-selling record by The Clovers (Atlantic).

Guy Who Invented Kissin', The
Words and music Charles Orr and Earl Griswold.
Hill and Range Songs, Inc.
Best-selling record by Ella Mae Morse (Capitol).

Half a Photograph
Words by Bob Russell, music by Hal Stanley.
Starstan Music Corp.
Best-selling record by Kay Starr (Capitol).

Help Me, Somebody
Words and music by Lowman Pauling.
Bess Music Co.
Best-selling record by The Five Royales (Apollo).

Here Comes That Heartache Again
Words by Roy Alfred, music by Al Frisch.
United Music Corp.
Best-selling record by Tony Bennett (Columbia).

Here's That Rainy Day
Words by Johnny Burke, music by James Van Heusen.
Burke & Van Heusen, Inc.
Introduced by John Raitt in *Carnival in Flanders* (musical).

He's in Love
Words and music by Robert Wright and George Forrest.
Frank Music Corp.
Adapted from Borodin's "Polovtsian Dances." Introduced by Hal Hackett in *Kismet* (musical).

Hey Joe
Words and music by Boudleaux Bryant.
Acuff-Rose Publications.
Best-selling record by Carl Smith (Columbia).

Hey! Mister Cotton-Picker
Words and music by Dok Stanford and Robert Mitchum.
Laurel Music Corp.
Best-selling record by Tennessee Ernie Ford (Capitol).

Hittin' on Me
Words and music by Buddy Johnson.
Sophisticate Music, Inc.
Best-selling record by Buddy Johnson (Mercury).

Ho Ho Song, The
Words and music by Red Buttons, Joe Darion, and Jack Wolf.
Arbee Music Publishing Co.
Introduced and best-selling record by Red Buttons (Columbia).

Hold Me Close, see **Embrasse.**

Hold Me, Thrill Me, Kiss Me, see 1952.

Honeymoon on a Rocket Ship
Words and music by Johnnie Masters.
Peer International Corp.
Best-selling record by Hank Snow (RCA Victor).

Hound Dog, see 1956.

Hurt
Words and music by Jimmie Crane and Al Jacobs.
Miller Music Corp.
First recorded by Roy Hamilton (Epic). Best-selling record in 1963 by Timi Yuro (Liberty).

I Am in Love
Words and music by Cole Porter.
Buxton Hill Music Corp.
Introduced by Peter Cookson in *Can-Can* (musical).

I Could Be Happy with You (English)
Words and music by Sandy Wilson.
Chappell & Co., Inc.
Introduced in the original London production of *The Boy Friend* (musical) by Anne Rogers and Anthony Hayes; in the New York production by Julie Andrews and John Hewer.

I Couldn't Keep from Crying
Words and music by Marty Robbins.
Fred Rose Music, Inc.
Best-selling record by Marty Robbins (Columbia).

I Forgot More Than You'll Ever Know
Words and music by Cecil A. Null.
Travis Music Co.
Best-selling record by The Davis Sisters (RCA Victor).

I Get So Lonely, see **Oh, Baby Mine.**

I Love Paris
Words and music by Cole Porter.
Buxton Hill Music Corp.
Introduced by Lilo in *Can-Can* (musical). Best-selling records, instrumentals, by Les Baxter and his Orchestra (Capitol) and Michel Legrand and his Orchestra (Columbia).

I Love You
Words and music by B. Grimes (pseudonym for Billy Barton).
American Music, Inc.
Best-selling record in 1953 and 1954 by Ginny Wright and Jim Reeves (Fabor).

I Need You Now
Words and music by Jimmie Crane and Al Jacobs.
Miller Music Corp.
Best-selling record in 1954 by Eddie Fisher (RCA Victor).

I Really Don't Want To Know
Words by Howard Barnes, music by Don Robertson.
Hill and Range Songs, Inc.
Best-selling records by Les Paul and Mary Ford (Capitol) and Eddy Arnold (RCA Victor).

I See the Moon
Words and music by Meredith Willson.
Plymouth Music Co., Inc.
Introduced by The Mariners on *The Arthur Godfrey Show* (television show).

I Understand Just How You Feel
Words and music by Pat Best.
Jubilee Music.
Best-selling record in 1954 by The Four Tunes (Jubilee). Revived in 1961 with best-selling record by The G-Clefs (Terrance).

I Want You To Be My Baby
Words and music by Jon Hendricks.
Victory Music Co.
Best-selling record in 1955 by Georgia Gibbs (Mercury).

I'd Rather Die Young
Words and music by Beasley Smith, Billy Vaughn, and Randy Wood.
Randy-Smith Music Corp.
Best-selling record by The Hilltoppers (Dot).

Idle Gossip
Words by Floyd Huddleston, music by Joseph Meyer.
Redd Evans Music Co.
Best-selling records by Perry Como (released in England only) and in 1954 by Tony Alamo (Majar).

If You Love Me (Really Love Me) (French)
English words by Geoffrey Parsons, French words by Edith Piaf, music by Marguerite Monnot.
Duchess Music Corp./France Music Co.
Introduced under its original title, "Hymne a l'Amour," in 1949 by Edith Piaf. Best-selling record in 1954 by Kay Starr (Capitol).

If You Loved Me Truly
Words and music by Cole Porter.
Buxton Hill Music Corp.
Introduced by the ensemble in *Can-Can* (musical).

I'll Be True to You
Words and music by William McLemore.
Angel Music, Inc.
Best-selling record in 1954 by Faye Adams (Herald).

I'll Go On Alone
Words and music by Marty Robbins.
Fred Rose Music, Inc.
Best-selling record by Webb Pierce (Decca).

I'll Never Stand in Your Way
Words and music by Fred Rose and Hy Heath.
Milene Music.
Best-selling record by Joni James (M-G-M).

I'm Just Your Fool
Words and music by Buddy Johnson.
Sophisticate Music, Inc.
Best-selling record in 1954 by Buddy Johnson (Mercury).

I'm Mad
Words and music by Willie Mabon.
Republic Music Corp.
Best-selling record by Willie Mabon (Chess).

I'm Walking behind You (English)
Words and music by Billy Reid.
Peter Maurice Co., Ltd., London, England/Leeds Music Corp.
Best-selling record in 1953 and 1954 by Eddie Fisher (RCA Victor).

I'm Walking the Dog
Words and music by A. Grisham.
Cedarwood Publishing Co., Inc.
Best-selling record by Webb Pierce (Decca).

I'm Your Girl
Words by Oscar Hammerstein II, music by Richard Rodgers.
Williamson Music, Inc.
Introduced by Isabel Bigley and Bill Hayes in *Me and Juliet* (musical).

In the Mission at St. Augustine
Words and music by Jack Chiarelli.
Republic Music Corp.
Introduced by Sammy Kaye and his Orchestra.

Is It Any Wonder
Words and music by Archie Gottler, Bob Hayes, and Roy Rodde.
Midway Music Co.
Best-selling record by Joni James (M-G-M).

Is Zat You, Myrtle?
Words and music by Bill Carlisle, Charles Louvin, and Ira Louvin.
Acuff-Rose Publications.
Best-selling record by The Carlisles (Mercury).

Istanbul, not Constantinople
Words by Jimmy Kennedy, music by Nat Simon.
Alamo Music, Inc.
Best-selling record by The Four Lads (Columbia).

It's All Right with Me
Words and music by Cole Porter.
Buxton Hill Music Corp.
Introduced by Peter Cookson in *Can-Can* (musical).

It's Been So Long
Words and music by Autry Grisham.
Cedarwood Publishing Co., Inc.
Best-selling record by Webb Pierce (Decca).

It's Love
Words by Betty Comden and Adolph Green, music by Leonard Bernstein.
Chappell & Co., Inc./G. Schirmer, Inc.
Introduced by Edith Adams and George Gaynes in *Wonderful Town* (musical).

Joey's Theme
Music by Eddy Manson.
Cherio Music Publishers, Inc.
Instrumental introduced by Eddy Manson playing the harmonica on the soundtrack of *The Little Fugitive* (film).

Johnny Is the Boy for Me
Words by Marcel Stellman and Paddy Roberts, music by Les Paul.
Iris-Trojan Music Corp.
Best-selling record by Les Paul and Mary Ford (Capitol).

Jones Boy, The
Words by Mann Curtis, music by Vic Mizzy.
George Pincus Music Corp.
Best-selling record by The Mills Brothers (Decca).

Just Another Polka
Words and music by Frank Loesser and Milton De Lugg.
Frank Music Corp.
Best-selling record by Jo Stafford (Columbia).

Just Call Me Lonesome
Words and music by Rex Griffin.
Valley Publishers, Inc.
Best-selling record in 1955 and 1956 by Eddy Arnold (RCA Victor).

Just Wait 'Till I Get You Alone
Words and music by Felice Bryant and Boudleaux Bryant.
Acuff-Rose Publications.
Best-selling record by Carl Smith (Columbia).

Just Walking in the Rain, also known as **Walkin' in the Rain**
Words and music by Johnny Bragg and Robert S. Riley.
Golden West Melodies, Inc.
Introduced and recorded by The Prisonaires, inmates of the Tennessee State Penitentiary (Sun). Best-selling record in 1956 by Johnnie Ray (Columbia).

Keep It Gay
Words by Oscar Hammerstein II, music by Richard Rodgers.
Williamson Music, Inc.
Introduced by Mark Dawson and Bob Fortier, then reprised by Joan McCracken and Buzz Miller in *Me and Juliet* (musical).

Knothole
Words and music by Bill Carlisle and Virginia Suber.
Acuff-Rose Publications.
Best-selling record by The Carlisles (Mercury).

La Seine, see **The River Seine,** 1953; see **You Will Find Your Love in Paris,** 1958.

Let Me Be the One
Words by W. S. Stevenson and P. Blevins, music by J. Hobson.
Four Star Sales Co.
Best-selling record in 1953 and 1954 by Hank Locklin (Four Star).

Let Me Go Devil!
Words and music by Jenny Lou Carson.
Rumbalero Music, Inc.
Best-selling record by George Shaw (Decca). Rewritten in 1954 as "Let Me Go Lover!"

Let Me Know
Words and music by Slim Willet.
Four Star Sales Co.
Best-selling record by Slim Willet (King).

Lighthouse
Words and music by Jim Lowe.
Frederick Music Co.
Best-selling record by Rusty Draper (Mercury).

Limelight, see **Eternally.**

Little Bit in Love, A
Words by Betty Comden and Adolph Green, music by Leonard Bernstein.
Chappell & Co., Inc./G. Schirmer, Inc.
Introduced by Edith Adams in *Wonderful Town* (musical).

Little Boy and the Old Man, The, also known as **Little Child (Daddy Dear)**
Words and music by Wayne Shanklin.
Mayfair Music Corp.
Introduced by Frankie Laine and Jimmy Boyd (Columbia). In its French adaptation, "L'Homme et L'Enfant," introduced successfully in France by Tania and Eddie Constantine. Re-adapted into English in 1956 under the title, "Little Child (Daddy Dear)" and re-introduced by Eddie Albert and Sondra Lee (Kapp).

Little Child (Daddy Dear), see **The Little Boy and the Old Man.**

Live and Let Live
Words and music by Cole Porter.
Buxton Hill Music Corp.
Introduced by Lilo in *Can-Can* (musical).

Love Is for the Very Young, see **The Bad and the Beautiful.**

Love Theme from *The Robe*
Music by Alfred Newman.
Robbins Music Corp.
Theme from *The Robe* (film).

Love, You Didn't Do Right by Me
Words and music by Irving Berlin.
Irving Berlin Music Corp.
Introduced by Rosemary Clooney in *White Christmas* (film, 1954).

Lover's Quarrel, A
Words and music by Vic McAlpin and Newt Richardson.
Melody Trails, Inc.
Best-selling record by Sarah Vaughan (Columbia).

Make Love to Me
Words by Bill Norvas and Allan Copeland, music by Leon Roppolo, Paul Mares, Benny Pollack, George Brunies, Mel Stitzel, and Walter Melrose.
Melrose Music Corp.
From the jazz instrumental, "Tin Roof Blues," originally introduced by the New Orleans Rhythm Kings in 1923. Best-selling record in 1954 by Jo Stafford (Columbia).

Mama (He Treats Your Daughter Mean)
Words and music by Johnny Wallace and Herbert J. Lance.
Marvin Music Co.
Best-selling record by Ruth Brown (Atlantic).

Mama, Come Get Your Baby Boy
Words and music by Leon Merritt and Alvin Alton.
Adams-Vee & Abbott, Inc.
Best-selling record by Eddy Arnold (RCA Victor).

Man with the Banjo (German)
English words by Robert Mellin, music by Fritz Schulz Reichel.
Peter Schaeffers Musikverlag, Berlin, Germany, 1952/Robert Mellin, Inc.
Original German title, "Banjo Benny." Best-selling record in the United States in 1954 by The Ames Brothers (RCA Victor).

Many Times (Belgian)
English words by Jessie Barnes, music by Felix Stahl.
World Music Co., Brussels, Belgium/Screen Gems-Columbia Music, Inc.
Introduced in the United States as an instrumental by Percy Faith and his Orchestra (Columbia). Best-selling record by Eddie Fisher (RCA Victor).

Marriage Type Love
Words by Oscar Hammerstein II, music by Richard Rodgers.
Williamson Music, Inc.
Introduced by Arthur Maxwell and Helena Scott in *Me and Juliet* (musical).

Matilda, Matilda
Words and music by Harry Thomas.
Duchess Music Corp.
Calypso song. Best-selling record by Harry Belafonte (RCA Victor).

Melancholy Serenade
Music by Jackie Gleason.
Jaglea Music Co.
Theme song of *The Jackie Gleason Show* (television comedy series). Best-selling record by Jackie Gleason and his Orchestra (Capitol).

Melba Waltz, The, also known as **Dream Time**
Words by Norman Newell, music by Mischa Spoliansky.
Bregman, Vocco & Conn, Inc.
Introduced by Patrice Munsel. From *Melba* (film).

Mercy, Mr. Percy
Words and music by Mae Moten.
Savoy Music Co.
Best-selling record by Varetta Dillard (Savoy).

Merry Little Minuet, see 1958.

Mexican Joe
Words and music by Mitchell Torok.
American Music, Inc.
Best-selling record by Jim Reeves (RCA Victor).

Money Honey
Words and music by Jesse Stone.
Walden Music Corp.
Best-selling records in 1953 by Clyde McPhatter (Atlantic) and in 1954 by The Drifters (Atlantic).

Moon Is Blue, The
Words by Sylvia Fine, music by Herschel Burke Gilbert.
Joy Music, Inc.
Title song of *The Moon Is Blue* (film). Nominated for Academy Award, 1953. Best-selling record by The Sauter-Finegan Orchestra, with vocal by Sally Sweetland (RCA Victor).

My Bonnie Lassie (Scotch)
Words and music by Roy C. Bennett, Sid Tepper, and Marion McClurg.
James S. Kerr, Glasgow, Scotland, 1952/Blossom Music Corp.
Published in the United Kingdom under the title, "Scotland the Brave." Best-selling record in 1955 by The Ames Brothers (RCA Victor).

My Jealous Eyes (That Turned from Blue to Green)
Words by Mack David, music by Martita (Marjorie Cummings).
Famous Music Corp.
Best-selling record by Patti Page (Mercury).

My One and Only Heart
Words by Al Stillman, music by Robert Allen.
Roncom Music Co.
Best-selling record by Perry Como (RCA Victor).

My One and Only Love
Words by Robert Mellin, music by Guy Wood.
Sherwin Music, Inc.
First recorded by Frank Sinatra (Capitol).

Mystery Street (French)
English words by Bob Howard, music by Jacques Plante and M. Philippe-Gérard.
Éditions du Lido, Paris, France/Robert Mellin, Inc.
Best-selling record by June Valli (RCA Victor).

Mystery Train
Words and music by Sam C. Phillips and Herman Parker, Jr.
Hi-Lo Music, Inc./Hill and Range Songs, Inc.
Best-selling record in 1955 and 1956 by Elvis Presley (RCA Victor).

Never Give Anything Away
Words and music by Cole Porter.
Buxton Hill Music Corp.
Introduced by Lilo in *Can-Can* (musical).

Night of My Nights
Words and music by Robert Wright and George Forrest.
Frank Music Corp.
Adapted from Borodin's piano composition, "Serenade." Introduced by Richard Kiley in *Kismet* (musical).

No Other Love
Words by Oscar Hammerstein II, music by Richard Rodgers.
Williamson Music, Inc.
Adapted from a theme from Rodger's score to the "Beneath the Southern Cross" episode of *Victory at Sea,* television series first telecast in 1952 and 1953. Introduced by Isabel Bigley and Bill Hayes in *Me and Juliet* (musical). Best-selling record by Perry Como (RCA Victor).

Non Dimenticar, also known as **Don't Forget** (Italian)
English words by Shelley Dobbins, Italian words by Michele Galdieri, music by P. G. Redi.
Redi-Ponti-De Laurentiis, Milan, Italy, 1952/Hollis Music, Inc.
Original title, "T'ho Voluto Bene." Introduced in *Anna* (Italian film). Best-selling record by Nat "King" Cole (Capitol).

North Wind
Words and music by Rodney Morris.
Travis Music Co.
Best-selling record by Slim Whitman (Imperial).

Not Since Nineveh
Words and music by Robert Wright and George Forrest.
Frank Music Corp.
Adapted from Borodin's "Polovtsian Dances." Introduced by Joan Diener and Henry Calvin in *Kismet* (musical).

Now That I'm in Love
Words and music by K. C. Rogan (pseudonym for Johnny Burke).
Burke & Van Heusen, Inc.
Adapted from Rossini's "William Tell Overture." Best-selling record by Patti Page (Mercury).

"O", also known as **Oh!, see 1919.**

O Mein Papa, see **Oh! My Pa-pa.**

Off Shore
Words by Steve Graham, music by Leo Diamond.
Hanover Music Corp.
First recording, instrumental, by Leo Diamond (Ambassador). Best-selling record, instrumental, by Richard Hayman (Mercury).

Oh, Baby Mine (I Get So Lonely)
Words and music by Pat Ballard.
Melrose Music Corp.
Best-selling record in 1954 by The Four Knights (Capitol).

Oh! My Pa-pa (Swiss)
English words by John Turner and Geoffrey Parsons, German words and music by Paul Burkhard.
Musikverlag und Bühnenvertrieb Zurich, A. G., Zurich, Switzerland, 1948, 1950/Shapiro, Bernstein & Co., Inc.
As "O Mein Papa," introduced by Lys Assia in *Fireworks* (Swiss musical). Best-selling records by Eddie Fisher (RCA Victor) and, instrumentally, by Eddie Calvert and his Orchestra (Essex).

Ohio
Words by Betty Comden and Adolph Green, music by Leonard Bernstein.
Chappell & Co., Inc./G. Schirmer, Inc.
Introduced by Rosalind Russell and Edith Adams in *Wonderful Town* (musical).

One Lonely Night
Words by Elthea Peale, music by John Benson Brooks.
Laurel Music Corp.
Best-selling record by Al Martino (Capitol).

One Scotch, One Bourbon, One Beer
Words and music by Rudolph Toombs.
Travis Music Co.
Best-selling record by Amos Milburn (Aladdin).

Oo! What You Do to Me
Words and music by Kay Twomey, Fred Wise, and Ben Weisman.
Joy Music, Inc.
Introduced by Patti Page.

Open Up Your Heart
Words and music by Stuart Hamblen.
Hamblen Music Co., Inc.
Best-selling record in 1955 by the Cowboy Church Sunday School (Decca).

P.S. I Love You, see 1934.

Pa-paya Mama
Words and music by George Sandler, Larry Coleman, and Norman Gimbel.
Travis Music Co.
Best-selling record by Perry Como (RCA Victor).

Paris Canaille (French)
French words and music by Léo Ferré.
Les Nouvelles Éditions Meridian, Paris, France/Leeds Music Corp.
Introduced in France by Léo Ferré.

Please Don't Leave Me
Words and music by Antoine "Fats" Domino.
Travis Music Co.
Best-selling record by Fats Domino (Imperial).

Please Love Me
Words by Jules Taub, music by Riley King.
Modern Music Publishing Co.
Best-selling record by B. B. King (RPM).

Please Play Our Song (Mister Record Man)
Words and music by Bob Marcus and Larry Stewart.
Travis Music Co.
Best-selling record by Don Cornell (Coral).

Popo the Puppet
Words and music by Sylvia Fine.
Pickwick Music Corp.
Introduced by Danny Kaye in *On the Riviera* (film).

Quiet Girl, A
Words by Betty Comden and Adolph Green, music by Leonard Bernstein.
Chappell & Co., Inc./G. Schirmer, Inc.
Introduced by George Gaynes in *Wonderful Town* (musical).

Rags to Riches
Words and music by Richard Adler and Jerry Ross.
Saunders Publications, Inc.
Best-selling record in 1953 and 1954 by Tony Bennett (Columbia).

Ramblin' Man, see 1951.

Re-enlistment Blues
Words and music by James Jones, Robert Wells, and Fred Karger.
Barton Music Corp.
Introduced by Merle Travis in *From Here to Eternity* (film).

Return to Paradise
Words by Ned Washington, music by Dimitri Tiomkin.
Remick Music Corp.
Theme from *Return to Paradise* (film). Best-selling record by Percy Faith and his Orchestra (Columbia).

Ricochet
Words and music by Larry Coleman, Joe Darion, and Norman Gimbel.
Travis Music Co.
Best-selling record in 1953 and 1954 by Teresa Brewer (Coral).

River, The (Italian)
English words by Robert Mellin, music by C. Concina.
Edizioni Leonardi, Milan, Italy, 1952/Robert Mellin, Inc.
Best-selling record, instrumental, by Mitch Miller with Percy Faith and his Orchestra (Columbia).

River Seine, The (French)
English words by Allan Roberts and Alan Holt, French words by Flavien Monod and Guy La Farge, music by Guy La Farge.
Royalty, Éditions Musicales, Paris, France, 1948/Remick Music Corp., 1953, 1958.
First English-language version of "La Seine." A new version with lyrics by Mack Gordon, entitled "You Will Find Your Love in Paris," published in 1958.

Robe of Calvary
Words and music by Kathleen Twomey, Fred White, Robert St. Clair, and Elaine Rivers.
Hill and Range Songs, Inc.
Best-selling record by The Orioles (Jubilee).

(We're Gonna) Rock around the Clock
Words and music by Max C. Freedman and Jimmy De Knight.
Myers Music.
Used in 1955 behind the opening titles of *The Blackboard Jungle* (film). Best-selling record in 1955 by Bill Haley and The Comets (Decca).

Roo Roo Kangaroo
Words by Al Hoffman, music by John Clark McClellan and James Roma.
Milber Enterprises Corp.
Best-selling record by Jimmy Roma (Rainbow).

Ruby
Words by Mitchell Parish, music by Heinz Roemheld.
Miller Music Corp.
Theme melody from *Ruby Gentry* (film). Best-selling records, instrumentals, by Les Baxter and his Orchestra (Capitol) and Richard Hayman and his Orchestra (Mercury).

Sadie Thompson's Song, also known as **The Blue Pacific Blues**
Words by Ned Washington, music by Lester Lee.
Mills Music, Inc.
Introduced in *Miss Sadie Thompson* (film). Nominated for Academy Award, 1953.

St. George and the Dragonet
Special words by Stan Freberg and Daws Butler, music by Walter Schumann.
Hill and Range Songs, Inc./Alamo Music, Inc.
Parody of the *Dragnet* television show, utilizing the Walter Schumann themes. Best-selling record by Stan Freberg (Capitol).

Sands of Time
Words and music by Robert Wright and George Forrest.
Frank Music Corp.
Adapted from Borodin's "In the Steppes of Central Asia." Introduced by Richard Oneto, Alfred Drake, and Doretta Morrow in *Kismet* (musical).

Santa Baby
Words and music by Joan Javits, Phil Springer, and Tony Springer.
T. M. Music, Inc.
Best-selling record by Eartha Kitt (RCA Victor).

Satin Doll, see 1958.

Satisfaction Guaranteed
Words and music by Kay Twomey, Fred Wise, and Ben Weisman.
Alamo Music, Inc.
Best-selling record by Carl Smith (Columbia).

Say It with Your Heart
Words and music by Norman Kaye and Steve Nelson.
Robbins Music Corp.
Best-selling record by Bob Carroll (Derby).

Sayonara
Words and music by Irving Berlin.
Irving Berlin Music Corp.
Introduced in 1957 in *Sayonara* (film). Best-selling record in 1957 by Eddie Fisher (RCA Victor).

Second Star to the Right, The
Words by Sammy Cahn, music by Sammy Fain.
Walt Disney Music Co.
Introduced in *Peter Pan* (cartoon film).

Secret Love
Words by Paul Francis Webster, music by Sammy Fain.
Remick Music Corp.
Introduced by Doris Day in *Calamity Jane* (film). Academy Award-winning song, 1953. Best-selling record in 1953 and 1954 by Doris Day (Columbia).

Send My Baby Back to Me
Words by Bob Hilliard, music by Milton De Lugg.
Edwin H. Morris & Co., Inc.
Best-selling record by Sunny Gale (RCA Victor).

Seven Lonely Days
Words and music by Earl Shuman, Alden Shuman, and Marshall Brown.
Jefferson Music Co., Inc.
Best-selling record by Georgia Gibbs (Mercury) and Bonnie Lou (King).

Shake a Hand
Words and music by Joe Morris.
Merrimac Music Corp.
Best-selling records by Faye Adams (Herald) and Red Foley (Decca).

Shane, see **The Call of the Far-Away Hills.**

Siamese Cat Song, The
Words and music by Peggy Lee and Sonny Burke.
Walt Disney Music Co.
Introduced by Peggy Lee in 1955 on the soundtrack of *The Lady and the Tramp* (cartoon film).

Side by Side, see 1927.

Slowly
Words and music by Tommy Hill and Webb Pierce.
Cedarwood Publishing Co., Inc.
Best-selling record in 1954 by Webb Pierce (Decca).

Solfeggio, see **Song of the Nairobi Trio.**

Somebody Bad Stole de Wedding Bell (Who's Got de Ding Dong?)
Words by Bob Hilliard, music by Dave Mann.
Edwin H. Morris & Co., Inc.
Best-selling record in 1954 by Georgia Gibbs (Mercury).

Somewhere (There Is Someone)
Words and music by Charles Nathan and Dave Heisler.
Travis Music Co.
Introduced by Lou Monte (Decca).

Song from the Moulin Rouge, The, also known as **Where Is Your Heart** (French)
Words by William Engvick, music by Georges Auric.
Screen Gems-Columbia Music, Inc.
Theme from *Moulin Rouge* (film). Original title, "Le Long de la Seine," with French words by Jacques Larue. Best-selling record by Percy Faith and his Orchestra, vocal by Felicia Sanders (Columbia).

Song of the Nairobi Trio, also known as **Solfeggio**
Music by Robert Maxwell.
Robbins Music Corp.
Best-selling record by Robert Maxwell (M-G-M).

Sorta on the Border
Words and music by Irving Gordon.
Edwin H. Morris & Co., Inc.
Best-selling record by Tony Martin (RCA Victor).

Sous les Ponts de Paris, see **Under the Bridges of Paris.**

Spanish Fireball
Words and music by Daniel James Welch.
Lowery Music Co.
Best-selling record by Hank Snow (RCA Victor).

Strange
Words by John Latouche, music by Marvin Fisher.
Marvin Music Co.
Introduced by Nat "King" Cole.

Strange Things Are Happening
Words and music by Red Buttons, Allan Walker, and Elliot Lawrence.
Helayne Music Publishing Co., Inc.
Best-selling record by Red Buttons (Columbia).

Stranger in Paradise
Words and music by Robert Wright and George Forrest.
Frank Music Corp.
Based on a theme from the "Polovtsian Dances" from the opera, *Prince Igor,* by Borodin. Introduced by Richard Kiley and Doretta Morrow in *Kismet* (musical). Best-selling records in 1954 by Tony Bennett (Columbia) and The Four Aces (Decca).

Suddenly (German)
Words by Dorcas Cochran, music by Richard Heuberger.
Brenner Music, Inc.
Music based on "Komm mit Mir ins Chambre Separe," by Heuberger. Best-selling record in 1954 by Percy Faith and his Orchestra (Columbia).

Swedish Rhapsody, also known as **Midsummer Vigil** (Swedish)
New music and adaptation by Percy Faith from music based on folk themes by Hugo Alfven.
Cromwell Music, Inc.
Words by Carl Sigman added in 1954. Best-selling record, instrumental, by Percy Faith and his Orchestra (Columbia).

Teach Me Tonight
Words by Sammy Cahn, music by Gene de Paul.
The Hub Music Co.
First recorded by Janet Brace (Decca). Best-selling records in 1954 by The De Castro Sisters (Abbott) and Jo Stafford (Columbia).

Tell Me a Story
Words and music by Terry Gilkyson.
Montclare Music Corp.
Best-selling record by Frankie Laine and Jimmy Boyd (Columbia).

Tell Me You're Mine, see 1939.

Terry Theme, The, see **Eternally.**

That Hound Dog in the Window
Words and music by Bob Merrill.
Joy Music, Inc.
Parody of "That Doggie in the Window." Best-selling record by Homer and Jethro (RCA Victor).

That's Amoré, also known as **That's Love**
Words and music by Jack Brooks and Harry Warren.
Paramount Music Corp.
Introduced by Dean Martin in *The Caddy* (film). Nominated for Academy Award, 1953. Best-selling record in 1954 by Dean Martin (Capitol).

That's Entertainment
Words by Howard Dietz, music by Arthur Schwartz.
Chappell & Co., Inc.
Introduced by Fred Astaire, Nannette Fabray, and (dubbed for Cyd Charisse) the voice of India Adams in *The Band Wagon* film).

There Stands the Glass, see 1951.

Things That I Used To Do
Words and music by Eddie "Guitar Slim" Jones.
Venice Music, Inc.
Best-selling record in 1954 by Guitar Slim (Specialty).

This Orchid Means Goodbye
Words and music by Buck Bryant and Mark Webb.
Travis Music Co.
Best-selling record by Carl Smith (Columbia).

Thunder and Lightning (Lightning and Thunder)
Words by Marshall Barer, music by Paul Campbell.
Folkways Music Publishers, Inc.
Best-selling record by Georgia Gibbs (Mercury).

Till We Two Are One
Words by Tom Glazer, music by Larry Martin and Billy Martin.
Shapiro, Bernstein & Co., Inc.
Best-selling record in 1954 by George Shaw (Decca).

Today, I Love Ev'rybody
Words by Dorothy Fields, music by Harold Arlen.
Harwin Music Corp.
Introduced in *The Farmer Takes a Wife* (film).

Too Much Lovin' (Much Too Much)
Words and music by Lowman Pauling.
Bess Music Co.
Best-selling record by The Five Royales (Apollo).

Toys
Words and music by Bob Merrill.
Joy Music, Inc.
Introduced by Eileen Barton.

Trade Mark
Words and music by Porter Wagoner and Gary Walker.
Hill and Range Songs, Inc.
Best-selling record by Carl Smith (Columbia).

Tropicana
Music by Bernie Wayne.
Eastwick Music Co.
Best-selling record, instrumental, by Monty Kelly (Essex).

(I Love You) Twice As Much
Words and music by Royce Swain.
Porgie Music Corp.
Best-selling record by The Mills Brothers (Decca).

Twisted
Words by Annie Ross, music by Wardell Gray.
Prestige Music Co., Inc.
Text set to an improvised jazz solo by tenor saxophonist Wardell Gray. Best-selling record by Annie Ross (Prestige).

Typewriter, The
Music by Leroy Anderson.
Mills Music, Inc.
Introduced by Leroy Anderson and his Orchestra (Decca).

Under the Bridges of Paris (French)
English words by Dorcas Cochran, French words by J. Rodor, music by Vincent Scotto.
H. Delormel, Paris, France, 1914/Éditions Fortin, Paris, France, 1952/Hill and Range Songs, Inc.
Original title, "Sous les Ponts de Paris."

Uska Dara (Turkish)
Words and music by Stella Lee.
Robert Mellin, Inc.
Adapted from a Turkish popular song. First recorded by Eydie Gormé (Coral) in Turkish and English. Best-selling record, in Turkish, by Eartha Kitt (RCA Victor).

Vaya con Dios (May God Be with You)
Words and music by Larry Russell, Inez James, and Buddy Pepper.
Ardmore Music Corp.
Introduced by Anita O'Day (Mercury). Best-selling record by Les Paul and Mary Ford (Capitol).

Velvet Glove, The
Words and music by Harold Spina.
Edwin H. Morris & Co., Inc.
Best-selling record by Hugo Winterhalter and Henri René and their Orchestra (RCA Victor).

Very Necessary You, The
Words by Johnny Burke, music by James Van Heusen.
Burke & Van Heusen, Inc.
Introduced by Kevin Scott and Pat Stanley in *Carnival in Flanders* (Musical).

Very Special Day, A
Words by Oscar Hammerstein II, music by Richard Rodgers.
Williamson Music, Inc.
Introduced by Isabel Bigley in *Me and Juliet* (musical).

Wake Up Irene
Words and music by Weldon Allard and Johnny Hatchcock.
Brazos Valley Music, Inc.
Best-selling record in 1954 by Hank Thompson (Capitol).

Walkin' in the Rain, see **Just Walking in the Rain.**

Weary Blues from Waitin', see 1951.

Whale of a Tale, A
Words and music by Al Hoffman and Norman Gimbel.
Wonderland Music Co.
Introduced by Kirk Douglas in *20,000 Leagues under the Sea* (film).

When Loves Goes Wrong
Words by Harold Adamson, music by Hoagy Carmichael.
Leo Feist, Inc.
Introduced by Marilyn Monroe and the voice of Eileen Wilson in *Gentlemen Prefer Blondes* (film).

When Mexican Joe Met Jole Blon
Words and music by Sheb Wooley.
Aberbach, Inc./Brenner Music, Inc.
Best-selling record by Hank Snow (RCA Victor).

Where Is Your Heart, see **The Song from the Moulin Rouge.**

Wild Horses
Words and music by K. C. Rogan (pseudonym for Johnny Burke).
George Simon, Inc.
Adapted from Robert Schumann's "Wild Horseman." Best-selling record by Perry Como (RCA Victor).

Wild, Wild Young Men, see 1955.

With These Hands, see 1950.

Woke Up This Morning
Words and music by Riley King and Jules Taub.
Modern Music Publishing Co.
Best-selling record by B. B. King (RPM).

Woman
Words and music by Dick Gleason.
Studio Music Co.
Introduced by Johnny Desmond (Coral). Best-selling record by José Ferrer and Rosemary Clooney (Columbia). Released on a single record along with its sequel, entitled "Man."

Wrong Note Rag
Words by Betty Comden and Adolph Green, music by Leonard Bernstein.
Chappell & Co., Inc./G. Schirmer, Inc.
Introduced by Rosalind Russell and Edith Adams in *Wonderful Town* (musical).

Y'All Come, see **You All Come.**

Yellow Roses
Words and music by Kenny Devine and Sam Nichols.
Travis Music Co.
Best-selling record in 1955 by Hank Snow (RCA Victor).

You All Come, also known as **Y'All Come**
Words and music by Arlie Duff.
Starday Music.
Best-selling record by Arlie Duff (Starday).

You Alone (Solo Tu)
Words by Al Stillman, music by Robert Allen.
Roncom Music Co.
Best-selling record by Perry Como (RCA Victor).

You Are Not My First Love
Words and music by Bart Howard and Peter Windsor.
Walden Music Corp.
Introduced by Mabel Mercer.

You Better Not Do That
Words and music by Tommy Collins.
Central Songs, Inc.
Best-selling record in 1954 by Tommy Collins (Capitol).

You You You (German)
English words by Robert Mellin, German words by Walter Rothenberg, music by Lotar Olias.
Edition Accord, Berlin, Germany, 1952/ Robert Mellin, Inc.
Best-selling record by The Ames Brothers (RCA Victor).

You're So Much a Part of Me
Words and music by Richard Adler and Jerry Ross.
Frank Music Corp.
Introduced by Carleton Carpenter and Elaine Dunn in *John Murray Anderson's Almanac* (revue).

Zsa Zsa
Music by Bernie Wayne.
Sunbeam Music Corp.
Dedicated to Zsa Zsa Gabor. Best-selling record by Bernie Wayne and his Orchestra (Coral).

1954

Airegin, see 1963.

All of You
Words and music by Cole Porter.
Buxton Hill Music Corp.
Introduced by Don Ameche in 1955 in *Silk Stockings* (musical).

Allentown Jail
Words and music by Irving Gordon.
Bourne, Inc.

Alone Too Long
Words by Dorothy Fields, music by Arthur Schwartz.
Rugby Music Corp.
Introduced by Wilbur Evans and Shirley Booth in *By the Beautiful Sea* (musical).

Am I in Love?
Words by Ted Varnick, music by Nick Acquaviva.
Miller Music Corp.
Best-selling record by Joni James (M-G-M).

Ànema e Core, also known as **With All My Heart and Soul** (Italian)
English words by Mann Curtis and Harry Akst, Italian words by Tito Manlio, music by Salve d'Esposito.
Edizioni Musical Film, Milan, Italy, 1950/Leeds Music Corp.
Introduced by Ferruccio Tagliavini in the Italian film, *Ànema e Core*. Featured in *John Murray Anderson's Almanac* (revue). Best-selling record by Eddie Fisher (RCA Victor). An earlier English-language version, entitled "Until," recorded by Dinah Shore (RCA Victor).

Angels in the Sky
Words and music by Dick Glasser.
Ridgeway Music.
Best-selling record in 1956 by The Crew Cuts (Mercury).

Annie Had a Baby
Words and music by Henry Glover and Lois Mann.
Jay & Cee Music Corp.
Best-selling record by The Midnighters (Federal).

Anything Can Happen-Mambo
Words by Sid Wayne, music by Joe Sherman.
Beechwood Music Corp.
Best-selling record by Dolores Hawkins (Epic).

As Far As I'm Concerned
Words and music by Dale Parker.
Hill and Range Songs, Inc.
Best-selling record by Red Foley (Decca).

Athena
Words by Bert Pollack, music by Hugh Martin and Ralph Blane.
Leo Feist, Inc.
Theme from *Athena* (film). Best-selling record by Don Cornell (Coral).

Autumn in Rome
Words and music by Sammy Cahn and Paul Weston from an original score by Alessandro Cicognini.
Cromwell Music, Inc.
From *Indiscretion of an American Wife* (film).

Back Track! (French)
English words by Lee Wilson and Lynn Russell, French words by Pierre Delanoe, music by Gilbert Becaud.
France Music Co./Duchess Music Corp.
Introduced in France under its original title, "Passe Ton Chemin," by Gilbert Becaud. Introduced in the United States by Sammy Davis, Jr.

Back Up Buddy
Words and music by Boudleaux Bryant.
Acuff-Rose Publications.
Best-selling record by Carl Smith (Columbia).

Backward, Turn Backward (O' Time in Your Flight)
Words and music by Dave Coleman.
Travis Music Co.
Introduced by Jane Froman.

Bag's Groove, see 1962.

Bamboo Cage, see **Smellin' of Vanilla**

Bandit, The, also known as **O Cangaceiro** (Brazilian)
English words by John Turner and Michael Carr, music by Alfredo Ricardo de Nascimento.
Peter Maurice Music Co., Ltd., London, England, 1953/Leeds Music Corp.
Title song from *O Cangaceiro* (Brazilian film). Best-selling record by Percy Faith and his Orchestra (Columbia).

Bazoom, see **I Need Your Lovin'.**

Be Kind to Your Parents
Words and music by Harold Rome.
Chappell & Co., Inc./Florence Music Co., Inc.
Introduced by Florence Henderson and Lloyd Reese in *Fanny* (musical).

Berry Tree, The
Words and adapted music by Saul Chaplin.
Miller Music Corp.
Based on the traditional folk song, "The Next Big River." From *Many Rivers To Cross* (film). Best-selling record by Bill Hayes (Cadence).

Beware of It
Words and music by Cy Coben.
R.F.D. Music Publishing Co.
Best-selling record by Johnnie and Jack (RCA Victor).

Bless Your Beautiful Hide
Words by Johnny Mercer, music by Gene de Paul.
Robbins Music Corp.
Introduced by Howard Keel in *Seven Brides for Seven Brothers* (film).

Blossom Fell, A (English)
Words and music by Howard Barnes, Harold Cornelius, and Dominic John.
John Fields Music Co. Ltd., London, England/Shapiro, Bernstein & Co., Inc.
Best-selling record in 1955 by Nat "King" Cole (Capitol).

Blue Bird Waltz
Music by Frank Yankovic and Joe Trolli.
Mills Music, Inc.
Best-selling record by Frank Yankovic (Columbia).

Blue Monk
Music by Thelonious Monk.
Thelonious Music.
Introduced by Thelonious Monk (Prestige).

Bridges at Toko-Ri, The
Music by Lyn Murray.
Famous Music Corp.
Love theme from *The Bridges at Toko-Ri* (film).

Cara Mia
Words and music by Tulio Trapani and Lee Lange.
Leo Feist, Inc.
Best-selling record in 1956 by David Whitfield (produced in England) (London).

Cinnamon Sinner
Words and music by Lincoln Chase.
Raleigh Music, Inc.
Best-selling record by Tony Bennett (Columbia).

Come Back Baby
Words and music by Ray Charles.
Progressive Music Publishing Co., Inc.
Best-selling record in 1955 by Ray Charles (Atlantic).

Count Your Blessings Instead of Sheep, see 1952.

Courtin' in the Rain
Words and music by T. Texas Tyler.
Four Star Sales Co.
Best-selling record by T. Texas Tyler (Four Star).

Crazy 'bout Ya, Baby
Words by Pat Barrett, music by Rudi Maugeri.
Sunbeam Music Corp.
Best-selling record by The Crew Cuts (Mercury).

Cross over the Bridge
Words and music by Bennie Benjamin and George Weiss.
Laurel Music Corp.
Best-selling record by Patti Page (Mercury).

Cry, Cry Darling
Words and music by Jimmy Newman and Joseph D. Miller.
Acuff-Rose Publications.
Best-selling record by Jimmy Newman (Dot).

Cuddle Me
Words and music by Ronnie Gaylord.
Vincent Music Co.
Best-selling record by Ronnie Gaylord (Mercury).

Cuz You're So Sweet
Words and music by John Kane.
Tree Publishing Co., Inc.
Best-selling record in 1955 by Simon Crum (Capitol).

Danger! Heartbreak Ahead
Words and music by Carl Stutz and Carl Barefoot.
Robbins Music Corp.
Best-selling record by Jaye P. Morgan (RCA Victor).

Dim, Dim the Lights (I Want Some Atmosphere)
Words and music by Beverly Ross and Julius Dixon.
Republic Music Corp.
Best-selling record by Bill Haley and The Comets (Decca).

Dissertation on the State of Bliss, also known as **Love and Learn**
Words by Ira Gershwin, music by Harold Arlen.
Harwin Music Corp.
Introduced by Bing Crosby in *The Country Girl* (film).

Distant Melody
Words by Betty Comden and Adolph Green, music by Jule Styne.
Edwin H. Morris & Co., Inc.
Introduced by Mary Martin in *Peter Pan* (musical).

Don't Drop It
Words and music by Terry Fell.
American Music, Inc.
Best-selling record by Carl Smith (Columbia).

Don't Go to Strangers
Words by Redd Evans, music by Arthur Kent and Dave Mann.
Jefferson Music Co., Inc.
Best-selling record by Vaughn Monroe (RCA Victor).

Don't You Know
Words and music by Ray Charles.
Progressive Music Publishing Co., Inc.
Best-selling record by Ray Charles (Atlantic).

Dream, Dream, Dream
Words by Mitchell Parish, music by Jimmy McHugh.
Leo Feist, Inc.

Earth Angel (Will You Be Mine)
Words and music by Jesse Belvin.
Dootsie Williams, Inc.
Best-selling records in 1955 by The Penguins (Dooto) and The Crew Cuts (Mercury).

Even Tho'
Words and music by Willie Jones, Curt Peeples, and Webb Pierce.
Acuff-Rose Publications.
Best-selling record by Webb Pierce (Decca).

Fanny
Words and music by Harold Rome.
Chappell & Co., Inc./Florence Music Co., Inc.
Introduced by William Tabbert in *Fanny* (musical). Used as main theme of 1961 film version.

Finger of Suspicion Points at You, The
Words and music by Paul Mann and Al Lewis.
Pickwick Music Corp.
Introduced in England and best-selling record by Dicky Valentine (London).

Fly Me to the Moon, also known as **In Other Words**
Words and music by Bart Howard.
Almanac Music, Inc.
Introduced by Felicia Sanders. First recording by Kaye Ballard (Decca). Best-selling record in 1962 by Joe Harnell (Kapp).

From the Vine Came the Grape, see **1949.**

Funny Thing
Words by Carl Sigman, music by Arthur Williams.
United Music Corp.
Best-selling record by Tony Bennett (Columbia).

Gelsomina, see **Love Theme from *La Strada*.**

Gilly Gilly Ossenfeffer Katzenellen Bogen by the Sea
Words and music by Al Hoffman and Dick Manning.
Beaver Music Publishing Corp.
Best-selling record by The Four Lads (Columbia).

Girl! a Girl!, A
Words and music by Bennie Benjamin, George Weiss, and Al Bandini.
Valando Music Corp.
Best-selling record by Eddie Fisher (RCA Victor).

Goodnight, Sweetheart, Goodnight, see **Goodnight, Well It's Time To Go.**

Goodnight, Well It's Time To Go
Words and music by Calvin Carter and James Hudson.
Arc Music Corp./Conrad Publishing Co., Inc.
Original title, "Goodnight, Sweetheart, Goodnight." Best-selling records by The McGuire Sisters (Coral), Johnnie and Jack (RCA Victor), and The Spaniels (Vee Jay).

Gotta Have Me Go with You
Words by Ira Gershwin, music by Harold Arlen.
Harwin Music Corp.
Introduced by Judy Garland in *A Star Is Born* (film).

Green Years
Words and music by Don Reid and Arthur Altman.
Harms, Inc.
Best-selling record by Eddie Fisher (RCA Victor).

Hajji Baba
Words by Ned Washington, music by Dimitri Tiomkin.
Remick Music Corp.
Introduced by Nat "King" Cole in *The Adventures of Hajji Baba* (film).

Hang Up
Words by Dorothy Fields, music by Arthur Schwartz.
Rugby Music Corp.
Introduced by Mae Barnes in *By the Beautiful Sea* (musical).

Happy Habit
Words by Dorothy Fields, music by Arthur Schwartz.
Rugby Music Corp.
Introduced by Mae Barnes in *By the Beautiful Sea* (musical).

Happy Wanderer, The (Val-de Ri — Val-de Ra) (German)
English words by Antonia Ridge, German words by Fl. Siegesmund and Edith Möller, music by Friedrich Wilhelm Möller.
Bosworth & Co., Ltd., London, England; Cologne, Germany/Sam Fox Publishing Co., Inc.
From the German song, "Der Fröhliche Wanderer." Introduced by The Oberkirchen Children's Choir. Best-selling records by Henri René (RCA Victor) and Frank Weir (London).

He
Words by Jack Mullan, music by Jack Richards.
Avas Music Publishing Co., Inc.
Best-selling record by Al Hibbler (Decca).

Heart of a Fool, The
Words by Hal David, music by Frank Weldon.
Joy Music, Inc.
Best-selling record by Val Anthony (Essex).

Heartbreaker
Words and music by Ahmet Ertegun.
Progressive Music Publishing Co., Inc.
Best-selling record by Ray Charles (Atlantic).

Hearts of Stone
Words by Eddy Ray, music by Rudy Jackson.
Regent Music Corp./Travis Music Co.
Best-selling records in 1955 by The Fontane Sisters (Dot), Otis Williams and The Charms (De Luxe), and Red Foley (Decca).

Hep Cat Baby
Words and music by Cy Coben.
Alamo Music, Inc.
Best-selling record by Eddy Arnold (RCA Victor).

Here
Words and music by Dorcas Cochran and Harold Grant.
Hill and Range Songs, Inc.
Based on the aria, "Caro Nome," from Verdi's opera, *Rigoletto*. Best-selling record by Tony Martin (RCA Victor).

Hernando's Hideaway
Words and music by Richard Adler and Jerry Ross.
Frank Music Corp.
Introduced by Carol Haney in *The Pajama Game* (musical). Best-selling record by Archie Bleyer and his Orchestra (Cadence).

Hey There
Words and music by Richard Adler and Jerry Ross.
Frank Music Corp.
Introduced by John Raitt in *The Pajama Game* (musical). Best-selling record by Rosemary Clooney (Columbia).

High and the Mighty, The
Words by Ned Washington, music by Dimitri Tiomkin.
M. Witmark & Sons.
Theme from *The High and the Mighty* (film). Nominated for Academy Award, 1954. Best-selling records, instrumentals, by Leroy Holmes and his Orchestra (M-G-M), Victor Young and his Orchestra (Decca), and Les Baxter and his Orchestra (Capitol).

Hit and Run Affair
Words and music by Don Roseland, Ray Cormier, and Mel Van.
Duchess Music Corp.
Best-selling record by Perry Como (RCA Victor).

Hold 'em Joe
Words and music by Harry Thomas.
Folkways Music Publishers, Inc.
Introduced by Harry Belafonte in *John Murray Anderson's Almanac* (revue).

Hold Me in Your Arms
Words and music by Ray Heindorf, Charles Henderson, and Don Pippin.
Artists Music, Inc.
Introduced by Doris Day in *Young at Heart* (film).

Hold My Hand, see 1950.

Home Is Where the Heart Is
Words by Sammy Cahn, music by Sammy Fain.
M. Witmark & Sons.
Introduced in *Three Sailors and a Girl* (film).

Honey Hush
Words and music by Lou Willie Turner.
Progressive Music Publishing Co., Inc.
Best-selling record in 1953 and 1954 by Joe Turner (Atlantic).

Honey Love
Words and music by Clyde McPhatter and J. Gerald.
Progressive Music Publishing Co., Inc.
Best-selling record by The Drifters (Atlantic).

Honeycomb
Words and music by Bob Merrill.
Joy Music, Inc.
Best-selling record in 1957 by Jimmie Rodgers (Roulette).

Honky Tonk Girl
Words and music by Gladwyn E. "Chuck" Harding and Hank Thompson.
Brazos Valley Music, Inc.
Best-selling record by Hank Thompson (Capitol).

Horse with the Easter Bonnet, The
Words and music by Al Hoffman and Dick Manning.
Ben Bloom Music Corp.
From a story by Jane Thayer. Introduced by Gene Autry.

House of Flowers
Words by Truman Capote and Harold Arlen, music by Harold Arlen.
Harwin Music Corp.
Introduced by Diahann Carroll and Rawn Spearman in *House of Flowers* (musical).

Huckleberry Finn
Music by Richard Hayman, John Sbarra, Jr., and Joseph Di Buono.
Paxwin Music Corp.
Best-selling record, instrumental, by Richard Hayman and his Orchestra (Mercury).

Hurts Me to My Heart
Words and music by Charles Singleton and Rose Marie McCoy.
Monument Music, Inc.
Best-selling record by Faye Adams (Herald).

I Can't Tell a Waltz from a Tango
Words and music by Al Hoffman and Dick Manning.
Harman Music, Inc.
Best-selling record by Patti Page (Mercury).

I Could Have Told You
Words by Carl Sigman, music by James Van Heusen.
United Music Corp.
Best-selling record by Frank Sinatra (Capitol).

I Cried
Words and music by Michael Elias and Billy Duke.
Moonlight Music, Inc.
Best-selling record by Patti Page (Mercury).

I Didn't Want To Do It
Words and music by Adolph Smith and Harry Gladstone.
Travis Music Co.
Best-selling record by The Spiders (Imperial).

I Don't Hurt Anymore
Words by Jack Rollins, music by Don Robertson.
Hill and Range Songs, Inc./Rumbalero Music, Inc.
Best-selling records in 1954 by Dinah Washington (Mercury) and in 1954 and 1955 by Hank Snow (RCA Victor).

I Got a Woman (I Got a Sweetie)
Words and music by Ray Charles.
Progressive Music Pubilshing Co., Inc.
Best-selling record in 1955 by Ray Charles (Atlantic).

I Have To Tell You
Words and music by Harold Rome.
Chappell & Co., Inc./Florence Music Co., Inc.
Introduced by Florence Henderson in *Fanny* (musical).

I Left My Heart in San Francisco
Words by Douglass Cross, music by George Cory.
General Music Publishing Co., Inc.
Intoduced by Claramae Turner. Best-selling record in 1962 by Tony Bennett (Columbia).

I Like Myself
Words by Betty Comden and Adolph Green, music by André Previn.
Leo Feist, Inc.
Introduced by Gene Kelly in *It's Always Fair Weather* (film).

I Like You
Words and music by Harold Rome.
Chappell & Co., Inc./Florence Music Co., Inc.
Introduced by William Tabbert and Ezio Pinza in *Fanny* (musical).

I Love You Madly
Words and music by Charles Jones.
Angel Music, Inc.
Original rhythm and blues version introduced by Charlie and Ray (Herald). Best-selling record by The Four Coins (Epic).

I Need Your Lovin', also known as Bazoom
Words and music by Jerry Leiber and Mike Stoller.
Quintet Music, Inc.
Best-selling record by The Cheers (Capitol).

I Never Felt More Like Falling in Love
Words by Ralph Freed, music by Robert Allen.
Korwin Music, Inc.
Best-selling record in 1957 by Tony Bennett (Columbia).

I Never Has Seen Snow
Words by Truman Capote and Harold Arlen, music by Harold Arlen.
Harwin Music Corp.
Introduced by Diahann Carroll in *House of Flowers* (musical).

I Speak to the Stars
Words by Paul Francis Webster, music by Sammy Fain.
M. Witmark & Sons.
Introduced by Doris Day in *Lucky Me* (film).

I Want You All to Myself
Words and music by John Koch and Roy Carroll.
Skidmore Music Co., Inc.
Best-selling record by Kitty Kallen (Decca).

I Won't Grow Up
Words by Carolyn Leigh, music by Mark Charlap.
Edwin H. Morris & Co., Inc.
Introduced by Mary Martin in *Peter Pan* (musical).

If I Give My Heart to You
Words and music by Jimmie Crane, Al Jacobs, and Jimmy Brewster.
Miller Music Corp.
First recording by Denise Lor (Majar). Best-selling record by Doris Day (Columbia).

If You Ain't Lovin' (You Ain't Livin')
Words and music by Tommy Collins.
Central Songs, Inc.
Best-selling record in 1954 and 1955 by Faron Young (Capitol).

If You Don't, Somebody Else Will
Words and music by Johnny Mathis, Jimmy Lee, and Geraldine Hamilton.
Acuff-Rose Publications.
Best-selling records by Jimmy and Johnny (Chess) and Ray Price (Columbia).

I'll Be There If You Ever Want Me
Words and music by Rusty Gabbard and Ray Price.
Ernest Tubb Music, Inc.
Best-selling record by Ray Price (Columbia).

I'll Cry Tomorrow
Words and music by Dave Dreyer, Lillian Roth, and Gerald Marks.
Marlong Music Corp.
Promotional tie-in song for Lillian Roth's autobiography, *I'll Cry Tomorrow*.

I'm a Fool To Care, see 1948.

I'm Always Hearing Wedding Bells (German)
English words by Robert Mellin, German words by Fred Rauch, music by Herbert Jarczyk.
Quint-Musikverlag, Munich, Germany/Robert Mellin, Inc.
Original title, "Hochzeitsglocken," from the German film of the same name. Best-selling record in 1955 by Eddie Fisher (RCA Victor).

I'm Flying
Words by Carolyn Leigh, music by Mark Charlap.
Edwin H. Morris & Co., Inc.
Introduced by Mary Martin, Kathy Nolan, Richard Harrington, and Joseph Stafford in *Peter Pan* (musical).

I'm Just a Country Boy
Words and music by Fred Brooks and Marshall Barer.
Folkways Music Publishers, Inc.
Best-selling record by Harry Belafonte (RCA Victor).

I'm Not at All in Love
Words and music by Richard Adler and Jerry Ross.
Frank Music Corp.
Introduced by Janis Paige in *The Pajama Game* (musical).

I'm Ready
Words and music by Willie Dixon.
Arc Music Corp.
Best-selling record by Muddy Waters (Chess).

I'm Your Hoochie Cooche Man, see 1957.

In Other Words, see **Fly Me to the Moon.**

In Paris and in Love
Words by Leo Robin, music by Sigmund Romberg.
Chappell & Co., Inc.
Introduced by Jeanmaire and David Atkinson in *The Girl in Pink Tights* (musical).

In the Chapel in the Moonlight, see 1936.

Indiscretion
Words and music by Sammy Cahn and Paul Weston from an original score by Alessandro Cicognini.
Cromwell Music, Inc.
From *Indiscretion of an American Wife* (film). Best-selling record by Jo Stafford (Columbia).

It May Sound Silly
Words and music by Ivory Joe Hunter.
Progressive Music Publishing Co., Inc.
Best-selling record by Ivory Joe Hunter (Atlantic).

It Tickles
Words and music by Tommy Collins and Wanda Collins.
Central Songs, Inc.
Best-selling record in 1955 by Tommy Collins (Capitol).

It's a Chemical Reaction
Words and music by Cole Porter.
Buxton Hill Music Corp.
Introduced by Hildegarde Neff in 1955 in *Silk Stockings* (musical).

It's a New World
Words by Ira Gershwin, music by Harold Arlen.
Harwin Music Corp.
Introduced by Judy Garland in *A Star Is Born* (film).

It's a Woman's World
Words by Sammy Cahn, music by Cyril Mockridge.
Robbins Music Corp.
Introduced by The Four Aces, behind the titles, on the soundtrack of *Woman's World* (film).

It's the Going Home Together
Words by John Latouche, music by Jerome Moross.
Chappell & Co., Inc.
Introduced by Stephen Douglass and Priscilla Gillette in *The Golden Apple* (musical).

I've Been Thinking
Words and music by Boudleaux Bryant.
Acuff-Rose Publications.
Best-selling record in 1954 and 1955 by Eddy Arnold (RCA Victor).

I've Got My Eyes on You
Words and music by Paul Winley.
Progressive Music Publishing Co., Inc.
Best-selling record by The Clovers (Atlantic).

I've Got To Crow
Words by Carolyn Leigh, music by Mark Charlap.
Edwin H. Morris & Co., Inc.
Introduced by Mary Martin in *Peter Pan* (musical)

Jeru
Music by Gerry Mulligan.
Beechwood Music Corp.
Recorded in 1949 by Miles Davis and his Orchestra (Capitol).

Jilted
Words and music by Robert Colby and Dick Manning.
Travis Music Co.
Best-selling record by Red Foley (Decca).

Joey
Words and music by Herb Wiener, James J. Kriegsman, and Salmirs-Bernstein.
Dorothy Music.
Best-selling record by Betty Madigan (M-G-M).

Johnny Guitar
Words by Peggy Lee, music by Victor Young.
Victor Young Publications, Inc.
Introduced by Peggy Lee in *Johnny Guitar* (film).

Johnny Guitar, see **My Restless Lover.**

Josephine
Words and music by Cole Porter.
Buxton Hill Music Corp.
Introduced by Gretchen Wyler in 1955 in *Silk Stockings* (musical).

Kiss Me and Kill Me with Love
Words by Dan Shapiro, music by Sammy Fain.
Chappell & Co., Inc.
Introduced by Jane Kean and Mark Dawson in *Ankles Aweigh* (musical).

Kisses Don't Lie
Words and music by Pearl Butler and George Sherry.
Cedarwood Publishing Co., Inc.
Best-selling record in 1954 and 1955 by Carl Smith (Columbia).

Knock on Wood
Words and music by Sylvia Fine.
Famous Music Corp.
Introduced by Danny Kaye in *Knock on Wood* (film).

La Ronde, also known as **Merry-Go-Round (French)**
Words by Dorcas Cochran, music by Oscar Straus.
Paris Choudens, Éditeur, Paris, France, 1950/Hill and Range Songs, Inc. for words/Alamo Music, Inc. for music.
Theme from *La Ronde* (French film). An earlier version, by Cochran and Straus, entitled "Love Makes the World Go 'round," copyrighted in 1951.

Land of Dreams
Words by Norman Gimbel, music by Eddie Heywood.
Vogue Music, Inc.
Best-selling record, instrumental, by Hugo Winterhalter and his Orchestra, featuring Eddie Heywood at the piano (RCA Victor).

Lazy Afternoon
Words by John Latouche, music by Jerome Moross.
Chappell & Co., Inc.
Introduced by Kaye Ballard in *The Golden Apple* (musical).

Le Grisbi, see **The Touch.**

Let Me Go Lover!
Words and music by Jenny Lou Carson, special lyrics by Al Hill.
Rumbalero Music, Inc.
A 1953 version, by Jenny Lou Carson, entitled "Let Me Go Devil!" rewritten at the suggestion of Mitch Miller for a CBS *Studio One* television show. Best-selling record in 1955 by Joan Weber (Columbia).

Let Me Love You
Words and music by Bart Howard.
Leeds Music Corp.
Introduced by Mabel Mercer.

Ling Ting Tong
Words and music by Mable Godwin.
St. Louis Music Corp.
Best-selling records by The Five Keys (Capitol) and Otis Williams and The Charms (De Luxe).

Lisa
Music by Franz Waxman.
Paramount Music Corp.
Theme from *Rear Window* (film).

Lisbon Antigua, also known as In Old Lisbon (Portuguese)
English words by Harry Dupree, Portuguese words by José Galhardo and Amadeu do Vale, music by Raul Portela.
Sassetti y Cia, Lisbon, Portugal, 1937/Southern Music Publishing Co., Inc.
Original title, "Lisboa Antigua." Best-selling record in 1956 by Nelson Riddle and his Orchestra (Capitol).

Little Mama
Words and music by Carmen Taylor, Willis Carroll, Ahmet Ertegun, and Jerry Wexler.
Progressive Music Publishing Co., Inc.
Best-selling record by The Clovers (Atlantic).

Little Shoemaker, The (French)
English words by Geoffrey Parsons and John Turner, French words by Francis Lamarque, music by Rudi Revil.
Les Éditions Tropicales, Paris, France, 1953/Bourne, Inc.
Original French title, "Le Petit Cordonnier." Best-selling records by The Gaylords (Mercury) and Hugo Winterhalter and his Orchestra (RCA Victor).

Little Things Mean a Lot
Words and music by Edith Lindeman and Carl Stutz.
Leo Feist, Inc.
Best-selling record by Kitty Kallen (Decca).

Live Fast, Love Hard, Die Young
Words and music by Joe Allison.
Central Songs, Inc.
Best-selling record by Faron Young (Capitol).

Lonesome Polecat
Words by Johnny Mercer, music by Gene de Paul.
Robbins Music Corp.
Introduced by Bill Lee in *Seven Brides for Seven Brothers* (film).

Long John
Words by Arnold Sundgaard, music by Paul Campbell.
Folkways Music Publishers, Inc.
Best-selling record by Lonnie Donegan (Mercury).

Loose Talk
Words and music by Freddie Hart and Ann Lucas.
Central Songs, Inc.
Best-selling record in 1954 and 1955 by Carl Smith (Columbia).

Lose That Long Face
Words by Ira Gershwin, music by Harold Arlen.
Harwin Music Corp.
Introduced by Judy Garland in *A Star Is Born* (film).

Losing Hand
Words and music by Charles Calhoun.
Progressive Music Publishing Co., Inc.
Best-selling record by Ray Charles (Atlantic).

Lost in Loveliness
Words by Leo Robin, music by Sigmund Romberg.
Chappell & Co., Inc.
Introduced by David Atkinson in *The Girl in Pink Tights* (musical).

Love I You (You I Love)
Words and music by Sammy Carlisi.
Cool Music Co.
Best-selling record by The Gaylords (Mercury).

Love Is a Very Light Thing
Words and music by Harold Rome.
Chappell & Co., Inc./Florence Music Co., Inc.
Introduced by Ezio Pinza in *Fanny* (musical).

Love Me
Words and music by Mike Stoller and Jerry Leiber.
Hill and Range Songs, Inc./Quintet Music, Inc.
Best-selling record in 1956 and 1957 by Elvis Presley (RCA Victor).

Love Theme from *La Strada* (Italian)
English words by Don Raye, original Italian version by M. Galdieri and N. Rota.
R.P.D. Radiofilmusica Ponti-De Laurentiis, Industrie Musicali, Milan, Italy/Leeds Music Corp.
Theme from *La Strada* (Italian film). Also known by the titles, "Gelsomina," "Traveling down a Lonely Road," and, in its initial English-language version, "You and You Alone."

Lovey Dovey
Words and music by Ahmet Ertegun and Memphis Curtis.
Progressive Music Publishing Co., Inc.
Best-selling record by The Clovers (Atlantic).

Lovin' Spree
Words by Joan Springer, music by Phil Springer.
Joy Music, Inc.
Best-selling record by Eartha Kitt (RCA Victor).

Magic Circle
Words and music by Bennie Benjamin and George Weiss.
Laurel Music Corp.
Best-selling record by Rusty Draper (Mercury).

Magic Tango, The (French)
English words by Jimmy Kennedy, music by M. Philippe-Gérard.
Chappell & Co., Inc.
Best-selling record, instrumental, by Hugo Winterhalter and his Orchestra (RCA Victor).

Make Her Mine
Words by Sammy Gallop, music by Chester Conn.
Bregman, Vocco & Conn, Inc.
Best-selling record by Nat "King" Cole (Capitol).

Make Yourself Comfortable
Words and music by Bob Merrill.
Rylan Music Corp.
Best-selling record by Sarah Vaughan (Mercury).

Making Believe
Words and music by Jimmy Work.
Acuff-Rose Publications.
Best-selling record in 1955 by Kitty Wells (Decca) and Jimmy Work (Dot).

Mama Doll Song, The
Words by Charles Tobias, music by Nat Simon.
Lear Music, Inc.
Best-selling record by Patti Page (Mercury).

Mambo Baby
Words and music by Charles Singleton and Rose Marie McCoy.
M & M Music Co.
Best-selling record by Ruth Brown (Atlantic).

Mambo Italiano
Words and music by Bob Merrill.
Rylan Music Corp.
Best-selling record by Rosemary Clooney (Columbia).

Man That Got Away, The
Words by Ira Gershwin, music by Harold Arlen.
Harwin Music Corp.
Introduced by Judy Garland in *A Star Is Born* (film). Nominated for Academy Award, 1954.

Man Upstairs, The
Words and music by Dorinda Morgan, Harold Stanley, and Gerry Manners.
Starstan Music Corp.
Best-selling record by Kay Starr (Capitol).

Melancholy Me
Words and music by Joe Thomas and Howard Biggs.
Travis Music Co.
Best-selling record by Eddy Howard (Mercury).

Melody of Love
Words by Tom Glazer, music by H. Engelmann.
Theodore Presser Co./Shapiro, Bernstein & Co., Inc.
Music originally copyrighted in 1903. First revived in 1942 with an accompanying recitation entitled "Whisper That You Love Me." Subsequently revived as "Melody of Love" with a best-selling instrumental record by Billy Vaughn and his Orchestra (Dot). First vocal version, with new lyrics, recorded by Tony Martin and Dinah Shore (RCA Victor). Best-selling vocal version by The Four Aces (Decca).

Mess Around
Words and music by Ahmet Ertegun.
Progressive Music Publishing Co., Inc.
Best-selling record by Ray Charles (Atlantic).

Midnight Sun
Words and music by Sonny Burke and Lionel Hampton.
Crystal Music Publishers, Inc.
Adapted from an instrumental composition introduced in 1948 by Lionel Hampton and his Orchestra.

Miss America
Words and music by Bernie Wayne.
Command Music Co., Inc.
Official song of the annual Miss America Pageant at Atlantic City, New Jersey.

Mister Sandman
Words and music by Pat Ballard.
Edwin H. Morris & Co., Inc.
Best-selling record by The Chordettes (Cadence).

Money Burns a Hole in My Pocket
Words by Bob Hilliard, music by Jule Styne.
Chappell & Co., Inc.
Introduced by Dean Martin in *Living It Up* (film).

More and More
Words and music by Merle Kilgore and Webb Pierce.
Travis Music Co./Cedarwood Publishing Co., Inc.
Best-selling record in 1954 and 1955 by Webb Pierce (Decca).

More Love Than Your Love
Words by Dorothy Fields, music by Arthur Schwartz.
Rugby Music Corp.
Introduced by Wilbur Evans in *By the Beautiful Sea* (musical).

My Everything (You're My Everything)
Words and music by Jim Wilson and Marvin Lacy.
Hill and Range Songs, Inc.
Best-selling record by Eddy Arnold (RCA Victor).

My Friend
Words and music by Ervin Drake and Jimmy Shirl.
George Paxton, Inc.
Introduced by Eddie Fisher (RCA Victor).

My Heart Won't Say Goodbye
Words by Leo Robin, music by Sigmund Romberg.
Chappell & Co., Inc.
Introduced by David Atkinson in *The Girl in Pink Tights* (musical).

My Own True Love
Words by Mack David, music by Max Steiner.
Remick Music Corp.
Vocal version of Steiner's "Tara's Theme" from the score of *Gone with the Wind* (film).

My Restless Lover, also known as Johnny Guitar
Words and music by Pembroke Davenport.
Chappell & Co., Inc.
Original title, "Johnny Guitar," but title changed because of conflict with film of same name. Best-selling record by Patti Page (Mercury).

My Son, My Son (English)
Words by Bob Howard and Melville Farley, music by Eddie Calvert.
Edward Kassner Music Co., Ltd., London, England/Ross Jungnickel, Inc.
Best-selling record by Vera Lynn (London).

Napoleon
Words and music by Vic Abrams.
Nom Music, Inc.
Based on Tchaikowsky's "1812 Overture." Introduced by Mitch Miller, his Chorus, and his Orchestra (Columbia).

Naughty Lady of Shady Lane, The
Words and music by Sid Tepper and Roy C. Bennett.
George Paxton, Inc.
Best-selling record in 1955 by The Ames Brothers (RCA Victor).

Never-Never Land
Words by Betty Comden and Adolph Green, music by Jule Styne.
Edwin H. Morris & Co., Inc.
Introduced by Mary Martin in *Peter Pan* (musical).

New Town Is a Blue Town, A
Words and music by Richard Adler and Jerry Ross.
Frank Music Corp.
Introduced by John Raitt in *The Pajama Game* (musical).

Night Watch, The
Words and music by Cindy Walker.
Copar-Forrest Music Corp.
Best-selling record by Red Foley (Decca).

(My Baby Don't Love Me) No More
Words by Julie De John and Dux De John, music by Leo J. De John.
Maple Leaf Music Publishing Co., Inc.
Best-selling record in 1955 by The De John Sisters (Epic).

No One but You
Words by Jack Lawrence, music by Nicholas Brodszky.
Leo Feist, Inc.
Introduced by Carlos Thompson in *Flame and the Flesh* (film).

O Cangaceiro, see **The Bandit.**

Oh, That'll Be Joyful
Words and music by Jack McVea, Jake Porter, and Paul Campbell.
Ludlow Music, Inc.

Oh What a Dream, see **What a Dream.**

On the Waterfront
Words by John Latouche, music by Leonard Bernstein.
J. J. Robbins, Inc.
Adapted from a theme from *On the Waterfront* (film).

One by One
Words and music by Jim Anglin, Johnnie Wright, and Jack Anglin.
Acuff-Rose Publications.
Best-selling record by Kitty Wells and Red Foley (Decca).

Oop Shoop
Words and music by Joe Josea.
Flair Publishing Co.
Best-selling record by The Crew Cuts (Mercury).

Papa Loves Mambo
Words and music by Al Hoffman, Dick Manning, and Bix Reichner.
Shapiro, Bernstein & Co., Inc.
Best-selling record by Perry Como (RCA Victor).

Paris Loves Lovers
Words and music by Cole Porter.
Buxton Hill Music Corp.
Introduced by Don Ameche and Hildegarde Neff in 1955 in *Silk Stockings* (musical).

Plantation Boogie
Music by Lenny Dee.
Copar-Forrest Music Corp.
Best-selling record, instrumental, by Lenny Dee (Decca).

Pledging My Love
Words and music by Ferdinand Washington and Don D. Robey.
Wemar Music Corp./Lion Publishing Co., Inc.
Best-selling record in 1955 by Johnny Ace (Duke).

Positively No Dancing
Words by Carolyn Leigh, music by Martin Roman.
Weiss & Barry, Inc.
Best-selling records by Alan Dean (M-G-M) and Karen Chandler (Coral).

Pretend You Don't See Her
Words and music by Steve Allen.
Rosemeadow Publishing Corp.
Best-selling record in 1957 by Jerry Vale (Columbia).

Quien Sera, see Sway.

Rain, Rain, Rain
Words and music by Jay McConologue.
Maple Leaf Music Publishing Co., Inc.
Best-selling record by Frankie Laine and The Four Lads (Columbia).

Ready, Willing and Able
Words and music by Al Rinker, Floyd Huddleston, and Dick Gleason.
Daywin Music, Inc.
Introduced by Doris Day in *Young at Heart* (film).

Release Me
Words and music by Eddie Miller and W. S. Stevenson.
Four Star Sales Co.
Best-selling records by Ray Price (Columbia), Jimmy Heap (Capitol), and Kitty Wells (Decca).

Restless Heart
Words and music by Harold Rome.
Chappell & Co., Inc./Florence Music Co., Inc.
Introduced by William Tabbert in *Fanny* (musical).

River of No Return
Words by Ken Darby, music by Lionel Newman.
Simon House, Inc.
Introduced by Tennessee Ernie Ford and Marilyn Monroe in *River of No Return* (film).

Rock Love
Words and music by Henry Glover.
Lois Publishing Co.
Best-selling record in 1955 by The Fontane Sisters (Dot).

Rose Marie, see 1924.

Runaround
Words and music by Cirino Celacrai.
Regent Music Corp.
Best-selling record by The Chuckles ("X").

Satin and Silk
Words and music by Cole Porter.
Buxton Hill Music Corp.
Introduced by Gretchen Wyler in 1955 in *Silk Stockings* (musical).

Saving My Love (For You), see 1958.

Search Is Through, The
Words by Ira Gershwin, music by Harold Arlen.
Harwin Music Corp.
Introduced by Bing Crosby in *The Country Girl* (film).

Sexy Ways
Words and music by Henry Ballard.
Armo Music Corp.
Best-selling record by The Midnighters (Federal).

Shadow Woman
Words and music by Arthur Hamilton.
Saunders Publications, Inc.
Introduced by Julie London.

Shake, Rattle, and Roll
Words and music by Charles Calhoun.
Progressive Music Publishing Co., Inc.
Introduced by Joe Turner. Best-selling records by Elvis Presley (RCA Victor), Bill Haley and The Comets (Decca), and Joe Turner (Atlantic).

Sh-Boom (Life Could Be a Dream)
Words and music by James Keyes, Claude Feaster, Carl Feaster, Floyd F. McRae, and James Edwards.
St. Louis Music Corp./Progressive Music Publishing Co., Inc.
Best-selling records by The Chords (Cat) and The Crew Cuts (Mercury).

Signpost
Words by Ben Raleigh, music by Larry Coleman.
Moonlight Music, Inc.
Introduced by Eileen Barton.

Silk Stockings
Words and music by Cole Porter.
Buxton Hill Music Corp.
Introduced by Don Ameche in 1955 in *Silk Stockings* (musical).

Sincerely
Words and music by Harvey Fuqua and Alan Freed.
Regent Music Corp.
Best-selling record in 1955 by The McGuire Sisters (Coral).

Singing the Blues
Words and music by Melvin Endsley.
Acuff-Rose Publications.
Introduced and best-selling country and western record in 1956 and 1957 by Marty Robbins (Columbia). Best-selling popular record in 1956 and 1957 by Guy Mitchell (Columbia).

Skokiaan (Northern Rhodesian)
Words by Tom Glazer, music by August Msarurgwa.
Gallo, Ltd., Johannesburg, South Africa/Shapiro, Bernstein & Co., Inc.
Named for a South African Zulu drink. Introduced in South Africa by The Bulawayo Sweet Rhythms Band on Gallotone Records. Best-selling records in the United States by The Four Lads (Columbia) and Ralph Marterie (Mercury).

Sleepin' Bee, A
Words by Truman Capote and Harold Arlen, music by Harold Arlen.
Harwin Music Corp.
Introduced by Diahann Carroll, Dolores Harper, Ada Moore, and Enid Mosier in *House of Flowers* (musical).

Small Talk
Words and music by Richard Adler and Jerry Ross.
Frank Music Corp.
Introduced by Janis Paige and John Raitt in *The Pajama Game* (musical).

Smellin' of Vanilla, also known as **Bamboo Cage**
Words by Truman Capote and Harold Arlen, music by Harold Arlen.
Harwin Music Corp.
Introduced by Dolores Harper, Enid Mosier, and Ada Moore in *House of Flowers* (musical).

Smile
Words by John Turner and Geoffrey Parsons, music by Charles Chaplin.
Bourne, Inc.
Music written by Chaplin in 1936 for *Modern Times* (film).

Sobbin' Women
Words by Johnny Mercer, music by Gene de Paul.
Robbins Music Corp.
Introduced by Howard Keel in *Seven Brides for Seven Brothers* (film).

Song from *Désirée,* The, also known as **We Meet Again**
Words by Ken Darby, music by Alfred Newman.
Miller Music Corp.
Theme from *Désirée* (film), interpolated behind the opening titles as part of Alex North's score for the film.

Song of the Barefoot Contessa
Music by Mario Nascimbene.
Chappell & Co., Inc.
Theme from *The Barefoot Contessa* (film).

Sparkling Brown Eyes, also known as **Sparkling Blue Eyes,** see 1939.

Spring Spring Spring
Words by Johnny Mercer, music by Gene de Paul.
Robbins Music Corp.
Introduced by chorus of "Brothers" and girls in *Seven Brides for Seven Brothers* (film).

Steam Heat
Words and music by Richard Adler and Jerry Ross.
Frank Music Corp.
Introduced by Carol Haney, Buzz Miller, and Pat Gennaro in *The Pajama Game* (musical).

Stolen Moments
Words by Sid Wayne, music by Joe Sherman.
Tannen Music, Inc.
Best-selling record in 1957 by Hank Snow (RCA Victor).

Strange Sensation
Words and music by Kay Twomey, Fred Wise, and Ben Weisman.
Joy Music, Inc.
Based on the tango, "La Cumparsita." Best-selling record by June Valli (RCA Victor).

Such a Night
Words and music by Lincoln Chase.
Raleigh Music, Inc./Elvis Presley Music, Inc.
Best-selling records by Johnnie Ray (Columbia) and The Drifters (Atlantic).

Sway, also known as Quien Sera (Mexican)
English words by Norman Gimbel, Spanish words and music by Pablo Beltran Ruiz.
Editorial Mexicana De Musica Internacional S.A., Mexico, 1953/Peer International Corp.
Best-selling record by Dean Martin (Capitol).

Swedish Rhapsody, see 1953.

Take My Love
Words by Helen Deutsch, music by Bronislau Kaper.
Leo Feist, Inc.
Introduced in *The Glass Slipper* (film). Best-selling record by Eddie Fisher (RCA Victor).

Tend To Your Business
Words and music by Dave Bartholomew.
Travis Music Co.
Best-selling record in 1951 by James Wayne (Specialty).

Tender Shepherd
Words by Carolyn Leigh, music by Mark Charlap.
Edwin H. Morris & Co., Inc.
Introduced by Margalo Gillmore, Kathy Nolan, Richard Harrington, and Joseph Stafford in *Peter Pan* (musical).

Thank You for Calling
Words and music by Cindy Walker.
Blackwood Music, Inc.
Best-selling record by Jo Stafford (Columbia).

Thanks a Lot, but No Thanks
Words by Betty Comden and Adolph Green, music by André Previn.
Leo Feist, Inc.
Introduced by Dolores Gray in *It's Always Fair Weather* (film).

That's All I Want from You
Words and music by M. Rotha (pseudonym for Fritz Rotter).
Weiss & Barry, Inc.
Best-selling record in 1955 by Jaye P. Morgan (RCA Victor).

That's What I Like
Words by Bob Hilliard, music by Jule Styne.
Stratford Music Corp.
Introduced by Dean Martin in *Living It Up* (film). Best-selling record by Don, Dick, and Jimmy (Crown).

There Once Was a Man
Words and music by Richard Adler and Jerry Ross.
Frank Music Corp.
Introduced by John Raitt and Janis Paige in *The Pajama Game* (musical).

There'll Be No Teardrops Tonight, see 1949.

There's Only One of You
Words by Al Stillman, music by Robert Allen.
Korwin Music, Inc.
Best-selling record in 1958 by The Four Lads (Columbia).

They Were Doin' the Mambo
Words and music by Don Raye and Sonny Burke.
Mayfair Music Corp.
Best-selling record by Vaughn Monroe (RCA Victor).

This Ole House
Words and music by Stuart Hamblen.
Hamblen Music Co., Inc.
Introduced by Stuart Hamblen. Best-selling records in 1954 by Rosemary Clooney (Columbia) and in 1954 and 1955 by Stuart Hamblen (RCA Victor).

Three Coins in the Fountain
Words by Sammy Cahn, music by Jule Styne.
Robbins Music Corp.
Introduced by Frank Sinatra, behind the titles, on the soundtrack of *Three Coins in the Fountain* (film). Academy Award-winning song, 1954. Best-selling records by Frank Sinatra (Capitol) and The Four Aces (Decca).

Till Then
Words and music by Guy Wood, Sol Marcus, and Eddie Seiler.
Pickwick Music Corp.
Best-selling record by The Hilltoppers (Dot).

Time for Parting
Words by Betty Comden and Adolph Green, music by André Previn.
Leo Feist, Inc.
Introduced by Gene Kelly, Dan Dailey, and Michael Kidd in *It's Always Fair Weather* (film).

Tina Marie
Words and music by Bob Merrill.
Roncom Music Co.
Best-selling record by Perry Como (RCA Victor).

Too Bad
Words and music by Cole Porter.
Buxton Hill Music Corp.
Introduced in 1955 in *Silk Stockings* (musical).

Touch, The (French)
English words by Norman Gimbel, French words by Marc Lanjean, music by Jean Wiener.
Éditions Ray Ventura, Paris, France/Duchess Music Corp.
French title, "Le Grisbi." Theme, played by Wiener on the harmonica, from *Touchez Pas au Grisbi* (French film).

Traveling Down a Lonely Road, see **Love Theme from *La Strada.***

True Love Goes On and On
Words and music by Richard Adler and Jerry Ross.
Frank Music Corp.
Best-selling record by Burl Ives with Gordon Jenkins and his Orchestra (Decca).

Tweedlee Dee
Words and music by Winfield Scott.
Progressive Music Publishing Co., Inc.
Introduced by LaVern Baker. Best-selling record in 1955 by Georgia Gibbs (Mercury).

Two Hearts
Words and music by Otis Williams and Henry Stone.
St. Louis Music Corp.
Best-selling record by Pat Boone (Dot).

Two Ladies in de Shade of de Banana Tree
Words by Truman Capote and Harold Arlen, music by Harold Arlen.
Harwin Music Corp.
Introduced by Ada Moore and Enid Mosier in *House of Flowers* (musical).

Two of Us
Words and music by Pony Sherrell and Phil Moody.
American Academy of Music, Inc.
Introduced by Tony Curtis and Gloria De Haven in *So This Is Paris* (film).

Vera Cruz
Words by Sammy Cahn, music by Hugo Friedhofer.
Leo Feist, Inc.
Recorded by Tony Martin for use behind the opening titles of *Vera Cruz* (film). Vocal version deleted from the film prior to its premiere.

Wake the Town and Tell the People
Words by Sammy Gallop, music by Jerry Livingston.
Joy Music, Inc.
Best-selling record in 1955 by Les Baxter and his Orchestra (Capitol).

Wanted
Words and music by Jack Fulton and Lois Steele.
M. Witmark & Sons.
Best-selling record by Perry Como (RCA Victor).

We Meet Again, see **The Song from *Désirée.***

Wedding Bells, see I'm Always Hearing Wedding Bells.

Welcome Home
Words and music by Harold Rome.
Chappell & Co., Inc./Florence Music Co., Inc.
Introduced by Ezio Pinza in *Fanny* (musical).

Wendy
Words by Betty Comden and Adolph Green, music by Jule Styne.
Edwin H. Morris & Co., Inc.
Introduced by Mary Martin in *Peter Pan* (musical).

We've Gone Too Far
Words and music by Hank Thompson and Billy Gray.
Hill and Range Songs, Inc./Texoma Music Corp.
Best-selling record by Hank Thompson (Capitol).

What a Dream, also known as Oh What a Dream
Words and music by Chuck Willis.
Berkshire Music, Inc.
Best-selling record by Ruth Brown (Atlantic).

What Ev'ry Girl Should Know
Words by Robert Wells, music by David Holt.
Daywin Music, Inc.
Best-selling record by Doris Day (Columbia).

What It Was, Was Football
Words and music by Andy Griffith.
Bentley Music Co.
A comedy monologue. Best-selling record by Andy Griffith (Capitol).

What-Cha Gonna Do Now
Words and music by Tommy Collins.
Central Songs, Inc.
Best-selling record by Tommy Collins (Capitol).

When You're in Love
Words by Johnny Mercer, music by Gene de Paul.
Robbins Music Corp.
Introduced by Jane Powell and Howard Keel in *Seven Brides for Seven Brothers* (film).

Whither Thou Goest
Words and music by Guy Singer.
Brenner Music, Inc./Kavelin Music.
Best-selling record by Les Paul and Mary Ford (Capitol).

With All My Heart and Soul, see Ànema e Core.

Without Love
Words and music by Cole Porter.
Buxton Hill Music Corp.
Introduced by Hildegarde Neff in 1955 in *Silk Stockings* (musical).

Wonderful, Wonderful Day
Words by Johnny Mercer, music by Gene de Paul.
Robbins Music Corp.
Introduced by Jane Powell in *Seven Brides for Seven Brothers* (film).

Work with Me Annie
Words and music by Henry "Hank" Ballard.
Lois Publishing Co.
Best-selling record by The Midnighters (Federal).

You and You Alone, see **Love Theme from *La Strada.***

You Can't Have My Love.
Words and music by Chuck Harding, Marty Roberts, Hank Thompson, and Billy Gray.
Brazos Valley Music, Inc.
Best-selling record by Wanda Jackson and Billy Gray (Decca).

You Don't Have To Go
Words and music by Matcher James Reed.
Travis Music Co./Conrad Publishing Co., Inc.
Best-selling record in 1955 by Jimmy Reed (Vee Jay).

You Upset Me, Baby
Words by Maxwell Davis, music by Joe Josea.
Modern Music Publishing Co.
Best-selling record by B. B. King (RPM).

You Will Wear Velvet
Words by Douglass Cross, music by George Cory.
General Music Publishing Co., Inc.
Introduced by Mabel Mercer.

Young and Foolish
Words by Arnold B. Horwitt, music by Albert Hague.
Chappell & Co., Inc.
Introduced by David Daniels and Gloria Marlowe in *Plain and Fancy* (musical).

Young at Heart
Words by Carolyn Leigh, music by Johnny Richards.
Cherio Music Publishers, Inc.
From the melody of a song called "Moonbeam," written by Richards in 1939. Introduced and best-selling record by Frank Sinatra (Capitol). Subsequently used as title song of *Young at Heart* (film).

Your Cash Ain't Nothin' but Trash
Words and music by Charles Calhoun.
Progressive Music Publishing Co., Inc.
Best-selling record by The Clovers (Atlantic).

You're Not Mine Anymore
Words and music by Webb Pierce and The Wilburn Brothers.
Cedarwood Publishing Co., Inc.
Best-selling record by Webb Pierce (Decca).

You're Still My Baby
Words and music by Chuck Willis.
Berkshire Music, Inc.
Best-selling record by Chuck Willis (Okeh).

1955

Adelaide
Words and music by Frank Loesser.
Frank Music Corp.
Introduced by Frank Sinatra in *Guys and Dolls* (film).

Ain't It a Shame, see **Ain't That a Shame.**

Ain't That a Shame, also known as **Ain't It a Shame**
Words and music by Antoine "Fats" Domino and Dave Bartholomew.
Travis Music Co.
Best-selling records by Fats Domino (Imperial) and Pat Boone (Dot).

Ain't That Lovin' You Baby
Words and music by Jimmy Reed.
Conrad Publishing Co., Inc.
Best-selling record in 1956 by Jimmy Reed (Vee Jay).

All at Once, also known as **Déjà** (French)
English words by Dorcas Cochran, French words by Eddy Marnay, music by Emil Stern.
Les Nouvelles Éditions Meridian, Paris, France, 1954/Ludlow Music, Inc.
Introduced in the United States by Felicia Sanders.

All at Once You Love Her
Words by Oscar Hammerstein II, music by Richard Rodgers.
Williamson Music, Inc.
Introduced by William Johnson, Judy Tyler, and Jerry La Zarre and reprised by Helen Traubel in *Pipe Dream* (musical). Best-selling record by Perry Como (RCA Victor).

All by Myself
Words and music by Antoine "Fats" Domino and Dave Bartholomew.
Travis Music Co.
Best-selling record by Fats Domino (Imperial).

All Right
Words and music by Faron Young.
Lancaster Music Publications, Inc.
Best-selling record by Faron Young (Capitol).

Alright, Okay, You Win
Words and music by Sid Wyche.
Munson Music Co.
Best-selling record by Count Basie and his Orchestra, vocal by Joe Williams (Clef and Verve).

Are You Mine?
Words by Don Grashey, music by Jim Amadeo and Myrna Petrunka.
Jamie Music Publishing Co.
Best-selling records by Ginny Wright and Tom Tall (Fabor) and Myrna Lorrie and Buddie Devol (Decca).

Arrivederci, Roma, also known as **Goodbye to Rome (Italian)**
Words by Carl Sigman, music by Renato Rascel (pseudonym for Renato Ranucci).
Edizioni Kramer, Milan, Italy, 1954/Reg Connelly Music, Inc.
Introduced in the United States by The Three Suns (RCA Victor). Best-selling record by Georgia Gibbs (Mercury). Sung by Mario Lanza in 1958 in *The Seven Hills of Rome* (film).

As I Love You
Words and music by Ray Evans and Jay Livingston.
Northern Music Corp.
Best-selling record in 1959 by Shirley Bassey (produced in England) (Philips).

As Long As I Live, see 1946.

At My Front Door (Crazy Little Mama Song)
Words and music by John C. Moore and Ewart G. Abner, Jr.
Conrad Publishing Co., Inc.
Best-selling record by The El Dorados (Vee Jay) and Pat Boone (Dot).

Autumn Leaves, see 1950.

Ballad of Davy Crockett, The
Words by Tom Blackburn, music by George Bruns.
Wonderland Music Co.
Introduced by Fess Parker in the title role in *Davy Crockett at the Alamo* (Disneyland television production). Best-selling records by Bill Hayes (Cadence) and Tennessee Ernie Ford (Capitol).

Band of Gold
Words by Bob Musel, music by Jack Taylor.
Ludlow Music, Inc.
Introduced by Kit Carson, formerly known as Liza Morrow (Mars and Capitol). Best-selling record in 1955 and 1956 by Don Cherry (Columbia).

Banjo's Back in Town, The
Words and music by Earl Shuman, Alden Shuman, and Marshall Brown.
World Music, Inc.
Best-selling record by Teresa Brewer (Coral).

Beautiful Lies
Words and music by Jack Rhodes.
Central Songs, Inc.
Best-selling record in 1955 and 1956 by Jean Shepard (Capitol).

Believe in Me (Italian)
English words by Carl Sigman, Italian words and music by Icini.
Pickwick Music Corp.
Original title, "Credimi." Best-selling record by Connie Francis (M-G-M).

Bernie's Tune, see 1953.

Bible Tells Me So, The
Words and music by Dale Evans.
Paramount-Roy Rogers Music Co., Inc.
Introduced by Roy Rogers and Dale Evans. Best-selling record by Don Cornell (Coral).

Birmin'ham
Words and music by Hugh Martin and Ralph Blane.
Saunders Publications, Inc.
Introduced by Rosalind Russell and Eddie Albert in *The Girl Rush* (film).

Black Denim Trousers and Motorcycle Boots
Words and music by Mike Stoller and Jerry Leiber.
Quintet Music, Inc.
Best-selling record by The Cheers and Les Baxter and his Orchestra (Capitol).

Blue Mirage (Don't Go) (German)
Words by Sam Coslow, music by Lotar Olias.
Teoton-Verlag, Munich, Germany, 1954/The B. F. Wood Music Co., Inc.
Original title, "Fata Morgana." First United States recording, instrumental, by Guy Lombardo and his Royal Canadians (Decca).

Blue Star, also known as **The Medic Theme**
Words by Edward Heyman, music by Victor Young.
Victor Young Publications, Inc.
Theme from *Medic* (television series). Best-selling record, instrumental, by Les Baxter and his Orchestra (Capitol).

Blue Suede Shoes
Words and music by Carl Lee Perkins.
Hi-Lo Music, Inc./Hill and Range Songs, Inc.
Sung by Elvis Presley in *G.I. Blues* (film). Best-selling records in 1956 by Carl Perkins (Hi-Lo) and Elvis Presley (RCA Victor).

Blues from *Kiss Me Deadly,* also known as **I'd Rather Have the Blues**
Words and music by Frank De Vol.
Paxwin Music Corp.
Introduced by Nat "King" Cole in *Kiss Me Deadly* (film).

Bo Diddley
Words and music by E. McDaniels.
Arc Music Corp.
Best-selling record by Bo Diddley (Checker).

Bonnie Blue Gal
Words by William Engvick, music by Jessie Cavanaugh.
Hollis Music, Inc.
Adaptation of the Civil War song, "Bonnie Blue Flag." Best-selling record by Mitch Miller, his Orchestra, and his Chorus (Columbia).

Boom Boom Boomerang
Words and music by Lonnie Coleman.
Dandelion Music Co.
Best-selling record by The De Castro Sisters (Abbott).

Bop-Ting-a-Ling
Words and music by Winfield Scott.
Progressive Music Publishing Co., Inc.
Best-selling record by LaVern Baker (Atlantic).

Born to Sing the Blues
Words by Lenny Adelson, music by Imogene Carpenter.
United Music Corp.
Best-selling record by Vic Damone (Mercury).

Burn That Candle
Words and music by Winfield Scott.
Roosevelt Music Co., Inc.
Best-selling record by Bill Haley and The Comets (Decca).

Cattle Call, The, see 1934.

C'est a Hambourg, see **The Left Bank.**

C'est la Vie
Words by Stella Unger, music by Victor Young.
Chappell & Co., Inc.
Introduced by Robert Clary, Beatrice Arthur, and Kurt Kasznar in *Seventh Heaven* (musical).

C'est la Vie
Words and music by Edward R. White and Mack Wolfson.
Planetary Music Publishing Corp.
Best-selling record by Sarah Vaughan (Mercury).

Chee Chee-oo Chee (Sang the Little Bird) (Italian)
English words by John Turner and Geoffrey Parsons, music by Severio Seracini.
Edizioni Musicali Tevere, Italy/The Peter Maurice Music Co., Ltd., London, England/Hill and Range Songs, Inc.
Winner at San Remo (Italy) Song Festival. Best-selling record by Perry Como and Jaye P. Morgan (RCA Victor).

Cherry Pink and Apple Blossom White, see 1951.

Close Your Eyes
Words and music by Chuck Willis.
Tideland Music Publishing Corp.
Best-selling record by The Five Keys (Capitol).

Come Next Spring
Words by Lenny Adelson, music by Max Steiner.
Frank Music Corp.
Introduced by Tony Bennett in *Come Next Spring* (film).

Convicted
Words and music by Leon René.
Leon René Publications.
Best-selling record by Oscar McLollie (Class).

Crazy Otto Rag, The
Words and music by Edward R. White, Mack Wolfson, Hugo B. Peretti, and Luigi Creatore.
George Pincus Music Corp.
Best-selling record by Crazy Otto (Decca).

Croce di Oro
Words by Bob Haring, music by Kim Gannon.
Shapiro, Bernstein & Co., Inc.
Best-selling record by Patti Page (Mercury).

Cryin', Prayin', Wishin', Waitin'
Words and music by C. Stewart, J. Smith, and D. Dill.
Dart Music Co.
Best-selling record by Hank Snow (RCA Victor).

Daddy O
Words and music by Louie Innis, Buford Abner, and Charlie Gore.
Lois Publishing Co.
Best-selling record in 1955 and 1956 by The Fontane Sisters (Dot).

Dance with Me Henry, also known as **The Wallflower**
Words and music by Johnny Otis, Hank Ballard, and Etta James.
Modern Music Publishing Co./Lois Publishing Co.
Original rhythm and blues version, entitled "The Wallflower," introduced by Etta James (Modern). Best-selling record by Georgia Gibbs (Mercury).

Devil or Angel
Words and music by Blanche Carter.
Progressive Music Publishing Co., Inc.
Best-selling record by The Clovers (Atlantic).

Django
Music by John Lewis.
M.J.Q. Music, Inc.
Introduced by The Modern Jazz Quartet and dedicated to French jazz guitarist Django Reinhardt.

Dogface Soldier, see 1942.

Domani (Tomorrow)
Words by Tony Velona, music by Ulpio Minucci.
Montauk Music, Inc.
Best-selling record by Julius La Rosa (Cadence).

Don't Be Angry
Words and music by Napoleon Brown, Fred Madison, and Rose Marie McCoy.
Republic Music Corp./Savoy Music Co.
Best-selling records by Nappy Brown (Savoy) and The Crew Cuts (Mercury).

Don't Let Her Go
Words by Aaron Schroeder, music by Abner Silver.
United Music Corp.
Best-selling record by Frank Sinatra (Capitol).

Don't Stay Away Too Long
Words and music by Al Hoffman and Dick Manning.
Bourne, Inc.
Best-selling record by Eddie Fisher (RCA Victor).

Don't Take It Out on Me
Words and music by Hank Thompson.
Brazos Valley Music, Inc.
Best-selling record by Hank Thompson (Capitol).

Door Is Still Open to My Heart, The
Words and music by Chuck Willis.
Berkshire Music, Inc.
Best-selling record by The Cardinals (Atlantic).

Dream Along with Me (I'm on My Way to a Star)
Words and music by Carl Sigman.
Roncom Music Co.
Theme song of *The Perry Como Show* (television series).

Dungaree Doll!
Words by Ben Raleigh, music by Sherman Edwards.
Edward B. Marks Music Corp.
Best-selling record by Eddie Fisher (RCA Victor).

Eat, Drink and Be Merry
Words and music by Celia Ferguson and Sandra Ferguson.
Earl Barton Music Co.
Best-selling record in 1956 by Porter Wagoner (RCA Victor).

Elephants Tango, The
Music by Bernie Landes.
Regent Music Corp.
Best-selling record by Lawrence Welk and his Orchestra (Coral).

Everybody's Got a Home but Me
Words by Oscar Hammerstein II, music by Richard Rodgers.
Williamson Music, Inc.
Introduced by Judy Tyler in *Pipe Dream* (musical). Best-selling record in 1956 by Eddie Fisher (RCA Victor).

Experience Unnecessary
Words and music by Gladys Shelley, Hugo Peretti, and Luigi Creatore.
George Pincus Music Corp.
Best-selling record by Sarah Vaughan (Mercury).

Farewell
Words by Tom Blackburn, music by George Bruns.
Wonderland Music Co.
Introduced by Fess Parker in the title role in *Davy Crockett at the Alamo* (Disneyland television production).

Feel So Good
Words and music by Leonard Lee.
Travis Music Co.
Best-selling record by Shirley and Lee (Aladdin).

Flip Flop and Fly
Words and music by Charles Calhoun and Lou Willie Turner.
Progressive Music Publishing Co., Inc.
Best-selling record by Joe Turner (Atlantic).

Fool for You, A
Words and music by Ray Charles.
Progressive Music Publishing Co., Inc.
Best-selling record by Ray Charles (Atlantic).

Fooled
Words by Mann Curtis, music by Doris Tauber.
Harms, Inc.
Best-selling record by Perry Como (RCA Victor).

Forever Darling
Words by Sammy Cahn, music by Bronislau Kaper.
Leo Feist, Inc.
Introduced by Desi Arnaz in *Forever Darling* (film). Best-selling record in 1956 by The Ames Brothers (RCA Victor).

Forgive My Heart
Words by Sammy Gallop, music by Chester Conn.
Bregman, Vocco & Conn, Inc.
Best-selling record by Nat "King" Cole (Capitol).

Forgive This Fool
Words and music by Bill Cook.
Travis Music Co.
Best-selling record by Roy Hamilton (Epic).

Forgotten Dreams
Music by Leroy Anderson.
Mills Music, Inc.
Best-selling record in 1957 by Leroy Anderson and his Orchestra (Decca).

Freddy
Words and music by Sheldon Harnick, Peter Pan, and Steve Kirk.
Duchess Music Corp.
Introduced by French singer Annie Corday. Best-selling record by Connie Francis (M-G-M).

Girl Upstairs, The
Words by Sammy Cahn, music by Alfred Newman.
Robbins Music Corp.
Adapted from the theme from *The Seven Year Itch* (film).

Give Me Love
Words and music by Cindy Walker.
Aberbach, Inc.
Best-selling record by The McGuire Sisters (Cadence).

Go Back You Fool
Words and music by Don Robertson and Hal Blair.
Hill and Range Songs, Inc.
Best-selling record by Faron Young (Capitol).

Goodbye, Old Girl
Words and music by Richard Adler and Jerry Ross.
Frank Music Corp.
Introduced by Robert Shafer and Stephen Douglass in *Damn Yankees* (musical).

Goodbye to Rome, see **Arrivederci, Roma.**

Great Pretender, The
Words and music by Buck Ram.
Panther Music Corp.
Introduced by The Platters (Mercury).

Greenbacks
Words and music by Renald Richard.
Progressive Music Publishing Co., Inc.
Best-selling record in 1954 by Ray Charles (Atlantic).

Gum Drop
Words and music by Rudy Toombs.
R-T Publishing Co.
Best-selling record by The Crew Cuts (Mercury).

Happiness Street (Corner Sunshine Square)
Words and music by Mack Wolfson and Edward R. White.
Planetary Music Publishing Corp.
Best-selling record in 1956 by Georgia Gibbs (Mercury).

Hard To Get
Words and music by Jack Segal.
M. Witmark & Sons.
Introduced by Giselle MacKenzie on *Justice* (television dramatic program).

Hawk-Eye
Words and music by Boudleaux Bryant.
Acuff-Rose Publications.
Best-selling record by Frankie Laine (Columbia).

He Needs Me
Words and music by Arthur Hamilton.
Mark VII Music.
Introduced by Peggy Lee in *Pete Kelly's Blues* (film).

Heart
Words and music by Richard Adler and Jerry Ross.
Frank Music Corp.
Introduced by Russ Brown, Jimmie Komack, Nathaniel Frey, and Albert Linville in *Damn Yankees* (musical). Best-selling record by Eddie Fisher (RCA Victor).

Heart of Paris (French)
English words by Mitchell Parish, French words by Jacques La Rue, music by Georges Auric.
Societé d'Éditions Musicales Internationales, Paris, France, 1954/ The B. F. Wood Music Co., Inc.
Original French title, "Coeur de Mon Coeur."

He's a Tramp, see 1952.

Hey, Doll Baby
Words and music by Titus Turner.
Progressive Music Publishing Co., Inc.
Best-selling record by The Clovers (Atlantic).

Hey, Mr. Banjo
Words and music by Freddy Morgan and Norman Malkin.
Mills Music, Inc.
Best-selling record by The Sunnysiders (Kapp).

(There's No Place Like) Home for the Holidays
Words by Al Stillman, music by Robert Allen.
Roncom Music Co.
Best-selling record by Perry Como (RCA Victor).

Honey-Babe
Words by Paul Francis Webster, music by Max Steiner.
M. Witmark & Sons.
Based on a traditional air. Marching song from *Battle Cry* (film). Best-selling record by Art Mooney and his Orchestra (M-G-M).

How Can I Replace You
Words by Sammy Gallop, music by James Van Heusen.
United Music Corp.
Best-selling record by Tony Bennett (Columbia).

How Far Is Heaven
Words and music by Jimmie Davis and Tillman Franks.
Peer International Corp.
Best-selling record in 1956 by Kitty Wells (Decca).

How Important Can It Be?
Words and music by Bennie Benjamin and George Weiss.
Aspen Music Corp.
Best-selling record by Joni James (M-G-M).

Hummingbird
Words and music by Don Robertson.
Ross Jungnickel, Inc.
Introduced by Don and Lou Robertson (Epic). Best-selling record by Les Paul and Mary Ford (Capitol).

I Don't Believe You've Met My Baby
Words and music by Autry Inman.
Tree Publishing Co., Inc.
Best-selling record by The Louvin Brothers (Capitol).

I Don't Care
Words and music by Webb Pierce and Cindy Walker.
Cedarwood Publishing Co., Inc.
Best-selling record by Webb Pierce (Decca).

I Feel Like Crying
Words and music by Lewi Werly Fairburn.
Mallory Music Publications.
Best-selling record in 1956 by Carl Smith (Columbia).

I Forgot To Remember To Forget
Words and music by Stanley A. Kesler and Charles A. L. Feathers.
Hi-Lo Music, Inc.
Best-selling record in 1956 by Elvis Presley (RCA Victor).

I Gotta Go Get My Baby
Words and music by Marvin Rainwater and Kay Adelman.
Four Star Sales Co.
Best-selling record by Teresa Brewer (Coral).

I Hear You Knocking
Words and music by Dave Bartholomew and Pearl King.
Travis Music Co.
Best-selling records in 1955 by Smiley Lewis (Imperial) and in 1955 and 1956 by Gale Storm (Dot).

I Live for Only You (Argentine)
English words by Al Hoffman and Jessie Cavanaugh, Spanish words by Manuel Ortiz Guerrero, music by José Asuncion Flores.
Fermata do Brasil, Sao Paulo, Brazil/Hollis Music, Inc.
From the Latin-American popular song, "India." Introduced by Jerry Vale (Columbia).

I Want You To Be My Baby, see 1953.

I Wish You Love (French)
English words by Lee Wilson, French words and music by Charles Trenet.
Éditions Salabert, Paris, France, 1946/Leeds Music Corp.
Original French title, "Que Reste-t-il de Nos Amours." Introduced by Keely Smith. Identified with Felicia Sanders. Best-selling record in 1964 by Gloria Lynne (Everest).

I'd Rather Have the Blues, see **Blues from *Kiss Me Deadly*.**

If I May
Words and music by Charles Singleton and Rose Marie McCoy.
Roosevelt Music Co., Inc.
Best-selling record by Nat "King" Cole (Capitol).

I'll Cry Tomorrow
Words by Johnny Mercer, music by Alex North.
Robbins Music Corp.
From *I'll Cry Tomorrow* (film biography of Lillian Roth). Recorded by Susan Hayward (M-G-M) and Lillian Roth (Coral).

I'll Never Know
Words by Roy Jordan, music by Ulpio Minucci.
Maple Leaf Music Publishing Co., Inc.
Best-selling record by The Four Lads (Columbia).

I'll Never Stop Loving You
Words by Sammy Cahn, music by Nicholas Brodszky.
Leo Feist, Inc.
Introduced by Doris Day in *Love Me or Leave Me* (film). Nominated for Academy Award, 1955.

I'm Gonna Laugh You out of My Life
Words and music by Cy Coleman and Joseph A. McCarthy.
Jefferson Music Co., Inc.
Best-selling record by Nat "King" Cole (Capitol).

I'm with You
Words by Johnny Mercer, music by Bobby Troup.
Commander Publications.
Introduced by Bobby Troup.

Impatient Years, The
Words by Sammy Cahn, music by James Van Heusen.
Barton Music Corp.
From the musical version of Thornton Wilder's *Our Town* (television production).

In the Jailhouse Now, see 1928.

India, see **I Live for Only You.**

Innamorata (Sweetheart)
Words by Jack Brooks, music by Harry Warren.
Paramount Music Corp.
Introduced by Dean Martin in *Artists and Models* (film).

It Isn't Right, see 1952.

It's a Great Life If You Don't Weaken
Words and music by Joe Allison, Audrey Allison, and Faron Young.
Central Songs, Inc.
Best-selling record in 1955 and 1956 by Faron Young (Capitol).

It's Almost Tomorrow
Words by Wade Buff, music by Eugene H. Adkinson.
Northern Music Corp.
Best-selling record in 1955 and 1956 by The Dream Weavers (Decca).

It's Love Baby (24 Hours a Day)
Words and music by Ted Jarrett.
Excellorec Music Co.
Best-selling record by Louis Brooks (Excello).

I've Been Searching
Words and music by Murphy Maddux.
Valley Publishers, Inc./Singing River Publishing Co., Inc.
Best-selling record in 1956 and 1957 by Kitty Wells (Decca).

I've Changed
Words and music by Danny Dill.
Cedarwood Publishing Co., Inc.
Best-selling record in 1956 by Carl Smith (Columbia).

Jamaica Farewell
Words and music by Lord Burgess.
Shari Music Publishing Corp.
Adaptation of a West Indian folk song. Best-selling record by Harry Belafonte (RCA Victor).

Just Call Me Lonesome, see 1953.

Kentuckian Song, The
Words and music by Irving Gordon.
Frank Music Corp.
Introduced in *The Kentuckian* (film). Best-selling record by The Hilltoppers (Dot).

Ko Ko Mo, I Love You So
Words and music by Forest Wilson, Jake Porter, and Eunice Levy.
Vogue Music, Inc.
Original rhythm and blues version by Combo No. 64, Gene and Eunice (Combo). Best-selling record by Perry Como (RCA Victor).

Land of the Pharaohs
Words by Ned Washington, music by Dimitri Tiomkin.
Remick Music Corp.
Adapted from a theme from *Land of the Pharaohs* (film).

Learnin' the Blues
Words and music by Dolores Vicki Silvers.
Barton Music Corp.
Introduced and best-selling record by Frank Sinatra (Capitol).

Left Bank, The (French)
French words by Claude Delecluse and Michelle Senlis, music by Marguerite Monnot.
Enoch & Cie, Paris, France/Cromwell Music, Inc.
French title, "C'est a Hambourg." Introduced instrumentally in the United States by Les Elgart and his Orchestra.

Legend of Wyatt Earp, The
Words by Harold Adamson, music by Harry Warren.
Four Jays Music Co.
Theme song of *The Life and Legend of Wyatt Earp* (television production).

Let It Ring
Words and music by Joan Edwards and Lyn Duddy.
Artists Music, Inc.
Best-selling record by Doris Day (Columbia).

Little Love Can Go a Long, Long Way, A
Words by Paul Francis Webster, music by Sammy Fain.
Northern Music Corp.
Introduced in *Ain't Misbehavin'* (film). Best-selling record by The Dream Weavers (Decca).

Lonely Nights
Words and music by Zell Sanders.
Dare Music Co.
Best-selling record by The Hearts (Baton).

Longest Walk, The
Words by Eddie Pola, music by Fred Spielman.
Advanced Music Corp.
Best-selling record by Jaye P. Morgan (RCA Victor).

Love among the Young
Words by Norman Gimbel, music by Alec Wilder.
Vogue Music, Inc.
Introduced by Rosemary Clooney (Columbia).

Love and Marriage
Words by Sammy Cahn, music by James Van Heusen.
Maraville Music Corp.
Introduced by Frank Sinatra in the musical version of Thornton Wilder's *Our Town* (television production).

Love Has Joined Us Together
Words and music by Billy Dawn Smith and Marguerite James (pseudonym for Teddy Powell).
Maggie Music Co., Inc.
Best-selling record by Ruth Brown and Clyde McPhatter (Atlantic).

Love Is a Many-Splendored Thing
Words by Paul Francis Webster, music by Sammy Fain.
Miller Music Corp.
Title song from *Love Is a Many-Splendored Thing* (film). Academy Award-winning song, 1955. Introduced by The Four Aces. Best-selling records by The Four Aces (Decca) and Don Cornell (Coral).

Love, Love, Love
Words and music by Ted Jarrett.
Cedarwood Publishing Co., Inc./Babb Music Publishers.
Best-selling record in 1955 and 1956 by Webb Pierce (Decca).

Love Me or Leave Me, see 1928.

Mabelline, also known as **Maybellene**
Words and music by Chuck Berry, Russ Fratto, and Alan Freed.
Arc Music Corp.
Best-selling record by Chuck Berry (Chess).

Mainliner
Words and music by Stuart Hamblen.
Hamblen Music Co., Inc.
Best-selling record by Hank Snow (RCA Victor).

Mambo Bacan, see **Woman of the River.**

Mambo Rock
Words and music by Bix Reichner, Mildred Phillips, and Jimmy Ayre.
Myers Music.
Best-selling record by Bill Haley and The Comets (Decca).

Man Doesn't Know, A
Words and music by Richard Adler and Jerry Ross.
Frank Music Corp.
Introduced by Stephen Douglass in *Damn Yankees* (musical).

Man from Laramie, The
Words by Ned Washington, music by Lester Lee.
Columbia Pictures Music Corp.
From *The Man from Laramie* (film). Best-selling record by The Voices of Walter Schumann (Capitol).

Man in a Raincoat (Canadian)
Words and music by Warwick Webster.
BMI Canada Ltd./Associated Music Publishers, Inc.
Introduced in Canada and the United States by Priscilla Wright (Unique).

Man with a Dream, A
Words by Stella Unger, music by Victor Young.
Chappell & Co., Inc.
Introduced by Ricardo Montalban in *Seventh Heaven* (musical).

Marianne
Words and music by Terry Gilkyson, Frank Miller, and Richard Dehr.
Montclare Music Corp.
Adapted from a Bahaman folk song. Best-selling records in 1957 by Terry Gilkyson and The Easy Riders (Columbia) and The Hilltoppers (Dot).

Marty
Words by Paddy Chayefsky, music by Harry Warren.
Cromwell Music, Inc.
"Inspired by" *Marty* (film).

Maybellene, see **Mabelline.**

Medic Theme, The, see **Blue Star.**

Memories Are Made of This
Words and music by Terry Gilkyson, Richard Dehr, and Frank Miller.
Montclare Music Corp.
Best-selling record by Dean Martin (Capitol).

Merry-Go-Round (French)
English words by Jack Lawrence, French words by Jean Renoir, music by George Van Parys.
Les Nouvelles Éditions Meridian, Paris, France, 1954/Southern Music Publishing Co., Inc.
French title, "Complainte de la Butte." From Jean Renoir's *French Can-Can* (French film). Introduced in the United States by Percy Faith and his Orchestra (Columbia).

Missing You
Words and music by Red Sovine and Dale E. Noe.
Valley Publishers, Inc.
Best-selling record in 1957 by Webb Pierce (Decca).

Misty
Words by Johnny Burke, music by Erroll Garner.
Vernon Music Corp./Octave Music Publishing Corp.
Introduced, as an instrumental, in 1954 by The Erroll Garner Trio (Mercury). Best-selling record in 1956 by Garner with Mitch Miller and his Orchestra (Columbia). Best-selling vocal record by Johnny Mathis (Columbia).

Moments To Remember
Words by Al Stillman, music by Robert Allen.
Beaver Music Publishing Corp.
Best-selling record by The Four Lads (Columbia).

Most of All
Words and music by Alan Freed and Harvey Fuqua.
Arc Music Corp.
Best-selling record by The Moonglows (Chess).

My Babe
Words and music by Willie Dixon.
Arc Music Corp.
Best-selling record by Little Walter (Checker).

My Believing Heart
Words and music by Jimmy Crane and Al Jacobs.
Valando Music Corp.
Best-selling record by Joni James (M-G-M).

My Bonnie Lassie, see 1953.

My Boy, Flat Top
Words and music by John F. Young, Jr. and Boyd Bennett.
Lois Publishing Co.
Best-selling record by Boyd Bennett (King).

My Lips Are Sealed
Words and music by Ben Weisman, Hal Blair, and Bill Peppers.
Hill and Range Songs, Inc.
Best-selling record in 1956 by Jim Reeves (RCA Victor).

My Love's a Gentle Man
Words by Roy Jordan, music by Ulpio Minucci.
Montauk Music, Inc.
Introduced by Dorothy Collins. Best-selling record by Felicia Sanders (Columbia).

My Personal Possession
Words and music by Charles Singleton and Rose Marie McCoy.
Roosevelt Music Co., Inc.
Introduced by Nat "King" Cole (Capitol).

Mystery Train, see 1953.

Near to You
Words and music by Richard Adler and Jerry Ross.
Frank Music Corp.
Introduced by Stephen Douglass and Shannon Bolin in *Damn Yankees* (musical).

Need Your Love So Bad
Words and music by John Metis, Jr.
Lois Publishing Co.
Best-selling record by Little Willie John (King).

Next Time It Happens, The
Words by Oscar Hammerstein II, music by Richard Rodgers.
Williamson Music, Inc.
Introduced by Judy Tyler and William Johnson in *Pipe Dream* (musical).

No Arms Can Ever Hold You (Like These Arms of Mine)
Words and music by Art Crafer and Jimmy Nebb.
Gil Music Corp.
Best-selling record by Pat Boone (Dot).

Not As a Stranger
Words by Buddy Kaye, music by James Van Heusen.
Maraville Music Corp.
Introduced as incidental, interpolated dance music in *Not As a Stranger* (film). Best-selling record by Frank Sinatra (Capitol).

Nothing Ever Changes My Love for You
Words by Jack Segal, music by Marvin Fisher.
Marvin Music Co.
Best-selling record by Nat "King" Cole (Capitol).

Nuttin' for Christmas
Words and music by Sid Tepper and Roy C. Bennett.
Ross Jungnickel, Inc.
Best-selling record by Barry Gordon and Art Mooney and his Orchestra (M-G-M).

Occasional Man, An
Words and music by Hugh Martin and Ralph Blane.
Saunders Publications, Inc.
Introduced by Gloria De Haven in *The Girl Rush* (film).

Only You
Words and music by Buck Ram and Ande Rand.
Wildwood Music, Inc.
Best-selling record by The Platters (Mercury). Revived in 1959 with best-selling record, instrumental, by Frank Pourcel and his Orchestra (recorded in France) (Capitol).

Open Up Your Heart, see 1953.

Pepper-Hot Baby
Words and music by Alicia Evelyn.
Travis Music Co.
Best-selling record by Jaye P. Morgan (RCA Victor).

Pet Me, Poppa
Words and music by Frank Loesser.
Frank Music Corp.
Introduced by Vivian Blaine in *Guys and Dolls* (film).

Pete Kelly's Blues
Words by Sammy Cahn, music by Ray Heindorf.
Mark VII Music.
Introduced by Ella Fitzgerald in *Pete Kelly's Blues* (film).

(My Heart Goes) Piddily Patter Patter
Words and music by Charles Singleton and Rose Marie McCoy.
Edward B. Marks Music Corp.
Introduced under the title "Pitter Patter" by Nappy Brown (Savoy). Best-selling record by Patti Page (Mercury).

Play Me Hearts and Flowers (I Wanna Cry)
Words by Mann Curtis, music by Sanford Green.
Advanced Music Corp.
Introduced by Johnny Desmond on *Philco Playhouse* (television dramatic program).

Poor Me
Words and music by Dave Bartholomew and Antoine "Fats" Domino.
Travis Music Co.
Best-selling record by Fats Domino (Imperial).

Por Favor ("Please . . .")
Words and music by Noel Sherman and Joe Sherman.
Paxwin Music Corp.
Best-selling record by Vic Damone (Mercury).

Prodigal, The (Love Theme)
Music by Bronislau Kaper.
Miller Music Corp.
Love theme from *The Prodigal* (film).

Que Sera, Sera, also known as **Whatever Will Be, Will Be**
Words and music by Jay Livingston and Ray Evans.
Artists Music, Inc.
Introduced by Doris Day in *The Man Who Knew Too Much* (film). Academy Award-winning song, 1956. Best-selling record by Doris Day (Columbia).

Reconsider Baby
Words and music by Lowell Fulson.
Arc Music Corp.
Best-selling record by Lowell Fulson (Checker).

Relax-Ay-Voo
Words by Sammy Cahn, music by Arthur Schwartz.
Leeds Music Corp.
Introduced by Dean Martin and Jerry Lewis in *You're Never Too Young* (film).

Rhythm 'n' Blues (Mama's Got the Rhythm, Papa's Got the Blues)
Words and music by Jules Loman and Buddy Kaye.
Vernon Music Corp.
Best-selling record by The McGuire Sisters (Coral).

Richest Man in the World, The
Words and music by Boudleaux Bryant.
Acuff-Rose Publications.
Best-selling record by Eddy Arnold (RCA Victor).

Rock and Roll Waltz
Words by Roy Alfred, music by Shorty Allen.
Travis Music Co.
Best-selling record by Kay Starr (RCA Victor).

(We're Gonna) Rock around the Clock, see 1953.

Rollin' Stone
Words and music by Robert S. Riley.
Excellorec Music Co.
Best-selling records by The Marigolds (Excello) and The Fontane Sisters (Dot).

Rose Tattoo
Words by Jack Brooks, music by Harry Warren.
Paramount Music Corp.
Written for, but never used in, *The Rose Tattoo* (film). Vocal version introduced by Perry Como (RCA Victor).

Run Boy
Words and music by Hy Heath.
Milene Music.
Best-selling record in 1956 by Ray Price (Columbia).

Sailor Boys Have Talk to Me in English
Words by Bob Hilliard, music by Milton De Lugg.
Edwin H. Morris & Co., Inc.
Introduced in *Ziegfeld Follies Las Vegas* (nightclub revue). Best-selling record by Rosemary Clooney (Columbia).

Same Old Saturday Night
Words by Sammy Cahn, music by Frank Reardon.
Barton Music Corp.
Best-selling record by Frank Sinatra (Capitol).

Sand and the Sea, The
Words and music by Hal Hester and Barry Parker.
Paxwin Music Corp.
Best-selling record by Nat "King" Cole (Capitol).

Santo Natale
Words and music by Al Hoffman, Dick Manning, and Belle Nardone.
Larry Spier, Inc.
Best-selling record by David Whitfield (London).

Satisfied Mind, A
Words and music by Red Hayes and Jack Rhodes.
Starday Music.
Best-selling records by Red and Betty Foley (Decca), Jean Shepard (Capitol), and Porter Wagoner (RCA Victor).

Seasons of My Heart
Words and music by George Jones and Darrell Edwards.
Starday Music.
Best-selling record in 1956 by Jim Newman (Dot).

See You Later, Alligator
Words and music by Robert Guidry.
Arc Music Corp.
Introduced by Bill Haley and The Comets in *Rock around the Clock* (film). Best-selling record in 1956 by Bill Haley and The Comets (Decca).

Seventeen
Words and music by John Young, Jr., Chuck Gorman, and Boyd Bennett.
Lois Publishing Co.
Best-selling records by Boyd Bennett and his Rockets (King) and The Fontane Sisters (Dot).

Shifting, Whispering Sands, The, see 1950.

Shoeless Joe from Hannibal Mo.
Words and music by Richard Adler and Jerry Ross.
Frank Music Corp.
Introduced by Rae Allen and Baseball Players in *Damn Yankees* (musical).

Siamese Cat Song, The, see 1953.

Sincerely Yours
Words by Paul Francis Webster, music by Liberace.
M. Witmark & Sons.
Introduced by Liberace in *Sincerely Yours* (film).

Sing a Rainbow
Words and music by Arthur Hamilton.
Mark VII Music.
Introduced by Peggy Lee in *Pete Kelly's Blues* (film).

Sixteen Tons, see 1947.

Slowly, with Feeling
Words by Don George, music by Mark "Moose" Charlap.
Planetary Music Publishing Corp.
Best-selling record by Sarah Vaughan (Mercury).

Sluefoot
Words and music by Johnny Mercer.
Robbins Music Corp.
Introduced by Fred Astaire and Ray Anthony and his Orchestra in *Daddy Long Legs* (film).

Smack Dab in the Middle
Words and music by Charles E. Calhoun.
Roosevelt Music Co., Inc.
Popularized by Joe Williams with Count Basie and his Orchestra.

Smoke from Your Cigarette
Words and music by Harold Johnson.
Beacon Music Co.
Best-selling record by Lillian Leach and The Mellows (Davis).

So Fine
Words and music by Johnny Otis.
Eldorado Music Co.
Best-selling record in 1958 and 1959 by The Fiestas (Old Town).

Soft Summer Breeze
Words by Judy Spencer, music by Eddie Heywood.
Regent Music Corp.
Best-selling record, instrumental, in 1956 by Eddie Heywood (Mercury).

Soldier Boy
Words and music by Theodore Williams, Jr. and David Jones.
Bryden Music, Inc./Elvis Presley Music, Inc.
Best-selling record by The Four Fellows (Glory).

Solitaire
Music by Erroll Garner.
Octave Music Publishing Corp.
Instrumental introduced by Erroll Garner. Words added in 1960 by Steve Allen.

Someone You Love
Words and music by Steven Michaels.
Bradshaw Music, Inc.
Best-selling record by Nat "King" Cole (Capitol).

Someone's Been Sending Me Flowers
Words by Sheldon Harnick, music by David Baker.
Leeds Music Corp.
Introduced by Dody Goodman in *Shoestring Revue* (revue).

Something's Gotta Give
Words and music by Johnny Mercer.
Robbins Music Corp.
Introduced by Fred Astaire in *Daddy Long Legs* (film). Nominated for Academy Award, 1955. Best-selling records by Sammy Davis, Jr. (Decca) and The McGuire Sisters (Coral).

Song of the Dreamer
Words and music by Eddie Tex Curtis.
Ludlow Music, Inc.
Best-selling record by Eddie Fisher (RCA Victor).

Speedoo
Words and music by Esther Navarro.
Benell Music Publishing Co.
Best-selling record by The Cadillacs (Josie).

Spring Can Really Hang You Up the Most
Words by Fran Landesman, music by Tommy Wolf.
Wolf-Mills Music, Inc.
Introduced in the original St. Louis production of *The Nervous Set* (musical).

Steamboat
Words and music by Buddy Lucas.
Progressive Music Publishing Co., Inc.
Best-selling record by The Drifters (Atlantic).

Story Untold, A
Words and music by LeRoy Griffin and Marty Wilson.
Tideland Music Publishing Corp.
Best-selling records by The Crew Cuts (Mercury) and The Nutmegs (Herald).

Strange Lady in Town
Words by Ned Washington, music by Dimitri Tiomkin.
M. Witmark & Sons.
Introduced in *Strange Lady in Town* (film). Best-selling record by Frankie Laine (Columbia).

Suddenly There's a Valley
Words and music by Chuck Meyer and Biff Jones.
Hill and Range Songs, Inc./Hillary Music, Inc./Bamboo Music, Inc.
Best-selling records by Gogi Grant (Era) and Jo Stafford (Columbia).

Summertime in Venice (Italian)
English words by Carl Sigman, Italian words by Pinchi, music by Icini.
Soc. An. Metron, Milan, Italy/Pickwick Music Corp.
Italian title, "Tempo d'Estate (A Venezia)." Love theme from *Summertime* (film).

Sweet and Gentle (Cuban)
English words by George Thorn, Spanish words and music by Otilio Portal.
Peer y Compania, S.L., Havana, Cuba, 1953/Peer International Corp.
A "mambo-cha-cha." Original Cuban title, "Me lo Dijo Adela." Best-selling record in the United States by Georgia Gibbs (Mercury).

Sweet Dreams
Words and music by Don Gibson.
Acuff-Rose Publications.
Best-selling record in 1956 by Faron Young (Capitol).

Sweet Heartaches
Words and music by Nat Simon and Jimmy Kennedy.
George Pincus Music Corp.
Best-selling record by Eddie Fisher (RCA Victor).

Sweet Thursday
Words by Oscar Hammerstein II, music by Richard Rodgers.
Williamson Music, Inc.
Introduced by Helen Traubel in *Pipe Dream* (musical).

Teen Age Prayer
Words and music by Bix Reichner and Bernie Lowe.
La Salle Music Publishers, Inc.
Best-selling record in 1956 by Gale Storm (Dot).

(Love Is) Tender Trap, The
Words by Sammy Cahn, music by James Van Heusen.
Barton Music Corp.
Introduced by Frank Sinatra in *The Tender Trap* (film). Nominated for Academy Award, 1955.

That Do Make It Nice
Words and music by Eddy Arnold, Fred Ebb, and Paul Klein.
T. M. Music, Inc.
Best-selling record by Eddy Arnold (RCA Victor).

That's All Right
Words and music by Arthur Crudup.
St. Louis Music Corp.
Best-selling record by Marty Robbins (Columbia).

That's All There Is to That
Words and music by Clyde Otis and Kelly Owens.
Vogue Music, Inc.
Best-selling record in 1956 by Nat "King" Cole (Capitol).

Theme from *East of Eden*
Music by Leonard Rosenman.
M. Witmark & Sons.
Theme from *East of Eden* (film).

Theme from *Picnic*
Words by Steve Allen, music by George Duning.
Columbia Pictures Music Corp.
Introduced in *Picnic* (film). Best-selling records in 1956 by The McGuire Sisters (Cadence) and, in an instrumental medley with the 1934 song, "Moonglow," by Morris Stoloff and his Orchestra (Decca) and George Cates and his Orchestra (Coral).

Theme from *Rebel without a Cause*
Music by Leonard Rosenman.
M. Witmark & Sons.
Theme from *Rebel without a Cause* (film).

There She Goes
Words and music by Eddie Miller, Durwood Haddock, and W. S. Stevenson.
Four Star Sales Co.
Best-selling record by Carl Smith (Columbia).

These Hands
Words and music by Eddie Noack.
Hill and Range Songs, Inc.
Best-selling record in 1955 and 1956 by Hank Snow (RCA Victor).

This Little Girl of Mine
Words and music by Ray Charles.
Progressive Music Publishing Co., Inc.
Best-selling record by Ray Charles (Atlantic) and in 1958 by The Everly Brothers (Cadence).

Times Two, I Love You
Words and music by Jack Fulton and Lois Steele.
Mayfair Music Corp.
Best-selling record by The Three Chuckles ("X").

To Love Again
Words by Ned Washington, music by Morris Stoloff and George Sidney.
Columbia Pictures Music Corp.
Adapted from Chopin's "E-flat Nocturne." Theme from *The Eddy Duchin Story* (film). Performed on the soundtrack by Carmen Cavallaro. Best-selling record by The Four Aces (Decca).

To You My Love (French)
English words by Jack Lawrence, French words and music by Louis Gasté.
Éditions Louis Gasté, Paris, France, 1953/Leeds Music Corp.
Best-selling record by Nick Noble (Mercury).

Too Young To Go Steady
Words by Harold Adamson, music by Jimmy McHugh.
Robbins Music Corp.
Introduced in *Strip for Action* (musical). Best-selling record by Nat "King" Cole (Capitol).

Toy Tiger
Music by Henry Mancini and Herman Stein.
Northern Music Corp.
From *The Private War of Major Benson* (film). Best-selling record by Henri René and his Orchestra (RCA Victor).

Tropical Meringue
English words by Lawrence Elow and Don Marsh, Spanish words and music by Rafael Muñoz.
Edward B. Marks Music Corp.
Best-selling record by Percy Faith and his Orchestra (Columbia).

Trouble with Harry, The
Words by Floyd Huddleston and Herb Eiseman, music by Mark McIntyre.
Frank Music Corp.
"Inspired by" *The Trouble with Harry* (film). Best-selling record in 1956 by Alfi and Harry (Liberty).

Tutti Frutti
Words and music by Richard Penniman, D. La Bostrie, and Joe Lubin.
Venice Music, Inc.
Best-selling records by Little Richard (Specialty) and Pat Boone (Dot).

24 Hours a Day (365 a Year)
Words and music by Rudy Toombs and Henry Glover.
R-T Publishing Co.
Best-selling record by Georgia Gibbs (Mercury).

Two Lost Souls
Words and music by Richard Adler and Jerry Ross.
Frank Music Corp.
Introduced by Gwen Verdon and Stephen Douglass in *Damn Yankees* (musical).

Unchained Melody
Words by Hy Zaret, music by Alex North.
Frank Music Corp.
Theme music from *Unchained* (film). Nominated for Academy Award, 1955. Best-selling instrumental record by Les Baxter and his Orchestra (Capitol). Best-selling vocal record by Al Hibbler (Decca).

Unsuspecting Heart
Words by Freddy James, music by Joe Beal, Bob Singer, and Joe Shank.
Tee Pee Music Co., Inc.
Best-selling record by George Shaw (Decca).

Verdict, The
Words by Glen Moore, music by Alan Freed.
Nom Music, Inc.
Best-selling record by The Five Keys (Capitol).

Wallflower, The, see **Dance with Me Henry.**

Wedding, The
Words and music by Pat Gaston, Bobby Williams, and Jacqueline McCoy.
St. Louis Music Corp.
Best-selling record by The Solitaires (Old Town).

(In the) Wee Small Hours (Of the Morning)
Words by Bob Hilliard, music by David Mann.
Redd Evans Music Co.
Best-selling record by Frank Sinatra (Capitol).

We're Gonna Be in High Society
Words and music adapted by Dan Swan, Allan Copeland, and Mort Green.
Leeds Music Corp.
Adapted from the traditional New Orleans jazz band marching tune, "High Society." Vocal version introduced by Jo Stafford (Columbia).

What Am I Worth
Words and music by Darrell Edwards and George Jones.
Starrite Publishing Co.
Best-selling record in 1956 by George Jones (Starday).

What Is a Husband? (What Is a Wife?)
Words and music by Bill Katz, Ruth Roberts, and Gene Piller.
Vernon Music Corp.
Introduced on *The Garry Moore Show* (television program). Best-selling record by Steve Allen (Coral).

What Is a Wife?, see **What Is a Husband?**

What'cha Gonna Do?
Words and music by Ahmet Ertegun.
Progressive Music Publishing Co., Inc.
Best-selling record by The Drifters (Atlantic).

Whatever Lola Wants (Lola Gets)
Words and music by Richard Adler and Jerry Ross.
Frank Music Corp.
Introduced by Gwen Verdon in *Damn Yankees* (musical).

Whatever Will Be, Will Be, see **Que Sera, Sera.**

When the Sea Is All around Us
Words by Sheldon Harnick, music by David Baker.
Leeds Music Corp.
Introduced by James Harwood in *Shoestring Revue* (revue). Later associated with Dorothy Loudon.

When You Dance
Words and music by Andrew Jones and L. Kirkland.
Angel Music, Inc.
Best-selling record in 1956 by The Turbans (Herald).

Where Is That Someone for Me
Words by Stella Unger, music by Victor Young.
Chappell & Co., Inc.
Introduced by Gloria De Haven in *Seventh Heaven* (musical).

Where Will the Dimple Be?
Words and music by Bob Merrill and Al Hoffman.
Roger Music, Inc.
Best-selling record by Rosemary Clooney (Columbia).

Who's Got the Pain?
Words and music by Richard Adler and Jerry Ross.
Frank Music Corp.
Introduced by Gwen Verdon in *Damn Yankees* (musical).

Why, Baby, Why
Words and music by George Jones and Darrell Edwards.
Starday Music.
Best-selling records in 1956 by Webb Pierce (Decca) and George Jones (Starday).

Why Don't You Write Me
Words and music by Laura Hollins.
Golden State Songs.
Best-selling record by The Jacks (RPM).

Wild, Wild Young Men
Words and music by Ahmet Ertegun.
Progressive Music Publishing Co., Inc.
Best-selling record in 1953 by Ruth Brown (Atlantic).

Wildwood Flower
Words and music by Hank Thompson.
Brazos Valley Music, Inc.
Best-selling record by Hank Thompson (Capitol).

Winter of My Discontent
Words by Ben Ross Berenberg, music by Alec Wilder.
Ludlow Music, Inc.
Introduced by Mabel Mercer.

Witchcraft
Words and music by Dave Bartholomew and Pearl King.
Travis Music Co./Elvis Presley Music, Inc.
Best-selling record by Elvis Presley (RCA Victor).

Woman Alone with the Blues
Words and music by Willard Robison.
Mayfair Music Corp.
Identified with Peggy Lee.

Woman in Love, A
Words and music by Frank Loesser.
Frank Music Corp.
Introduced by Frank Sinatra in the film version of *Guys and Dolls*. Best-selling record by Frankie Laine (Columbia).

Woman of the River, also known as Mambo Bacan (Italian)
Italian words by Franco Giordano, music by Roman Vatro.
R.P.D. Radiofilmusica Ponti De Laurentiis, Italy/Hollis Music, Inc.
Introduced in *Woman of the River* (Italian film).

Yaller Yaller Gold
Words by Tom Blackburn, music by George Bruns.
Wonderland Music Co.
Introduced by Fess Parker in *Davy Crockett and Mike Fink* (television show).

Year after Year
Words and music by Bart Howard.
Almanac Music, Inc.
Introduced by Mabel Mercer.

Yellow Rose of Texas, The
Words and music adapted by Don George.
Planetary Music Publishing Corp.
From an anonymous minstrel song of the 1860's. First revived by conductor Richard Bales in his album, *The Confederacy* (Columbia). Best-selling records by Mitch Miller and his Orchestra and Chorus (Columbia) and Johnny Desmond (Coral).

Yellow Roses, see 1953.

Yonder Comes a Sucker
Words and music by Jim Reeves.
Tree Publishing Co., Inc.
Best-selling record by Jim Reeves (RCA Victor).

You and Me
Words and music by Johnnie Wright, Jack Anglin, and Jim Anglin.
Brenner Music, Inc.
Best-selling record in 1956 by Red Foley and Kitty Wells (Decca).

You Are My Love
Words and music by Jimmie Nabbie.
Jubilee Music.
Best-selling record by Joni James (M-G-M).

You Don't Know Me
Words and music by Cindy Walker and Eddy Arnold.
Hill and Range Songs, Inc./Brenner Music, Inc.
Best-selling record in 1956 by Eddy Arnold (RCA Victor). Revived in 1962 with best-selling record by Ray Charles (ABC Paramount).

Young Ideas
Words by Chuck Sweeney, music by Moose Charlap.
Harms, Inc.
Introduced in *The King and Mrs. Candle* (television musical). Introduced on records by Tony Martin (RCA Victor).

You're Free To Go
Words and music by Don Robertson and Lou Herscher.
Ross Jungnickel, Inc.
Best-selling record in 1956 by Carl Smith (Columbia).

Zambezi, also known as **Sweet African** (South Africa)
Words by Bob Hilliard, music by Nico Carstens and Anton De Waal.
Carstens-De Waal Publications, Johannesburg, South Africa, 1954/ Shapiro, Bernstein & Co., Inc.
Best-selling record by Lou Busch and his Orchestra (Capitol).

1956

A.B.C.'s of Love, The
Words and music by George Goldner and Richard Barrett.
Nom Music, Inc.
Best-selling record by Frankie Lymon and The Teenagers (Gee).

According to My Heart
Words and music by Gary Walker.
Cedarwood Publishing Co., Inc.
Best-selling record in 1956 and 1957 by Jim Reeves (RCA Victor).

After the Lights Go Down Low
Words and music by Alan White and Leroy Lovett.
Harvard Music, Inc.
Best-selling record by Al Hibbler (Decca).

Ain't Got No Home
Words and music by Clarence Henry.
Arc Music Corp.
Best-selling record in 1956 and 1957 by Clarence "Frogman" Henry (Argo).

Allegheny Moon
Words and music by Al Hoffman and Dick Manning.
Joy Music, Inc.
Best-selling record by Patti Page (Mercury).

Am I Losing You?
Words and music by Jim Reeves.
Rondo Music.
Best-selling record in 1957 by Jim Reeves (RCA Victor).

Anastasia
Words by Paul Francis Webster, music by Alfred Newman.
Leo Feist, Inc.
Theme melody from *Anastasia* (film). Best-selling record by Pat Boone (Dot).

Angels in the Sky, see 1954.

Any Way You Want Me (That's How I Will Be)
Words and music by Aaron Schroeder and Cliff Owens.
Ross Jungnickel, Inc.
Best-selling record by Elvis Presley (RCA Victor).

April Age, The
Words by William Engvick, music by Alec Wilder.
Hollis Music, Inc.

Ariane
Words by Johnny Mercer, music by Matty Malneck.
Commander Publications.
From *Love in the Afternoon* (film).

Armen's Theme, also known as Yesterday and You
Music by Ross Bagdasarian.
ABC Music Corp.
Instrumental introduced by David Seville (pseudonym for Bagdasarian) and his Orchestra (Liberty).

Around the World
Words by Harold Adamson, music by Victor Young.
Liza Music Corp.
Theme from *Around the World in 80 Days* (film). Best-selling instrumental record by Victor Young and his Orchestra (Decca). Best-selling vocal record by Jane Morgan (Kapp).

Ascot Gavotte
Words by Alan Jay Lerner, music by Frederick Loewe.
Chappell & Co., Inc.
Introduced by members of the ensemble in *My Fair Lady* (musical).

Ask Me (German)
English words by Sunny Skylar, German words by Carl Niessen, music by Heino Gaze.
ABC Music Corp.
Best-selling record by Nat "King" Cole (Capitol).

Autumn Concerto (Italian)
English words by Paul Siegel, Italian words by Danpa, music by Camillo Bargoni.
Edizioni Luisiana, Milan, Italy/Symphony House Music Publishers Corp.
Original title, "Concerto d'Autumno." Best-selling record, instrumental, by Richard Hayman and his Orchestra (Mercury). New English words written in 1957 by Al Stillman with the alternate titles, "My Heart Reminds Me" and "And That Reminds You" (see 1957).

Autumn Waltz, The
Words by Bob Hilliard, music by Cy Coleman.
Shapiro, Bernstein & Co., Inc.
Introduced by Tony Bennett (Columbia).

Away All Boats
Words by Lenny Adelson, music by Frank Skinner and Albert Skinner.
Northern Music Corp.
Adapted from the theme from *Away All Boats* (film).

Baby Doll
Words by Bernie Hanighen, music by Kenyon Hopkins.
Remick Music Corp.
Adapted from the theme from *Baby Doll* (film). Best-selling vocal record by Andy Williams (Cadence).

Bad Luck
Words and music by Jules Taub and Sam Ling.
Belmar Music Publishing Co.
Best-selling record by B. B. King (RPM).

Banana Boat Song, The, also known as Day-O
Words and music by Erik Darling, Bob Carey, and Alan Arkin.
Edward B. Marks Music Corp./Bryden Music, Inc.
Introduced by The Tarriers. Best-selling records in 1956 and 1957 by Harry Belafonte (RCA Victor) and The Tarriers (Glory).

Be-Bop-a-Lula
Words and music by Gene Vincent and Sheriff Tex Davis.
Lowery Music Co.
Best-selling record by Gene Vincent (Capitol).

Bells Are Ringing
Words by Betty Comden and Adolph Green, music by Jule Styne.
Stratford Music Corp.
Introduced by the chorus in *Bells Are Ringing* (musical).

Big D
Words and music by Frank Loesser.
Frank Music Corp.
Introduced by Susan Johnson and Shorty Long in *The Most Happy Fella* (musical).

Blackboard of My Heart
Words and music by Lyle Gaston and Hank Thompson.
Texoma Music Corp.
Best-selling record by Hank Thompson (Capitol).

Blanche
Words and music by Frank Stropoli, Anthony Grochowski, Joseph Francavilla, and Nick Cutrone.
A.D.T. Enterprises, Inc.
Best-selling record by The Three Friends (Lido).

Blueberry Hill, see 1940.

Bo Weevil
Words and music by Antoine "Fats" Domino and Dave Bartholomew.
Travis Music Co.
Best-selling record by Fats Domino (Imperial).

Boppin' the Blues
Words and music by Carl Lee Perkins and Howard "Curley" Griffin.
Hi-Lo Music, Inc.
Best-selling record by Carl Perkins (Sun).

Born To Be with You
Words and music by Don Robertson.
Mayfair Music Corp.
Best-selling record by The Chordettes (Cadence).

Bus Stop Song, The, also known as **A Paper of Pins**
Words and music by Ken Darby.
Miller Music Corp.
Introduced by The Four Lads on the soundtrack of *Bus Stop* (film).

Call Me
Words and music by Clyde Otis and Belford C. Hendricks.
Vogue Music, Inc./Noma Music, Inc./Amano Music Corp.
Introduced by Johnny Mathis (Columbia).

Can I Steal a Little Love?
Words and music by Phil Tuminello.
Northern Music Corp.
From *Rock, Pretty Baby* (film). Best-selling record by Frank Sinatra (Capitol).

Can You Find It in Your Heart
Words by Al Stillman, music by Robert Allen.
M. Witmark & Sons.
Best-selling record by Tony Bennett (Columbia).

Canadian Sunset
Words by Norman Gimbel, music by Eddie Heywood.
Vogue Music, Inc.
Best-selling instrumental record by Hugo Winterhalter and his Orchestra (RCA Victor). Best-selling vocal record by Andy Williams (Cadence).

Can't We Be Sweethearts
Words and music by Herbert Cox and George Goldner.
Nom Music, Inc.
Best-selling record by The Cleftones (Gee).

Cara Mia, see 1954.

Casual Look, A
Words and music by Ed Wells.
Limax Music, Inc.
Best-selling record by The Six Teens (Flip).

'Cause I Love You
Words and music by Webb Pierce and Danny Dill.
Cedarwood Publishing Co., Inc.
Best-selling record by Webb Pierce (Decca).

Chain Gang
Words and music by Sol Quasha and Herb Yakus.
George Pincus Music Corp.
Best-selling record by Bobby Scott (ABC Paramount). Revived in 1960 with best-selling record by Sam Cooke (RCA Victor).

Chella Llà (Italian)
English words by Al Hoffman and Dick Manning, Italian words by U. Bertini, music by S. Taccani.
La Cicala Casa Editrice Musicale S.R.L., Milan, Italy/Leeds Music Corp.

Cherry Lips
Words and music by Winfield Scott.
Atlantic Music Corp./Neil Music, Inc.
Best-selling record by The Robins (Whippet).

Cheyenne
Words by Stan Jones, music by William Lava.
M. Witmark & Sons.
Theme from *Cheyenne* (television series).

Chincherinchee (English)
Words and music by John Jerome.
John Fields Music Co., Ltd., London, England/Roncom Music Co.
Best-selling record by Perry Como (RCA Victor).

Church Bells May Ring
Words and music by Morty Craft and The Willows.
Ray Maxwell Music Publishing Co.
Best-selling record by The Willows (Melba).

Cinco Robles, also known as **Five Oaks**
Words by Larry Sullivan, music by Dorothy Wright.
Hillary Music, Inc./Bamboo Music, Inc.
Introduced by Russell Arms (Era). Best-selling record in 1956 and 1957 by Les Paul and Mary Ford (Capitol).

Cindy, Oh Cindy
Words and music by Bob Barron and Burt Long.
Edward B. Marks Music Corp./Bryden Music, Inc.
Adapted from a Georgia Sea Island chantey. Introduced by Vince Martin. Best-selling record by Eddie Fisher (RCA Victor).

City of Angels
Words and music by Nick Jovan and Bev Dusham.
Valleydale Music, Inc.
Best-selling record by The Highlights (Bally).

Closer You Are, The
Words and music by Earle Lewis and Morgan C. Robinson.
Spinning Wheel Music Corp./Starfire Music Corp.
Best-selling record by The Channels (Whirlin' Disc).

Conscience, I'm Guilty
Words and music by Jack Rhodes.
Central Songs, Inc.
Best-selling record by Hank Snow (RCA Victor).

Crazy Arms
Words and music by Chuck Seals and Ralph Mooney.
Champion Music Corp./Pamper Music, Inc.
Best-selling record in 1956 and 1957 by Ray Price (Columbia).

Crazy in the Heart
Words by William Engvick, music by Alec Wilder.
Regent Music Corp.
Introduced by Peggy Lee.

Day-O, see **The Banana Boat Song.**

Delilah Jones, see **The Man with the Golden Arm.**

Don't Be Cruel (To a Heart That's True)
Words and music by Otis Blackwell and Elvis Presley.
Travis Music Co./Elvis Presley Music, Inc.
Best-selling record by Elvis Presley (RCA Victor).

Don't Cry
Words and music by Frank Loesser.
Frank Music Corp.
Introduced by Art Lund and Jo Sullivan in *The Most Happy Fella* (musical).

Don't Forbid Me
Words and music by Charles Singleton.
Roosevelt Music Co., Inc.
Best-selling record in 1957 by Pat Boone (Dot).

Don't Laugh
Words and music by Rebe Gosdin.
Acuff-Rose Publications.
Best-selling record in 1957 by The Louvin Brothers (Capitol).

Down in Mexico
Words and music by Jerry Leiber and Mike Stoller.
Tiger Music, Inc.
Best-selling record by The Coasters (Atco).

Dreamy
Music by Erroll Garner.
Octave Music Publishing Corp.
Introduced by Erroll Garner. Lyrics added in 1960 by Sydney Shaw.

Drown in My Tears
Words and music by Henry Glover.
Jay & Cee Music Corp.
Best-selling record by Ray Charles (Atlantic).

Earthbound
Words and music by Jack Taylor, Clive Richardson, and Bob Musel.
Robert Mellin, Inc.
Best-selling record by Sammy Davis, Jr. (Decca).

Eddie, My Love
Words and music by Aaron Collins, Maxwell Davis, and Sam Ling.
Modern Music Publishing Co.
Best-selling records by The Teen-Queens (RPM) and The Fontane Sisters (Dot).

11th Hour Melody
Words by Carl Sigman, music by King Palmer.
George Paxton, Inc.
Best-selling record by Al Hibbler (Decca).

English Muffins and Irish Stew
Words by Bob Hilliard, music by Moose Charlap.
Shapiro, Bernstein & Co., Inc.
Introduced by Sylvia Syms.

Fabulous Character
Words and music by Bennie Benjamin and Sol Marcus.
Valando Music Corp.
Best-selling record by Sarah Vaughan (Mercury).

Fever
Words and music by John Davenport and Eddie Cooley.
Jay & Cee Music Corp.
Best-selling record in 1956 by Little Willie John (King) and in 1958 by Peggy Lee (Capitol).

First Born
Words and music by John Lehman.
Bradshaw Music, Inc.
Best-selling record by Tennessee Ernie Ford (Capitol).

Flowers Mean Forgiveness
Words and music by Al Frisch, Mack Wolfson, and Edward R. White.
Barton Music Corp.
Best-selling record by Frank Sinatra (Capitol).

Folsom Prison Blues
Words and music by Johnny Cash.
Hi-Lo Music, Inc.
Best-selling record by Johnny Cash (Sun).

Fool, The
Words and music by Naomi Ford.
Malapi Music/Desert Palms Publishing Co.
Best-selling record by Sanford Clark (Dot).

For Rent
Words and music by James Loden and Jack Morrow.
Vanguard Songs.
Best-selling record by Sonny James (Capitol).

Forty Days and Forty Nights
Words and music by Bernie Roth.
Arc Music Corp.
Best-selling record by Muddy Waters (Chess).

(I'll Always Be Your) Fraulein
Words and music by Lawton Williams.
Travis Music Co.
Best-selling records in 1957 by Bobby Helms (Decca) and Kitty Wells (Decca).

Friendly Persuasion, also known as **Thee I Love**
Words by Paul Francis Webster, music by Dimitri Tiomkin.
Leo Feist, Inc.
From *Friendly Persuasion* (film). Nominated for Academy Award, 1956. Best-selling record by Pat Boone (Dot).

From the Candy Store on the Corner (To the Chapel on the Hill)
Words and music by Bob Hilliard.
Shapiro, Bernstein & Co., Inc.
Best-selling record by Tony Bennett (Columbia).

From the First Hello to the Last Goodbye
Words and music by Johnny Burke.
Cavalcade Music Corp.
Best-selling record by Jane Morgan (Kapp).

Game of Love, The
Words by Matt Dubey, music by Harold Carr.
Chappell & Co., Inc.
Introduced by Ethel Merman in *Happy Hunting* (musical).

Garden of Eden
Words and music by Dennise Haas Norwood.
Republic Music Corp.
Best-selling record by Joe Valino (Vik).

Get Me to the Church on Time
Words by Alan Jay Lerner, music by Frederick Loewe.
Chappell & Co., Inc.
Introduced by Stanley Holloway in *My Fair Lady* (musical).

Ghost Town
Words by Ted Varnick, music by Nick Acquaviva.
Cromwell Music, Inc.
Best-selling record by Don Cherry (Columbia).

Giant, also known as **This Then Is Texas**
Words by Paul Francis Webster, music by Dimitri Tiomkin.
M. Witmark & Sons.
Adapted from a theme from *Giant* (film).

Give Us This Day
Words by Buddy Kaye, music by Bobby Day.
Valando Music Corp./Wizell & Day Music Corp.
Best-selling record by Joni James (M-G-M).

Glendora
Words and music by Ray Stanley.
American Music, Inc.
Best-selling record by Perry Como (RCA Victor).

Go Away with Me
Words and music by Dan Welch.
Lowery Music Co.
Best-selling record in 1957 by The Wilburn Brothers (Decca).

Go On with the Wedding
Words and music by Arthur Korb, Charles Purvis, and Milton Yakus.
George Pincus Music Corp.
Best-selling record by Patti Page (Mercury).

Gonna Get Along without You Now, see 1951.

Good Rockin' Tonight
Words and music by Roy Brown.
Blue Ridge Publishing Co.
Best-selling record in 1959 by Pat Boone (Dot).

Graduation Day
Words and music by Joe Sherman and Noel Sherman.
Travis Music Co.
Best-selling record by The Rover Boys (ABC Paramount).

Green Door, The
Words by Marvin Moore, music by Bob Davie.
T. M. Music, Inc.
Best-selling record in 1956 and 1957 by Jim Lowe (Dot).

Green Fields
Words and music by Terry Gilkyson, Richard Dehr, and Frank Miller.
Montclare Music Corp.
Introduced by The Easy Riders in 1956. Best-selling record in 1959 by The Brothers Four (Columbia).

Guaglioni, also known as **The Man Who Plays the Mandolino** (Italian)
English words by Alan Bergman and Marilyn Keith, Italian words by Nisa, music by Fanciulla.
Accordo Edizione Musicale Milano, Milan, Italy/Fred Raphael Music, Inc.
Introduced in the United States in 1957 in *10,000 Bedrooms* (film). Best-selling record, in Italian, by Renato Carasone (Capitol).

Hallelujah I Love Her So
Words and music by Ray Charles.
Progressive Music Publishing Co., Inc.
Best-selling records in 1956 by Ray Charles (Atlantic) and in 1959 by Peggy Lee (Capitol).

Hands Off
Words and music by Jay McShann and Priscilla Bowman.
Conrad Publishing Co., Inc.
Best-selling record by Jay McShann and Priscilla Bowman (Vee Jay).

Happy To Make Your Acquaintance
Words and music by Frank Loesser.
Frank Music Corp.
Introduced by Jo Sullivan, Robert Weede, and Susan Johnson in *The Most Happy Fella* (musical).

Happy Whistler
Music by Don Robertson.
Don Robertson Music Corp.
Best-selling record, instrumental, by Don Robertson (Capitol).

Heartbreak Hotel
Words and music by Mae Boren Axton, Tommy Durden, and Elvis Presley.
Tree Publishing Co., Inc.
Best-selling record by Elvis Presley (RCA Victor).

Hey! Jealous Lover
Words and music by Sammy Cahn, Kay Twomey, and Bee Walker.
Barton Music Corp.
Best-selling record by Frank Sinatra (Capitol).

Historia de un Amor, see **The Story of Love.**

Hold Everything (Till I Get Home)
Words and music by Red Hayes and Buddy Dee.
Starday Music.
Best-selling record by Red Sovine and Webb Pierce (Decca).

Honky Tonk
Words by Henry Glover, music by Bill Doggett, Billy Butler, Shape Sheppard, and Clifford Scott.
Islip Music Publishing Co./W & K Publishing Corp.
Best-selling record, instrumental, in 1956 and 1957 by Bill Doggett (King).

Honky Tonk Man
Words and music by Johnny Horton, Tillman Franks, and Howard Hausey.
Cedarwood Publishing Co., Inc.
Best-selling record by Johnny Horton (Columbia).

Hoping That You're Hoping
Words and music by Betty E. Harrison.
Cedarwood Publishing Co., Inc.
Best-selling record by The Louvin Brothers (Capitol).

Hot Diggity
Words and music by Al Hoffman and Dick Manning.
Roncom Music Co.
Adapted from Chabrier's "Espana Rhapsody." Best-selling record by Perry Como (RCA Victor).

Hotta Chocolotta
Words by Milton Drake, music by Vic Mizzy.
Beaver Music Publishing Corp.
Best-selling record by Ella Fitzgerald (Verve).

Hound Dog
Words and music by Jerry Leiber and Mike Stoller.
Elvis Presley Music, Inc./Lion Publishing Co., Inc.
Originally copyrighted in 1953, listing Leiber, Stoller, and Johnny Otis as authors and composers and Valjo Publishing Co. as publisher. Introduced by Willie Mae Thornton. Best-selling records in 1953 by Willie Mae Thornton (Peacock) and in 1956 by Elvis Presley (RCA Victor).

House with Love in It, A
Words by Sylvia Dee, music by Sid Lippman.
Redd Evans Music Co.
Best-selling record by The Four Lads (Columbia).

How Little We Know (How Little It Matters How Little We Know)
Words by Carolyn Leigh, music by Philip Springer.
Melrose Music Corp.
Introduced by Frank Sinatra.

I Almost Lost My Mind, see 1950.

I Believe in You
Words and music by Johnny Mitchell, Robert Carr, and Sam Weiss.
Sea-Lark Enterprises, Inc.
Best-selling record in 1955 by Robert and Johnny (Old Town).

I Can't Love You Enough
Words and music by Dorian Burton, Howard Plummer, Jr., and LaVern Baker.
Progressive Music Publishing Co., Inc.
Best-selling record by LaVern Baker (Atlantic).

I Could Have Danced All Night
Words by Alan Jay Lerner, music by Frederick Loewe.
Chappell & Co., Inc.
Introduced by Julie Andrews in *My Fair Lady* (musical). Best-selling record by Sylvia Syms (Decca).

I Dreamed
Words and music by Charles Grean and Marvin Moore.
T. M. Music, Inc.
Best-selling record by Betty Johnson (Bally).

I Love You, Samantha
Words and music by Cole Porter.
Buxton Hill Music Corp.
Introduced by Bing Crosby in *High Society* (film).

I Miss You Already
Words and music by Marvin Rainwater and Faron Young.
Tree Publishing Co., Inc.
Best-selling record in 1957 by Faron Young (Capitol).

I Promise To Remember
Words and music by Jimmy Castor and Jimmy Smith.
Patricia Music Publishing Corp.
Best-selling record by Frankie Lymon and The Teenagers (Gee).

I Remember When, see 1952.

I Take the Chance
Words and music by Ira Louvin and Charles Louvin.
Acuff-Rose Publications.
Best-selling record by J. E. and Maxine Brown (RCA Victor).

I Walk the Line
Words and music by John R. Cash.
Hi-Lo Music, Inc.
Best-selling record in 1956 and 1957 by Johnny Cash (Sun).

I Wanna Do More, see **I Want To Do More.**

I Want To Be Loved (But Only by You), see 1947.

I Want To Do More, also known as **I Wanna Do More**
Words and music by Jerry Leiber and Mike Stoller.
Tiger Music, Inc.
Best-selling record by Ruth Brown (Atlantic).

I Want You, I Need You, I Love You
Words by Maurice Mysels, music by Ira Kosloff.
Elvis Presley Music, Inc.
Best-selling record by Elvis Presley (RCA Victor).

I Want You To Be My Girl
Words and music by George Goldner and Richard Barrett.
Nom Music, Inc.
Best-selling record by Frankie Lymon and The Teenagers (Gee).

I Was the One
Words and music by Aaron Schroeder, Claude De Metruis, Hal Blair, and Bill Peppers.
Ross Jungnickel, Inc.
Best-selling record by Elvis Presley (RCA Victor).

If I Had My Druthers
Words by Johnny Mercer, music by Gene de Paul.
Commander Publications.
Introduced by Peter Palmer and dancers in *L'il Abner* (musical).

If'n
Words by Matt Dubey, music by Harold Carr.
Chappell & Co., Inc.
Introduced by Gordon Polk and Virginia Gibson in *Happy Hunting* (musical).

I'll Be Home
Words and music by Ferdinand Washington and Stan Lewis.
Arc Music Corp./Lion Publishing Co., Inc.
Best-selling records in 1955 and 1956 by Pat Boone (Dot) and The Flamingos (Checker).

I'll Remember (In the Still of the Nite)
Words and music by Fredericke Parris.
Angel Music, Inc.
Best-selling record by The Five Satins (Ember).

I'll Remember Today
Words by William Engvick, music by Edith Piaf.
Hollis Music, Inc.
Best-selling record by Patti Page (Mercury).

I'm a One-Woman Man
Words and music by Johnny Horton and Tillman Franks.
Cedarwood Publishing Co., Inc.
Best-selling record by Johnny Horton (Columbia).

I'm an Ordinary Man
Words by Alan Jay Lerner, music by Frederick Loewe.
Chappell & Co., Inc.
Introduced by Rex Harrison in *My Fair Lady* (musical).

I'm Available
Words and music by Jerry Bock, Larry Holofcener, and George Weiss.
Laurel Music Corp.
Introduced by Chita Rivera in *Mr. Wonderful* (musical).

I'm Coming Home
Words and music by Johnny Horton.
Golden West Melodies, Inc.
Best-selling record in 1957 by Johnny Horton (Columbia).

I'm in Love Again
Words and music by Antoine "Fats" Domino and Dave Bartholomew.
Travis Music Co.
Best-selling record by Fats Domino (Imperial).

I'm So in Love with You
Words and music by Sonny James and John Skye.
Sure-Fire Music Co., Inc.
Best-selling record by The Wilburn Brothers (Decca).

Impossible
Words and music by Steve Allen.
Rosemeadow Publishing Corp.
Best-selling record by Nat "King" Cole (Capitol).

In the Middle of the House
Words and music by Bob Hilliard.
Shapiro, Bernstein & Co., Inc.
Best-selling record by Vaughn Monroe (RCA Victor).

In Your Own Sweet Way
Music by Dave Brubeck.
Derry Music Co.
Jazz instrumental introduced by The Dave Brubeck Quartet.

Invitation, see 1952.

Island in the Sun
Words and music by Harry Belafonte and Irving Burgess.
Clara Music Publishing Corp.
Introduced by Harry Belafonte in *Island in the Sun* (film).

It Hurts To Be in Love
Words and music by Rudy Toombs and Julius Dixon.
Lois Publishing Co.
Best-selling record in 1957 by Annie Laurie (De Luxe).

It Only Hurts for a Little While
Words by Mack David, music by Fred Spielman.
Advanced Music Corp.
Best-selling record by The Ames Brothers (RCA Victor).

Italian Theme, The (Italian)
English words by Buddy Kaye, music by Angelo Giacomazzi and Clyde Hamilton.
Edizioni Musicali Accordo, Milan, Italy/World Wide Music Co., Ltd., London, England/The Peter Maurice Music Co., Ltd.
Best-selling record by Cyril Stapleton and his Orchestra (London).

It's Better in the Dark
Words by Sammy Cahn, music by James Van Heusen.
Leeds Music Corp.
Best-selling record by Tony Martin (RCA Victor).

It's Too Late
Words and music by Chuck Willis.
Progressive Music Publishing Co., Inc./Tideland Music Publishing Corp.
Best-selling record by Chuck Willis (Atlantic).

I've Got a New Heartache
Words and music by Wayne Walker.
Cedarwood Publishing Co., Inc.
Best-selling record in 1956 and 1957 by Ray Price (Columbia).

I've Got Five Dollars and It's Saturday Night, see 1950.

I've Grown Accustomed to Her Face
Words by Alan Jay Lerner, music by Frederick Loewe.
Chappell & Co., Inc.
Introduced by Rex Harrison in *My Fair Lady* (musical).

Ivory Tower
Words and music by Jack Fulton and Lois Steele.
Melrose Music Corp.
Best-selling records by Cathy Carr (Fraternity), Gale Storm (Dot), and Otis Williams (De Luxe).

Jivin' Around
Words and music by J. Gray, Ernie Freeman, and John Dolphin.
Travis Music Co.
Best-selling record by Ernie Freeman (Chess).

Joey, Joey, Joey
Words and music by Frank Loesser.
Frank Music Corp.
Introduced by Art Lund in *The Most Happy Fella* (musical).

Johnny Concho's Theme, also known as Wait for Me
Words by Dick Stanford, music by Nelson Riddle.
Barton Music Corp.
From *Johnny Concho* (film). Introduced by Frank Sinatra.

Jubilation T. Cornpone
Words by Johnny Mercer, music by Gene de Paul.
Commander Publications.
Introduced by Stubby Kaye in *L'il Abner* (musical).

Juke Box Baby
Words and music by Joe Sherman and Noel Sherman.
Paxwin Music Corp.
Best-selling record by Perry Como (RCA Victor).

Julie
Words by Tom Adair, music by Leith Stevens.
Artists Music, Inc.
Introduced by Doris Day on the soundtrack of *Julie* (film). Nominated for Academy Award, 1956.

Just in Time
Words by Betty Comden and Adolph Green, music by Jule Styne.
Stratford Music Corp.
Introduced by Sydney Chaplin and Judy Holliday in *Bells Are Ringing* (musical).

Just Walking in the Rain, see 1953.

Just You Wait
Words by Alan Jay Lerner, music by Frederick Loewe.
Chappell & Co., Inc.
Introduced by Julie Andrews in *My Fair Lady* (musical).

(My Heart Goes) Ka-Ding-Dong
Words and music by Robert Jordan and John J. McDermott, Jr.
Greta Music Corp.
Best-selling record by The G-Clefs (Pilgrim).

Kiss Me Another
Words by Fred Ebb, music by Charles Friedman.
Edward B. Marks Music Corp.
Best-selling record by Georgia Gibbs (Mercury).

Knee Deep in the Blues
Words and music by Melvin Endsley.
Acuff-Rose Publications.
Best-selling record in 1957 by Marty Robbins (Columbia).

Late, Late Show, The
Words by Roy Alfred, music by Murray Berlin.
Nom Music, Inc.
Best-selling record by Dakota Staton (Capitol).

Laugh, I Thought I'd Die
Words by Fran Landesman, music by Tommy Wolf.
Buckeye Publishing Co.
Interpolated by Richard Hayes in 1959 in *The Nervous Set* (musical).

Lay Down Your Arms (Swedish)
English words by Paddy Roberts, Swedish words and music by Ake Gerhard and Leon Land.
Lelands Musikförlag, Stockholm, Sweden/Francis, Day and Hunter, Ltd., London, England/Ludlow Music, Inc.
Original Swedish title, "Ann-Caroline." Introduced in England by Anne Shelton. Best-selling record in the United States by The Chordettes (Cadence).

Le Gamin de Paris (French)
English words by Allan Roberts, French words by Mick Micheyl, music by André Mares.
Éditions Metropolitaines, Paris, France, 1951/Leeds Music Corp.

Let the Good Times Roll
Words and music by Leonard Lee.
Travis Music Co./Atlantic Music Corp.
Best-selling record by Shirley and Lee (Aladdin).

Lili Maebelle
Words and music by Richard Barrett, Tommy Vastola, and Raymond Briggs.
Nom Music, Inc.
Best-selling record in 1955 by The Valentines (Rama).

Lipstick and Candy and Rubber Sole Shoes
Words and music by Bob Haymes.
Jimskip Music, Inc.
Best-selling record by Julius La Rosa (RCA Victor).

Lisbon Antigua, see **1954.**

Little Child (Daddy Dear), see **The Little Boy and the Old Man, 1953.**

Little Girl of Mine
Words by George Goldner and Herbert Cox.
Nom Music, Inc.
Best-selling record by The Cleftones (Gee).

Little Rosa
Words and music by Red Sovine and Webb Pierce.
Cedarwood Publishing Co., Inc.
Best-selling record by Red Sovine and Webb Pierce (Decca).

Lonely Street
Words and music by Kenny Sowder, W. S. Stevenson, and Carl Belew.
Four Star Sales Co., Inc.
Best-selling record in 1959 by Andy Williams (Cadence).

Long Before I Knew You
Words by Betty Comden and Adolph Green, music by Jule Styne.
Stratford Music Corp.
Introduced by Judy Holliday and Sydney Chaplin in *Bells Are Ringing* (musical).

Long Tall Sally
Words and music by Enotris Johnson, Richard Penniman, and Robert A. Blackwell.
Venice Music, Inc.
Best-selling records by Little Richard (Specialty) and Pat Boone (Dot).

Love in a Home
Words by Johnny Mercer, music by Gene de Paul.
Commander Publications.
Introduced by Peter Palmer and Edith Adams in *Li'l Abner* (musical).

Love in the Afternoon
Words by Johnny Mercer, music by Matty Malneck.
Commander Publications.
From *Love in the Afternoon* (film).

Love! Love! Love!
Words and music by Teddy McRae, Sid Wyche, and Sunny David.
Progressive Music Publishing Co., Inc.
Best-selling record by The Clovers (Atlantic).

Love Me Tender
Words and music by Elvis Presley and Vera Matson.
Elvis Presley Music, Inc.
Adapted from the song, "Aura Lea," with words by W. W. Fosdick and music by George R. Poulton. A favorite of the Union Army during the Civil War, the melody has also been used for the popular West Point song "Army Blue." New version introduced by Elvis Presley in *Love Me Tender* (film). Best-selling record in 1957 by Elvis Presley (RCA Victor). Revived in 1963 with best-selling record by Richard Chamberlain (M-G-M).

M.T.A., The
Words and music by Jacqueline Steiner and Bess Hawes.
Atlantic Music Corp.
Originally written for the 1948 elections as a campaign song protesting crowded conditions in the Boston, Massachusetts subways. Melody based on "The Wreck of the Old '97." Initials signify "Metropolitan Transit Authority." Best-selling record by The Kingston Trio (Capitol).

Mack the Knife, also known as Moritat (German)
English words by Marc Blitzstein, German words by Bertolt Brecht, music by Kurt Weill.
Universal Editions, Berlin, Germany, 1928/Harms, Inc.
Originally introduced by Kurt Gerron in Brecht and Weill's *Die Dreigroschenoper* in Berlin in 1928. First recorded in the United States by Lotte Lenya. Blitzstein's English-language version introduced in 1952 in a concert performance at Brandeis University. Introduced by Scott Merrill in the off-Broadway production of *The Threepenny Opera* in 1954. Best-selling instrumental record in 1956, under the title, "Theme from *The Threepenny Opera*," by The Dick Hyman Trio (M-G-M). Best-selling vocal records in 1957 by Louis Armstrong (Columbia), in 1959 by Bobby Darin (Atco), and in 1962 by Ella Fitzgerald (Verve).

Madly in Love
Words by Ogden Nash, music by Vernon Duke.
Saunders Publications, Inc.
Introduced by Tammy Grimes in *The Littlest Revue* (revue).

(You've Got) Magic Touch, The
Words and music by Buck Ram.
Panther Music Corp.
Best-selling record by The Platters (Mercury).

Main Title Theme, see **The Man with the Golden Arm.**

Mama from the Train (A Kiss, a Kiss)
Words and music by Irving Gordon.
Remick Music Corp.
Introduced and best-selling record by Patti Page (Mercury).

Mama, Teach Me To Dance
Words and music by Al Hoffman and Dick Manning.
Roncom Music Co.
Best-selling record by Eydie Gormé (ABC Paramount).

Man Who Plays the Mandolino, The, see **Guaglioni.**

Man with the Golden Arm, The
Words by Sammy Cahn, music by James Van Heusen.
Barton Music Corp.
Written for, but never used in, *The Man with the Golden Arm* (film).

Man with the Golden Arm, The
Words and music by Elmer Bernstein and Sylvia Fine.
Dena Music, Inc.
Main title theme from *The Man with the Golden Arm* (film). Best-selling records by Morris Stoloff and his Orchestra (Decca) and Elmer Bernstein and his Orchestra (Decca). Vocal version entitled "Delilah Jones."

Married I Can Always Get
Words and music by Gordon Jenkins.
Leeds Music Corp.
Introduced by Gordon Jenkins and his Orchestra and Chorus in *Manhattan Tower.*

Mary Ann
Words and music by Ray Charles.
Progressive Music Publishing Co., Inc.
Best-selling record by Ray Charles (Atlantic).

Miracle of Love
Words and music by Bob Merrill.
Rylan Music Corp.
Best-selling record by Eileen Rodgers (Columbia).

Mr. Wonderful
Words and music by Jerry Bock, Larry Holofcener, and George Weiss.
Laurel Music Corp.
Introduced by Olga James in *Mr . Wonderful* (musical).

Molly-O
Words and music by Elmer Bernstein and Sylvia Fine.
Dena Music, Inc.
Based on a theme from *The Man with the Golden Arm* (film).

Money Tree, The
Words by Cliff Ferre, music by Mark McIntyre.
Frank Music Corp.
First recorded by Margaret Whiting (Capitol).

Moonglow, see **Theme from *Picnic,*** 1955; see 1934.

Moonlight Gambler
Words by Bob Hilliard, music by Phil Springer.
Edwin H. Morris & Co., Inc.
Best-selling record in 1956 and 1957 by Frankie Laine (Columbia).

Moonlight Love
Words by Mitchell Parish, music by Dominico Savino.
J. Jobert, Paris, France.
Adaptation of Debussy's "Clair de Lune." Best-selling record by Perry Como (RCA Victor).

More
Words by Tom Glazer, music by Alex Alstone.
Shapiro, Bernstein & Co., Inc.
Best-selling record by Perry Como (RCA Victor).

Moritat, see Mack the Knife.

Most Happy Fella, The
Words and music by Frank Loesser.
Frank Music Corp.
Introduced by Robert Weede in *The Most Happy Fella* (musical).

Mu-Cha-Cha
Words by Betty Comden and Adolph Green, music by Jule Styne.
Stratford Music Corp.
Introduced by Judy Holliday and Peter Gennaro in *Bells Are Ringing* (musical).

Mutual Admiration Society
Words by Matt Dubey, music by Harold Carr.
Chappell & Co., Inc.
Introduced by Ethel Merman in *Happy Hunting* (musical).

My Baby Left Me
Words and music by Arthur Crudup.
Elvis Presley Music, Inc.
Best-selling record by Elvis Presley (RCA Victor).

My Dream Sonata
Words by Mack David, music by James Van Heusen.
United Music Corp.
Best-selling record by Nat "King" Cole (Capitol).

My Happiness Forever
Words and music by Jerome "Doc" Pomus.
Progressive Music Publishing Co., Inc.
Best-selling record by LaVern Baker (Atlantic).

My Heart Is So Full of You
Words and music by Frank Loesser.
Frank Music Corp.
Introduced by Robert Weede in *The Most Happy Fella* (musical).

My Prayer, see 1939.

Namely You
Words by Johnny Mercer, music by Gene de Paul.
Commander Publications.
Introduced by Edith Adams and Peter Palmer in *L'il Abner* (musical).

Never Leave Me
Words and music by Gordon Jenkins.
Leeds Music Corp.
Introduced by Gordon Jenkins and his Orchestra and Chorus in *Manhattan Tower.*

Never Mind
Words by George Weiss, music by Jerry Bock.
Valando Music Corp.
Best-selling record by Dinah Shore (RCA Victor).

New-Fangled Tango, A
Words by Matt Dubey, music by Harold Carr.
Chappell & Co., Inc.
Introduced by Ethel Merman, Virginia Gibson, Leon Belasco, and the chorus in *Happy Hunting* (musical).

Next Time You See Me
Words and music by Bill Harvey and Earl Forest.
Lion Publishing Co., Inc.
Best-selling record in 1957 by Little Junior Parker (Duke).

Night Lights
Words by Sammy Gallop, music by Chester Conn.
Bregman, Vocco & Conn, Inc.
Best-selling record by Nat "King" Cole (Capitol).

Ninety Nine Years (Dead or Alive)
Words by Sid Wayne, music by John Benson Brooks.
Joy Music, Inc.
Best-selling record by Guy Mitchell (Columbia).

No Money Down
Words and music by Chuck Berry.
Arc Music Corp.
Best-selling record by Chuck Berry (Chess).

No, Not Much
Words by Al Stillman, music by Robert Allen.
Beaver Music Publishing Corp.
Best-selling record by The Four Lads (Columbia).

No Other One
Words and music by Ivory Joe Hunter and Clyde Otis.
Vogue Music, Inc.
Best-selling record by Eddie Fisher (RCA Victor).

Now! Baby, Now!
Words by Sammy Cahn, music by Nicholas Brodszky.
Robbins Music Corp.
Introduced in *The Opposite Sex* (film).

Now You Has Jazz
Words and music by Cole Porter.
Buxton Hill Music Corp.
Introduced by Bing Crosby and Louis Armstrong in *High Society* (film).

Oh, What a Night
Words and music by Marvin Junior and John Funches.
Conrad Publishing Co., Inc.
Best-selling record by The Dells (Vee Jay).

Old Cape Cod
Words and music by Claire Rothrock, Milt Yakus, and Allan Jeffrey.
George Pincus Music Corp.
Best-selling record in 1956 and 1957 by Patti Page (Mercury).

On London Bridge
Words and music by Sid Tepper and Roy C. Bennett.
Ross Jungnickel, Inc.
Best-selling record by Jo Stafford (Columbia).

On the Street Where You Live
Words by Alan Jay Lerner, music by Frederick Loewe.
Chappell & Co., Inc.
Introduced by Michael King in *My Fair Lady* (musical). Best-selling record by Vic Damone (Columbia).

One Finger Piano (German)
English words by Charles Friedman, German words by Theo Hansen, music by Fred Hilger.
Edward B. Marks Music Corp.
Original German title, "Ich Spiel' Klavier mit Einem Finger." Best-selling record by The Dick Hyman Trio, vocal by The Naturals (M-G-M).

Other Woman, The
Words and music by Jessie Mae Robinson.
Favorite Music, Inc.
Introduced by Sarah Vaughan (Mercury).

Out of Sight, out of Mind
Words and music by Ivory Joe Hunter and Clyde Otis.
Nom Music, Inc.
Best-selling record by The Five Keys (Capitol).

Paper of Pins, A, see **The Bus Stop Song.**

Party's Over, The
Words by Betty Comden and Adolph Green, music by Jule Styne.
Stratford Music Corp.
Introduced by Judy Holliday in *Bells Are Ringing* (musical).

Petticoats of Portugal
Words and music by Michael Durso, Mel Mitchell, and Murl Kahn.
Brent Music Corp.
Best-selling record by Dick Jacobs and his Orchestra (Coral).

Pink Sweater Angel
Words by Aaron Schroeder, music by Guy Wood.
Planetary Music Publishing Corp.
Best-selling record by Johnnie Ray (Columbia).

Pleadin' for Love
Words and music by Larry Birdsong.
Excellorec Music Co.
Best-selling record by Larry Birdsong (Excello).

Please, Please, Please
Words and music by James Brown and Johnny Terry.
Lois Publishing Co.
Best-selling record by James Brown (Federal).

Poor Man's Riches
Words and music by Benny Barnes and Dee Marais.
Starrite Publishing Co.
Best-selling record by Benny Barnes (Starday).

Poor People of Paris, The (French)
English words by Jack Lawrence, French words by René Rouzoud, music by Marguerite Monnot.
René Rouzoud-Marguerite Monnot, Paris, France, 1954/Reg Connelly Music, Inc.
Introduced under its original title, "Le Goualante de Pauvre Jean" in Paris by Edith Piaf. Best-selling record, instrumental, in the United States by Les Baxter and his Orchestra (Capitol).

Port-au-Prince
Words by Bernie Wayne and Miriam Lewis, music by Bernie Wayne.
Edward B. Marks Music Corp.
Best-selling record, instrumental, by Nelson Riddle and his Orchestra (Capitol).

Portuguese Washerwomen, The (French)
Music by André Popp and Roger Lucchesi.
Paul Beuscher, Paris, France, 1954/Remick Music Corp.
Best-selling record, instrumental, by Joe "Fingers" Carr (pseudonym for Lou Busch) and his Orchestra (Capitol).

Preacher, The
Words and music by Horace Silver.
Silhouette Music Corp.
Jazz composition introduced by Horace Silver.

Rain in Spain, The
Words by Alan Jay Lerner, music by Frederick Loewe.
Chappell & Co., Inc.
Introduced by Rex Harrison, Julie Andrews, and Robert Coote in *My Fair Lady* (musical).

Ready Teddy
Words and music by John Marascalco and Robert Blackwell.
Venice Music, Inc./Elvis Presley Music, Inc.
Best-selling record by Little Richard (Specialty).

Rebel in Town
Words by Lenny Adelson, music by Les Baxter.
Saunders Publications, Inc.
Introduced in *Rebel in Town* (film).

Repeat after Me
Words and music by Gordon Jenkins.
Leeds Music Corp.
From the television production of *Manhattan Tower*. Best-selling record by Patti Page (Mercury).

Repenting
Words and music by Gary Walker.
Valley Publishers, Inc.
Best-selling record in 1957 by Kitty Wells (Decca).

Rip It Up
Words and music by Robert A. Blackwell and John Marascalco.
Venice Music, Inc.
Best-selling record by Little Richard (Specialty).

Rock Island Line
New words and music by Lonnie Donegan.
Hollis Music, Inc.
Adapted from a traditional American folk song first recorded by Huddie Ledbetter (Leadbelly). Best-selling record by Lonnie Donegan (London).

Rock-a-Bye Your Baby with a Dixie Melody, see 1918.

Roll Over Beethoven
Words and music by Chuck Berry.
Arc Music Corp.
Best-selling record by Chuck Berry (Chess). Revived in 1964 with best-selling record by The Beatles (Capitol).

Rose and a Baby Ruth, A
Words and music by John Loudermilk.
Bentley Music Co.
Best-selling record by George Hamilton IV (ABC Paramount).

Round and Round
Words and music by Lou Stallman and Joe Shapiro.
Tideland Music Publishing Corp./Pinelawn Music Publishing Co., Inc.
Best-selling record in 1956 and 1957 by Perry Como (RCA Victor).

Sadie's Shawl (English)
Music by Nico Carstens and Sam Lorraine.
Jerome Music Co., Ltd., London, England/Roncom Music Co.
Best-selling record, instrumental, by Robert Sharples and his Orchestra (London).

St. Theresa of the Roses
Words by Remus Harris, music by Arthur Strauss.
Dennis Music Co., Inc.
Best-selling record by Billy Ward (Decca).

Searchers (Ride Away)
Words and music by Stan Jones.
M. Witmark & Sons.
Introduced in *The Searchers* (film).

See-Saw
Words and music by Roquel Davis, Charles Sutton, and Harry Pratt.
Arc Music Corp.
Best-selling record by The Moonglows (Chess).

Sermonette, see 1958.

Seven Days
Words and music by Willis Carroll and Carmen Taylor.
Progressive Music Publishing Co., Inc.
Best-selling record by Clyde McPhatter (Atlantic).

Shape of Things, The
Words and music by Sheldon Harnick.
Saunders Publications, Inc.
Introduced by Charlotte Rae in *The Littlest Revue* (revue).

Show Me
Words by Alan Jay Lerner, music by Frederick Loewe.
Chappell & Co., Inc.
Introduced by Julie Andrews in *My Fair Lady* (musical).

Show Must Go On
Words by Roy Alfred, music by Al Frisch.
United Music Corp.
Best-selling record by Dinah Washington (Mercury).

Silver Threads and Golden Needles
Words and music by Dick Reynolds and Jack Rhodes.
Central Songs, Inc.
Best-selling record in 1963 by The Springfields (recorded in England) (Philips).

Since I Met You Baby
Words and music by Ivory Joe Hunter.
Progressive Music Publishing Co., Inc.
Best-selling record in 1956 and 1957 by Ivory Joe Hunter (Atlantic).

Singing the Blues, see 1954.

Slippin' and Slidin'
Words and music by Richard Penniman, Edwin Bocage, James Smith, and Albert Collins.
Venice Music, Inc./Bess Music Co.
Best-selling record by Little Richard (Specialty).

So Doggone Lonesome
Words and music by Johnny Cash.
Hi-Lo Music, Inc./Hill and Range Songs, Inc.
Best-selling record by Johnny Cash (Sun).

So Long
Words and music by Antoine "Fats" Domino and Dave Bartholomew.
Travis Music Co.
Best-selling record by Fats Domino (Imperial).

Somebody, Somewhere
Words and music by Frank Loesser.
Frank Music Corp.
Introduced by Jo Sullivan in *The Most Happy Fella* (musical).

Somebody Up There Likes Me
Words by Sammy Cahn, music by Bronislau Kaper.
Leo Feist, Inc.
From *Somebody Up There Likes Me* (film). Best-selling record by Perry Como (RCA Victor).

Song for a Summer Night
Words and music by Robert Allen.
Cromwell Music, Inc.
Introduced by Mitch Miller and his Orchestra in *Song for a Summer Night* (Westinghouse *Studio One* television production). Best-selling record by Mitch Miller and his Orchestra (Columbia).

Speak, My Love (Italian)
English words by Roberta Heller, music by Ero Valladi.
Casa Editrice Ambrosiana, Milan, Italy, 1954/Harvard Music, Inc.
Best-selling record by Vic Damone (Mercury).

Spring in Maine
Words by Carolyn Leigh, music by Steve Allen.
Edwin H. Morris & Co., Inc.
Introduced by Margaret Whiting (Capitol).

Standing on the Corner
Words and music by Frank Loesser.
Frank Music Corp.
Introduced by Shorty Long, Alan Gilbert, John Henson, and Roy Lazarus in *The Most Happy Fella* (musical). Best-selling record by The Four Lads (Columbia).

Still
Words and music by Dorian Burton and Howard Plummer.
Progressive Music Publishing Co., Inc.
Best-selling record by LaVern Baker (Atlantic).

Story of Love, The (Mexican)
English words by George Thorn, Spanish words and music by Carlos Almaran.
Editorial Mexicana de Musica Internacional, S.A., Mexico, 1955/Peer International Corp.
Original title, "Historia de un Amor." Popularized by The Trio Los Panchos.

Stranded in the Jungle
Words and music by Ernestine Smith and James Johnson.
Shag Publications/Peer International Corp.
Best-selling record by The Cadets (Modern).

Sugartime
Words and music by Charlie Phillips and Odis Echols.
Nor Va Jak Music, Inc.
Best-selling record in 1958 by The McGuire Sisters (Coral).

Sweet Old-Fashioned Girl, A
Words and music by Bob Merrill.
Valyr Music Corp.
Best-selling record by Teresa Brewer (Coral).

Talk to Me
Words and music by Eddie Snyder, Stanley Kahan, and Rudy Vallee.
Barton Music Corp.
Best-selling record by Frank Sinatra (Capitol).

Tangled Mind
Words and music by Ted Daffan and Herman Shoss.
Hill and Range Songs, Inc.
Best-selling record in 1957 by Hank Snow (RCA Victor).

Teacher's Pet
Words and music by Joe Lubin.
Daywin Music, Inc.
Introduced by Doris Day in 1958 in *Teacher's Pet* (film).

Tear Fell, A
Words and music by Dorian Burton and Eugene Randolph.
Progressive Music Publishing Co., Inc.
Best-selling record by Teresa Brewer (Coral).

Teen Age Crush
Words and music by Audrey Allison and Joe Allison.
Central Songs, Inc.
Best-selling record in 1957 by Tommy Sands (Capitol).

Teen-Age Love
Words and music by George Goldner and Al Joseph Cooper.
Nom Music, Inc.
Best-selling record by Frankie Lymon and The Teenagers (Gee).

Thee I Love, see **Friendly Persuasion.**

Theme from *Baby Doll*
Music by Kenyon Hopkins.
Remick Music Corp.
Theme from *Baby Doll* (film).

Theme from *The Proud Ones*
Words by Johnny Desmond, music by Ruth Keddington.
Weiss & Barry, Inc.
From *The Proud Ones* (film). Recorded by Lionel Newman and his Orchestra, with whistling by Muzzy Marcellino (Columbia). Best-selling record by Nelson Riddle and his Orchestra (Capitol).

Theme from *The Swan*
Music by Bronislau Kaper.
Miller Music Corp.
Theme from *The Swan* (film).

Theme from *The Threepenny Opera,* see **Mack the Knife.**

There You Go
Words and music by Johnny Cash.
Knox Music, Inc.
Best-selling record in 1957 by Johnny Cash (Sun).

There's Never Been Anyone Else but You
Words by Paul Francis Webster, music by Dimitri Tiomkin.
M. Witmark & Sons.
Adapted from a theme from *Giant* (film).

This Could Be the Start of Something
Words and music by Steve Allen.
Rosemeadow Publishing Corp.
Introduced by Les Brown and his Band of Renown.

This Is What I Call Love
Words by Matt Dubey, music by Harold Carr.
Chappell & Co., Inc.
Introduced by Ethel Merman in *Happy Hunting* (musical).

This Land Is Your Land
Words and music by Woody Guthrie.
Ludlow Music, Inc.
Adapted from a folk melody used by the Carter Family for their songs, "When the World's on Fire" and "Little Darling Pal of Mine." Later Guthrie version introduced by The Weavers. Best-selling record in 1963 by The New Christy Minstrels (Columbia).

Thousand Miles Away, A
Words and music by James Sheppard and William H. Miller.
Nom Music, Inc.
Best-selling record in 1956 and 1957 by The Heartbeats (Rama).

Tonight You Belong to Me, see 1926.

Too Close for Comfort
Words and music by Jerry Bock, Larry Holofcener, and George Weiss.
Laurel Music Corp.
Introduced by Sammy Davis, Jr. in *Mr. Wonderful* (musical).

Too Much
Words and music by Bernard Weinman.
Elvis Presley Music, Inc./Southern Belle Music Publishers.
Best-selling record in 1956 and 1957 by Elvis Presley (RCA Victor).

Too Much Monkey Business
Words and music by Chuck Berry.
Arc Music Corp.
Best-selling record by Chuck Berry (Chess).

Tra La La
Words and music by Johnny Parker.
Snapper Music, Inc.
Introduced by LaVern Baker in *Rock, Rock, Rock* (film).

Train of Love
Words and music by Johnny Cash.
Knox Music, Inc.
Best-selling record in 1957 by Johnny Cash (Sun).

Transfusion
Words and music by Jimmy Drake.
Paul Barrett Music, Inc.
Best-selling record by Norvus Nervous (Dot).

Treasure of Love
Words and music by J. Shapiro and Lou Stallman.
Progressive Music Publishing Co., Inc.
Best-selling record by Clyde McPhatter (Atlantic).

True Love
Words and music by Cole Porter.
Buxton Hill Music Corp.
Introduced by Bing Crosby and Grace Kelly in *High Society* (film). Nominated for Academy Award, 1956. Best-selling record in 1956 and 1957 by Bing Crosby and Grace Kelly (Capitol).

Twelfth of Never
Words by Paul Francis Webster, music by Jerry Livingston.
Empress Music, Inc.
Melody adapted from "The Riddle Song," a folk song from Kentucky, but probably of earlier English origin. Best-selling record by Johnny Mathis (Columbia).

Twenty Feet of Muddy Water
Words and music by Bill Smith.
Central Songs, Inc.
Best-selling record by Sonny James (Capitol).

Two Different Worlds
Words by Sid Wayne, music by Al Frisch.
Princess Music Publishing Corp.
Best-selling record by Don Rondo (Jubilee).

Uncle Pen, see 1951.

Upon the Mountain
Words and music by Nathaniel Montague and Ewart G. Abner, Jr.
Conrad Publishing Co., Inc.
Best-selling record by The Magnificents (Vee Jay).

Walk Hand in Hand
Words and music by Johnny Cowell.
Republic Music Corp.
Introduced by Canadian singer Denny Vaughan (Kapp). Best-selling record by Tony Martin (RCA Victor).

Walk Up
Words and music by Bart Howard.
Almanac Music, Inc.
Introduced by Mabel Mercer.

Walkin' after Midnight
Words by Don Hecht, music by Alan Block.
Four Star Sales Co.
Best-selling record in 1957 and 1958 by Patsy Cline (Decca).

War and Peace
Words by Wilson Stone, music by Nino Rota.
Famous Music Corp.
Adapted from a theme from *War and Peace* (film). Best-selling record by Vic Damone (Mercury).

Warm
Words by Sid Jacobson, music by Jimmy Krondes.
Fred Fisher Music Co., Inc.
Introduced by Johnny Mathis (Columbia).

Warm All Over
Words and music by Frank Loesser.
Frank Music Corp.
Introduced by Jo Sullivan in *The Most Happy Fella* (musical).

Wasted Words
Words and music by Don Gibson.
Acuff-Rose Publications.
Best-selling record in 1956 and 1957 by Ray Price (Columbia).

Wayward Wind
Words and music by Stan Lebowsky and Herb Newman.
Hillary Music, Inc./Bamboo Music, Inc.
Best-selling record by Gogi Grant (Era).

What Would I Do without You
Words and music by Ray Charles.
Progressive Music Publishing Co., Inc.
Best-selling record by Ray Charles (Atlantic).

What Would You Do (If Jesus Came to Your House)
Words and music by Hugh Ashley and Lois Blanchard.
Earl Barton Music Co.
Best-selling record by Porter Wagoner (RCA Victor).

Whatcha' Gonna Do When Your Baby Leaves You
Words and music by Chuck Willis.
Tideland Music Publishing Corp./Progressive Music Publishing Co., Inc.
Best-selling record by Fats Domino (Imperial).

When Sunny Gets Blue
Words by Jack Segal, music by Marvin Fisher.
Marvin Music Co.
Best-selling record by Johnny Mathis (Columbia).

Who Needs You
Words by Al Stillman, music by Robert Allen.
Korwin Music, Inc.
Best-selling record in 1956 and 1957 by The Four Lads (Columbia).

Why Can't the English
Words by Alan Jay Lerner, music by Frederick Loewe.
Chappell & Co., Inc.
Introduced by Rex Harrison in *My Fair Lady* (musical).

Why Do Fools Fall in Love
Words and music by Frank Lymon and George Goldner.
Patricia Music Publishing Corp.
Best-selling record by Frankie Lymon and The Teenagers (Gee) and Gale Storm (Dot).

With a Little Bit of Luck
Words by Alan Jay Lerner, music by Frederick Loewe.
Chappell & Co., Inc.
Introduced by Stanley Holloway in *My Fair Lady* (musical).

Without Love (There Is Nothing)
Words and music by Danny Small.
Suffolk Music, Inc./Progressive Music Publishing Co., Inc.
Best-selling record in 1957 by Clyde McPhatter (Atlantic).

Without You
Words and music by J. D. Miller.
Acuff-Rose Publications.
Best-selling record by Eddie Fisher (RCA Victor).

Wonderful! Wonderful!
Words by Ben Raleigh, music by Sherman Edwards.
Edward B. Marks Music Corp.
Best-selling record by Johnny Mathis (Columbia). Revived in 1963 with best-selling record by The Tymes (Parkway).

Wouldn't It Be Loverly?
Words by Alan Jay Lerner, music by Frederick Loewe.
Chappell & Co., Inc.
Introduced by Julie Andrews in *My Fair Lady* (musical).

Wringle Wrangle
Words and music by Stan Jones.
Walt Disney Music Co.
Introduced by Fess Parker in *Westward Ho the Wagons!* (film).

Written on the Wind
Words by Sammy Cahn, music by Victor Young.
Northern Music Corp.
Introduced by The Four Aces, behind the opening titles, on the soundtrack of *Written on the Wind* (film). Nominated for Academy Award, 1956.

Yes, I Know Why
Words and music by Webb Pierce.
Cedarwood Publishing Co., Inc.
Best-selling record by Webb Pierce (Decca).

Yesterday and You, see **Armen's Theme.**

You Are the One
Words and music by Pat Patterson.
Starday Music.
Best-selling record by Carl Smith (Columbia).

You Can't Run Away from It
Words by Johnny Mercer, music by Gene de Paul.
Columbia Pictures Music Corp.
From *You Can't Run Away from It* (film). Best-selling record by The Four Aces (Decca).

You Done Me Wrong
Words and music by Ray Price and Shirley Jones.
Cedarwood Publishing Co., Inc.
Best-selling record by Ray Price (Columbia).

You Don't Owe Me a Thing
Words and music by Marty Robbins.
Fred Rose Music, Inc.
Introduced by Marty Robbins. Best-selling record in 1957 by Johnnie Ray (Columbia).

You Got Me Dizzy
Words and music by Jimmy Reed and Ewart Abner, Jr.
Conrad Publishing Co., Inc.
Best-selling record in 1957 by Jimmy Reed (Vee Jay).

You Gotta Be My Baby
Words and music by George Jones.
Starrite Publishing Co.
Best-selling record by George Jones (Starday).

You Gotta Love Everybody
Words and music by Bill Norvas and Kay Thompson.
Edwin H. Morris & Co., Inc.
Best-selling record in 1958 by Della Reese (Jubilee).

Young Love
Words and music by Ric Cartey and Carole Joyner.
Lowery Music Co., Inc.
Introduced by Ric Cartey. Subsequently used as title song for *Young Love* (film). Best-selling records in 1957 by Tab Hunter (Dot) and Sonny James (Capitol).

You're Mine
Words and music by Wade Buff and Gene Adkinson.
Northern Music Corp.
Best-selling record by Robert and Johnny (Old Town).

You're Running Wild
Words and music by Ray Edenton and Don Winters.
Acuff-Rose Publications.
Best-selling record by The Louvin Brothers (Capitol).

You're Sensational
Words and music by Cole Porter.
Buxton Hill Music Corp.
Introduced by Frank Sinatra in *High Society* (film).

You're Still Mine
Words by Eddie Thorpe, music by Faron Young.
Lancaster Music Publications, Inc.
Best-selling record by Faron Young (Capitol).

You're the Reason I'm in Love
Words and music by Jack Morrow.
Beechwood Music Corp.
Best-selling record in 1957 by Sonny James (Capitol).

1957

Affair To Remember, An
Words by Harold Adamson and Leo McCarey, music by Harry Warren.
Leo Feist, Inc.
Introduced by Vic Damone, behind the titles, on the soundtrack of *An Affair To Remember* (film). Nominated for Academy Award, 1957. Best-selling record by Vic Damone (Columbia).

Ain't That Love
Words and music by Ray Charles.
Progressive Music Publishing Co., Inc.
Best-selling record by Ray Charles (Atlantic).

Aisle, The, see **To the Aisle.**

All of These and More
Words by Sheldon Harnick, music by Jerry Bock.
Sunbeam Music Corp.
Introduced by Barbara McNair and Lonnie Satin in *Body Beautiful* (musical).

All Shook Up
Words and music by Otis Blackwell and Elvis Presley.
Travis Music Co./Elvis Presley Music, Inc.
Best-selling record by Elvis Presley (RCA Victor).

All the Way
Words by Sammy Cahn, music by Jimmy Van Heusen.
Maraville Music Corp.
From *The Joker Is Wild* (film). Academy Award-winning song, 1957. Introduced and best-selling record by Frank Sinatra (Capitol).

Almost Paradise
Words and music by Norman Petty.
Peer International Corp.
Introduced by The Norman Petty Trio (M-G-M). Best-selling record, instrumental, by Roger Williams (Kapp).

Alone
Words by Selma Craft, music by Morton Craft.
Selma Music Corp.
Best-selling record by The Shepherd Sisters (Lance).

America
Words by Stephen Sondheim, music by Leonard Bernstein.
Chappell & Co., Inc./G. Schirmer, Inc.
Introduced by Chita Rivera, Marilyn Cooper, Reri Grist, and "The Shark Girls" in *West Side Story* (musical).

And That Reminds You, see **My Heart Reminds Me.**

Anne Marie
Words and music by Cindy Walker.
Open Road Music, Inc.
Best-selling record by Jim Reeves (RCA Victor).

April Love
Words by Paul Francis Webster, music by Sammy Fain.
Leo Feist, Inc.
Introduced by Pat Boone in *April Love* (film). Nominated for Academy Award, 1957.

Are You Sincere
Words and music by Wayne Walker.
Cedarwood Publishing Co., Inc.
Best-selling record in 1958 by Andy Williams (Cadence).

At the Hop
Words and music by A. Singer, J. Medora, and D. White.
Sea-Lark Enterprises, Inc./Singular Music Publishing Co., Inc.
Best-selling record by Danny and The Juniors (ABC Paramount).

Band of Angels
Words by Carl Sigman, music by Max Steiner.
M. Witmark & Sons.
From *Band of Angels* (film).

Battle of New Orleans, The
Words and music by Jimmy Driftwood.
Warden Music Co., Inc.
Written, according to folklorist Oscar Brand, to the tune of "The Eighth of January," an 1815 fiddle tune composed to celebrate the United States victory at New Orleans. Best-selling record in 1959 by Johnny Horton (Columbia).

Be-Bop Baby
Words and music by Pearl Lendhurst.
Travis Music Co.
Best-selling record by Ricky Nelson (Imperial).

Bernadine
Words and music by Johnny Mercer.
Palm Springs Music Co.
Introduced by Pat Boone in *Bernadine* (film).

Black Slacks
Words and music by Joe Bennett and Jimmy Denton.
Pamco Music, Inc.
Best-selling record by Joe Bennett and The Sparkletones (ABC Paramount).

Blue, Blue Day
Words and music by Don Gibson.
Acuff-Rose Publications.
Best-selling record by Don Gibson (RCA Victor).

Blue Doll
Words and music by Boudleaux Bryant.
Acuff-Rose Publications.
Best-selling record by Jim Reeves (RCA Victor).

Blue Monday
Words and music by Dave Bartholomew and Antoine "Fats" Domino.
Travis Music Co.
Introduced by Fats Domino in *The Girl Can't Help It* (film). Best-selling record by Fats Domino (Imperial).

Bonjour Tristesse
Words by Arthur Laurents, music by Georges Auric.
Carlot Music, Inc.
From *Bonjour Tristesse* (film). Best-selling record by Gogi Grant (RCA Victor).

Bony Moronie
Words and music by Larry Williams.
Venice Music, Inc.
Best-selling record by Larry Williams (Specialty).

Book of Love
Words and music by Warren Davis, George Malone, and Charles Patrick.
Arc Music Corp./Keel Music Co.
Best-selling record in 1958 by The Monotones (Argo).

Boy on a Dolphin (Greek)
English words by Paul Francis Webster, Greek words by J. Fermanoglou, music by Takis Morakis, adapted by Hugo W. Friedhofer.
Franciscos Depastas, Athens, Greece/Robbins Music Corp.
From the Greek song, "Tinafto." Introduced by Julie London in *Boy on a Dolphin* (film).

Butterfly
Words and music by Bernie Lowe and Kal Mann.
Ross Jungnickel, Inc.
Best-selling records by Andy Williams (Cadence) and Charlie Gracie (Cameo).

Buzz Buzz Buzz
Words and music by J. Gray and R. Byrd.
Cash Songs.
Best-selling record by The Hollywood Flames (Ebb).

Bye Bye Love
Words and music by Felice Bryant and Boudleaux Bryant.
Acuff-Rose Publications.
Best-selling records by The Everly Brothers (Cadence) and Webb Pierce (Decca).

Ca, C'est l'Amour
Words and music by Cole Porter.
Buxton Hill Music Corp.
Introduced by Taina Elg in *Les Girls* (film). Best-selling record by Tony Bennett (Columbia).

Calypso Joe
Words and music by Marge O'Neale and Fred Darian.
Edwin H. Morris & Co., Inc.
Best-selling record by Nat "King" Cole (Capitol).

Calypso Melody
Words and music by Larry Clinton.
Cromwell Music, Inc.
Best-selling record, instrumental, by David Rose and his Orchestra (M-G-M).

Catch a Falling Star
Words and music by Paul Vance and Lee Pockriss.
Marvin Music Co.
Best-selling record by Perry Como (RCA Victor).

Chances Are
Words by Al Stillman, music by Robert Allen.
Korwin Music, Inc.
Best-selling record by Johnny Mathis (Columbia).

Chantez, Chantez
Words by Albert Gamse, music by Irving Fields.
Chantez Music, Inc.
Introduced by Dinah Shore.

China Gate
Words by Harold Adamson, music by Victor Young.
Victor Young Publications, Inc.
Introduced by Nat "King" Cole in *China Gate* (film).

Cocoanut Sweet
Words by E. Y. Harburg, music by Harold Arlen.
Harwin Music Corp.
Introduced by Adelaide Hall and Lena Horne in *Jamaica* (musical).

Cocoanut Woman
Words and music by Harry Belafonte.
Clara Music Publishing Corp.
Calypso song. Best-selling record by Harry Belafonte (RCA Victor).

(You Can't Lose the Blues with) Colors
Words and music by Irving Berlin.
Irving Berlin Music Corp.
Introduced by Rosemary Clooney (Columbia).

Come Go with Me
Words and music by C. E. Quick.
Gil Music Corp./Fee Bee Music.
Best-selling record by the Del Vikings (Dot).

Come to Me
Words by Peter Lind Hayes, music by Robert Allen.
Korwin Music, Inc.
Introduced in *Come to Me* (television production). Best-selling record by Johnny Mathis (Columbia).

Cool
Words by Stephen Sondheim, music by Leonard Bernstein.
Chappell & Co., Inc./G. Schirmer, Inc.
Introduced by Mickey Calin and "The Jets" in *West Side Story* (musical).

Cool Baby
Words and music by Otis Blackwell.
B.R.S. Music Corp.
Best-selling record by Charlie Gracie (Cameo).

Could This Be Magic
Words and music by Hiram Johnson and Richard Blandon.
Sea-Lark Enterprises, Inc.
Best-selling record by The Dubs (Gone).

Dark Moon
Words and music by Ned Miller.
Jamie Music Publishing Co.
Best-selling records by Bonnie Guitar (Dot) and Gale Storm (Dot).

Day the Rains Came, The (French)
English words by Carl Sigman, French words by Pierre Delanoe, music by Gilbert Becaud.
Garland Music, Inc./France Music Co.
Original title, "Le Jour ou la Pluie Viendra." Introduced by Gilbert Becaud. Best-selling record in the United States by Jane Morgan (Kapp).

Diana
Words and music by Paul Anka.
Spanka Music Corp.
Best-selling record by Paul Anka (ABC Paramount).

Did You Close Your Eyes When We Kissed
Words and music by Bob Merrill.
Chappell & Co., Inc.
Introduced by Gwen Verdon and George Wallace in *New Girl in Town* (musical).

Do I Love You Because You're Beautiful
Words by Oscar Hammerstein II, music by Richard Rodgers.
Williamson Music, Inc.
Introduced by Jon Cypher and Julie Andrews in *Cinderella* (television musical).

Don't
Words and music by Jerry Leiber and Mike Stoller.
Elvis Presley Music, Inc.
Best-selling record by Elvis Presley (RCA Victor).

Don't Let Go
Words and music by Jesse Stone.
Roosevelt Music Co., Inc.
Best-selling records by Roy Hamilton (Epic) and Billy Williams (Coral).

Empty Arms
Words and music by Ivory Joe Hunter.
Desiard Music Co., Inc.
Best-selling record by Ivory Joe Hunter (Atlantic).

Everyone's Laughing
Words and music by Calvin Carter.
Conrad Publishing Co., Inc.
Best-selling record by The Spaniels (Vee Jay).

Fabulous
Words by Jon Sheldon, music by Harry Land.
Rice Mill Publishing Co., Inc.
Best-selling record by Charlie Gracie (Cameo).

Face in the Crowd, A
Words by Budd Schulberg, music by Tom Glazer.
Remick Music Corp.
Introduced by Andy Griffith in *A Face in the Crowd* (film).

Fallen Star, A
Words and music by James Joiner.
Tree Publishing Co., Inc.
Best-selling records by Ferlin Husky (Capitol) and Jimmy Newman (Dot).

Farther up the Road
Words and music by J. Veasey and Don Robey.
Lion Publishing Co., Inc.
Best-selling record by Bobby "Blue" Bland (Duke).

Fascination (French)
English words by Dick Manning, music by F. D. Marchetti.
Southern Music Publishing Co., Inc.
New adaptation of Marchetti's 1904 "Fascination," a "valse tzigane" with lyrics by Maurice de Féraudy. Theme from *Love in the Afternoon* (film). Best-selling record by Jane Morgan (Kapp).

Fire Down Below
Words by Ned Washington, music by Lester Lee.
Columbia Pictures Music Corp.
From *Fire Down Below* (film).

First Date, First Kiss, First Love
Words by Mary Stovall and Dan Welch, music by Dan Welch.
Lowery Music Co.
Best-selling record by Sonny James (Capitol).

Florence
Words and music by Julius McMichaels and Paul Winley.
Sylvia Music Publishing Co., Inc./Ninny Publishing Co.
Best-selling record by The Paragons (Winley).

Forgotten Dreams, **see 1955.**

Forsaking All Others
Words by Rhoda Roberts and Melvin Unger, music by Kenny Jacobson.
Nom Music, Inc.
Best-selling record by Don Rondo (Jubilee).

Four Walls
Words and music by Marvin Moore and George Campbell.
Travis Music Co.
Best-selling record by Jim Reeves (RCA Victor).

Freight Train
Words and music by Paul James and Fred Williams.
The Peter Maurice Music Co., Ltd., New York.
Introduced in England and best-selling record by The Clyde McDevitt Skiffle Group, vocal by Nancy Wiskey (Chic).

Gee, Officer Krupke
Words by Stephen Sondheim, music by Leonard Bernstein.
Chappell & Co., Inc./G. Schirmer, Inc.
Introduced by Eddie Roll, Grove Dale, and "The Jets" in *West Side Story* (musical).

Geisha Girl
Words and music by Lawton Williams.
Travis Music Co.
Best-selling record by Hank Locklin (RCA Victor).

Get a Job
Words and music by The Silhouettes.
Wildcat Music, Inc./Kae Williams Music Inc.
Best-selling record in 1958 by The Silhouettes (Ember).

Gift of Love, The
Words by Paul Francis Webster, music by Sammy Fain.
Robbins Music Corp.
From *The Gift of Love* (film). Best-selling record by Vic Damone (Columbia).

Girl with the Golden Braids, The
Words and music by Stanley Kahan and Eddie Snyder.
Roncom Music Co.
Best-selling record by Perry Como (RCA Victor).

Going to the River
Words and music by Antoine "Fats" Domino and Dave Bartholomew.
Travis Music Co.
Best-selling record in 1953 by Fats Domino (Imperial).

Golden Striker, The
Music by John Lewis.
Rayven Music Co., Inc.
Introduced by The Modern Jazz Quartet on the soundtrack of *No Sun in Venice* (French film).

Gone, see 1952.

Gonna Find Me a Bluebird
Words and music by Marvin Rainwater.
Acuff-Rose Publications.
Best-selling record by Marvin Rainwater (M-G-M).

Good Intentions
Words by Carolyn Leigh, music by Cy Coleman.
Edwin H. Morris & Co., Inc.

Goodnight My Someone
Words and music by Meredith Willson.
Frank Music Corp.
Introduced by Barbara Cook in *The Music Man* (musical).

Great Balls of Fire
Words and music by Jack Hammer and Otis Blackwell.
Hill and Range Songs, Inc.
Featured in *Jamboree* (film). Best-selling record by Jerry Lee Lewis (Sun).

Half of My Heart
Words by Ned Washington, music by George W. Duning.
Columbia Pictures Music Corp.
From *Jeanne Eagels* (film).

Happy, Happy Birthday Baby
Words and music by Margo Sylvia and Gilbert Lopez.
Arc Music Corp./Donna Music Publishing Co.
Best-selling record by The Tune Weavers (Checker).

He's Got the Whole World in His Hands
Words and music by Geoff Love.
Chappell & Co., Inc.
Adapted from a traditional gospel song. Best-selling record in 1958 by Laurie London (produced in England) (Capitol).

Hey, Schoolgirl
Words by Arthur Garfunkel, music by Paul Simon.
Village Music Co.
Best-selling record by Tom and Jerry (Big).

Holiday for Love
Words and music by Webb Pierce, Wayne P. Walker, and A. R. Peddy.
Cedarwood Publishing Co., Inc.
Best-selling record by Webb Pierce (Decca).

Home of the Blues
Words and music by Johnny Cash, G. Douglas, and L. McAlpin.
Hi-Lo Music, Inc.
Best-selling record by Johnny Cash (Sun).

Honest I Do
Words and music by Jimmy Reed and Ewart G. Abner, Jr.
Conrad Publishing Co., Inc.
Best-selling record by Jimmy Reed (Vee Jay).

Honeycomb, see 1954.

Honky Tonk Song
Words and music by Mel Tillis and Buck Peddy.
Tree Publishing Co., Inc./Cedarwood Publishing Co., Inc.
Best-selling record by Webb Pierce (Decca).

How Green Was My Valley
Words by Paul Francis Webster, music by Alfred Newman.
Robbins Music Corp.
Love theme from the score written for the 1941 film, *How Green Was My Valley.*

Hula Love
Words and music by Buddy Knox.
Nom Music, Inc.
Best-selling record by Buddy Knox (Roulette).

I Beg of You
Words and music by Rose Marie McCoy and Kelly Owens.
Elvis Presley Music, Inc.
Best-selling record in 1958 by Elvis Presley (RCA Victor).

I Feel Pretty
Words by Stephen Sondheim, music by Leonard Bernstein.
Chappell & Co., Inc./G. Schirmer, Inc.
Introduced by Carol Lawrence, Marilyn Cooper, Carmen Guiterrez, and Elizabeth Taylor in *West Side Story* (musical).

I Found My Girl in the U. S. A.
Words and music by Jimmie Skinner.
Starday Music.
Best-selling record by Jimmie Skinner (Mercury).

I Heard the Bluebirds Sing, see 1952.

I Just Don't Know
Words by Joseph Stone, music by Robert Allen.
Korwin Music, Inc.
Best-selling record by The Four Lads (Columbia).

I Like Your Kind of Love
Words and music by Melvin Endsley.
Acuff-Rose Publications.
Best-selling record by Andy Williams (Cadence).

I Never Felt More Like Falling in Love, see 1954.

I Never Felt This Way Before
Words by Mack Gordon, music by Josef Myrow.
Blackstone Music, Inc.
Introduced by Eddie Fisher and Debbie Reynolds in *Bundle of Joy* (film).

I Stayed Too Long at the Fair
Words and music by Billy Barnes.
Tylerson Music Co.
Introduced by Joyce Jameson in *The Billy Barnes Revue* (revue). Popularized by Barbra Streisand in 1963.

I Thought It Was Over
Words by Kermit Goell, music by Fred Spielman.
Remick Music Corp.

I Walk a Little Faster
Words by Carolyn Leigh, music by Cy Coleman.
Edwin H. Morris & Co., Inc.

I Want To Know
Words and music by Ray Charles.
Progressive Music Publishing Co., Inc.
Best-selling record by Ray Charles (Atlantic).

I Won't Be the Fool Anymore
Words and music by James Sheppard and Joe Thomas.
Nom Music, Inc.
Best-selling record by The Heartbeats (Rama).

I'm Available
Words and music by Dave Burgess.
Golden West Melodies, Inc.
Introduced by Margie Rayburn (Liberty).

I'm Gonna Be a Wheel Someday
Words and music by Dave Bartholomew and Antoine "Fats" Domino.
Travis Music Co.
Best-selling record by Fats Domino (Imperial).

I'm Gonna Sit Right Down and Write Myself a Letter, see 1935.

I'm Stickin' with You
Words and music by James Bowen and Buddy Knox.
Nom Music, Inc.
Best-selling record by Jimmy Bowen (Roulette).

I'm Tired
Words and music by Melvin Tillis, Ray Price, and A. R. Peddy.
Cedarwood Publishing Co., Inc.
Best-selling record by Webb Pierce (Decca).

I'm Waiting Just for You, see 1951.

I'm Walkin'
Words and music by Antoine "Fats" Domino and Dave Bartholomew.
Travis Music Co.
Best-selling record by Fats Domino (Imperial). Featured by Ricky Nelson in his singing debut on the *Ozzie and Harriet* (Nelson) television series in April 1957.

I'm Your Hoochie Cooche Man
Words and music by Willie Dixon.
Arc Music Corp.
Best-selling record in 1954 by Muddy Waters (Chess).

In My Own Little Corner
Words by Oscar Hammerstein II, music by Richard Rodgers.
Williamson Music, Inc.
Introduced by Julie Andrews in *Cinderella* (television musical).

In the Middle of an Island
Words and music by Nick Acquaviva and Ted Varnick.
Mayfair Music Corp.
Best-selling record by Tony Bennett (Columbia).

Independent (On My Own)
Words by Betty Comden and Adolph Green, music by Jule Styne.
Stratford Music Corp.
Introduced by Sydney Chaplin in *Bells Are Ringing* (musical).

Interlude
Words by Paul Francis Webster, music by Frank Skinner.
Northern Music Corp.
Theme from *Interlude* (film).

Is It Wrong?
Words and music by Warren MacPherson.
Copar-Forrest Music Corp.
Best-selling record by Warner Mack (Decca).

It's All Right
Words and music by Ray Charles.
Progressive Music Publishing Co., Inc.
Best-selling record by Ray Charles (Atlantic).

It's Good To Be Alive
Words and music by Bob Merrill.
Valyr Music Corp.
Introduced by Gwen Verdon in *New Girl in Town* (musical).

It's Not for Me To Say
Words by Al Stillman, music by Robert Allen.
Korwin Music, Inc.
Introduced in *Lizzie* (film). Best-selling record by Johnny Mathis (Columbia).

It's You
Words and music by Meredith Willson.
Frank Music Corp.
Introduced by The Buffalo Bills in *The Music Man* (musical).

It's You I Love
Words and music by Antoine "Fats" Domino and Dave Bartholomew.
Travis Music Co.
Best-selling record by Fats Domino (Imperial).

Ivy Rose
Words and music by Al Hoffman and Dick Manning.
Roncom Music Co.

Jailhouse Rock
Words and music by Jerry Leiber and Mike Stoller.
Elvis Presley Music, Inc.
Introduced by Elvis Presley in *Jailhouse Rock* (film). Best-selling record by Elvis Presley (RCA Victor).

Jenny, Jenny
Words and music by Enotris Johnson and Richard Penniman.
Venice Music, Inc.
Best-selling record by Little Richard (Specialty).

Jim Dandy
Words and music by Lincoln Chase.
Raleigh Music, Inc./Progressive Music Publishing Co., Inc.
Best-selling record by LaVern Baker (Atlantic).

Jingle-Bell Rock
Words and music by Joe Beal and Jim Boothe.
Rosarita Music, Inc.
Best-selling record by Bobby Helms (Decca).

Jo-Ann
Words and music by John Cunningham and James Cunningham.
Figure Music, Inc.
Best-selling record by The Playmates (Roulette).

Joey's Song
Words by Sammy Gallop, music by Joe Reisman.
Shapiro, Bernstein & Co., Inc.
Best-selling record, instrumental, by Joe Reisman and his Orchestra (RCA Victor).

Joker, The
Words and music by Billy Myles.
Angel Music, Inc.
Best-selling record by Billy Myles (Ember).

Just Because
Words and music by Lloyd Price.
Pamco Music, Inc.
Best-selling record by Lloyd Price (ABC Paramount).

Just Between You and Me
Words and music by Lee Cathy and Jack Keller.
Paxwin Music Corp.
Best-selling record by The Chordettes (Cadence).

Just Born (To Be Your Baby)
Words and music by Luther Dixon and Billy Dawn Smith.
Paxwin Music Corp.
Best-selling record by Perry Como (RCA Victor).

Just My Luck
Words by Sheldon Harnick, music by Jerry Bock.
Sunbeam Music Corp.
Introduced by Mindy Carson in *Body Beautiful* (musical).

Just One More
Words and music by George Jones.
Starrite Publishing Co.
Best-selling record in 1956 by George Jones (Starday).

Katsumi Love Theme
Music by Franz Waxman.
M. Witmark & Sons.
Theme from *Sayonara* (film). Adapted version with lyrics by Carl Sigman entitled "The Mountains beyond the Moon."

Keep A-Knockin'
Words and music by Richard Penniman.
Venice Music, Inc./Duchess Music Corp.
Best-selling record by Little Richard (Specialty).

Kiss That Rocked the World, The
Words and music by Joe Sherman and Noel Sherman.
Edward B. Marks Music Corp.
Best-selling record by Dinah Shore (RCA Victor).

Kiss Them for Me
Words by Carroll Coates, music by Lionel Newman.
Miller Music Corp.
Introduced by The McGuire Sisters in *Kiss Them for Me* (film).

Kisses Sweeter Than Wine, see 1951.

Lasting Love
Words and music by Hunt Stevens and Jack Ackerman.
Travis Music Co.
Best-selling record by Sal Mineo (Epic).

Let It Be Me (French)
English words by Mann Curtis, French words by Pierre Delanoe, music by Gilbert Becaud.
France Music Co., 1955, 1957, 1960.
Original title, "Je T'Appartiens." Introduced by Gilbert Becaud. English-language version introduced by Jill Corey in *Climax* (television dramatic series). Best-selling record in 1960 by The Everly Brothers (Cadence).

Let Me Be Loved
Words and music by Jay Livingston and Ray Evans.
Livingston & Evans Music Co.
End-title theme from *The James Dean Story* (film).

Lida Rose
Words and music by Meredith Willson.
Frank Music Corp.
Introduced by Bill Spangenberg, Wayne Ward, Al Shea, and Vern Reed in *The Music Man* (musical).

Liechtensteiner Polka (German)
Words and music by Edmund Kötscher and R. Lindt.
Minerva Music (M. Bohm), Berlin, Germany/Burlington Music Corp.
Best-selling record by Will Glahe and his Orchestra (London).

Lights of Paris
Words by Charles Henderson, music by Hugo Friedhofer.
Robbins Music Corp.
Love theme from *The Sun Also Rises* (film).

Lilac Chiffon
Words by Peter Lind Hayes, music by Robert Allen.
Korwin Music, Inc.
Introduced by Julie London on *Kraft Theatre* (television dramatic show).

Lips of Wine
Words by Shirley Wolfe, music by Sy Soloway.
Mack Martin Music Co.
Best-selling record by Andy Williams (Cadence).

Little Biscuit
Words by E. Y. Harburg, music by Harold Arlen.
Harwin Music Corp.
Introduced by Ossie Davis and Josephine Premice in *Jamaica* (musical).

Little Bitty Pretty One
Words and music by Robert Byrd.
Recordo Music Publishers.
Best-selling record by Thurston Harris (Aladdin).

Little Darlin'
Words and music by Maurice Williams.
Excellorec Music Co.
Best-selling record by The Diamonds (Mercury).

Lonely Island
Words and music by Eden Ahbez.
Panther Music Corp.
Best-selling record by Sam Cooke (Keen).

Long Hot Summer, The
Words by Sammy Cahn, music by Alex North.
Leo Feist, Inc.
Introduced by Jimmie Rodgers, behind the titles, on the soundtrack of *The Long Hot Summer* (film).

Long Lonely Nights
Words and music by Lee Andrews, Bernice Davis, Douglas Henderson, and Mimi Uniman.
Arc Music Corp./G & H Music Publishing House, Inc.
Best-selling records by Lee Andrews and The Hearts (Chess) and Clyde McPhatter (Atlantic).

Look at 'er
Words and music by Bob Merrill.
Valyr Music Corp.
Introduced by George Wallace in *New Girl in Town* (musical).

Love Is a Golden Ring
Words and music by Richard Dehr, Frank Miller, and Terry Gilkyson.
Montclare Music Corp.
Best-selling record by Frankie Laine (Columbia).

Love Is Strange
Words and music by Ethel Smith and Mickey Baker.
Jonware Music Corp.
Best-selling record in 1956 and 1957 by Mickey and Sylvia (Groove and Vik).

Love Letters in the Sand, see 1931.

Love Me to Pieces
Words and music by Melvin Endsley.
Acuff-Rose Publications.
Introduced by Jill Corey on *Studio One Summer Theatre* (television dramatic show).

Love Theme from *A Farewell to Arms*
Words by Paul Francis Webster, music by Mario Nascimbene.
Leo Feist, Inc.
From *A Farewell to Arms* (film).

Lovely Night, A
Words by Oscar Hammerstein II, music by Richard Rodgers.
Williamson Music, Inc.
Introduced by Julie Andrews, Ilka Chase, Kaye Ballard, and Alice Ghostley in *Cinderella* (television musical).

Loving You
Words and music by Jerry Leiber and Mike Stoller.
Elvis Presley Music, Inc.
Best-selling record by Elvis Presley (RCA Victor).

Lucille
Words and music by Albert Collins and Richard Penniman.
Venice Music, Inc.
Best-selling record by Little Richard (Specialty).

Lucky Lips
Words and music by Jerry Leiber and Mike Stoller.
Tiger Music, Inc.
Best-selling record by Ruth Brown (Atlantic). International hit in 1963 by British singer Cliff Richard (Epic).

Lullaby in Blue
Words by Mack Gordon, music by Josef Myrow.
Blackstone Music, Inc.
Introduced by Eddie Fisher and Debbie Reynolds in *Bundle of Joy* (film).

Magic Moments
Words by Hal David, music by Burt F. Bacharach.
Famous Music Corp.
Best-selling record by Perry Como (RCA Victor).

Mama Guitar
Words by Budd Schulberg and Tom Glazer, music by Tom Glazer.
Remick Music Corp.
Introduced by Andy Griffith in *A Face in the Crowd* (film).

Mama Look a Booboo
Words and music by Lord Melody (Fitzroy Alexander).
Duchess Music Corp.
Best-selling record by Harry Belafonte (RCA Victor).

Man on Fire
Words by Paul Francis Webster, music by Sammy Fain.
Robbins Music Corp.
Title song of *Man on Fire* (film).

Mangos
Words by Sid Wayne, music by Dee Libbey.
Redd Evans Music Co.
Introduced by Micki Marlo in *Ziegfeld Follies* (revue). Best-selling record by Rosemary Clooney (Columbia).

Maria
Words by Stephen Sondheim, music by Leonard Bernstein.
Chappell & Co., Inc./G. Schirmer, Inc.
Introduced by Larry Kert in *West Side Story* (musical). Best-selling record by Johnny Mathis (Columbia).

Marian the Librarian
Words and music by Meredith Willson.
Frank Music Corp.
Introduced by Robert Preston and Boys and Girls in *The Music Man* (musical).

Marianne, see 1955.

Meaning of the Blues, The
Words and music by Bobby Troup and Leah Worth.
Northern Music Corp.
Introduced by Julie London in *The Great Man* (film).

Melodie d'Amour (French)
English words by Leo Johns, music by Henri Salvador.
Éditions Transatlantiques, Paris, France, 1949/Imperia Music Co., Ltd., London, England/Rayven Music Co., Inc.
From the French song, "Maladie d'Amour." English-language version introduced by Edmundo Ros and his Orchestra in England. Best-selling record by The Ames Brothers (RCA Victor).

Mi Casa, Su Casa (My House Is Your House)
Words and music by Al Hoffman and Dick Manning.
Post Music, Inc.
Best-selling record by Perry Como (RCA Victor).

Miss Ann
Words and music by Richard Penniman and Enotris Johnson.
Venice Music, Inc.
Best-selling record by Little Richard (Specialty).

Missing You, see 1955.

Mr. Lee
Words and music by Heather Dixon, Helen Gathers, Emma Ruth Pought, Laura Webb, and Jannie Pought.
Progressive Music Publishing Co., Inc.
Best-selling record by The Bobbettes (Atlantic).

Moonlight Swim
Words by Sylvia Dee, music by Ben Weisman.
Charles N. Daniels, Inc.
Best-selling records by Anthony Perkins (Epic) and Nick Noble (Mercury).

Mountains beyond the Moon, The
Words by Carl Sigman, music by Franz Waxman.
M. Witmark & Sons.
Adapted from "Katsumi Love Theme" from *Sayonara* (film).

My Heart Is an Open Book
Words by Hal David, music by Lee Pockriss.
Post Music, Inc.
Best-selling record by Carl Dobkins, Jr. (Decca).

My Heart Reminds Me, also known as **And That Reminds You (Italian)**
Words by Al Stillman, music by Camillo Bargoni.
Symphony House Music Publishers Corp.
Adapted from "Autumn Concerto" (see 1956). Best-selling record by Kay Starr (Capitol) entitled "My Heart Reminds Me." Best-selling record by Della Reese (Jubilee) entitled "And That Reminds You."

My, How the Time Goes By
Words by Carolyn Leigh, music by Cy Coleman.
Edwin H. Morris & Co., Inc.
Introduced by Patti Page.

My Shoes Keep Walking Back to You
Words and music by Lee Ross and Bob Wills.
Valley Publishers, Inc.
Best-selling record by Ray Price (Columbia).

My Special Angel
Words and music by Jimmy Duncan.
Blue Grass Music.
Best-selling record by Bobby Helms (Decca).

My Wish Came True
Words and music by Ivory Joe Hunter.
Desiard Music Co., Inc.
Best-selling record in 1959 by Elvis Presley (RCA Victor).

Napoleon
Words by E. Y. Harburg, music by Harold Arlen.
Harwin Music Corp.
A revised version of a song originally introduced in 1937 by June Clyde in *Hooray for What?* (revue). New song introduced by Lena Horne in *Jamaica* (musical).

Never Till Now
Words by Paul Francis Webster, music by Johnny Green.
Robbins Music Corp.
From *Raintree County* (film).

Next in Line
Words and music by Johnny Cash.
Knox Music, Inc.
Best-selling record by Johnny Cash (Sun).

Ninety-Nine Ways
Words and music by Anthony September.
Rice Mill Publishing Co., Inc.
Best-selling record by Tab Hunter (Dot).

No Love (But Your Love)
Words and music by Billy Myles.
Weiss & Barry, Inc.
Best-selling record by Johnny Mathis (Columbia).

No One Ever Tells You
Words and music by Carroll Coates and Hub Atwood.
Weiss & Barry, Inc.
Best-selling record by Frank Sinatra (Capitol).

Oh Julie
Words and music by Kenneth R. Moffitt and Noel Ball.
Excellorec Music Co.
Best-selling record by The Crescendos (Nasco).

On My Mind Again
Words and music by Dean Beard, Elmer Ray, and Slim Willet.
Slim Willet Songs.
Best-selling record by Billy Walker (Columbia).

One Hand, One Heart
Words by Stephen Sondheim, music by Leonard Bernstein.
Chappell & Co., Inc./G. Schirmer, Inc.
Introduced by Larry Kert and Carol Lawrence in *West Side Story* (musical).

One Is a Lonely Number
Words by Paul Francis Webster, music by Nicholas Brodszky.
Miller Music Corp.
Introduced by Tony Martin in *Let's Be Happy* (film).

One Night
Words and music by Dave Bartholomew and Pearl King.
Elvis Presley Music, Inc./Travis Music Co.
Best-selling record in 1958 by Elvis Presley (RCA Victor).

Only Trust Your Heart
Words by Sammy Cahn, music by Nicholas Brodszky.
Leo Feist, Inc.
Introduced by Dean Martin in *10,000 Bedrooms* (film).

Our Anniversary
Words and music by Jesse Murphy and James Freeman.
Angel Music Inc.
Best-selling record by The Five Satins (Ember).

Over the Mountain, across the Sea
Words and music by Rex Garvin.
Arc Music Corp.
Best-selling record by Johnnie and Joe (Chess).

Padre (French)
English words by Paul Francis Webster, French words by Jacques Larue, music by Alain Romans.
Éditions Pigalle, Paris, France/Charles N. Daniels, Inc.
Introduced in the United States by Lola Dee (Mercury). Best-selling record by Tony Arden.

Pamela Throws a Party
Music by Robert Allen.
Korwin Music, Inc.
Best-selling record, instrumental, by Joe Reisman and his Orchestra (RCA Victor).

Party Doll
Words and music by Jimmy Bowen and Buddy Knox.
Patricia Music Publishing Corp.
Best-selling records by Buddy Knox (Roulette) and Steve Lawrence (Coral).

Peanuts
Words and music by Joe Cook.
Cranford Music Corp.
Best-selling record by Little Joe and The Thrillers (Okeh).

Peggy Sue
Words and music by Jerry Allison, Buddy Holly, and Norman Petty.
Nor Va Jak Music, Inc.
Best-selling record in 1958 by Buddy Holly (Decca).

Plaything
Words and music by Samuel Underwood and Henry Underwood.
Renda Music Publishers/Pontra Music Corp.
Best-selling record by Ted Newman (Rev).

Please Don't Blame Me
Words and music by Marty Robbins.
Fred Rose Music, Inc.
Best-selling record by Marty Robbins (Columbia).

Please Say You Want Me
Words and music by Donald Hayes.
Blackwood Music, Inc.
Best-selling record by The Schoolboys (Okeh).

Poor Man's Roses, A (Or a Rich Man's Gold)
Words by Bob Hilliard, music by Milton De Lugg.
Shapiro, Bernstein & Co., Inc.
Best-selling record by Patti Page (Mercury).

Pretend You Don't See Her, see 1954.

Pretty To Walk With
Words by E. Y. Harburg, music by Harold Arlen.
Harwin Music Corp.
Introduced by Lena Horne in *Jamaica* (musical).

Promise Her Anything (But Give Her Love)
Words and music by Roy Alfred.
Planetary Music Publishing Corp.
Best-selling record by Dean Martin (Capitol).

Push the Button
Words by E. Y. Harburg, music by Harold Arlen.
Harwin Music Corp.
Introduced by Lena Horne in *Jamaica* (musical).

Put a Light in the Window
Words by Rhoda Roberts, music by Kenny Jacobson.
Planetary Music Publishing Corp.
Best-selling record by The Four Lads (Columbia).

Queen of the Senior Prom
Words and music by Ed Penny, Jack Richards, and Stella Lee.
Carnegie Music Corp.
Best-selling record by The Mills Brothers (Decca).

Rainbow
Words and music by Russ Hamilton.
Robbins Music Corp.
Best-selling record by Russ Hamilton (Kapp).

Rang, Tang, Ding, Dong
Words and music by Alvin Williams.
Bess Music Co.
Best-selling record by The Cellos (Apollo).

Raunchy
Music by Bill Justis, Jr. and Sidney Manker.
Hi-Lo Music, Inc.
Best-selling record, instrumental, by Bill Justis (Phillips-International).

Remember You're Mine
Words and music by Kal Mann and Bernie Lowe.
Lowe Music Corp.
Best-selling record by Pat Boone (Dot).

Return to Me (Ritorna a Me)
Words and music by Carmen Lombardo and Danny Di Minno.
Southern Music Publishing Co., Inc.
Best-selling record by Dean Martin (Capitol), sung in English and Italian.

Ride on a Rainbow, A
Words by Leo Robin, music by Jule Styne.
Robin-Styne Music Corp./Chappell & Co., Inc.
Introduced by Jane Powell in *Ruggles of Red Gap* (television musical).

Right Time, The
Words and music by Ozzie Cadena and Lew Herman.
Planemar Music Co.
Best-selling record in 1959 by Ray Charles (Atlantic).

River Kwai March, The (English)
Music by Malcolm Arnold.
Columbia Pictures Music Corp.
From *The Bridge on the River Kwai* (film). Best-selling record, in an arrangement that included the "Colonel Bogey March," by Mitch Miller and his Orchestra (Columbia).

Rock and Roll Music
Words and music by Chuck Berry.
Arc Music Corp.
Best-selling record by Chuck Berry (Chess).

Rock Your Little Baby To Sleep
Words and music by Buddy Knox.
Nom Music, Inc.
Best-selling record by Buddy Knox (Roulette).

Rock-a-Billy
Words and music by Woody Harris and Eddie V. Deane.
Joy Music, Inc.
Best-selling record by Guy Mitchell (Columbia).

Rosie Lee
Words and music by Jerry Carr.
Duchess Music Corp./Bridgeport Music.
Best-selling record by The Mello-Tones (Gee).

Savannah
Words by E. Y. Harburg, music by Harold Arlen.
Harwin Music Corp.
Introduced by Ricardo Montalban in *Jamaica* (musical).

Sayonara, see 1953.

School Day (Ring! Ring! Goes the Bell)
Words and music by Chuck Berry.
Arc Music Corp.
Best-selling record by Chuck Berry (Chess).

Search for Paradise
Words by Ned Washington and Lowell Thomas, music by Dimitri Tiomkin.
M. Witmark & Sons.
Theme from *Search for Paradise* (film).

Searchin'
Words and music by Jerry Leiber and Mike Stoller.
Tiger Music, Inc.
Best-selling record by The Coasters (Atco).

Send for Me
Words and music by Ollie Jones.
Paxwin Music Corp.
Best-selling record by Nat "King" Cole (Capitol).

Send Me Some Lovin'
Words by Leo Price and John S. Marascalco, music by Leo Price.
Venice Music, Inc.
Best-selling record by Little Richard (Specialty).

Seventy Six Trombones
Words and music by Meredith Willson.
Frank Music Corp.
Introduced by Robert Preston and Boys and Girls in *The Music Man* (musical).

Shake Me I Rattle (Squeeze Me I Cry)
Words and music by Hal Hackaday and Charles Naylor.
Coliseum Music, Inc.
Introduced by The Lennon Sisters. Best-selling record in 1963 by Marian Worth (Columbia).

Shenandoah Rose
Words by Paul Francis Webster, music by Jerry Livingston.
Planetary Music Publishing Corp.
Best-selling record by Johnny Desmond (M-G-M).

Short Fat Fannie
Words and music by Larry Williams.
Venice Music, Inc.
Best-selling record by Larry Williams (Specialty).

Short Shorts
Words by Bob Gaudio and Bill Dalton, music by Bill Crandall and Tom Austin.
Figure Music, Inc./Admiration Music, Inc.
Best-selling record by The Royal Teens (ABC Paramount).

Sick and Tired
Words and music by Dave Bartholomew and Christopher Kenner.
Travis Music Co.
Best-selling record by Fats Domino (Imperial).

Silhouettes
Words and music by Frank C. Slay, Jr. and Bob Crewe.
Regent Music Corp.
Best-selling record by The Rays (Cameo).

Sing Boy, Sing
Words and music by Tommy Sands and Rod McKuen.
Snyder Music Corp.
Introduced by Tommy Sands in *Sing Boy, Sing* (film).

Singing the Blues, see 1954.

Sittin' in the Balcony
Words and music by John Loudermilk.
Bentley Music Co.
Best-selling records by Johnny Dee (Colonial) and Eddie Cochran (Liberty).

Slow Walk
Words and music by Sil Austin, Irving Siders, and Connie Moore.
Norbay Music, Inc.
Best-selling records by Sil Austin (Mercury) and Bill Doggett (King).

So Rare, see 1937.

Soft Sands
Words by Carroll Coates, music by Lou Stein.
Weiss & Barry, Inc.
Best-selling record by The Rover Boys (Vik).

Something's Coming
Words by Stephen Sondheim, music by Leonard Bernstein.
Chappell & Co., Inc./G. Schirmer, Inc.
Introduced by Larry Kert in *West Side Story* (musical).

Somewhere
Words by Stephen Sondheim, music by Leonard Bernstein.
Chappell & Co., Inc./G. Schirmer, Inc.
Introduced by Reri Grist in *West Side Story* (musical).

Song of Raintree County, The
Words by Paul Francis Webster, music by Johnny Green.
Robbins Music Corp.
Introduced by Nat "King" Cole, behind the titles, on the soundtrack of *Raintree County* (film).

Souvenir d'Italie (Italian)
English words by Carl Sigman, Italian words by Scarnicci Tarabusi, music by L. Luttazzi.
Edizioni Musicali Liberty, Milan, Italy, 1954/Leeds Music Corp.
Featured in *Souvenir d'Italie* (Italian film) and in *Danger, Girl at Play* (English film).

Stairway to the Sea (Italian)
English words by Albert A. Beach, Italian words by Enzo Bonagura, music by Giuseppe Cioffi.
Italian Book Co., 1948/Leeds Music Corp.
Original title, "Scalinatella." English-language version introduced by Johnny Mathis (Columbia).

Start Movin'
Words and music by David Hill and Bobby Stevenson.
Travis Music Co.
Best-selling record by Sal Mineo (Epic).

Stay Here with Me (Italian)
English words by Milt Gabler, Italian words by Verde and Domenico Modugno, music by Domenico Modugno.
Edizioni Curci, Milan, Italy, 1957, 1958, 1960/Leeds Music Corp.
Performed under its original title, "Resta Cu'mme," in *Bay of Naples* (film).

Stolen Moments, see 1954.

Stood Up
Words and music by Dub Dickerson and Erma Herrold.
Travis Music Co.
Best-selling record in 1958 by Ricky Nelson (Imperial).

Stop the World (And Let Me Off)
Words by W. S. Stevenson, music by Carl Belew.
Four Star Sales Co.
Best-selling record in 1958 by Johnnie and Jack (RCA Victor).

Story of My Life, The
Words by Hal David, music by Burt F. Bacharach.
Famous Music Corp.
Best-selling record by Marty Robbins (Columbia).

Stroll, The
Words and music by Clyde Otis and Nancy Lee.
Vogue Music, Inc.
Best-selling record in 1958 by The Diamonds (Mercury).

Sugar Moon
Words and music by Danny Wolf.
Gallatin Music Corp.
Best-selling record in 1958 by Pat Boone (Dot).

Summer Love
Words and music by George Weiss.
Valando Music Corp.
Best-selling record by Joni James (M-G-M).

Susie Q
Words and music by Dale Hawkins, Stanley Lewis, and Eleanor Broadwater.
Arc Music Corp.
Best-selling record by Dale Hawkins (Checker).

Swanee River Rock
Words and music by Ray Charles.
Progressive Music Publishing Co., Inc.
Based on "The Old Folks at Home." Best-selling record by Ray Charles (Atlantic).

Take It Slow, Joe
Words by E. Y. Harburg, music by Harold Arlen.
Harwin Music Corp.
Introduced by Lena Horne in *Jamaica* (musical).

Tales of Wells Fargo
Words and music by Mort Greene and Stanley J. Wilson.
Marlen Music Co.
Theme of *Tales of Wells Fargo* (television series).

Tammy
Words and music by Jay Livingston and Ray Evans.
Northern Music Corp.
Introduced by Debbie Reynolds in *Tammy and the Bachelor* (film). Nominated for Academy Award, 1957. Best-selling records by The Ames Brothers (RCA Victor) and Debbie Reynolds (Coral).

Teacher, Teacher
Words by Al Stillman, music by Robert Allen.
Korwin Music, Inc.
Best-selling record in 1958 by Johnny Mathis (Columbia).

(Let Me Be Your) Teddy Bear
Words and music by Bernie Lowe and Kal Mann.
Gladys Music, Inc.
Introduced by Elvis Presley in *Loving You* (film). Best-selling record by Elvis Presley (RCA Victor).

Teenager's Romance, A
Words and music by David Gillam.
Aztec Music, Inc.
Best-selling record by Ricky Nelson (Verve).

That Face
Words by Alan Bergman and Lew Spence, music by Lew Spence.
Empress Music, Inc.
Introduced by Fred Astaire.

That'll Be the Day
Words and music by Jerry Allison, Buddy Holly, and Norman Petty.
Nor Va Jak Music, Inc.
Best-selling record by Buddy Holly and The Crickets (Brunswick).

That's Why
Words and music by Berry Gordy, Jr., Gwendolyn Gordy, and Tyran Carlo.
Pearl Music Co., Inc.
Best-selling record in 1959 by Jackie Wilson (Brunswick).

That's Why I Was Born
Words and music by O. O. Merritt and Vin Roddie.
The Janfra Music Publishing Co./Planetary Music Publishing Corp.
Introduced by Janice Harper.

There Is Something on Your Mind
Words and music by Cecil "Big Jay" McNeely.
Mercedes Music Co.
Best-selling record in 1959 by Big Jim McNeely (Swingin').

3:10 to Yuma
Words by Ned Washington, music by George W. Duning.
Columbia Pictures Music Corp.
Introduced by Frankie Laine, behind the titles, on the soundtrack of *3:10 to Yuma* (film).

Three Ways To Love You
Words and music by Eve Jay and Julius Dixon.
Travis Music Co.
Best-selling record by Kitty Wells (Decca).

Through the Eyes of Love
Words by Albert A. Beach, music by Sid Lippman.
Pickwick Music Corp.
Introduced by Doris Day (Columbia).

Till
Words by Carl Sigman, music by Charles Danvers.
Chappell & Co., Inc.
Introduced by Tony Bennett (Columbia).

Till There Was You
Words and music by Meredith Willson.
Frank Music Corp.
Introduced by Barbara Cook and Robert Preston in *The Music Man* (musical).

To Be in Love!
Words and music by Bart Howard.
Wintergreen Music, Inc.
Popularized by Johnny Mathis.

To the Aisle, also known as **The Aisle**
Words and music by Billy Dawn Smith and Stuart Wiener.
Wemar Music Corp.
Best-selling record by The Five Satins (Ember).

Tonight
Words by Stephen Sondheim, music by Leonard Bernstein.
Chappell & Co., Inc./G. Schirmer, Inc.
Introduced by Larry Kert and Carol Lawrence in *West Side Story* (musical). Best-selling record, instrumental, in 1961 by Ferrante and Teicher (United Artists).

Tonight My Heart She Is (Will Be) Crying
Words and music by Vic Abrams, Irving Reid, and Moishe.
Nom Music, Inc.
Introduced by El Boy with Ralph Sayho and his Calypso Singers. Best-selling record by Eddie Fisher (RCA Victor).

Treat Me Nice
Words and music by Mike Stoller and Jerry Leiber.
Elvis Presley Music, Inc.
Introduced by Elvis Presley in *Jailhouse Rock* (film).

Two Shadows on Your Window
Words and music by Mickey Baker and Robert Taylor.
Hill and Range Songs, Inc./Ben-Ghazi Enterprises, Inc.
Best-selling record by Jim Reeves (RCA Victor).

Valley of Tears
Words and music by Antoine "Fats" Domino and Dave Bartholomew.
Travis Music Co.
Best-selling record by Fats Domino (Imperial).

Very Special Love, A
Words and music by Robert Allen.
Korwin Music, Inc.
Best-selling record by Johnny Nash (ABC Paramount).

Wagon Train
Words and music by Henri René and Bob Russell.
Marlen Music Co.
Title theme from *Wagon Train* (television series).

Waitin' in School
Words and music by Johnny Burnette and Dorsey Burnette.
Travis Music Co.
Best-selling record in 1958 by Ricky Nelson (Imperial).

Wake Up, Little Susie
Words and music by Boudleaux Bryant and Felice Bryant.
Acuff-Rose Publications.
Best-selling record by The Everly Brothers (Cadence).

Waltz for a Ball
Music by Richard Rodgers.
Williamson Music, Inc.
Introduced in *Cinderella* (television musical).

What Good Does It Do?
Words by E. Y. Harburg, music by Harold Arlen.
Harwin Music Corp.
Introduced by Ricardo Montalban, Ossie Davis, and Austine Rios in *Jamaica* (musical).

Whispering Bells
Words and music by C. E. Quick.
Gil Music Corp./Fee Bee Music.
Best-selling record by The Del Vikings (Dot).

White Silver Sands
Words and music by Charles G. "Red" Matthews.
Sharina Music Co.
First recorded by Dave Gardner (O-J). Best-selling record by Don Rondo (Jubilee). Revived in 1960 with best-selling record, instrumental, by Bill Black's Combo (Hi).

White Sport Coat, A (And a Pink Carnation)
Words and music by Marty Robbins.
Fred Rose Music, Inc.
Best-selling record by Marty Robbins (Columbia).

Whole Lot-ta Shakin' Goin' On
Words and music by Dave Williams and Sunny David.
Valley Publishers, Inc./Cherio Music Publishers, Inc.
Best-selling record by Jerry Lee Lewis (Sun).

Why Baby Why
Words and music by Luther Dixon and Larry Harrison.
Paxwin Music Corp.
Best-selling record by Pat Boone (Dot).

Why Do You Have To Go
Words and music by Verne Allison and Ewart G. Abner, Jr.
Conrad Publishing Co., Inc.
Best-selling record by The Dells (Vee Jay).

Why Don't They Understand
Words and music by Jack Fishman and Joe Henderson.
Henderson Music, Ltd., London, England/Hollis Music, Inc.
Best-selling record in 1958 by George Hamilton IV (ABC Paramount).

Why Why
Words and music by Wayne P. Walker, Mel Tillis, and George Sherry.
Cedarwood Publishing Co., Inc.
Best-selling record by Carl Smith (Columbia).

Wild Is the Wind
Words by Ned Washington, music by Dimitri Tiomkin.
Ross Jungnickel, Inc.
Introduced in *Wild Is the Wind* (film). Nominated for Academy Award, 1957. Best-selling record by Johnny Mathis (Columbia).

Will I Ever Tell You
Words and music by Meredith Willson.
Frank Music Corp.
Introduced by Barbara Cook in *The Music Man* (musical).

Witchcraft
Words by Carolyn Leigh, music by Cy Coleman.
Edwin H. Morris & Co., Inc.
Introduced by Gerry Matthews in Julius Monk's *Take Five* (nightclub revue). Best-selling record by Frank Sinatra (Capitol).

With All My Heart
English and Italian words by Bob Marcucci and Pete De Angelis, music by Pete De Angelis.
Debmar Publishing Co., Inc.
Best-selling record by Jodie Sands (Chancellor).

With You on My Mind
Words by Charlotte Hawkins, music by Nat "King" Cole.
Muirfield Music Corp.
Best-selling record by Nat "King" Cole (Capitol).

Wondering
Words and music by Jack Schafer.
Egap Music, Inc.
Best-selling record by Patti Page (Mercury).

Yellow Bird
Words and music by Norman Luboff, Marilyn Keith, and Alan Bergman.
Walton Music Corp./Frank Music Corp.
Adapted from a West Indian folk song. Introduced by The Norman Luboff Choir. Best-selling record, instrumental, in 1961 by Arthur Lyman (Hi-Fi).

Yes Tonight, Josephine
Words and music by Winfield Scott and Dorothy Goodman.
Robert Astor Music Co., Inc.
Best-selling record by Johnnie Ray (Columbia).

You Need Hands (English)
Words and music by Roy Irwin.
Lakeview Music Co., London, England/Leeds Music Corp.
Best-selling record by Eydie Gormé (ABC Paramount).

You Send Me
Words and music by L. C. Cooke.
Higuera Publishing Co.
Best-selling record by Sam Cooke (Keen).

Young Blood
Words and music by Jerry Leiber, Mike Stoller, and Doc Pomus.
Tiger Music, Inc.
Best-selling record by The Coasters (Atco).

Your True Love
Words and music by Carl Lee Perkins.
Knox Music, Inc.
Best-selling record by Carl Perkins (Sun).

1958

All Grown Up
Words and music by Howard Hausey.
Buna Music Corp.
Best-selling record by Johnny Horton (Columbia).

All I Have To Do Is Dream
Words and music by Boudleaux Bryant.
Acuff-Rose Publications.
Best-selling record by The Everly Brothers (Cadence).

All Over Again
Words and music by Johnny Cash.
Johnny Cash Music, Inc.
Best-selling record by Johnny Cash (Columbia).

All the Time
Words and music by Jay Livingston and Ray Evans.
Livingston & Evans, Inc.
Introduced by Tony Randall and Jacquelyn McKeever in *Oh Captain!* (musical).

All-American Boy, The
Words and music by Bill Parsons and Orville Lunsford.
Buckeye Music, Inc.
Best-selling record by Bill Parsons (Fraternity).

Almost in Your Arms, also known as **Love Song from *Houseboat***
Words and music by Jay Livingston and Ray Evans.
Paramount Music Corp.
Introduced by Sophia Loren in *Houseboat* (film). Nominated for Academy Award, 1958.

Alone with You
Words and music by Faron Young, Lester Vanadore, and Roy Drusky.
Lancaster Music Publications, Inc.
Best-selling record by Faron Young (Capitol).

Am I That Easy To Forget?
Words and music by Carl Belew, W. S. Stevenson, and Shelby Singleton.
Four Star Sales Co., Inc.
Best-selling record in 1959 by Carl Belew (Decca).

Angel Baby
Words and music by Joe Penny.
Armo Music Corp.
Best-selling record by Dean Martin (Capitol).

Angel Smile
Words and music by Luther Dixon, Billy Dawn Smith, and Bert Keyes.
Paxwin Music Corp.
Best-selling record by Nat "King" Cole (Capitol).

Another Time, Another Place
Words and music by Jay Livingston and Ray Evans.
Famous Music Corp.
Introduced in *Another Time, Another Place* (film). Best-selling record by Don Cherry (Columbia).

Are You Really Mine?
Words and music by Al Hoffman, Dick Manning, and Mark Markwell.
Planetary Music Publishing Corp.
Best-selling record by Jimmie Rodgers (Roulette).

At the End of a Rainbow, see The End.

Baby Talk
Words and music by Melvin H. Schwartz.
Admiration Music, Inc./Ultra Music/Hillary Music, Inc.
Best-selling record by Jan and Dean (Dore).

Ballad of a Teenage Queen
Words and music by Jack H. Clement.
Knox Music, Inc.
Best-selling record by Johnny Cash (Sun).

Ballad of Paladin
Words and music by Johnny Western, Richard Boone, and Sam Rolfe.
Time Music Co., Inc.
Introduced by Johnny Western in *Have Gun, Will Travel* (television series).

Beats There a Heart So True
Words and music by Noel Sherman and Jack Keller.
Nom Music, Inc.
Best-selling record by Perry Como (RCA Victor).

Beep, Beep
Words and music by Donald Claps and Carl Cicchetti.
Patricia Music Publishing Corp./H & L Music Corp.
Best-selling record by The Playmates (Roulette).

Believe What You Say
Words and music by Johnny Burnette and Dorsey Burnette.
Eric Music, Inc.
Best-selling record by Ricky Nelson (Imperial).

Big Daddy
Words by Peter Udell, music by Lee Pockriss.
Empress Music, Inc.
Introduced in *Senior Prom* (film). Best-selling record by Jill Corey (Columbia).

Big Guitar, The
Music by Francis D. De Rosa, Robert Genovese, and Larry Coleman.
Time Music Co., Inc.
Best-selling record, instrumental, by Frank De Rosa and his D Men (Dot).

Big Man
Words and music by Glen Larson and Bruce Belland.
Beechwood Music Corp.
Best-selling record by The Four Preps (Capitol).

Billy Bayou
Words and music by Roger Miller.
Tree Publishing Co., Inc.
Best-selling record by Jim Reeves (RCA Victor).

Bimbombey
Words and music by Mack David, Hugo Peretti, and Luigi Creatore.
Planetary Music Publishing Corp.
Best-selling record by Jimmie Rodgers (Roulette).

Bing! Bang! Bong!
Words and music by Jay Livingston and Ray Evans.
Paramount Music Corp.
Introduced by Sophia Loren in *Houseboat* (film).

Bird Dog
Words and music by Boudleaux Bryant.
Acuff-Rose Publications.
Best-selling record by The Everly Brothers (Cadence).

Blob, The
Words by Mack David, music by Burt F. Bacharach.
Famous Music Corp.
From *The Blob* (film). Best-selling record by The Five Blobs (pseudonym for the multi-tracked voice of Bernie Knee) (Columbia).

Bluebell
Words by Paul Francis Webster, music by Jerry Livingston.
Frank Music Corp.
Best-selling record by Mitch Miller and his Orchestra and Chorus (Columbia).

Born Too Late
Words by Fred Tobias, music by Charles Strouse.
Mansion Music Corp.
Best-selling record by The Poni Tails (ABC Paramount).

Breathless
Words and music by Otis Blackwell.
Home Folks Music, Inc./Obie Music, Inc.
Best-selling record by Jerry Lee Lewis (Sun).

Cannon Ball
Music by Duane Eddy and Lee Hazlewood.
Gregmark Music Co.
Best-selling record, instrumental, in 1959 by Duane Eddy (Jamie).

Carol
Words and music by Chuck Berry.
Arc Music Corp.
Best-selling record by Chuck Berry (Chess).

Certain Smile, A
Words by Paul Francis Webster, music by Sammy Fain.
Miller Music Corp.
Introduced by Johnny Mathis in *A Certain Smile* (film). Nominated for Academy Award, 1958.

Cerveza
Music by Boots Brown.
Michele Publishing Co.
Best-selling record, instrumental, by Boots Brown (RCA Victor).

Cha-hua-hua
Music by Joe Lubin and I. J. Roth.
Daywin Music, Inc.
Best-selling record, instrumental, by The Pets (Arwin).

Chanson d'Amour
Words and music by Wayne Shanklin.
Thunderbird Music, Inc.
First recorded by Art and Dotty Todd (Era). Best-selling record by The Fontane Sisters (Dot).

Chantilly Lace
Words and music by J. P. Richardson.
Glad Music Co.
Best-selling record by Big Bopper (pseudonym for Richardson) (Mercury).

Children's Marching Song, The, also known as **This Old Man** (English)
Words and music adapted and arranged by Malcolm Arnold.
B. Feldman & Co., Ltd., London, England/Miller Music Corp.
Introduced by Ingrid Bergman and the Orphans' Chorus in *The Inn of the Sixth Happiness* (film). Best-selling record in 1959 by Mitch Miller and his Orchestra and Chorus (Columbia).

Chipmunk Song, The (Christmas Don't Be Late)
Words and music by Ross Bagdasarian.
Monarch Music Corp.
Best-selling record by David Seville (pseudonym for Bagdasarian) and The Chipmunks (Liberty).

City Lights
Words and music by Bill Anderson.
TNT Music, Inc.
Best-selling record by Ray Price (Columbia).

Closer Than a Kiss
Words by Sammy Cahn, music by James Van Heusen.
Edwin H. Morris & Co., Inc.
First recording by Vic Damone (Columbia).

C'mon Everybody
Words and music by Eddie Cochran and Jerry Capehart.
Metric Music Co.
Best-selling record by Eddie Cochran (Liberty).

Colt .45
Words by Douglas Heyes, music by Hal Hopper.
Remick Music Corp.
Theme from *Colt .45* (television series).

Come Prima, also known as **For the First Time** (Italian)
English words by Buck Ram, Italian words by M. Panzeri, music by Di Paola and Taccani.
Cicala Casa Editrice Musicale/A.M.C., Inc.
Introduced by Domenico Modugno. Best-selling Italian version by Tony Dalardo (Mercury).

Come to Me
Words and music by Marvin Johnson and Berry Gordy, Jr.
Jobete Music Co., Inc.
Best-selling record in 1959 by Marv Johnson (United Artists).

Come to the Supermarket (In Old Peking)
Words and music by Cole Porter.
Buxton Hill Music Corp.
Introduced by Cyril Ritchard in *Aladdin* (television production).

Come Walk with Me
Words and music by Burkett Graves.
Acuff-Rose Publications.
Best-selling record in 1959 by Stoney Cooper and Wilma Lee (Hickory).

Country Music Is Here To Stay
Words and music by Ferlin Husky.
Bee Gee Music Publications, Inc.
Best-selling record by Simon Crum (Capitol).

Crazy Love
Words and music by Paul Anka.
Spanka Music Corp.
Best-selling record by Paul Anka (ABC Paramount).

Curtain in the Window
Words and music by Lee Ross.
Pamper Music, Inc.
Best-selling record by Ray Price (Columbia).

Dance, Everyone, Dance
Words and musical adaptation by Sid Danoff.
Bourne, Inc.
Adapted from the Israeli song, "Hava Nagila." Best-selling record by Betty Madigan (Coral).

Dance Only with Me
Words by Betty Comden and Adolph Green, music by Jule Styne.
Stratford Music Corp.
Introduced by Vivian Blaine and Mitchell Gregg in *Say, Darling* (musical).

Dede Dinah
Words by Bob Marcucci, music by Peter De Angelis.
Debmar Publishing Co.
Best-selling record by Frankie Avalon (Chancellor).

Devoted to You
Words and music by Boudleaux Bryant.
Acuff-Rose Publications.
Best-selling record by The Everly Brothers (Cadence).

Diary, The
Words by Howard Greenfield, music by Neil Sedaka.
Screen Gems-Columbia Music, Inc.
Best-selling record in 1959 by Neil Sedaka (RCA Victor).

Dis-Donc, Dis-Donc (French)
English lyrics by Julian More, David Heneker, and Monty Norman, French lyrics by Alexandre Breffort, music by Marguerite Monnot.
Éditions Micro, Paris, France, 1956/Trafalgar Music Ltd., London, England/Chappell & Co., Inc.
Original French title, "Ah! Dis-Donc." Introduced by Colette Renard in the Paris production and by Elizabeth Seal in the London (1958) and New York (1960) productions of *Irma la Douce* (musical).

Do You Want To Dance?
Words and music by Bobby Freeman.
Clockus Music, Inc.
Best-selling record by Bobby Freeman (Josie).

Doncha' Think It's Time
Words and music by Clyde Otis and Willie Dixon.
Elvis Presley Music, Inc.
Best-selling record by Elvis Presley (RCA Victor).

Donde Esta Santa Claus? (Where Is Santa Claus?)
Words and music by Rod Parker, Al Greiner, and George Scheck.
Ragtime Music Corp.
Best-selling record by Augie Rios (Metro).

Donna
Words and music by Ritchie Valens.
Kemo Music Co.
Best-selling record by Ritchie Valens (Del-Fi).

Don't Ask Me Why
Words by Fred Wise, music by Ben Weisman.
Gladys Music, Inc.
Introduced by Elvis Presley in *King Creole* (film).

Don't Pity Me
Words by Sid Jacobson, music by Lou Stallman.
We Three Music, Inc.
Best-selling record by Dion and The Belmonts (Laurie).

Don't Take Your Guns to Town
Words and music by Johnny Cash.
Johnny Cash Music, Inc.
Best-selling record in 1959 by Johnny Cash (Columbia).

Dormi, Dormi, Dormi
Words by Sammy Cahn, music by Harry Warren.
Paramount Music Corp.
From *Rock-a-Bye Baby* (film). Best-selling record by Eydie Gormé (ABC Paramount).

Down the Aisle of Love
Words and music by The Quin-Tones.
Myra Music Co./Carney Music, Inc.
Best-selling record by The Quin-Tones (Hunt).

Drifting
Words by Kim Gannon, music by Bronislau Kaper.
M. Witmark & Sons.
Adapted from the theme from *Auntie Mame* (film). Introduced by David Allen.

Duke's Place
Words by Ruth Roberts, Bill Katz, and Robert Thiele, music by Duke Ellington.
Robbins Music Corp.
Based on "C Jam Blues," by Ellington, copyrighted in 1942.

Early in the Morning
Words and music by Bobby Darin and Woody Harris.
Post Music, Inc.
Best-selling record by Bobby Darin and The Rinky Dinks (Atco).

El Rancho Rock (Mexican)
Words by Ben Raleigh, music by Silvano R. Ramos.
Edward B. Marks Music Corp.
Based on "Alla en el Rancho Grande," copyrighted in 1934. Best-selling record by The Champs (Challenge).

Enchanted Island
Words by Al Stillman, music by Robert Allen.
Korwin Music, Inc.
Introduced by The Four Lads (Columbia).

(At) End, The (Of a Rainbow)
Words by Sid Jacobson, music by Jimmy Krondes.
Criterion Music Corp.
Best-selling record by Earl Grant (Decca).

Endless Sleep
Words and music by Jody Reynolds and Dolores Nance.
Johnstone-Montei, Inc./Elizabeth Music.
Best-selling record by Jody Reynolds (Demon).

Everybody Loves a Lover
Words by Richard Adler, music by Robert Allen.
Korwin Music, Inc.
Best-selling record by Doris Day (Columbia).

Fallin'
Words by Howard Greenfield, music by Neil Sedaka.
Screen Gems-Columbia Music, Inc.
Best-selling record by Connie Francis (M-G-M).

Falling Back to You
Words and music by Billy Phillips and Webb Pierce.
Cedarwood Publishing Co., Inc.
Best-selling record by Webb Pierce (Decca).

Fan Tan Fannie
Words by Oscar Hammerstein II, music by Richard Rodgers.
Williamson Music, Inc.
Introduced by Anita Ellis in *Flower Drum Song* (musical).

Femininity
Words and music by Jay Livingston and Ray Evans.
Livingston & Evans, Inc.
Introduced by Abbe Lane in *Oh Captain!* (musical).

Fever, see 1956.

Firefly
Words by Carolyn Leigh, music by Cy Coleman.
Edwin H. Morris & Co., Inc.
Best-selling record by Tony Bennett (Columbia).

First Anniversary
Words and music by Aaron Schroeder and Sid Wayne.
Planetary Music Publishing Corp.
Best-selling record in 1959 by Cathy Carr (Roulette).

For My Good Fortune
Words and music by Otis Blackwell and Bobby Stevenson.
Roosevelt Music Co., Inc.
Best-selling record by Pat Boone (Dot).

For the First Time, see **Come Prima.**

For Your Love
Words and music by Ed Townsend.
Beechwood Music Corp.
Best-selling record by Ed Townsend (Capitol).

Forbidden, see **Verboten!**

Forget Me Not
Words by Larry Kolber, music by Larry Martin.
Screen Gems-Columbia Music, Inc.
Best-selling record by The Kalin Twins (Decca).

Gee, but It's Lonely
Words and music by Phil Everly.
Acuff-Rose Publications.
Best-selling record by Pat Boone (Dot).

Gigi
Words by Alan Jay Lerner, music by Frederick Loewe.
Mara-Lane Music Corp.
Introduced by Louis Jourdan in *Gigi* (film). Academy Award-winning song, 1958. Best-selling record by Vic Damone (Columbia).

Ginger Bread
Words and music by Clint Ballard, Jr. and Hank Hunter.
Jimskip Music, Inc./Rambed Music Publishing Co., Inc.
Best-selling record by Frankie Avalon (Chancellor).

Girl on Page 44
Words by Richard Adler, music by Robert Allen.
Korwin Music, Inc.
Best-selling record by The Four Lads (Columbia).

Give It All You've Got
Words and music by Jay Livingston and Ray Evans.
Livingston & Evans, Inc.
Introduced by Susan Johnson in *Oh Captain!* (musical).

Give Myself a Party
Words and music by Don Gibson.
Acuff-Rose Publications.
Best-selling record by Don Gibson (RCA Victor).

Goodbye Baby
Words and music by Jack Scott.
Starfire Music Corp./Peer International Corp.
Best-selling record in 1959 by Jack Scott (Carlton).

Gotta Travel On
Words and music by Paul Clayton, Larry Ehrlich, Dave Lazer, Fred Hellerman, Pete Seeger, Lee Hays, and Ronnie Gilbert.
Sanga Music, Inc.
Best-selling record by Billy Grammer (Monument).

Grant Avenue
Words by Oscar Hammerstein II, music by Richard Rodgers.
Williamson Music, Inc.
Introduced by Pat Suzuki in *Flower Drum Song* (musical).

Guess Things Happen That Way
Words and music by Jack Clement.
Knox Music, Inc.
Best-selling record by Johnny Cash (Sun).

Half a Mind
Words and music by Roger Miller.
Tree Publishing Co., Inc.
Best-selling record by Ernest Tubb (Decca).

Hang Up My Rock and Roll Shoes
Words and music by Chuck Willis.
Rush Music Corp.
Best-selling record by Chuck Willis (Atlantic).

Hanging Tree, The
Words by Mack David, music by Jerry Livingston.
M. Witmark & Sons.
Introduced by Marty Robbins in *The Hanging Tree* (film). Nominated for Academy Award, 1959.

Hard Headed Woman
Words and music by Claude De Metruis.
Gladys Music, Inc.
Introduced by Elvis Presley in *King Creole* (film).

Hawaiian Wedding Song, The (Hawaiian)
English words by Al Hoffman and Dick Manning, Hawaiian words and music by Charles E. King.
Pickwick Music Corp.
"Ke Kali Nei Au," original Hawaiian version, published in 1928. Best-selling record in 1958 and 1959 by Andy Williams (Cadence).

Hibiscus
Words by Carolyn Leigh, music by Cy Coleman.
Melrose Music Corp.
Introduced by Jo Stafford (Columbia).

Hideaway
Words and music by Robert Goodman.
Jack Gold Music Co.
Best-selling record by The Esquires (Paris).

High School Confidential
Words and music by Ron Hargrave and Jerry Lee Lewis.
Penron Music Publications.
Introduced by Jerry Lee Lewis in *High School Confidential* (film).

Hot Spell
Words by Mack David, music by Burt F. Bacharach.
Famous Music Corp.
"Inspired by" *Hot Spell* (film).

House of Bamboo (English)
Words and music by Bill Crompton and Norman Murrells.
Sydney Bron Music Co., London, England/Criterion Music Corp.
Best-selling record by Earl Grant (Decca).

How the Time Flies
Words and music by Tommy Jarrett.
Thunderbird Music, Inc.
Best-selling record by Jerry Wallace (Challenge).

Hula Hoop Song, The
Words and music by Donna Kohler and Carl Maduri.
Shapiro, Bernstein & Co., Inc.
Best-selling record by Georgia Gibbs (Mercury).

Hundred Million Miracles, A
Words by Oscar Hammerstein II, music by Richard Rodgers.
Williamson Music, Inc.
Introduced by Miyoshi Umeki, Conrad Yama, Keye Luke, Juanita Hall, and Rose Quong in *Flower Drum Song* (musical).

I Adore You
Words and music by Cole Porter.
Buxton Hill Music Corp.
Introduced by Sal Mineo and Anna Maria Alberghetti in *Aladdin* (television production).

I Can't Get You out of My Heart (Ti Amo—Ti Voglio Amor)
Words and music by Danny Di Minno and Jimmy Crane.
Southern Music Publishing Co., Inc.
Best-selling record by Al Martino (20th Century-Fox).

I Can't Stop Loving You
Words and music by Don Gibson.
Acuff-Rose Publications.
Introduced by Don Gibson. Best-selling records in 1958 by Kitty Wells (Decca) and in 1962 by Ray Charles (ABC Paramount).

I Cried a Tear
Words and music by Al Julia and Fred Jay.
Progressive Music Publishing Co., Inc.
Best-selling record by LaVern Baker (Atlantic).

I Enjoy Being a Girl
Words by Oscar Hammerstein II, music by Richard Rodgers.
Williamson Music, Inc.
Introduced by Miyoshi Umeki in *Flower Drum Song* (musical).

I Got a Feeling
Words and music by Baker Knight.
Eric Music, Inc.
Best-selling record by Ricky Nelson (Imperial).

I Got Stung
Words and music by Aaron Schroeder and David Hill.
Gladys Music, Inc.
Best-selling record by Elvis Presley (RCA Victor).

I Had a Dream
Words and music by Ray Charles and Ricky Harper.
Progressive Music Publishing Co., Inc.
Best-selling record by Ray Charles (Atlantic).

I May Never Pass This Way Again
Words and music by Murray Wizell and Irving Melsher.
Oval Music Co.
Popularized in England with best-selling record by Robert Earl (Philips). Best-selling record in the United States by Perry Como (RCA Victor).

I Remember It Well
Words by Alan Jay Lerner, music by Frederick Loewe.
Mara-Lane Music Corp.
Introduced by Maurice Chevalier and Hermione Gingold in *Gigi* (film).

I Wonder Why
Words by Ricardo Weeks, music by Melvin Anderson.
Schwartz Music Co., Inc.
Best-selling record by Dion and The Belmonts (Laurie).

If Dreams Come True
Words by Al Stillman, music by Robert Allen.
Korwin Music, Inc.
Best-selling record by Pat Boone (Dot).

If I Had a Hammer

Words and music by Lee Hays and Pete Seeger.
Ludlow Music, Inc.
A "modern" folk song. Introduced by The Weavers. Revived in 1962 with best-selling record by Peter, Paul, and Mary (Warner Brothers) and in 1963 with best-selling record by Trini Lopez (Reprise).

I'll Wait for You

Words by Bob Marcucci, music by Peter De Angelis.
Debmar Publishing Co., Inc.
Best-selling record by Frankie Avalon (Chancellor).

I'm a Man

Words and music by Doc Pomus and Mort Shuman.
Rio Grande Music, Inc.
Best-selling record by Fabian (Chancellor).

I'm Glad I'm Not Young Anymore

Words by Alan Jay Lerner, music by Frederick Loewe.
Mara-Lane Music Corp.
Introduced by Maurice Chevalier in *Gigi* (film).

Indiscreet

Words by Sammy Cahn, music by James Van Heusen.
Edwin H. Morris & Co., Inc.
Based on the love theme from *Indiscreet* (film).

Irma la Douce (French)

English lyrics by Julian More, David Heneker, and Monty Norman, French lyrics by Alexandre Breffort, music by Marguerite Monnot.
Éditions Micro, Paris, France, 1956/Trafalgar Music Ltd., London, England/Chappell & Co., Inc.
Introduced by Colette Renard in the Paris production and by Elizabeth Seal in the London (1958) and New York (1960) productions of *Irma la Douce* (musical.)

It Amazes Me

Words by Carolyn Leigh, music by Cy Coleman.
Edwin H. Morris & Co., Inc.
Introduced on records by Tony Bennett (Columbia).

It Doesn't Matter Any More

Words and music by Paul Anka.
Spanka Music Corp.
Best-selling record in 1959 by Buddy Holly (Coral).

Itchy Twitchy Feeling

Words and music by James Oliver.
Saturn Music, Inc./Emkay Music.
Best-selling record by Bobby Hendricks (Sue).

It's All in the Game, see 1951.

It's Just a Matter of Time
Words and music by Brook Benton, Belford Hendricks, and Clyde Otis.
Eden Music, Inc.
Best-selling record in 1959 by Brook Benton (Mercury).

It's Just About Time
Words and music by Jack Clement.
Jack Clement Music, Inc.
Best-selling record by Johnny Cash (Sun).

It's Only Make Believe
Words and music by Conway Twitty and Jack Nance.
Marielle Music Publishing Corp.
Best-selling record by Conway Twitty (M-G-M).

It's Only the Beginning
Words and music by Aaron Schroeder and Sid Wayne.
Charles N. Daniels, Inc.
Best-selling record by The Kalin Twins (Decca).

It's Too Soon To Know, see 1947.

I've Had It
Words by Ray Ceroni and Carl Bonura, music by Ray Ceroni.
Brent Music Corp.
Best-selling record in 1959 by The Bell Notes (Time).

Java
Music by Freddy Friday, Allen Toussaint, and Alvin Tyler.
Tideland Music Publishing Corp.
Best-selling record in 1964 by Al Hirt and his Orchestra (RCA Victor).

Jenny-Lee
Words and music by Jan Berry and Arnie Ginsburg.
Daywin Music, Inc.
Adapted from the American Civil War song, "Aura Lea." Best-selling record by Jan and Arnie (Arwin).

Johnny B. Goode
Words and music by Chuck Berry.
Arc Music Corp.
Best-selling record by Chuck Berry (Chess).

Just a Dream
Words and music by Jimmy Clanton and Cosmo Matassa.
Ace Publishing Co., Inc./Maureen Music, Inc.
Best-selling record by Jimmy Clanton (Ace).

Just Young
Words and music by Lya S. Roberts.
Peer International Corp.
First recorded by Andy Rose (AAMCO). Best-selling record by Paul Anka (ABC Paramount).

Kathy-O
Words and music by Charles Tobias, Ray Joseph, and Jack Sher.
Northern Music Corp.
Introduced by The Diamonds on the soundtrack of *Kathy-O* (film).

Kewpie Doll
Words and music by Sid Tepper and Roy C. Bennett.
Leeds Music Corp.
Best-selling record by Perry Como (RCA Victor).

La Bamba
Words and music by William Clauson.
Beechwood Music Corp.
Best-selling record by Ritchie Valens (Del-Fi).

La Dee Dah
Words and music by Frank C. Slay, Jr. and Bob Crewe.
Conley Music, Inc.
Best-selling record by Billy and Lillie (Swan).

La Seine, see **You Will Find Your Love in Paris,** 1958; see **The River Seine,** 1953.

La Strada del' Amore, also known as **The Street of Love**
Words and music by Jack Reardon.
Sounds Music Co.
Best-selling record by Caterina Valente (Decca).

Lazy Mary (Italian)
English words by Lou Monte, Italian words and music by Paolo Citorello.
Shapiro, Bernstein & Co., Inc.
From the Italian song, "Luna Mezzo Mare." Best-selling record by Lou Monte (RCA Victor).

Lazy Summer Night
Words and music by Harold Spina.
Mickey Rooney Publishing Co./Spina Music.
From *Andy Hardy Comes Home* (film). Best-selling record by The Four Preps (Capitol).

Left Right out of Your Heart (Hi-Lee Hi-Lo Hi-Lup-Up-Up)
Words by Earl Shuman, music by Mort Garson.
Shapiro, Bernstein & Co., Inc.
Best-selling record by Patti Page (Mercury).

Let the Bells Keep Ringing
Words and music by Paul Anka.
Spanka Music Corp.
Best-selling record by Paul Anka (ABC Paramount).

Light of Love
Words and music by Charles Singleton.
Singleton Music, Inc.
Best-selling record by Peggy Lee (Capitol).

Like Young
Words by Paul Francis Webster, music by André Previn.
Robbins Music Corp.
Best-selling record, instrumental, by André Previn with David Rose and his Orchestra (M-G-M). First vocal record by Ann Henry (Dynasty).

Li'l Darlin'
Music by Neal Hefti.
Neal Hefti Music, Inc.
Introduced by Count Basie and his Orchestra.

Little Blue Man, The
Words and music by Fred Ebb and Paul Klein.
T.M. Music, Inc.
Best-selling record by Betty Johnson (Atlantic).

Little Drummer Boy, The
Words and music by Katherine Davis, Henry Onerati, and Harry Simeone.
Mills Music, Inc./Delaware Music Corp.
Best-selling record by The Harry Simeone Chorale (Mercury).

Little Star
Words and music by Vito Picone and Arthur Venosa.
Keel Music Co.
Best-selling record by The Elegants (Apt).

Little Susie
Music by Ray Bryant.
Brynor Music, Inc.
First recording, instrumental, by Ray Bryant (Signature). Best-selling record, instrumental, in 1960 by Ray Bryant (Columbia).

Lollipop
Words and music by Beverly Ross and Julius Dixon.
Edward B. Marks Music Corp.
Best-selling record by The Chordettes (Cadence).

Lonely Blue Boy
Words by Fred Wise, music by Ben Weisman.
May Music, Inc.
Best-selling record in 1959 and 1960 by Conway Twitty (M-G-M).

(I'm Just a) Lonely Boy
Words and music by Paul Anka.
Spanka Music Corp.
Best-selling record in 1959 by Paul Anka (ABC-Paramount). Featured in *Girlstown* (film).

Lonely One, The
Music by Lee Hazlewood and Duane Eddy.
Gregmark Music Co.
Best-selling record, instrumental, by Duane Eddy (Jamie).

Lonely Teardrops
Words and music by Berry Gordy, Jr., Gwen Gordy, and Tyran Carlo.
Pearl Music Co.,Inc.
Best-selling record in 1959 by Jackie Wilson (Brunswick).

Lonesome Town
Words and music by Baker Knight.
Eric Music, Inc.
Best-selling record by Ricky Nelson (Imperial).

Long Legged Ladies of Labrador
Words by Mack Discant, music by Charlotte Chait.
Planetary Music Publishing Corp.
Best-selling record by Morty Craft and his Orchestra (M-G-M).

Looking Back
Words and music by Clyde Otis, Brook Benton, and Belford Hendricks.
Eden Music, Inc./Sweco Music Corp.
Best-selling record by Nat "King" Cole (Capitol).

Love Eyes
Words by Norman Gimbel, music by Moose Charlap.
Saunders Publications, Inc.
Introduced by Ralph Young in *Whoop-Up* (musical).

Love Is All We Need
Words and music by Ben Raleigh and Don Wolf.
Travis Music Co.
Best-selling record by Tommy Edwards (M-G-M).

Love, Look Away
Words by Oscar Hammerstein II, music by Richard Rodgers.
Williamson Music, Inc.
Introduced by Arabella Hong in *Flower Drum Song* (musical).

Love Makes the World Go 'round (Yeah, Yeah)
Words and music by Ollie Jones.
Paxwin Music Corp.
Best-selling record by Perry Como (RCA Victor).

Love Song from *Houseboat,* see **Almost in Your Arms.**

Love Theme from *The Brothers Karamazov*
Music by Bronislau Kaper.
Robbins Music Corp.
From *The Brothers Karamazov* (film).

Love You Most of All
Words and music by B. Campbell.
Hermosa Music Corp.
Best-selling record by Sam Cooke (Keen).

Lover's Question, A
Words and music by Brook Benton and Jimmy Williams.
Eden Music, Inc./Progressive Music Publishing Co., Inc.
Best-selling record in 1959 by Clyde McPhatter (Atlantic).

Lucky Ladybug
Words and music by Frank C. Slay, Jr. and Bob Crewe.
Conley Music, Inc.
Best-selling record by Billy and Lillie (Swan).

Lullaby in Ragtime
Words and music by Sylvia Fine.
Dena Music, Inc.
Introduced by Danny Kaye and the dubbed voice of Eileen Wilson in *The Five Pennies* (film).

Mandolins in the Moonlight
Words and music by George Weiss and Aaron Schroeder.
Roncom Music Co.
Best-selling record by Perry Como (RCA Victor).

Manhattan Spiritual
Music by Billy Maxted.
Zodiac Music Corp.
Best-selling record in 1959 by The Reg Owen Orchestra (Palette).

Maverick
Words by Paul Francis Webster, music by David Buttolph.
M. Witmark & Sons.
Theme from *Maverick* (television series).

May You Always
Words and music by Larry Markes and Dick Charles.
Hecht & Buzzell, Inc.
Best-selling record in 1959 by The McGuire Sisters (Coral).

Maybe
Words and music by George Goldner.
Figure Music, Inc.
Best-selling record by The Chantels (End).

Melodie Perdue, see Willingly.

Merry Little Minuet
Words and music by Sheldon Harnick.
Sunbeam Music Corp.
Satire on the atom bomb introduced in 1953 by Orson Bean in *John Murray Anderson's Almanac* (revue). Used as special nightclub material by comedienne Charlotte Rae until publication in 1958. Best-selling record by The Kingston Trio (Capitol).

Mommy for a Day
Words and music by Buck Owens and Harlan Howard.
Travis Music Co.
Best-selling record in 1959 by Kitty Wells (Decca).

Moon-Talk
Words and music by Al Hoffman and Dick Manning.
Roncom Music Co.
Best-selling record by Perry Como (RCA Victor).

Morning Music of Montmartre, The
Words and music by Jay Livingston and Ray Evans.
Livingston & Evans, Inc.
Introduced by Susan Johnson in *Oh Captain!* (musical).

My Baby's Gone
Words and music by Hazel Houser.
Central Songs, Inc.
Best-selling record in 1959 by The Louvin Brothers (Capitol).

My True Love
Words and music by Jack Scott.
Starfire Music Corp.
Best-selling record by Jack Scott (Carlton).

Nel Blu, Dipinto di Blu, see Volare.

Never Be Anyone Else but You
Words and music by Baker Knight.
Eric Music, Inc.
Best-selling record in 1959 by Ricky Nelson (Imperial).

Never Before
Words by Norman Gimbel, music by Moose Charlap.
Saunders Publications, Inc.
Introduced by Julienne Marie in *Whoop-Up* (musical).

Night They Invented Champagne, The
Words by Alan Jay Lerner, music by Frederick Loewe.
Mara-Lane Music Corp.
Introduced by Leslie Caron, Louis Jourdan, and Hermione Gingold in *Gigi* (film).

No Chemise, Please!
Words and music by Gerry Granahan, Jodi D'Amour, and Arnold Goland.
Sunbeam Music Corp.
Best-selling record by Gerry Granahan (Sunbeam).

No One Knows
Words by Ken Hecht, music by Ernie Maresca.
Schwartz Music Co., Inc.
Best-selling record by Dion and The Belmonts (Laurie).

Nobody but You
Words and music by Dee Clark.
Gladstone Music, Inc.
Best-selling record by Dee Clark (Abner).

Nothing in Common
Words by Sammy Cahn, music by James Van Heusen.
Edwin H. Morris & Co., Inc.
Introduced by Bob Hope and Bing Crosby in *Paris Holiday* (film).

Now I Lay Me Down To Sleep
Words by Carolyn Leigh, music by Cy Coleman.
Mayfair Music Corp.
Best-selling record by Tony Bennett (Columbia).

Oh, Lonesome Me
Words and music by Don Gibson.
Acuff-Rose Publications.
Best-selling record by Don Gibson (RCA Victor).

Oh, Oh, I'm Falling in Love Again
Words and music by Al Hoffman, Dick Manning, and Mark Markwell (pseudonym for Hugo Peretti and Luigi Creatore).
Planetary Music Publishing Corp.
Best-selling record by Jimmie Rodgers (Roulette).

Old Man and the Sea, The
Music by Dimitri Tiomkin.
M. Witmark & Sons.
Theme from *The Old Man and the Sea* (film).

One Summer Night
Words and music by Danny Webb.
Melody Lane Publications, Inc.
Best-selling record by The Dandleers (AMP).

Only Man on the Island, The
Words by Bob Hilliard, music by Dave Mann.
Shapiro, Bernstein & Co., Inc.
Best-selling record by Vic Damone (Columbia).

Only the Lonely
Words by Sammy Cahn, music by James Van Heusen.
Maraville Music Corp.
Introduced and best-selling record by Frank Sinatra (Capitol).

Our Language of Love (French)
English lyrics by Julian More, David Heneker, and Monty Norman, French lyrics by Alexandre Breffort, music by Marguerite Monnot.
Éditions Micro, Paris, France, 1956/Trafalgar Music Ltd., London, England/Chappell & Co., Inc.
Original French title, "Avec les Anges." Introduced by Colette Renard in the Paris production and by Elizabeth Seal in the London (1958) and New York (1960) productions of *Irma la Douce* (musical).

Pansy (Italian)
English words by Jack Elliott, Italian words by Gigi Pisano, music by Furio Rendine.
Italian Book Co., 1953/Leeds Music Corp.
Introduced in Italy by Renato Carasone in 1953. Original title, "La Pansé."

Paris (Mexican)
Music by Perez Prado.
Editorial Mexicana de Musica Internacional, S.A., Mexico/Peer International Corp.
Best-selling record, instrumental, by Perez Prado and his Orchestra (RCA Victor).

Patricia (It's Patricia)
Words by Bob Marcus, music by Perez Prado.
Editorial Mexicana de Musica Internacional, S.A., Mexico/Peer International Corp.
Introduced and best-selling record by Perez Prado (RCA Victor).

Peek-a-Boo
Words and music by Jack Hammer.
Cole and Gale Music Distributors, Inc.
Best-selling record by The Cadillacs (Josie).

Pepito
Spanish words and music by Art Truscott and Carmen Taylor.
Raleigh Music, Inc.
Best-selling record, in Spanish, by Elena Madera (pseudonym for Carmen Taylor) (Decca). Subsequently a hit in Germany with best-selling record by Caterina Valente (Polydor).

Periwinkle Blue
Words by Paul Francis Webster, music by Jerry Livingston.
Artists Music, Inc.
Introduced by Doris Day (Columbia).

Philadelphia, U.S.A.
Words and music by Anthony Antonucci and Bill Borrelli, Jr.
Southern Music Publishing Co., Inc.
Best-selling record by The Nu-Tornados (Carlton).

Pink Shoelaces
Words and music by Mickie Grant.
Pioneer Publishing Co.
Best-selling record in 1959 by Dodie Stevens (Crystalette).

Poor Boy
Words by Mel Mitchell, music by David R. Sanderson.
Vogue Music, Inc./Parkwood Music Co.
Best-selling record in 1959 by The Royaltones (Jubilee).

Poor Little Fool
Words and music by Shari Sheeley.
Eric Music, Inc.
Best-selling record by Ricky Nelson (Imperial).

Primrose Lane
Words and music by George Callender and Wayne Shanklin.
Gladys Music, Inc.
Best-selling record in 1959 by Jerry Wallace (Challenge).

Problems
Words and music by Boudleaux Bryant and Felice Bryant.
Acuff-Rose Publications.
Best-selling record by The Everly Brothers (Cadence).

Promise Me Love
Words and music by Kay Thompson.
Kay Thompson Music, Inc.
Best-selling record by Andy Williams (Cadence).

Purple People Eater, The
Words and music by Sheb Wooley.
Cordial Music Co.
Best-selling record by Sheb Wooley (M-G-M).

Pussy Cat
Words by Sunny Skylar, music by Tom Glazer.
George Paxton, Inc.
Best-selling record by The Ames Brothers (RCA Victor).

Put Your Head on My Shoulder
Words and music by Paul Anka.
Spanka Music Corp.
Best-selling record by Paul Anka (ABC Paramount).

Queen of the Hop
Words and music by Woody Harris and Bobby Darin.
Walden Music Corp./Tweed Music Co.
Best-selling record by Bobby Darin (Atco).

Rags and Old Iron ("Aigs Ol' I-on")
Words by Oscar Brown, Jr., music by Oscar Brown, Jr. and Norman Curtis.
Edward B. Marks Music Corp.
Introduced by Oscar Brown, Jr.

Ramrod
Music by Al Casey.
Gregmark Music Co.
Best-selling record, instrumental, by Duane Eddy (Jamie).

Rawhide
Words by Milt Grant, music by Link Wray.
Andval Music.
Best-selling record, instrumental, by Link Wray (Epic).

Rawhide
Words by Ned Washington, music by Dimitri Tiomkin.
Erosa Music Publishing Corp.
Theme, sung by Frankie Laine behind the opening titles, of *Rawhide* (television series).

Rebel-Rouser
Music by Duane Eddy and Lee Hazlewood.
Valley Publishers, Inc.
Best-selling record, instrumental, by Duane Eddy (Jamie).

Rockhouse (Part I and Part II)
Music by Ray Charles.
Progressive Music Publishing Co., Inc.
Best-selling record, instrumental, by Ray Charles (Atlantic).

Rockin' Robin
Words and music by Jimmie Thomas.
Recordo Music Publishers.
Best-selling record by Bobby Day (Class).

Rumble
Music by Sy Oliver.
Sy Oliver Music Corp.
Best-selling record, instrumental, by Link Wray (Cadence).

Sail Along Silvery Moon, see 1937.

San Francisco Bay Blues
Words and music by Jesse Fuller.
Hollis Music, Inc.
Introduced by Jesse Fuller (Good Time Jazz).

Satin Doll
Words by Johnny Mercer, music by Billy Strayhorn and Duke Ellington.
Tempo Music, Inc.
Introduced by Duke Ellington and his Orchestra. From an instrumental composition published and recorded by Ellington in 1953.

Saving My Love (For You)
Words and music by Ron Hoffman.
Kenny Marlow.
Best-selling record in 1954 by Johnny Ace (Duke).

Say, Darling
Words by Betty Comden and Adolph Green, music by Jule Styne.
Stratford Music Corp.
Introduced by Johnny Desmond in *Say, Darling* (musical).

Secret, The
Words and music by Joe Lubin and I. J. Roth.
Daywin Music, Inc.
Best-selling record by Gordon MacRae (Capitol).

Secretly
Words and music by Al Hoffman, Dick Manning, and Mark Markwell.
Planetary Music Publishing Corp.
Best-selling record by Jimmie Rodgers (Roulette).

Señor Blues
Words and music by Horace Silver.
Ecaroh Music, Inc.
Introduced, as an instrumental, by Horace Silver.

Separate Tables
Words by Harold Adamson, music by Harry Warren.
Hecht & Buzzell, Inc.
Promotional song for *Separate Tables* (film). Best-selling record by Vic Damone (Columbia).

Sermonette
Words by Jon Hendricks, music by Julian Adderley.
Silhouette Music Corp.
From an instrumental composition recorded by Julian "Cannonball" Adderley in 1956. Best-selling record by Della Reese (RCA Victor).

She Was Only Seventeen (He Was One Year More)
Words and music by Marty Robbins.
Fred Rose Music, Inc.
Best-selling record by Marty Robbins (Columbia).

Skinny Minnie
Words and music by Bill Haley, Arrett "Rusty" Keefer, Catherine Cafra, and Milt Gabler.
Valley Brook Publications, Inc.
Best-selling record by Bill Haley and The Comets (Decca).

Smoke Gets in Your Eyes, see 1933.

So Fine, see 1955.

So Many Ways
Words and music by Bobby Stevenson.
Play Music, Inc.
Best-selling record in 1959 by Brook Benton (Mercury).

Somebody Touched Me
Words and music by Ahmet Ertegun.
Progressive Music Publishing Co., Inc.
Best-selling record by Ruth Brown (Atlantic).

Something's Always Happening on the River
Words by Betty Comden and Adolph Green, music by Jule Styne.
Stratford Music Corp.
Introduced by David Wayne in *Say, Darling* (musical). Best-selling record by Art Mooney and his Orchestra (M-G-M).

Song and Dance Man
Words by Bob Hilliard, music by Dave Mann.
Shapiro, Bernstein & Co., Inc.

Song from *Some Came Running,* also known as **To Love and Be Loved**
Words by Sammy Cahn, music by James Van Heusen.
Maraville Music Corp.
From *Some Came Running* (film). Introduced by Frank Sinatra (Capitol). Nominated for Academy Award, 1958.

Sorry for Myself?
Words by Norman Gimbel, music by Moose Charlap.
Saunders Publications, Inc.
Introduced by Sylvia Syms in *Whoop-Up* (musical).

Splish Splash
Words and music by Bobby Darin and Jean Murray.
Travis Music Co.
Best-selling record by Bobby Darin (Atco).

Stagger Lee
Words and music by Harold Logan and Lloyd Price.
Travis Music Co.
Best-selling record in 1959 by Lloyd Price (ABC-Paramount).

Stairway of Love
Words and music by Sid Tepper and Roy C. Bennett.
Planetary Music Publishing Corp.
Best-selling record by Marty Robbins (Columbia).

Stay
Words and music by Sid Tepper and Roy C. Bennett.
Planetary Music Publishing Corp.
Best-selling record by The Ames Brothers (RCA Victor).

Street of Love, The, see **La Strada del' Amore.**

Stupid Cupid
Words by Neil Sedaka, music by Howard Greenfield.
Screen Gems-Columbia Music, Inc.
Best-selling record by Connie Francis (M-G-M).

Sugarfoot
Words by Paul Francis Webster, music by Ray Heindorf and Max Steiner.
Remick Music Corp.
Theme from *Sugarfoot* (television series).

Sugartime, see 1956.

Summertime Blues
Words and music by Eddie Cochran and Jerry Capehart.
American Music, Inc.
Best-selling record by Eddie Cochran (Liberty).

Summertime Lies
Words and music by Alan Hood and Richard Loring.
Edwin H. Morris & Co., Inc.
Best-selling record by The Four Preps (Capitol).

Summertime, Summertime
Words and music by Tom Jameson and Sherm Feller.
Roxbury Music Co.
Best-selling record by The Jamies (Epic).

Sunday
Words by Oscar Hammerstein II, music by Richard Rodgers.
Williamson Music, Inc.
Introduced by Pat Suzuki and Larry Blyden in *Flower Drum Song* (musical).

Surprise
Words and music by Jay Livingston and Ray Evans.
Livingston & Evans, Inc.
Introduced by Jacquelyn McKeever in *Oh Captain!* (musical).

Susie Darlin
Words and music by Robin Luke.
Congressional Music Publications.
Best-selling record by Robin Luke (Dot).

Sweet Little Sixteen
Words and music by Chuck Berry.
Arc Music Corp.
Best-selling record by Chuck Berry (Chess).

Sweet Sixteen Bars
Music by Ray Charles.
Progressive Music Publishing Co., Inc.
Introduced by Ray Charles (Atlantic).

Swingin' Shepherd Blues, The (Canadian)
Words by Rhoda Roberts and Kenny Jacobson, music by Moe Koffman.
Nom Music, Inc.
Best-selling record by Moe Koffman and his Orchestra (Jubilee). From a Canadian-produced jazz Lp, *Cool and Hot Sax.*

Talk to Me, Talk to Me
Words and music by Joe Seneca.
Jay & Cee Music Corp.
Best-selling record by Little Willie John (King).

Tall Paul
Words and music by Bob Roberts, Bob Sherman, and Dick Sherman.
Music World Corp./Wonderland Music Co., Inc.
Best-selling record in 1959 by Annette (Disneyland).

Tears on My Pillow
Words and music by Sylvester Bradford and Al Lewis.
Gladys Music, Inc./Tricky Music, Inc.
Best-selling record by Little Anthony and The Imperials (End).

Tell All the World about You
Words and music by Ray Charles.
Progressive Music Publishing Co., Inc.
Introduced by Ray Charles (Atlantic).

Tell Him No
Words and music by Travis Pritchett.
Burnt Oak Publishing Co., Inc./Dorothy Music.
Best-selling record in 1959 by Travis and Bob (Sandy).

Tennessee Stud
Words and music by Jimmy Driftwood.
Warden Music Co., Inc.
Best-selling record by Eddy Arnold (RCA Victor).

Tequila
Music by Chuck Rio.
Jat Music, Inc./Modern Music Publishing Co.
Best-selling record, instrumental, by The Champs (Challenge).

Thank Heaven for Little Girls
Words by Alan Jay Lerner, music by Frederick Loewe.
Mara-Lane Music Corp.
Introduced by Maurice Chevalier in *Gigi* (film).

Thank You Pretty Baby
Words and music by Clyde Otis and Brook Benton.
Eden Music, Inc.
Best-selling record in 1959 by Brook Benton (Mercury).

That's What It's Like To Be Lonesome
Words and music by Bill Anderson.
Champion Music Corp./Tree Publishing Co., Inc.
Best-selling record in 1959 by Ray Price (Columbia).

Theme from *Auntie Mame*
Music by Bronislau Kaper.
M. Witmark & Sons.
Theme from *Auntie Mame* (film). Version with lyrics by Kim Gannon entitled "Drifting."

Theme from *Zorro*
Words by Norman Foster, music by George Bruns.
Walt Disney Music Co.
Theme from *Zorro* (television series). Introduced by Henry Calvin (Disneyland). Best-selling record by The Chordettes (Cadence).

There Is Only Paris for That (French)
English lyrics by Julian More, David Heneker, and Monty Norman, French lyrics by Alexandre Breffort, music by Marguerite Monnot.
Éditions Micro, Paris, France, 1956/Trafalgar Music Ltd., London, England/Chappell & Co., Inc.
Original French title, "Y'a Qu' Paris pour Ca." Introduced by Colette Renard in the Paris production and by Keith Michell in the London (1958) production and the New York (1960) production of *Irma la Douce* (musical).

There's Only One of You, see 1954.

This Happy Feeling
Words and music by Jay Livingston and Ray Evans.
Carrie Music Co., Inc.
Introduced by Debbie Reynolds in *This Happy Feeling* (film).

This Is All I Ask
Words and music by Gordon Jenkins.
Massey Music Co., Inc.
Best-selling record in 1963 by Tony Bennett (Columbia).

This Little Girl of Mine, see 1955.

This Little Girl's Gone Rockin'
Words and music by Bobby Darin and Mann Curtis.
Leeds Music Corp.
Best-selling record by Ruth Brown (Atlantic).

This Old Man, see **The Children's Marching Song.**

To Be Loved
Words and music by Tyran Carlo, Berry Gordy, Jr., and Gwen Gordy.
Pearl Music Co., Inc.
Best-selling record by Jackie Wilson (Brunswick).

To Know Him Is To Love Him
Words and music by Phil Spector.
Hillary Music, Inc./Bamboo Music, Inc.
Best-selling record by The Teddy Bears (Dore).

To Love and Be Loved, see **Song from *Some Came Running*.**

Tom Dooley
Traditional, arranged by Dave Guard.
Beechwood Music Corp.
An adaptation of an 1868 Blue Ridge Mountain song about a folk hero named Tom Dula. Best-selling record by The Kingston Trio (Capitol).

Tom Thumb's Tune
Words and music by Peggy Lee.
Robbins Music Corp.
Introduced by Russ Tamblyn in *Tom Thumb* (film).

Tomboy
Words and music by Joe Farrell and Jim Conway.
Roncom Music Co.
Best-selling record in 1959 by Perry Como (RCA Victor).

Too Much, Too Soon
Words by Al Stillman, music by Ernest Gold.
M. Witmark & Sons.
From *Too Much, Too Soon* (film).

Topsy II
Words by Edgar Battle, music by Edgar Battle and Edward Durham.
Cosmopolitan Music Publishers.
Drum solo based on "Topsy" from Battle and Durham's 1939 composition, *Uncle Tom's Cabin.* Best-selling record by Cozy Cole (Love).

Torero (Italian)
English words by Al Hoffman and Dick Manning, Italian words by Nisa, music by Renato Carosone.
Edizione Musicali EDIR, Milan, Italy/Leeds Music Corp.
Best-selling record by Renato Carosone (Capitol).

Tragedy
Words and music by Gerald H. Nelson and Fred B. Burch.
Bluff City Music Publishing Co., Inc./Dorothy Music.
Best-selling record in 1959 by Thomas Wayne (Fernwood).

Try Me
Words and music by James Brown.
Lois Publishing Co.
Best-selling record in 1959 by James Brown and The Famous Flames (Federal).

Try To Love Me Just As I Am
Words by Betty Comden and Adolph Green, music by Jule Styne.
Stratford Music Corp.
Introduced by Johnny Desmond in *Say, Darling* (musical).

Tupelo County Jail
Words and music by Webb Pierce and Mel Tillis.
Cedarwood Publishing Co., Inc.
Best-selling record by Webb Pierce (Decca).

Twenty-Six Miles
Words and music by Glenn Larson and Bruce Belland.
Beechwood Music Corp.
Best-selling record by The Four Preps (Capitol).

Twilight Time, see 1944.

Two Faces in the Dark
Words by Dorothy Fields, music by Albert Hague.
Chappell & Co., Inc.
Introduced by Bob Dixon in 1959 in *Redhead* (musical).

Verboten!, also known as **Forbidden**
Words by Mack David, music by Harry Sukman.
Leo Feist, Inc.
Introduced by Paul Anka on the soundtrack of *Verboten!* (film).

Vertigo
Words and music by Jay Livingston and Ray Evans.
Famous Music Corp.
"Inspired by" *Vertigo* (film).

Very Precious Love, A
Words by Paul Francis Webster, music by Sammy Fain.
M. Witmark & Sons.
Introduced in *Marjorie Morningstar* (film). Nominated for Academy Award, 1958. Best-selling record by Doris Day (Columbia).

Voice in My Heart, The
Words and music by Dave Franklyn.
Summit Music Corp.
Best-selling record by Eydie Gormé (ABC Paramount).

Volare, also known as **Nel Blu, Dipinto di Blu** (Italian)
English words by Mitchell Parish, Italian words by Domenico Modugno and F. Migliacci, music by Domenico Modugno.
Edizioni Curci, Milan, Italy/Robbins Music Corp.
Introduced by Domenico Modugno. Awarded First Prize, San Remo (Italy) Song Festival. Named "Song of the Year" by the National Academy of Recording Arts and Sciences. Best-selling record by Domenico Modugno (Decca). Revived in 1960 with best-selling record by Bobby Rydell (Cameo).

Waiting Game, The
Words by Bob Hilliard, music by Robert Allen.
Korwin Music, Inc.
Best-selling record by Harry Belafonte (RCA Victor).

Waltz at Maxim's
Words by Alan Jay Lerner, music by Frederick Loewe.
Mara-Lane Music Corp.
Introduced in *Gigi* (film).

Ways of a Woman in Love, The
Words and music by Charlie Rich and Bill Justis.
Hi-Lo Music, Inc.
Best-selling record by Johnny Cash (Sun).

Wear My Ring around Your Neck
Words and music by Bert Carroll and Russell Moody.
Elvis Presley Music, Inc./Rush Music Corp.
Best-selling record by Elvis Presley (RCA Victor).

Wedding, The
Words and music by Albert A. Beach and Guy Wood.
Criterion Music Corp.
Best-selling record by June Valli (Mercury).

We're Not Children
Words and music by Jay Livingston and Ray Evans.
Livingston & Evans, Inc.
Introduced by Jacquelyn McKeever and Paul Valentine in *Oh Captain!* (musical).

Western Movies
Words by Cliff Goldsmith, music by Fred Smith.
Elizabeth Music/Aries Music Co.
Best-selling record by The Olympics (Liberty).

What Am I Living For?
Words and music by Fred Jay and Art Harris.
Progressive Music Publishing Co., Inc./Rush Music Corp.
Best-selling record by Chuck Willis (Atlantic).

What Do I Care?
Words and music by Johnny Cash.
Johnny Cash Music, Inc.
Best-selling record by Johnny Cash (Columbia).

When
Words and music by Paul Evans and Jack Reardon.
Sounds Music Co.
Best-selling record by The Kalin Twins (Decca).

When the Boys Talk about the Girls
Words and music by Bob Merrill.
Valyr Music Corp./Favorite Music, Inc.
Best-selling record by Valerie Carr (Roulette).

Whole Lotta Loving
Words and music by Antoine "Fats" Domino and Dave Bartholomew.
Travis Music Co.
Best-selling record by Fats Domino (Imperial).

Who's Sorry Now, see 1923.

Willingly, also known as **Melodie Perdue** (French)
English words by Carl Sigman, French words by Jean Broussolle, music by Hubert Giraud.
Éditions Do Re Mi and Nouvelles Éditions Meridian, Paris, France/Shapiro, Bernstein & Co., Inc.
Best-selling record, in French, by Les Compagnons de la Chanson (Capitol).

Win Your Love for Me
Words and music by L. C. Cook.
Hermosa Music Corp.
Best-selling record by Sam Cooke (Keen).

Wishing for Your Love
Words and music by Sampson Horton.
Rayven Music Co., Inc.
Best-selling record by The Voxpoppers (Mercury).

Witch Doctor
Words and music by Ross Bagdasarian.
Monarch Music Corp.
Best-selling record by David Seville (pseudonym for Bagdasarian) (Liberty).

World Outside, The (English)
Words by Carl Sigman, music by Richard Addinsell.
Keith Prowse Music Publishing Co., Ltd., London, England/Chappell & Co., Inc.
Adapted from the theme from Addinsell's "Warsaw Concerto" (see 1942). Introduced by The Four Aces (Decca).

Yakety Yak
Words and music by Jerry Leiber and Mike Stoller.
Tiger Music, Inc.
Best-selling record by The Coasters (Atco).

You Are Beautiful
Words by Oscar Hammerstein II, music by Richard Rodgers.
Willamson Music, Inc.
Introduced by Ed Kenny and Juanita Hall in *Flower Drum Song* (musical).

You Are My Destiny
Words and music by Paul Anka.
Pamco Music, Inc.
Best-selling record by Paul Anka (ABC-Paramount).

You Cheated
Words and music by Don Burch.
Balcones Publishing Co.
Best-selling record by The Shields (Dot).

You Don't Know Him
Words and music by Jay Livingston and Ray Evans.
Livingston & Evans, Inc.
Introduced by Jacquelyn McKeever and Abbe Lane in *Oh Captain!* (musical).

You Fascinate Me So
Words by Carolyn Leigh, music by Cy Coleman.
Mayfair Music Corp.
Introduced by Jean Arnold in *Julius Monk's Demi-Dozen* (nightclub revue).

You Gotta Love Everybody, see 1956.

You Will Find Your Love in Paris (French)
English words by Mack Gordon, French words by Flavien Monod and Guy La Farge, music by Guy La Farge.
Royalty, Éditions Musicales, Paris, France, 1948/Remick Music Corp., 1953, 1958.
Second English-language version of "La Seine." Best-selling record by Patti Page (Mercury).

Young and Warm and Wonderful
Words by Hy Zaret, music by Lou Singer.
Frank Music Corp.
Best-selling record by Tony Bennett (Columbia).

Your Name Is Beautiful
Words and music by Diana Lampert and John Gluck.
Denny Music, Inc.
Best-selling record by Carl Smith (Columbia).

You're Making a Fool out of Me
Words and music by Tompall Glaser.
Be-Are Music Publications, Inc.
Best-selling record by Jimmy Newman (M-G-M).

You're So Right for Me
Words and music by Jay Livingston and Ray Evans.
Livingston & Evans, Inc.
Introduced by Edward Platt and Abbe Lane in *Oh Captain!* (musical).

You're the Nearest Thing to Heaven
Words by Johnny Cash, music by Hoydt Johnson and Jim Atkins.
Hi-Lo Music, Inc./E & M Publishing Co.
Best-selling record by Johnny Cash (Sun).

Zorro, see **Theme from *Zorro*.**

1959

Adventures in Paradise
Words by Dorcas Cochran, music by Lionel Newman.
Hastings Music Corp.
Theme from *Adventures in Paradise* (television series).

Alaskans, The, also known as **Gold Fever**
Words and music by Mack David and Jerry Livingston.
M. Witmark & Sons.
Theme from *The Alaskans* (television series).

All I Need Is the Girl
Words by Stephen Sondheim, music by Jule Styne.
Williamson Music, Inc./Stratford Music Corp.
Introduced by Paul Wallace and Sandra Church in *Gypsy* (musical).

Almost Grown
Words and music by Chuck Berry.
Arc Music Corp.
Best-selling record by Chuck Berry (Chess).

Along Came Jones
Words and music by Jerry Leiber and Mike Stoller.
Tiger Music, Inc.
Best-selling record by The Coasters (Atco).

Alvin's Harmonica
Words and music by Ross Bagdasarian.
Monarch Music Corp.
Best-selling record by David Seville (pseudonym for Bagdasarian) and The Chipmunks (Liberty).

Amigo's Guitar
Words and music by John D. Loudermilk, Kitty Wells, and Roy Bodkin.
Cedarwood Publishing Co., Inc.
Best-selling record by Kitty Wells (Decca).

Among My Souvenirs, see 1927.

Angels Listened In, The
Words and music by Billy Dawn Smith and Sid Faust.
Paxwin Music Corp.
Best-selling record by The Crests (Co-ed).

Another Sleepless Night
Words by Howard Greenfield, music by Neil Sedaka.
Screen Gems-Columbia Music, Inc.
Best-selling record by Jimmy Clanton (Ace).

Any Way the Wind Blows
Words by By Dunham, music by Marilyn Hooven and Joe Hooven.
Artists Music, Inc.
Introduced by Doris Day in *Please Don't Eat the Daisies* (film).

Anyone Would Love You
Words and music by Harold Rome.
Chappell & Co., Inc.
Introduced by Andy Griffith and Dolores Gray in *Destry Rides Again* (musical).

Apple Green
Words and music by Charlie Singleton.
Hollis Music, Inc.
Best-selling record in 1960 by June Valli (Mercury).

As I Love You, see 1955.

Baby (You've Got What It Takes)
Words and music by Murray Stein and Clyde Otis.
Vogue Music, Inc.
Best-selling record in 1960 by Dinah Washington and Brook Benton (Mercury).

Ballad of the Sad Young Men, The
Words by Fran Landesman, music by Tommy Wolf.
Empress Music, Inc.
Introduced by Tani Seitz in *The Nervous Set* (musical).

Battle Hymn of the Republic
Words by Julia Ward Howe, music attributed to William Steffe.
Public Domain.
The earliest known use of this music was for the hymn, "Say, Brothers, Will You Meet Me," attributed to William Steffe. The same melody was used for the anti-slavery song, "John Brown's Body." Also known as "Glory, Glory Hallelujah." Became a best-selling popular record in 1959 by The Mormon Tabernacle Choir (Columbia).

Battle of Kookamonga, The
Words by J. J. Reynolds and Jimmy Driftwood, music by Jimmy Driftwood.
Warden Music Co., Inc.
Parody of "The Battle of New Orleans." Best-selling record by Homer and Jethro (RCA Victor).

Battle of New Orleans, The, see 1957.

Be My Guest
Words and music by Antoine "Fats" Domino, John Marascalco, and Tommy Boyce.
Travis Music Co.
Best-selling record by Fats Domino (Imperial).

Be Prepared
Words by Richard Quine, music by Fred Karger.
Artists Music, Inc.
Introduced by Doris Day in *It Happened to Jane* (film).

Best Is Yet To Come, The
Words by Carolyn Leigh, music by Cy Coleman.
Edwin H. Morris & Co., Inc.
Introduced by Tony Bennett.

Best of Everything, The
Words by Sammy Cahn, music by Alfred Newman.
Miller Music Corp.
Introduced by Johnny Mathis in *The Best of Everything* (film). Nominated for Academy Award, 1959. Best-selling record by Johnny Mathis (Columbia).

Big Hunk o' Love, A
Words and music by Aaron Schroeder and Sid Wyche.
Elvis Presley Music, Inc.
Best-selling record by Elvis Presley (RCA Victor).

Big Hurt, The
Words and music by Wayne Shanklin.
Gladys Music, Inc.
Best-selling record by Toni Fisher (Signet).

Big Midnight Special
Words and music by Wilma Lee Cooper.
Acuff-Rose Publications.
Best-selling record by Wilma Lee and Stoney Cooper (Hickory).

Blackland Farmer
Words and music by Frankie Miller.
Peer International Corp.
Best-selling record by Frankie Miller (Starday).

Bobby Sox to Stockings
Words and music by Russell Faith, Clarence Wey Kehner, and R. di Cicco.
Debmar Publishing Co., Inc.
Best-selling record by Frankie Avalon (Chancellor).

Bonanza!
Words and music by Jay Livingston and Ray Evans.
Livingston & Evans, Inc.
Theme from *Bonanza!* (television series).

Bongo Rock
Music by Preston Epps and Arthur Egnoian.
Drive-In Music Co., Inc.
Best-selling record, instrumental, by Preston Epps (Original Sound).

Bonnie Come Back
Music by Lee Hazlewood and Duane Eddy.
Gregmark Music, Inc.
Best-selling record, instrumental, by Duane Eddy (Jamie).

Bourbon Street Beat
Words and music by Mack David and Jerry Livingston.
M. Witmark & Sons.
From *Bourbon Street Beat* (television series).

Boy without a Girl, A
Words and music by Sid Jacobson and Ruth Sexter.
Arch Music Co., Inc.
Best-selling record by Frankie Avalon (Chancellor).

Broken-Hearted Melody
Words by Hal David, music by Sherman Edwards.
Mansion Music Corp.
Best-selling record by Sarah Vaughan (Mercury).

Bronco
Words by Mack David, music by Jerry Livingston.
M. Witmark & Sons.
Theme from *Bronco* (television series).

Buon Natale (Means Merry Xmas to You)
Words by Bob Saffer, music by Bob Saffer and Nat Cole.
Ivan Mogull Music Corp.
Best-selling record by Nat "King" Cole (Capitol).

Charlie Brown
Words and music by Jerry Leiber and Mike Stoller.
Tiger Music, Inc.
Best-selling record by The Coasters (Atco).

Ciao, Ciao, Bambina (Italian)
English words by Mitchell Parish, Italian words by Domenico Modugno and Verde, music by Domenico Modugno.
Edizioni Curci S.R.L., Milan, Italy/Robbins Music Corp.
Introduced by Domenico Modugno at the 1959 San Remo (Italy) Song Festival. Awarded first prize under the original Italian title, "Piove."

Climb Ev'ry Mountain
Words by Oscar Hammerstein II, music by Richard Rodgers.
Williamson Music, Inc.
Introduced by Patricia Neway in *The Sound of Music* (musical).

Come into My Heart
Words and music by Lloyd Price and Harold Logan.
Prigan Music Corp.
Best-selling record by Lloyd Price (ABC Paramount).

Come Softly to Me
Words and music by Gary Troxel, Gretchen Christopher, and Barbara Ellis.
Cornerstone Publishing Co.
Best-selling record by The Fleetwoods (Dolphin).

Country Girl
Words and music by Roy Drusky.
Lancaster Music Publications, Inc.
Best-selling record by Faron Young (Capitol).

Crossfire
Music by T. J. Fowler and Tom King.
Vicki Music, Inc.
Best-selling record, instrumental, by Johnny and The Hurricanes (Warwick).

Dance with Me
Words and music by Louis Lebish, George Treadwell, Irv Nahan, and Elmo Glick (pseudonym for Jerry Leiber and Mike Stoller).
Tredlew Music, Inc./Tiger Music, Inc.
Best-selling record by The Drifters (Atlantic).

Dark Hollow
Words and music by Bill Browning.
Starday Music/Island Music Publishing Co.
Best-selling record by Jimmy Skinner (Mercury).

Deck of Cards, see 1948.

Does Your Chewing Gum Lose Its Flavor on the Bedpost Overnight?, see 1924.

Don't Tell Me Your Troubles
Words and music by Don Gibson.
Acuff-Rose Publications.
Best-selling record by Don Gibson (RCA Victor).

Don't You Know
Words and music by Bobby Worth.
Alexis Music, Inc.
An adaptation of Puccini's "Musetta's Waltz" from the opera, *La Boheme.* Best-selling record by Della Reese (RCA Victor).

Do-Re-Mi
Words by Oscar Hammerstein II, music by Richard Rodgers.
Williamson Music, Inc.
Introduced by Mary Martin and children in *The Sound of Music* (musical).

Dream Lover
Words and music by Bobby Darin.
Fern Music, Inc./Progressive Music Publishing Co., Inc./T.M. Music, Inc.
Best-selling record by Bobby Darin (Atco).

El Paso
Words and music by Marty Robbins.
Marty's Music Corp.
Best-selling record by Marty Robbins (Columbia).

Enchanted
Words and music by Buck Ram.
Choice Music, Inc.
Best-selling record by The Platters (Mercury).

Enchanted Sea, The
Words and music by Frank Metis and Randy Starr.
Volkwein Brothers, Inc.
First recorded by The Islanders (Mayflower). Best-selling record, instrumental, by Martin Denny (Liberty).

Endlessly
Words and music by Clyde Otis and Brook Benton.
Vogue Music, Inc.
Best-selling record by Brook Benton (Mercury).

Everybody Likes To Cha Cha Cha
Words and music by Barbara Campbell.
Kags Music.
Best-selling record by Sam Cooke (Keen).

Everything's Coming Up Roses
Words by Stephen Sondheim, music by Jule Styne.
Williamson Music, Inc./Stratford Music Corp.
Introduced by Ethel Merman in *Gypsy* (musical). Sung by the voice of Lisa Kirk for Rosalind Russell in the film version.

Face to the Wall
Words and music by Bill Anderson.
Champion Music Corp./Tree Publishing Co., Inc.
Best-selling record in 1960 by Faron Young (Capitol).

Fair Warning
Words and music by Harold Rome.
Chappell & Co., Inc.
Introduced by Dolores Gray in *Destry Rides Again* (musical).

Family Man
Words and music by J. A. Balthrop.
Starday Music.
Best-selling record by Frankie Miller (Starday).

Faraway Boy
Words and music by Frank Loesser.
Frank Music Corp.
Introduced by Ellen McCown in 1960 in *Greenwillow* (musical).

First Name Initial
Words and music by Aaron Schroeder and Martin Kalmanoff.
Walt Disney Music Co.
Best-selling record by Annette (Vista).

Five Feet High and Rising
Words and music by Johnny Cash.
Johnny Cash Music, Inc.
Best-selling record by Johnny Cash (Columbia).

Five Pennies, The
Words and music by Sylvia Fine.
Dena Music, Inc.
Introduced in *The Five Pennies* (film). Nominated for Academy Award, 1959.

Fool Such As I, A, see 1952.

Fools' Hall of Fame, The
Words and music by Aaron Schroeder and Wally Gold.
Spoone Music Corp.
Best-selling record by Pat Boone (Dot).

For a Penny
Words and music by Charles Singleton.
Roosevelt Music Co., Inc.
Best-selling record by Pat Boone (Dot).

Forty Miles of Bad Road
Music by Duane Eddy and Al Casey.
Gregmark Music Co.
Best-selling record by Duane Eddy (Jamie).

Frankie
Words by Howard Greenfield, music by Neil Sedaka.
Screen Gems-Columbia Music, Inc./Efsee Music, Inc.
Best-selling record by Connie Francis (M-G-M).

French Foreign Legion
Words by Aaron Schroeder, music by Guy Wood.
Barton Music Corp.
Best-selling record by Frank Sinatra (Capitol).

Funny (But I Still Love You)
Words and music by Ray Charles.
Progressive Music Publishing Co., Inc.
Best-selling record by Ray Charles (Atlantic).

Gentleman Jimmy
Words by Sheldon Harnick, music by Jerry Bock.
Sunbeam Music Corp.
Introduced by Eileen Rodgers and girls in *Fiorello!* (musical).

Gidget
Words by Patti Washington, music by Fred Karger.
Columbia Pictures Music Corp.
Introduced by James Darren in *Gidget* (film).

Go, Jimmy, Go
Words and music by Doc Pomus and Mort Shuman.
Bob Wills Music, Inc.
Best-selling record by Jimmy Clanton (Ace).

Gold Fever, see **The Alaskans.**

Good Rockin' Tonight, see 1956.

Goodbye, Jimmy, Goodbye
Words and music by Jack Vaughn.
Knollwood Music Corp.
Best-selling record by Kathy Linden (Felsted).

Green Fields, see 1956.

Grin and Bear It
Words and music by John D. Loudermilk and Marijohn Wilkin.
Cedarwood Publishing Co., Inc.
Best-selling record by Jimmy Newman (M-G-M).

Hallelujah I Love Her So, see 1956.

Handy Man
Words and music by Otis Blackwell and Jimmy Jones.
Travis Music Co.
Best-selling record by Jimmy Jones (Cub).

Happy Anniversary
Words by Al Stillman, music by Robert Allen.
Korwin Music, Inc.
Introduced by Mitzi Gaynor in *Happy Anniversary* (film). Best-selling record by The Four Lads (Columbia).

Happy Organ, The
Words and music by Ken Wood (pseudonym for Walter R. Moody) and David Clowney.
Dorothy Music.
Best-selling record by Dave "Baby" Cortez (Clock).

Hard Travelin'
Words and music by Woody Guthrie.
Ludlow Music, Inc.
Introduced by Woody Guthrie.

Hawaiian Eye
Words and music by Mack David and Jerry Livingston.
M. Witmark & Sons.
From *Hawaiian Eye* (television series).

Heartaches by the Number
Words and music by Harlan Howard.
Pamper Music, Inc.
Introduced by Ray Price. Best-selling record by Guy Mitchell (Columbia).

Heavenly
Words by Sydney Shaw, music by Burt F. Bacharach.
Cathryl Music Corp.
Introduced by Johnny Mathis (Columbia).

He'll Have To Go
Words and music by Joe Allison and Audrey Allison.
Central Songs, Inc.
Best-selling record by Jim Reeves (RCA Victor).

Here Comes Summer
Words and music by Jerry Keller.
Jaymar Music Publishing Co., Inc.
Best-selling record by Jerry Keller (Kapp).

Hey, Little Girl
Words and music by Bobby Stevenson and Otis Blackwell.
Obie Music, Inc.
Best-selling record by Dee Clark (Abner).

Hey, Little Lucy! (Don' Tcha Put No Lipstick On)
Words and music by Aaron Schroeder, George Weiss, and Sharon Silbert.
Moorpark Music Corp.
Best-selling record by Conway Twitty (M-G-M).

High Hopes
Words by Sammy Cahn, music by James Van Heusen.
Maraville Music Corp.
Introduced by Frank Sinatra and Eddie Hodges in *A Hole in the Head* (film). Academy Award-winning song, 1959. Best-selling record by Frank Sinatra and Eddie Hodges (Capitol).

Home
Words and music by Roger Miller.
Tree Publishing Co., Inc.
Best-selling record by Jim Reeves (RCA Victor).

Hound Dog Man
Words and music by Doc Pomus and Mort Shuman.
Fabulous Music, Inc.
Introduced by Fabian in *Hound Dog Man* (film).

Hushabye
Words and music by Doc Pomus and Mort Shuman.
Brittany Music, Inc.
Best-selling record by The Mystics (Laurie).

I Ain't Never
Words and music by Mel Tillis and Webb Pierce.
Cedarwood Publishing Co., Inc.
Best-selling record by Webb Pierce (Decca).

I Believe to My Soul
Words and music by Ray Charles.
Progressive Music Publishing Co., Inc.
Best-selling record by Ray Charles (Atlantic).

I Go Ape
Words by Howard Greenfield, music by Neil Sedaka.
Screen Gems-Columbia Music, Inc.
Best-selling record by Neil Sedaka (RCA Victor).

I Got a Wife
Words by Erwin Wenzlaff, music by Eddie Mascari.
MRC Music, Inc.
Best-selling record by The Mark IV (Mercury).

I Got Stripes
Words and music by Johnny Cash and Charlie Williams.
Johnny Cash Music, Inc.
Best-selling record by Johnny Cash (Columbia).

I Loves You Porgy, see 1935.

I Need Your Love Tonight
Words and music by Sid Wayne and Bix Reichner.
Gladys Music, Inc.
Best-selling record by Elvis Presley (RCA Victor).

I Only Have Eyes for You, see 1934.

I Say Hello
Words and music by Harold Rome.
Chappell & Co., Inc.
Introduced by Dolores Gray in *Destry Rides Again* (musical).

I Waited Too Long
Words by Howard Greenfield, music by Neil Sedaka.
Screen Gems-Columbia Music, Inc.
Best-selling record by LaVern Baker (Atlantic).

I Wanna Be Around
Words and music by Johnny Mercer and Sadie Vimmerstedt.
Commander Publications.
Written as the result of a title idea sent to Mercer by Mrs. Sadie Vimmerstedt, a Youngstown, Ohio housewife. Best-selling record in 1963 by Tony Bennett (Columbia).

I Want To Walk You Home
Words and music by Antoine "Fats" Domino.
Travis Music Co.
Best-selling record by Fats Domino (Imperial).

If I Had a Girl
Words and music by Sid Tepper and Roy C. Bennett.
Sigma Music, Inc.
Best-selling record in 1960 by Rod Lauren (RCA Victor).

I'll Be Easy To Find
Words and music by Bart Howard.
Johnny Mathis Music, Inc.
Introduced by Johnny Mathis.

I'll Be Satisfied
Words and music by Berry Gordy, Jr., Gwen Gordy, and Tyran Carlo.
Pearl Music Co., Inc.
Best-selling record by Jackie Wilson (Brunswick).

I'm Gonna Get Married
Words and music by Harold Logan and Lloyd Price.
Lloyd and Logan, Inc.
Best-selling record by Lloyd Price (ABC-Paramount).

I'm in Love Again
Words and music by Vic McAlpin and George Morgan.
Acuff-Rose Publications.

I'm Ready
Words and music by Al Lewis, Sylvester Bradford, and Antoine "Fats" Domino.
Post Music, Inc./Vanderbuilt Music Corp.
Best-selling record by Fats Domino (Imperial).

Imitation of Life
Words by Paul Francis Webster, music by Sammy Fain.
Northern Music Corp.
From *Imitation of Life* (film).

Inspiration
Words by Joe Lubin, music by I. J. Roth.
Daywin Music, Inc.
Introduced by Doris Day in *Pillow Talk* (film).

It Happened to Jane
Words and music by Joe Lubin and I. J. Roth.
Daywin Music, Inc.
Introduced by Doris Day in *It Happened to Jane* (film).

It Was I
Words and music by Gary Paxton.
T.M. Music, Inc./Desert Palms Publishing Co./Brent Music Corp.
Best-selling record by Skip and Flip (Brent).

It's Late
Words and music by Dorsey Burnette.
Eric Music, Inc.
Best-selling record by Ricky Nelson (Imperial).

It's Time To Cry
Words and music by Paul Anka.
Spanka Music Corp.
Best-selling record by Paul Anka (ABC Paramount).

I've Come of Age
Words by Sid Jacobson, music by Lou Stallman.
We Three Music, Inc.
Best-selling record by Billy Storm (Columbia).

I've Got a Lot To Learn about Life
Words by Fran Landesman, music by Tommy Wolf.
Empress Music, Inc.
Introduced by Tani Seitz in *The Nervous Set* (musical).

I've Run Out of Tomorrows
Words by Lewis Compton, music by Vernon Mize and Hank Thompson.
Brazos Valley Music, Inc.
Best-selling record by Hank Thompson (Capitol).

Jimmie Brown, the Newsboy, see 1931.

Jimmy Brown Song, The see **The Three Bells,** 1948.

Joanna
Words by Johnny Mercer, music by Henry Mancini.
Northridge Music, Inc.
Adapted from music written for *Peter Gunn* (television series).

Just a Little Too Much
Words and music by Johnny Burnette.
Hilliard Music Co.
Best-selling record by Ricky Nelson (Imperial).

Just Ask Your Heart
Words by Pete Damato and Joe Ricci, music by Diane De Nota.
Rambed Publishing Co., Inc.
Best-selling record by Frankie Avalon (Chancellor).

Just for Once
Words by Dorothy Fields, music by Albert Hague.
Chappell & Co., Inc.
Introduced by Gwen Verdon, Richard Kiley, and Leonard Stone in *Redhead* (musical).

Just Keep It Up (And See What Happens)
Words and music by Otis Blackwell.
Travis Music Co.
Best-selling record by Dee Clark (Abner).

Kansas City
Words and music by Jerry Leiber and Mike Stoller.
Armo Music Corp.
Originally copyrighted in 1952 under the title, "K.C. Loving." Best-selling record in 1959 by Wilbert Harrison (Fury).

Kissin' Time
Words and music by Leonard Frazier and James Frazier.
Claiborne Music.
Best-selling record by Bobby Rydell (Cameo).

Kookie, Kookie, Lend Me Your Comb
Words and music by Irving Taylor.
M. Witmark & Sons.
From *77 Sunset Strip* (television series). Best-selling record by Edward Byrnes and Connie Stevens (Warner Brothers).

Kookie's Love Song (While Dancing)
Words and music by Mack David and Howie Horwitz.
M. Witmark & Sons.
From *77 Sunset Strip* (television series). Best-selling record by Edward Byrnes, with Joanie Sommers and The Mary Kaye Trio (Warner Brothers).

La Plume de Ma Tante
Words and music by Al Hoffman and Dick Manning.
Korwin Music, Inc.
Best-selling record by Hugo and Luigi and their Orchestra and Children's Chorus (RCA Victor).

Last Ride, The
Words by Robert Halcomb, music by Ted Daffan.
Silver Star Music Publishing Co.
Best-selling record by Hank Snow (RCA Victor).

Laugh, I Thought I'd Die, see 1956.

Lavender Blue (Dilly, Dilly), see 1948.

Lawman
Words by Mack David, music by Jerry Livingston.
M. Witmark & Sons.
From *Lawman* (television series).

Let Me Entertain You
Words by Stephen Sondheim, music by Jule Styne.
Williamson Music, Inc./Stratford Music Corp.
Introduced by Sandra Church and company in *Gypsy* (musical).

Let's Love
Words and music by Richie Ferraris and Norman Kaye.
Cathryl Music Corp.
Best-selling record by Johnny Mathis (Columbia).

Life To Go
Words and music by George Jones.
Starrite Publishing Co.
Best-selling record by Stonewall Jackson (Columbia).

Lipstick on Your Collar
Words by Edna Lewis, music by George Goehring.
Joy Music, Inc.
Best-selling record by Connie Francis (M-G-M).

Little Dipper
Music by Robert Maxwell.
Maxwell Music Corp.
Best-selling record, instrumental, by The Micky Mozart Quintet (Roulette).

Little Lamb
Words by Stephen Sondheim, music by Jule Styne.
Williamson Music, Inc./Stratford Music Corp.
Introduced by Sandra Church in *Gypsy* (musical).

Little Space Girl
Words and music by Jessie Lee Turner.
Longhorn Music Co.
Best-selling record in 1960 by Jessie Lee Turner (Carlton).

Living Doll (English)
Words and music by Lionel Bart.
Peter Maurice Music Co., Ltd., London, England.
Introduced by Cliff Richard in *Serious Charge* (film). Best-selling record by Cliff Richard (ABC Paramount).

Lonely for You
Words and music by Gary Stites.
David Jones, Inc.
Best-selling record by Gary Stites (Carlton).

Lonely Goatherd, The
Words by Oscar Hammerstein II, music by Richard Rodgers.
Williamson Music, Inc.
Introduced by Mary Martin and children in *The Sound of Music* (musical).

Lonely Street, see 1956.

Long Black Veil
Words and music by Marijohn Wilkin and Danny Dill.
Cedarwood Publishing Co., Inc.
Best-selling record by Lefty Frizzell (Columbia).

Love Held Lightly
Words by Johnny Mercer, music by Harold Arlen.
Harwin Music Corp.
Introduced by Odette Myrtil in *Saratoga* (musical).

Love Is Like Champagne (French)
English words by Carl Sigman, French words by Jean Constantin, music by Norbert Glanzberg.
Comfura, Paris, France, 1958/Southern Music Publishing Co., Inc.
Under its original title, "Mon Monège, a Moi," introduced in the United States by Yves Montand.

Love Potion Number Nine
Words and music by Jerry Leiber and Mike Stoller.
Quintet Music, Inc.
Best-selling record by The Clovers (United Artists).

Love Theme from *Ben Hur*
Music by Miklos Rozsa.
Robbins Music Corp.
From *Ben Hur* (film).

Luther Played the Boogie
Words and music by Johnny Cash.
Hi-Lo Music, Inc.
Best-selling record by Johnny Cash (Sun).

Mack the Knife, see 1956.

Makin' Love
Words and music by Floyd Robinson.
Emerald Music Publishing Co.
Best-selling record by Floyd Robinson (RCA Victor).

Manhã de Carnaval (Brazilian)
Words by Antonio Maria, music by Luis Bonfa.
Éditions Musicales "France Vedettes," Paris, France/Ross Jungnickel, Inc.
Introduced by Breno Mello in *Black Orpheus,* Academy Award-winning French film, 1960.

Maria
Words by Oscar Hammerstein II, music by Richard Rodgers.
Williamson Music, Inc.
Introduced by Patricia Neway, Muriel O'Malley, Elizabeth Howell, and Karen Shepard in *The Sound of Music* (musical).

Marina (Belgian)
English words by Ray Maxwell, Italian words and music by Rocco Granata.
Class Music, Antwerp, Belgium/Atlantic Music Corp.
Best-selling record (in Italian) by the Dutch singer, Willi Alberti (London).

Marry Young
Words by Carolyn Leigh, music by Cy Coleman.
Edwin H. Morris & Co., Inc.
Introduced by Tony Bennett.

Mary Lou
Words and music by Ron Hawkins and Jacqueline Magill.
Patricia Music Publishing Corp.
Best-selling record by Ronnie Hawkins (Roulette).

Mating Game, The
Words by Lee Adams, music by Charles Strouse.
Robbins Music Corp.
Introduced by Debbie Reynolds in *The Mating Game* (film).

Midnight Flyer
Words and music by Mayme Watts and Robert Mosely.
Paxwin Music Corp.
Best-selling record by Nat "King" Cole (Capitol).

Milord (French)
English words by Bunny Lewis, French words by G. Moustaki, music by Marguerite Monnot.
Éditions Salabert, S.A., Paris, France/Alamo Music, Inc.
Introduced and international best-selling record by Edith Piaf (Capitol).

Mr. Blue
Words and music by Dewayne Blackwell.
Cornerstone Publishing Co.
Best-selling record by The Fleetwoods (Dolton).

Moanin'
Music by Bobby Timmons.
Estella Music Corp.
Introduced by Julian "Cannonball" Adderley and his Band, featuring Bobby Timmons at the piano. Lyrics by Jon Hendricks added in 1961.

Morgen, also known as **One More Sunrise** (German)
English words by Noel Sherman, German words and music by Peter Mösser.
Monopol-Verlag GmbH, Berlin, Germany/Llee Corp.
Best-selling record by the Yugoslav singer, Ivo Robic, singing in German (Laurie).

M-Squad
Music by William "Count" Basie.
Alaska Music Co., Inc.
Theme of *M-Squad* (television series).

Music of Home, The
Words and music by Frank Loesser.
Frank Music Corp.
Introduced by Bruce MacKay and Anthony Perkins in 1960 in *Greenwillow* (musical).

My Favorite Things
Words by Oscar Hammerstein II, music by Richard Rodgers.
Williamson Music, Inc.
Introduced by Patricia Neway and Mary Martin in *The Sound of Music* (musical).

My Happiness, see 1948.

My Wish Came True, see 1957.

Never Will I Marry
Words and music by Frank Loesser.
Frank Music Corp.
Introduced by Anthony Perkins in 1960 in *Greenwillow* (musical).

No Other Arms, No Other Lips, see 1952.

Oh! Carol
Words by Howard Greenfield, music by Neil Sedaka.
Screen Gems-Columbia Music, Inc.
Best-selling record by Neil Sedaka (RCA Victor).

Old Moon
Words by Waco Austin, music by O'Brien Fisher.
Travis Music Co./Sundown Music Co.
Best-selling record by Betty Foley (Bandera).

On an Evening in Roma, also known as **Sott'er Celo de Roma** (Italian)
English words by Nan Frederics, Italian words by U. Bertini, music by S. Taccani.
Edizioni Musicali Successo, Milan, Italy, 1957/Zodiac Music Corp.
Best-selling record by Dean Martin (Capitol).

On the Beach
Words by Steve Allen, music by Ernest Gold.
Planetary Music Publishing Corp.
From *On the Beach* (film).

Once Knew a Fella
Words and music by Harold Rome.
Chappell & Co., Inc.
Introduced by Andy Griffith in *Destry Rides Again* (musical).

One More Sunrise, see Morgen.

Only You, see 1955.

Partners
Words and music by Danny Dill.
Cedarwood Publishing Co., Inc.
Best-selling record by Jim Reeves (RCA Victor).

Peter Gunn Theme
Music by Henry Mancini.
Northridge Music, Inc., 1958, 1959.
From *Peter Gunn* (television series). Best-selling record by Ray Anthony (Capitol).

Petite Fleur, see 1952.

Pick Me Up on Your Way Down
Words and music by Harlan Howard.
Pamper Music, Inc.
Best-selling record by Charlie Walker (Columbia).

Pillow Talk
Words and music by Buddy Pepper and Inez James.
Artists Music, Inc.
Introduced by Doris Day and Rock Hudson in *Pillow Talk* (film).

Plain Jane
Words and music by Doc Pomus and Mort Shuman.
Rumbalero Music, Inc.
Best-selling record by Bobby Darin (Atco).

Poet's Dream, The (French)
English words by Mal Peters, French words and music by Charles Trenet.
France Music Co., 1951/Leeds Music Corp.
A new adaptation of "L'Âme des Poètes." Previous version, "At Last! At Last!" published in 1951.

Poison Ivy
Words and music by Jerry Leiber and Mike Stoller.
Tiger Music, Inc.
Best-selling record by The Coasters (Atco).

Politics and Poker
Words by Sheldon Harnick, music by Jerry Bock.
Sunbeam Music Corp.
Introduced by Howard Da Silva in *Fiorello!* (musical).

Poor Jenny
Words and music by Boudleaux Bryant and Felice Bryant.
Acuff-Rose Publications.
Best-selling record by The Everly Brothers (Cadence).

Poor Old Heartsick Me
Words and music by Helen Carter.
Acuff-Rose Publications.
Best-selling record by Margie Bowes (Hickory).

Pretty Blue Eyes
Words and music by Teddy Randazzo and Bob Weinstein.
Almimo Music, Inc.
Best-selling record by Steve Lawrence (ABC Paramount).

Pretty Girls Everywhere
Words and music by Eugene Church and Thomas Williams.
Recordo Music Publishers.
Best-selling record by Eugene Church (Class).

Puppy Love
Words and music by Paul Anka.
Spanka Music Corp.
Best-selling record in 1960 by Paul Anka (ABC Paramount).

Quiet Village, see 1951.

Rebel, The
Words by Richard Markowitz and Andrew Fenady, music by Richard Markowitz.
M. Witmark & Sons.
Theme from *The Rebel* (television series).

Red River Rock
Music by Tom King, Ira Mack, and Fred Mendelsohn.
Vicki Music, Inc.
Best-selling record, instrumental, by Johnny and The Hurricanes (Warwick).

Red River Rose
Words and music by Tommie Connor and Johnnie Reine.
Michael Reine Music Co., Ltd./Leeds Music Corp.
Best-selling record by The Ames Brothers (RCA Victor).

Reveille Rock
Words by I. Mack, music by C. Conatser and J. King.
Vicki Music, Inc.
Best-selling record, instrumental, by Johnny and The Hurricanes (Warwick).

Richard Diamond Theme
Music by Pete Rugolo.
Jimmy McHugh Music, Inc.
Theme of *The Richard Diamond Show* (television series).

Right Time, The, see 1957.

Ring-a Ling-a Lario
Words and music by Arthur Kent, Jerry Grant, and George Armond.
Planetary Music Publishing Corp.
Best-selling record by Jimmie Rodgers (Roulette).

Rio Bravo
Words by Paul Francis Webster, music by Dimitri Tiomkin.
M. Witmark & Sons.
Introduced by Dean Martin in *Rio Bravo* (film).

River Boat
Words and music by Bill Anderson.
Champion Music Corp./Tree Publishing Co., Inc.
Best-selling record by Faron Young (Capitol).

Robbin' the Cradle
Words and music by Anthony J. Bellusci.
Wonder Music Co., Inc.
Best-selling record by Tony Bellers (NRC).

Running Bear
Words and music by J. P. Richardson.
Big Bopper Music Co.
Best-selling record by Johnny Preston (Mercury).

Samba de Orfeu (Brazilian)
Portuguese words by Antonio Maria, music by Luis Bonfa.
Éditions Musicales "France Vedettes," Paris, France/Ross Jungnickel, Inc.
Introduced in *Black Orpheus,* Academy Award-winning French film, 1960.

Same Old Me
Words and music by Fuzzy Owen.
Pamper Music, Inc.
Best-selling record by Ray Price (Columbia).

Sandy
Words and music by Terry Fell.
American Music, Inc./Maravilla Music, Inc.
Best-selling record by Larry Hall (Strand).

Say, Man
Words and music by E. McDaniel.
Arc Music Corp.
Best-selling record by Bo Diddley (Checker).

Sea of Love
Words and music by George Khoury and Phil Battiste.
Kamar Publishing Co.
Best-selling record by Phil Phillips (Mercury).

Secret of Christmas, The
Words by Sammy Cahn, music by James Van Heusen.
Leo Feist, Inc.
Introduced by Bing Crosby in *Say One for Me* (film).

See You in September
Words by Sid Wayne, music by Sherman Edwards.
Jack Gold Music Co.
Best-selling record by The Tempos (Climax).

Set Him Free
Words and music by Skeeter Davis, Penny Moyer, and Marie Wilson.
Pamper Music, Inc.
Best-selling record by Skeeter Davis (RCA Victor).

77 Sunset Strip
Words and music by Mack David and Jerry Livingston.
M. Witmark & Sons.
Theme from *77 Sunset Strip* (television series).

She Say (Oom Dooby Doom)
Words and music by Barry Mann and Mike Anthony.
Travis Music Co.
Best-selling record by The Diamonds (Mercury).

Shimmy, Shimmy Ko-Ko Bop
Words and music by Bob Smith.
Lois Publishing Co.
Best-selling record in 1960 by Little Anthony and The Imperials (End).

Ship on a Stormy Sea
Words and music by Jimmy Clanton, Cosima Matassa, Seth David, and Malcolm Rebennack.
Ace Publishing Co., Inc./Figure Music, Inc.
Best-selling record by Jimmy Clanton (Ace).

Since I Don't Have You
Words by James Beaumont, Janet Vogel, Joseph Verscharen, Walter Lester, and John Taylor, music by Joseph Rock and Lennie Martin.
Calico Records, Inc.
Best-selling record by The Skyliners (Calico).

Since I Made You Cry
Words and music by Robert Mosely and Mayme Watts.
Paxwin Music Corp.
Best-selling record in 1960 by The Rivieras (Co-ed).

Sitting in the Back Seat
Words by Bob Hilliard, music by Lee Pockriss.
Post Music, Inc.
Best-selling record by Paul Evans and The Curls (Guaranteed).

Six Boys and Seven Girls
Words and music by Carl Sigman.
Pambill Music, Inc.
Best-selling record by Anita Bryant (Carlton).

16 Candles
Words and music by Luther Dixon and Allyson R. Khent.
Coronation Music, Inc./January Music Corp.
Best-selling record by The Crests (Co-ed).

Sixteen Going on Seventeen
Words by Oscar Hammerstein II, music by Richard Rodgers.
Williamson Music, Inc.
Introduced by Laurie Peters in *The Sound of Music* (musical).

Sleep Walk (Canadian)
Music by Ann Farina, John Farina, and Santo Farina.
T.M. Music, Inc.
Best-selling record, instrumental, by Santo and Johnny (Canadian-American).

Small World
Words by Stephen Sondheim, music by Jule Styne.
Williamson Music, Inc./Stratford Music Corp.
Introduced by Ethel Merman and Jack Klugman in *Gypsy* (musical).

Smokie, Part II
Music by William P. Black.
Jec Publishing Corp.
Best-selling record, instrumental, by Bill Black's Combo (Hi).

So Close
Words and music by Brook Benton, Clyde Otis, and Luther Dixon.
Eden Music, Inc.
Best-selling record by Brook Benton (Mercury).

Some People
Words by Stephen Sondheim, music by Jule Styne.
Williamson Music, Inc./Stratford Music Corp.
Introduced by Ethel Merman in *Gypsy* (musical).

Somebody's Back in Town
Words and music by Don Helms, Teddy Wilburn, and Doyle Wilburn.
Sure Fire Music Co., Inc.
Best-selling record by The Wilburn Brothers (Decca).

Sorry, I Ran All the Way Home
Words and music by Harry Giosasi and Artie Zwirn.
Figure Music, Inc.
Best-selling record by The Impalas (Cub).

Sound of Music, The
Words by Oscar Hammerstein II, music by Richard Rodgers.
Williamson Music, Inc.
Introduced by Mary Martin in *The Sound of Music* (musical).

Starbright
Words and music by Lee Pockriss and Paul J. Vance.
Cathryl Music Corp.
Introduced by Johnny Mathis (Columbia).

Staying Young
Words and music by Robert Merrill.
Valyr Music Corp.
Introduced by Walter Pidgeon in *Take Me Along* (musical).

Story of My Love, The
Words and music by Jack Nance and Conway Twitty (pseudonym for Harold Jenkins).
Marielle Music Publishing Corp.
Best-selling record by Conway Twitty (M-G-M).

Story of Our Love, The
Words by Tony Piano, music by Michael Coldin.
Cathryl Music Corp.
Best-selling record by Johnny Mathis (Columbia).

Strange Are the Ways of Love
Words by Ned Washington, music by Dimitri Tiomkin.
Leo Feist, Inc.
Introduced by Randy Sparks in *The Young Land* (film). Nominated for Academy Award, 1959.

Summertime Love
Words and music by Frank Loesser.
Frank Music Corp.
Introduced by Anthony Perkins in 1960 in *Greenwillow* (musical).

Sunday in New York
Words and music by Portia Nelson.
Mayfair Music Corp.
Introduced by Ceil Cabot and Gerry Matthews in *Julius Monk's Demi-Dozen* (nightclub revue).

Sweet Nothin's
Words and music by Ronnie Self.
Champion Music Corp.
Best-selling record in 1960 by Brenda Lee (Decca).

Sweeter Than You
Words and music by Baker Knight.
Hilliard Music Co.
Best-selling record by Ricky Nelson (Imperial).

Swingin' on a Rainbow
Words by Bob Marcucci, music by Pete De Angelis.
Debmar Publishing Co., Inc.
Best-selling record in 1960 by Frankie Avalon (Chancellor).

T.L.C., also known as **Tender Love and Care**
Words and music by Johnny Lehmann, Stan Lebowsky, and Herb Clarke.
Nom Music, Inc.
Best-selling record in 1960 by Jimmie Rodgers (Roulette).

Take a Message to Mary
Words and music by Felice Bryant and Boudleaux Bryant.
Acuff-Rose Publications.
Best-selling record by The Everly Brothers (Cadence).

Take Me Along
Words and music by Robert Merrill.
Valyr Music Corp.
Introduced by Jackie Gleason and Walter Pidgeon in *Take Me Along* (musical).

Talk That Talk
Words and music by Sid Wyche.
Merrimac Music Corp.
Best-selling record in 1960 by Jackie Wilson (Brunswick).

Talkin' 'bout You
Words and music by Ray Charles.
Progressive Music Publishing Co., Inc.
Introduced by Ray Charles (Atlantic).

Tallahassee Lassie
Words and music by Frank C. Slay, Jr., Bob Crewe, and Frederick A. Picariello.
Conley Music, Inc.
Best-selling record by Freddy Cannon (Swan).

Tear Drop (Canadian)
Music by Ann Farina, John Farina, and Santo Farina.
T.M. Music, Inc.
Best-selling record, instrumental, by Santo and Johnny (Canadian-American).

Teardrops on Your Letter
Words and music by Henry Glover.
Lois Publishing Co.
Best-selling record by Hank Ballard and The Midnighters (King).

Teardrops Will Fall
Words and music by Marion Smith and Dickey Doo.
Dee Dee/Palmina Music.
Best-selling record by Dickey Doo and The Don'ts (Swan).

Teddy
Words and music by Paul Anka.
Spanka Music Corp.
Best-selling record in 1960 by Connie Francis (M-G-M).

Teen Angel
Words and music by Jean Surrey and Red Surrey.
Acuff-Rose Publications.
Best-selling record in 1960 by Mark Dinning (M-G-M).

Teen Beat
Music by Sander Nelson and Arthur Egnoian.
Drive-In Music Co., Inc.
Best-selling record by Sandy Nelson (Original Sound).

Teenager in Love, A
Words and music by Jerome "Doc" Pomus and Mort Shuman.
Rumbalero Music, Inc.
Best-selling record by Dion and The Belmonts (Laurie).

Ten Thousand Drums
Words and music by Mel Tillis and Carl Smith.
Cedarwood Publishing Co., Inc.
Best-selling record by Carl Smith (Columbia).

Tender Love and Care, see **T.L.C.**

That's Enough
Words and music by Ray Charles.
Progressive Music Publishing Co., Inc.
Best-selling record by Ray Charles (Atlantic).

That's Why, see 1957.

Theme from *A Summer Place*
Music by Max Steiner.
M. Witmark & Sons.
Theme from *A Summer Place* (film). Best-selling record in 1961 and 1962 by Percy Faith and his Orchestra (Columbia).

Theme from *Peter Gunn*, see **Peter Gunn Theme.**

There Goes My Baby
Words and music by Benjamin Nelson, Lover Patterson, and George Treadwell.
Jot Music Co./Progressive Music Publishing Co., Inc.
Best-selling record by The Drifters (Atlantic).

There Is Something on Your Mind, see 1957.

There's a Big Wheel
Words and music by Don Gibson.
Acuff-Rose Publications.
Best-selling record by Wilma Lee and Stoney Cooper (Hickory).

They Came to Cordura
Words by Sammy Cahn, music by James Van Heusen.
Maraville Music Corp.
From *They Came to Cordura* (film). Best-selling record by Frank Sinatra (Capitol).

This Earth Is Mine
Words by Sammy Cahn, music by James Van Heusen.
Northern Music Corp.
From *This Earth Is Mine* (film).

This Friendly World
Words and music by Ken Darby.
Miller Music Corp.
Introduced by Fabian in *Hound Dog Man* (film).

This I Swear
Words by Joe Rock and The Skyliners, music by Lennie Martin.
Calico Records, Inc.
Best-selling record by The Skyliners (Calico).

This Should Go On Forever
Words by J. Miller, music by J. Miller and B. Jolivette.
Jamil Music.
Best-selling record by Rod Bernard (Argo).

Thousand Miles Ago, A
Words and music by Mel Tillis and Webb Pierce.
Cedarwood Publishing Co., Inc.
Best-selling record by Webb Pierce (Decca).

Three Stars
Words and music by Tommy Dee.
American Music, Inc.
Best-selling record by Tommy Dee and Carol Kay (Crest).

Tiger
Words and music by Ollie Jones.
Roosevelt Music Co., Inc./Rambed Publishing Co., Inc.
Best-selling record by Fabian (Chancellor).

Tijuana Jail, The
Words and music by Denny Thompson.
Travis Music Co.
Best-selling record by The Kingston Trio (Capitol).

'Til I Kissed You
Words and music by Don Everly.
Acuff-Rose Publications.
Best-selling record by The Everly Brothers (Cadence).

'Til Tomorrow
Words by Sheldon Harnick, music by Jerry Bock.
Sunbeam Music Corp.
Introduced by Ellen Hanley and company in *Fiorello!* (musical).

Time and the River
Words and music by Aaron Schroeder and Wally Gold.
Arch Music Co., Inc.
Best-selling record in 1960 by Nat "King" Cole (Capitol).

Together Wherever We Go
Words by Stephen Sondheim, music by Jule Styne.
Williamson Music, Inc./Stratford Music Corp.
Introduced by Ethel Merman, Sandra Church, and Jack Klugman in *Gypsy* (musical).

Too Much Tequila
Music by Dave Burgess.
Jat Music, Inc.
Best-selling record, instrumental, by The Champs (Challenge).

Touch of Pink, A
Words and music by Diane Lampert and Richard Loring.
Northern Music Corp.
From *The Wild and the Innocent* (film).

Tracy's Theme
Music by Robert Ascher.
Devon Music, Inc.
Introduced in *The Philadelphia Story* (television dramatic production). Best-selling record, instrumental, by Spencer Ross (pseudonym for Robert Mersey) and his Orchestra (Columbia).

Turn Me Loose
Words and music by Jerome "Doc" Pomus and Mort Shuman.
Frankie Avalon Music, Inc./Hill and Range Songs, Inc.
Best-selling record by Fabian (Chancellor).

Twixt Twelve and Twenty
Words and music by Aaron Schroeder and Fredda Gold.
Spoone Music Corp.
Best-selling record by Pat Boone (Dot).

Uh! Oh! (The Nutty Squirrels)
Words and music by Granville "Sascha" Burland and Don Elliott.
Jason Music, Inc.
Best-selling record by The Nutty Squirrels (Hanover).

Under Your Spell Again
Words and music by Dusty Rhodes and Buck Owens.
Central Songs, Inc.
Best-selling records by Buck Owens (Capitol) and Ray Price (Columbia).

Untouchables, The
Music by Nelson Riddle.
Desilu Music Corp.
From *The Untouchables* (television series).

Venus
Words and music by Ed Marshall.
Rambed Publishing Co., Inc./Lansdale Music Corp.
Best-selling record by Frankie Avalon (Chancellor).

Very Next Man, The
Words by Sheldon Harnick, music by Jerry Bock.
Sunbeam Music Corp.
Introduced by Patricia Wilson in *Fiorello!* (musical).

Village of St. Bernadette, The (English)
Words and music by Eula Parker.
Francis, Day & Hunter, Ltd., London, England/Ludlow Music, Inc.
Introduced in England by Anne Shelton. Best-selling United States record by Andy Williams (Cadence).

Walking Away Whistling
Words and music by Frank Loesser.
Frank Music Corp.
Introduced by Ellen McCown in 1960 in *Greenwillow* (musical).

Warm and Willing
Words and music by Jimmy McHugh, Jay Livingston, and Ray Evans.
Miller Music Corp.
From *A Private's Affair* (film).

Waterloo
Words and music by John Loudermilk and Marijohn Wilkin.
Cedarwood Publishing Co., Inc.
Best-selling record by Stonewall Jackson (Columbia).

Way Down Yonder in New Orleans, see 1922.

We Got Love
Words by Kal Mann, music by Bernie Lowe.
Kalmann Music, Inc./Lowe Music Corp.
Best-selling record by Bobby Rydell (Cameo).

What a Diff'rence a Day Makes, see 1934.

What Do I Care
Words by Al Stillman, music by Max Steiner.
M. Witmark & Sons.
Adapted from the theme from *The FBI Story* (film).

What in the World's Come Over You
Words and music by Jack Scott.
Starfire Music Corp.
Best-selling record by Jack Scott (Top Rank).

What Is Love?
Words and music by Lee Pockriss and Paul Vance.
Planetary Music Publishing Corp.
Best-selling record by The Playmates (Roulette).

What'd I Say
Words and music by Ray Charles.
Progressive Music Publishing Co., Inc.
Best-selling record by Ray Charles (Atlantic).

When Did I Fall in Love?
Words by Sheldon Harnick, music by Jerry Bock.
Sunbeam Music Corp.
Introduced by Ellen Hanley in *Fiorello!* (musical).

When It's Springtime in Alaska
Words and music by Tillman Franks.
Cajun Publishing Co.
Best-selling record by Johnny Horton (Columbia).

Where Were You on Our Wedding Day
Words and music by Harold Logan, Lloyd Price, and John Patton.
Pamco Music, Inc.
Best-selling record by Lloyd Price (ABC-Paramount).

Which One Is To Blame
Words and music by Redd Stewart and Sunny Dull.
Ridgeway Music.
Best-selling record by The Wilburn Brothers (Decca).

White Lightning
Words and music by Jape Richardson.
Glad Music Co.
Best-selling record by George Jones (Mercury).

Who Cares (For Me)
Words and music by Don Gibson.
Acuff-Rose Publications.
Best-selling record by Don Gibson (RCA Victor).

Who Shot Sam
Words and music by Darrell Edwards, Ray Jackson, and George Jones.
Glad Music Co./Starday Music.
Best-selling record by George Jones (Mercury).

Who Was That Lady?
Words by Sammy Cahn, music by James Van Heusen.
Saunders Publications, Inc.
Introduced by Dean Martin. From *Who Was That Lady?* (film).

Woo-Hoo
Words and music by George Donald McGraw.
Skidmore Music Co., Inc./McGraw Music Co.
Best-selling record by The Rock-a-Teens (Roulette).

Worried Man, A
Words and music by Dave Guard and Tom Glazer.
Harvard Music, Inc.
Adapted from a traditional American folk song. Part of the standard repertoire of The Carter Family, country and western artists. Best-selling record by The Kingston Trio (Capitol).

You Better Know It
Words and music by Jackie Wilson and Norm Henry.
Pearl Music Co., Inc.
Best-selling record by Jackie Wilson (Brunswick).

You Better Watch Yourself
Words and music by Walter Jacobs.
Arc Music Corp.
Best-selling record in 1954 by Little Walter (Checker).

You Got What It Takes
Words and music by B. Gordy and R. Davis.
Arc Music Corp.
Best-selling record by Marv Johnson (United Artists).

You Were Mine
Words and music by Paul Giacalone.
Dara Music Corp./Patsy Ann Music.
Best-selling record by The Fireflies (Ribbon).

You'll Never Get Away from Me
Words by Stephen Sondheim, music by Jule Styne.
Williamson Music, Inc./Stratford Music Corp.
Introduced by Ethel Merman and Jack Klugman in *Gypsy* (musical).

You're Gonna Miss Me
Words and music by Eddie Curtis.
Aida Music, Inc.
Best-selling record by Connie Francis (M-G-M).

You're So Fine
Words and music by Lance Finney, Bob West, and Willie Schofield.
West-Higgins Publishing Co.
Best-selling record by The Falcons (Unart).

You've Got Personality
Words and music by Harold Logan and Lloyd Price.
Lloyd and Logan, Inc.
Best-selling record by Lloyd Price (ABC-Paramount).

List of Titles

A

A.B.C.'s of Love, The, 1956.
Aba Daba Honeymoon, 1951.
Accidents Will Happen, 1950.
According to My Heart, 1956.
Acorn in the Meadow, 1953.
Adelaide, 1955.
Adelaide's Lament, 1950.
Adventures in Paradise, 1959.
Affair To Remember, An, 1957.
After the Lights Go Down Low, 1956.
Ain't Got No Home, 1956.
Ain't It a Shame, see Ain't That a Shame, 1955.
Ain't That a Shame, 1955.
Ain't That Love, 1957.
Ain't That Lovin' You Baby, 1955.
Airegin, 1954.
Aisle, The, see To the Aisle, 1957.
Alabama Jubilee, 1952.
Alaskans, The, 1959.
Alice in Wonderland, 1951.
All at Once, 1955.
All at Once You Love Her, 1955.
All by Myself, 1955.
All Grown Up, 1958.
All I Have To Do Is Dream, 1958.
All I Need Is the Girl, 1959.
All My Love, 1950.
All Night Long, 1951.
All of These and More, 1957.
All of You, 1954.
All Over Again, 1958.
All Right, 1955.
All Shook Up, 1957.
All the Time, 1958.
All the Way, 1957.
All-American Boy, The, 1958.
Allegheny Moon, 1956.
Allentown Jail, 1954.
Allez-Vous-En, Go Away, 1953.
Almost, 1951.
Almost Always, 1953.
Almost Grown, 1959.
Almost in Your Arms, 1958.
Almost Paradise, 1957.
Alone, 1957.
Alone at Last, 1952.
Alone Too Long, 1954.
Alone with You, 1958.
Along Came Jones, 1959.
Alright, Okay, You Win, 1955.
Alvin's Harmonica, 1959.
Always, Always, 1951.
Always Late (With Your Kisses), 1951.
Am I in Love, 1952.
Am I in Love?, 1954.
Am I Losing You?, 1956.
Am I That Easy To Forget?, 1958.
America, 1957.
American Beauty Rose, 1950.
Amigo's Guitar, 1959.
Among My Souvenirs, 1959.
Anastasia, 1956.
And So To Sleep Again, 1951.
And That Reminds You, see My Heart Reminds Me, 1957.
And This Is My Beloved, 1953.
And You'll Be Home, 1950.
Andiamo, 1950.
Ànema e Core, 1954.
Angel Baby, 1958.
Angel Eyes, 1953.
Angelina, 1953.
Angels in the Sky, 1954.
Angels Listened In, The, 1959.
Angel Smile, 1958.
Anna, 1953.
Anne Marie, 1957.
Annie Had a Baby, 1954.
Another Autumn, 1951.
Another Sleepless Night, 1959.
Another Time, Another Place, 1958.
Answer Me, My Love, 1953.
Anticipation Blues, 1950.
Any Time, 1951.
Any Way the Wind Blows, 1959.
Any Way You Want Me (That's How I Will Be), 1956.
Anyone Would Love You, 1959.
Anything Can Happen-Mambo, 1954.
Anywhere I Wander, 1952.
Apple Green, 1959.
April Age, The, 1956.
April in Portugal, 1953.
April Love, 1957.
A-Razz-A-Ma-Tazz, 1950.
Are You Mine?, 1955.
Are You Really Mine?, 1958.

Are You Sincere, 1957.
Are You Teasing Me?, 1952.
Ariane, 1956.
Armen's Theme, 1956.
A-round the Corner (Beneath the Berry Tree), 1950.
Around the World, 1956.
Arrivederci, Roma, 1955.
As Far As I'm Concerned, 1954.
As I Love You, 1955.
As Long As I Live, 1955.
Ascot Gavotte, 1956.
Asia Minor, 1951.
Ask Me, 1956.
At Last! At Last!, 1951.
At My Front Door (Crazy Little Mama Song), 1955.
At the End of a Rainbow, see The End, 1958.
At the Hop, 1957.
Athena, 1954.
Auf Wiederseh'n, Sweetheart, 1952.
Autumn Concerto, 1956.
Autumn in Rome, 1954.
Autumn Leaves, 1950.
Autumn Waltz, The, 1956.
Away All Boats, 1956.

B

Baby (You've Got What It Takes), 1959.
Baby, Baby, Baby, 1950.
Baby Doll, 1956.
Baby, Don't Do It, 1952.
Baby, Let Me Hold Your Hand, 1951.
Baby Talk, 1958.
Baby We're Really in Love, 1951.
Back Street Affair, 1952.
Back Track!, 1954.
Back Up Buddy, 1954.
Backward, Turn Backward (O' Time in Your Flight), 1954.
Bad and the Beautiful, The, 1953.
Bad, Bad Whiskey, 1950.
Bad Luck, 1956.
Bag's Groove, 1954.
Baión, The, 1953.
Ballad of a Teenage Queen, 1958.
Ballad of Davy Crockett, The, 1955.
Ballad of Paladin, 1958.
Ballad of the Sad Young Men, The, 1959.
Bamboo, 1950.
Bamboo Cage, see Smellin' of Vanilla, 1954.
Banana Boat Song, The, 1956.
Band of Angels, 1957.
Band of Gold, 1955.
Bandit, The, 1954.
Banjo's Back in Town, The, 1955.
Battle Hymn of the Republic, 1959.
Battle of Kookamonga, The, 1959.
Battle of New Orleans, The, 1957.
Baubles, Bangles, and Beads, 1953.
Bazoom, see I Need Your Lovin', 1954.
Be Anything (But Be Mine), 1952.
Be Kind to Your Parents, 1954.
Be Mine, 1950.
Be Mine Tonight, 1951.
Be My Guest, 1959.
Be My Life's Companion, 1951.
Be My Love, 1950.
Be Prepared, 1959.
Beats There a Heart So True, 1958.
Beautiful Brown Eyes, 1951.
Beautiful Lies, 1955.
Be-Bop Baby, 1957.
Be-Bop-a-Lula, 1956.
Because of You, 1951.
Because You're Mine, 1951.
Beep, Beep, 1958.
Believe in Me, 1955.
Believe What You Say, 1958.
Bell Bottom Blues, 1953.
Belle, Belle (My Liberty Belle), 1951.
Belle of the Ball, 1953.
Bells, 1952.
Bells Are Ringing, 1956.
Beloved, 1952.
Beloved, Be Faithful, 1950.
Bemsha Swing, 1952.
Bermuda, 1951.
Bernadine, 1957.
Bernie's Tune, 1953.
Berry Tree, The, 1954.
Best Is Yet To Come, The, 1959.
Best of Everything, The, 1959.
Best Thing for You, The, 1950.
Best Things Happen While You're Dancing, The, 1953.
Best Wishes, 1951.
Beware of It, 1954.
Bewitched, 1950.
Bible Tells Me So, The, 1955.
Big Black Giant, The, 1953.
Big D, 1956.
Big Daddy, 1958.

Big Guitar, The, 1958.
Big Hunk o' Love, A, 1959.
Big Hurt, The, 1959.
Big Mamou, 1953.
Big Man, 1958.
Big Midnight Special, 1959.
Bigger the Figure, The, 1952.
Billy Bayou, 1958.
Bim Bam Baby, 1952.
Bimbo, 1953.
Bimbombey, 1958.
Bing! Bang! Bong!, 1958.
Bird Dog, 1958.
Birmin'ham, 1955.
Birmingham Bounce, 1950.
Black Denim Trousers and Motorcycle Boots, 1955.
Black Night, 1951.
Black Slacks, 1957.
Blackberry Boogie, 1952.
Blackboard of My Heart, 1956.
Blackland Farmer, 1959.
Blacksmith Blues, The, 1952.
Blanche, 1956.
Bless Your Beautiful Hide, 1954.
Blob, The, 1958.
Bloodshot Eyes, 1950.
Blossom Fell, A, 1954.
Blow Out the Candle, 1952.
Blowing Wild, 1953.
Blue Bird Waltz, 1954.
Blue, Blue Day, 1957.
Blue Canary, 1953.
Blue Doll, 1957.
Blue Gardenia, 1953.
Blue Light Boogie, 1950.
Blue Mirage (Don't Go), 1955.
Blue Monday, 1957.
Blue Monk, 1954.
Blue Pacific Blues, The, see Sadie Thompson's Song, 1953.
Blue Shadows, 1950.
Blue Star, 1955.
Blue Suede Shoes, 1955.
Blue Tango, 1951.
Blue Velvet, 1951.
Blue Violins, 1951.
Bluebell, 1958.
Blueberry Hill, 1956.
Bluebird Island, 1951.
Blues from *Kiss Me Deadly*, 1955.
Blues in Advance, 1952.
Bo Diddley, 1955.
Bo Weevil, 1956.
Bobby Sox to Stockings, 1959.
Bonanza!, 1959.
Bongo Rock, 1959.
Bonjour Tristesse, 1957.
Bonne Nuit—Goodnight, 1951.
Bonnie Blue Gal, 1955.
Bonnie Come Back, 1959.
Bony Moronie, 1957.
Boogie Woogie Maxixe, 1953.
Book of Love, 1957.
Boom Boom Boomerang, 1955.
Booted, 1951.
Boppin' the Blues, 1956.
Bop-Ting-a-Ling, 1955.
Born To Be with You, 1956.
Born To Sing the Blues, 1955.
Born Too Late, 1958.
Boston Beguine, 1952.
Botch-a-Me, 1952.
Bourbon Street Beat, 1959.
Bourbon Street Parade, 1952.
Boutonniere, 1950.
Boy on a Dolphin, 1957.
Boy without a Girl, 1959.
Breakin' the Rules, 1953.
Breathless, 1958.
Bridges at Toko-Ri, The, 1954.
Bring Back the Thrill, 1950.
Broken Down Merry-Go-Round, 1950.
Broken-Hearted Melody, 1959.
Bronco, 1959.
Bumming Around, 1953.
Bundle of Southern Sunshine, A, 1951.
Bunny Hop, The, 1952.
Buon Natale (Means Merry Xmas to You), 1959.
Burn That Candle, 1955.
Bus Stop Song, The, 1956.
Bushel and a Peck, A, 1950.
Butterflies, 1953.
Butterfly, 1957.
Buzz, Buzz, Buzz, 1957.
Bye Bye Love, 1957.

C

Ca, C'est l'Amour, 1957.
Call Me, 1956.
Call of the Far-Away Hills, The, 1953.
Call Operator 210, 1952.
Calla, Calla, 1951.
Calypso Blues, 1950.
Calypso Joe, 1957.
Calypso Melody, 1957.
Can Anyone Explain (No! No! No!), 1950.

Can I Steal a Little Love?, 1956.
Can You Find It in Your Heart, 1956.
Canadian Sunset, 1956.
Can-Can, 1953.
Candy and Cake, 1950.
Cannon Ball, 1958.
Can't I, 1953.
Can't We Be Sweethearts, 1956.
Cara Mia, 1954.
Caravan, 1953.
Caribbean, 1953.
Carol, 1958.
Castle Rock, 1951.
Casual Look, A, 1956.
Catch a Falling Star, 1957.
Cattle Call, The, 1955.
'Cause I Love You, 1956.
Certain Smile, A, 1958.
Cerveza, 1958.
C'est a Hambourg, see The Left Bank, 1955.
C'est la Vie, 1955.
C'est Magnifique, 1953.
C'est Si Bon, 1950.
Cha-hua-hua, 1958.
Chain Gang, 1956.
Chains of Love, 1951.
Chances Are, 1957.
Changing Partners, 1953.
Chanson d'Amour, 1958.
Chantez, Chantez, 1957.
Chantilly Lace, 1958.
Charlie Brown, 1959.
Charmaine, 1952.
Chattanoogie Shoe Shine Boy, 1950.
Chee Chee-oo Chee (Sang the Little Bird), 1955.
Chella Llà, 1956.
Chelsea Bridge, 1952.
Cherokee Boogie, 1951.
Cherry Lips, 1956.
Cherry Pies Ought To Be You, 1950.
Cherry Pink and Apple Blossom White, 1951.
Cheyenne, 1956.
Chica Boo, 1951.
Chicago Style, 1952.
Children's Marching Song, The, 1958.
China Gate, 1957.
Chincherinchee, 1956.
Chipmunk Song, The (Christmas Don't Be Late), 1958.
Choo Choo Train, 1953.
Choo'n Gum, 1950.
Christmas in Killarney, 1950.
Church Bells May Ring, 1956.
Ciao, Ciao, Bambina, 1959.
Cincinnat-ti Dancing Pig, 1950.
Cinco Robles, 1956.
Cindy, Oh Cindy, 1956.
Cinnamon Sinner, 1954.
City Lights, 1958.
City of Angels, 1956.
Climb Ev'ry Mountain, 1959.
Clock, The, 1953.
Close Your Eyes, 1955.
Closer Than a Kiss, 1958.
Closer You Are, The, 1956.
C'mon Everybody, 1958.
Cocoanut Sweet, 1957.
Cocoanut Woman, 1957.
Cold, Cold Heart, 1951.
(You Can't Lose the Blues with) Colors, 1957.
Colt .45, 1958.
Come Along with Me, 1953.
Come Back Baby, 1954.
Come Go with Me, 1957.
Come into My Heart, 1959.
Come Next Spring, 1955.
Come On-a My House, 1950.
Come Prima, 1958.
Come Softly to Me, 1959.
Come to Me, 1957.
Come to Me, 1958.
Come to the Supermarket (In Old Peking), 1958.
Come Walk with Me, 1958.
Come What May, 1953.
Comes A-long A-Love, 1952.
Comment Allez-Vous? (How Are Things with You?), 1953.
Confirmation, 1953.
Congratulations to Someone, 1953.
Conscience, I'm Guilty, 1956.
Convicted, 1955.
Cool, 1957.
Cool Baby, 1957.
Could This Be Magic, 1957.
Count Every Star, 1950.
Count Your Blessings Instead of Sheep, 1952.
Country Girl, 1959.
Country Music Is Here To Stay, 1958.
Courtin' in the Rain, 1954.
Crawlin', 1953.
Crazy Arms, 1956.
Crazy 'bout Ya, Baby, 1954.
Crazy Heart, 1951.

Crazy in the Heart, 1956.
Crazy Love, 1958.
Crazy Man, Crazy, 1953.
Crazy Otto Rag, The, 1955.
Creep, The, 1953.
Croce di Oro, 1955.
Cross over the Bridge, 1954.
Crossfire, 1959.
Cry, 1951.
Cry, Cry Baby, 1950.
Cry, Cry Darling, 1954.
Cry Me a River, 1953.
Cry of the Wild Goose, The, 1950.
Cryin' Heart Blues, 1951.
Cryin', Prayin', Wishin', Waitin', 1955.
Crying in the Chapel, 1953.
Cuban Mambo, 1950.
Cuddle Buggin' Baby, 1950.
Cuddle Me, 1954.
Cupid's Boogie, 1950.
Curtain in the Window, 1958.
Cuz You're So Sweet, 1954.

D

Daddy, Daddy, 1952.
Daddy O, 1955.
Daddy's Little Boy, 1950.
Dance, Everyone, Dance, 1958.
Dance Me Loose, 1951.
Dance Only with Me, 1958.
Dance with Me, 1959.
Dance with Me Henry, 1955.
Dancin' with Someone (Longin' for You), 1953.
Danger! Heartbreak Ahead, 1954.
Dansero, 1953.
Dark Hollow, 1959.
Dark Is the Night, 1950.
Dark Moon, 1957.
Darn It Baby, That's Love, 1950.
Day of Jubilo, The, 1952.
Day the Rains Came, The, 1957.
Day-O, see The Banana Boat Song, 1956.
Dear Hearts and Gentle People, 1950.
Dear John, 1951.
Dear John Letter, A, 1953.
Dear Old Stockholm, 1951.
Dearie, 1950.
Death of Hank Williams, 1953.
Deceivin' Blues, 1950.
Deck of Cards, 1959.
Dede Dinah, 1958.
Delia's Gone, 1952.
Delicado, 1952.
Delilah Jones, see The Man with the Golden Arm, 1956.
Dennis the Menace, 1952.
Destination Moon, 1951.
Detour, 1951.
Devil or Angel, 1955.
Devoted to You, 1958.
Diana, 1957.
Diary, The, 1958.
Did Anyone Ever Tell You Mrs. Murphy, 1950.
Did You Close Your Eyes When We Kissed, 1957.
Didja Ever?, 1951.
Dim, Dim the Lights (I Want Some Atmosphere), 1954.
Dis-Donc, Dis-Donc, 1958.
Dissertation on the State of Bliss, 1954.
Distant Melody, 1954.
Django, 1955.
Do I Love You Because You're Beautiful, 1957.
Do Something for Me, 1950.
Do You Want To Dance?, 1958.
Does Your Chewing Gum Lose Its Flavor on the Bedpost Overnight?, 1959.
Dogface Soldier, 1955.
Doggie in the Window, see That Doggie in the Window, 1952.
Doggone It, Baby, I'm in Love, 1953.
Domani (Tomorrow), 1955.
Domino, 1950.
Don'cha Go 'way Mad, 1950.
Doncha' Think It's Time, 1958.
Donde Esta Santa Claus? (Where Is Santa Claus?), 1958.
Donna, 1958.
Don't, 1957.
Don't Ask Me Why, 1958.
Don't Be Angry, 1955.
Don't Be Cruel (To a Heart That's True), 1956.
Don't Call My Name, 1953.
Don't Cry, 1956.
Don't Deceive Me (Please Don't Go), 1953.
Don't Drop It, 1954.
Don't Ever Be Afraid To Go Home, 1952.
Don't Forbid Me, 1956.
Don't Forget, see Non Dimenticar, 1953.

Don't Go to Strangers, 1954.
Don't Just Stand There (When You Feel Like You're in Love), 1952.
Don't Laugh, 1956.
Don't Let Go, 1957.
Don't Let Her Go, 1955.
Don't Let the Stars Get in Your Eyes, 1953.
Don't Pity Me, 1958.
Don't Rock the Boat, Dear, 1950.
Don't Stay Away ('Till Love Grows Cold), 1952.
Don't Stay Away Too Long, 1955.
Don't Take It Out on Me, 1955.
Don't Take Your Guns to Town, 1958.
Don't Tell Me Your Troubles, 1959.
Don't You Know, 1954.
Don't You Know, 1959.
Don't You Know I Love You, 1951.
Door Is Still Open to My Heart, The, 1955.
Do-Re-Mi, 1959.
Dormi, Dormi, Dormi, 1958.
Double Crossing Blues, 1950.
Down in Mexico, 1956.
Down the Aisle of Love, 1958.
Down the Lane, 1950.
Down the Trail of Achin' Hearts, 1951.
Down Yonder, 1951.
Downhearted, 1953.
Dragnet, 1953.
Dream Along with Me (I'm on My Way to a Star), 1955.
Dream, Dream, Dream, 1954.
Dream Girl, 1952.
Dream Lover, 1959.
Dreamy, 1956.
Drifting, 1958.
Drown in My Tears, 1956.
Duke's Place, 1958.
Dungaree Doll!, 1955.

E

Early in the Morning, 1958.
Earth and the Sky, 1950.
Earth Angel (Will You Be Mine), 1954.
Earthbound, 1956.
Easy, Easy Baby, 1952.
Easy on the Eyes, 1952.
Eat, Drink and Be Merry, 1955.
Ebb Tide, 1953.
Ecstasy Tango, 1952.
Eddie, My Love, 1956.
Eddy's Song, 1953.
Eggbert, the Easter Egg, 1952.
Eh, Cumpari!, 1953.
Eight Days in a Week, 1952.
El Paso, 1959.
El Rancho Rock, 1958.
Elephants Tango, The, 1955.
11th Hour Melody, 1956.
Embrasse, 1953.
Empty Arms, 1957.
Enchanted, 1959.
Enchanted Island, 1958.
Enchanted Sea, The, 1959.
Enclosed, One Broken Heart, 1950.
(At) End, The (Of a Rainbow), 1958.
End of a Love Affair, The, 1950.
Endless Sleep, 1958.
Endlessly, 1959.
English Muffins and Irish Stew, 1956.
Enjoy Yourself (It's Later Than You Think), 1950.
Eternally, 1953.
Even Now, 1953.
Even Tho', 1954.
Every Day, see Every Day I Have the Blues, 1952.
Every Day I Have the Blues, 1952.
Ev'ry Street's a Boulevard in Old New York, 1952.
Everybody Likes To Cha Cha Cha, 1959.
Everybody Loves a Lover, 1958.
Everybody's Got a Home but Me, 1955.
Everyone's Laughing, 1957.
Everything's Coming Up Roses, 1959.
Experience Unnecessary, 1955.

F

Fabulous, 1957.
Fabulous Character, 1956.
Face in the Crowd, A, 1957.
Face to Face, 1953.
Face to the Wall, 1959.
Fair Warning, 1959.
Faith Can Move Mountains, 1952.
Fallen Star, A, 1957.
Fallin', 1958.
Falling Back to You, 1958.
Family Man, 1959.
Fan Tan Fannie, 1958.

Fancy Free, 1950.
Fandango, 1952.
Fanny, 1954.
Faraway Boy, 1959.
Farewell, 1955.
Farther up the Road, 1957.
Fascination, 1957.
Fat Man, The, 1950.
Fate, 1953.
Feel So Good, 1955.
Feet Up (Pat Him on the Po-Po), 1952.
Femininity, 1958.
Fever, 1956.
Finger of Suspicion Points at You, The, 1954.
Fini, 1953.
Fire Down Below, 1957.
Firefly, 1958.
First Anniversary, 1958.
First Born, 1956.
First Date, First Kiss, First Love, 1957.
First Name Initial, 1959.
Five Feet High and Rising, 1959.
Five Long Years, 1952.
Five Pennies, The, 1959.
5-10-15 Hours, 1952.
Flip Flop and Fly, 1955.
Florence, 1957.
Flowers Mean Forgiveness, 1956.
Fly Me to the Moon, 1954.
Follow the Fold, 1950.
Folsom Prison Blues, 1956.
Fool, The, 1956.
Fool, Fool, Fool, 1951.
Fool for You, A, 1955.
Fool Such As I, A, 1952.
Fool Was I, A, 1953.
Fooled, 1955.
Fools' Hall of Fame, The, 1959.
For a Penny, 1959.
For My Good Fortune, 1958.
For Rent, 1956.
For the First Time, see Come Prima, 1958.
For the Very First Time, 1952.
For You My Love, 1950.
For Your Love, 1958.
Forbidden, see Verboten!, 1958.
Forever and Always, 1952.
Forever Darling, 1955.
Forget Me Not, 1958.
Forgive My Heart, 1955.
Forgive This Fool, 1955.
Forgotten Dreams, 1955.
Forsaking All Others, 1957.
Forty Cups of Coffee, 1953.
Forty Days and Forty Nights, 1956.
Forty Miles of Bad Road, 1959.
Four Walls, 1957.
Frankie, 1959.
(I'll Always Be Your) Fraulein, 1956.
Freddy, 1955.
Free Home Demonstration, 1953.
Freight Train, 1957.
French Foreign Legion, 1959.
Friendly Islands, The, 1950.
Friendly Persuasion, 1956.
Friendly Star, 1950.
From Here to Eternity, 1953.
From the Candy Store on the Corner (To the Chapel on the Hill), 1956.
From the First Hello to the Last Goodbye, 1956.
From the Vine Came the Grape, 1954.
From This Moment On, 1950.
Frosty the Snow Man, 1950.
Fugue for Tinhorns, 1950.
Full Time Job, 1952.
Funny (But I Still Love You), 1959.
Funny (Not Much), 1952.
Funny Thing, 1954.

G

Gal Who Invented Kissin', The, 1952.
Gambler's Guitar, 1953.
Game of Love, The, 1956.
Gandy Dancers' Ball, The, 1952.
Garden of Eden, 1956.
Gee!, 1953.
Gee, Baby, 1951.
Gee, But It's Lonely, 1958.
Gee, Officer Krupke, 1957.
Geisha Girl, 1957.
Gelsomina, see Love Theme from *La Strada*, 1954.
Gentleman Jimmy, 1959.
Get a Job, 1957.
Get Me to the Church on Time, 1956.
Get Out Those Old Records, 1950.
Getting To Know You, 1951.
Ghost Town, 1956.
Giant, 1956.
Gidget, 1959.
Gift of Love, The, 1957.

Gigi, 1953.
Gigi, 1958.
Gilly Gilly Ossenfeffer Katzenellen Bogen by the Sea, 1954.
Ginger Bread, 1958.
Girl! a Girl!, A, 1954.
Girl in the Wood, 1951.
Girl on Page 44, 1958.
Girl Upstairs, The, 1955.
Girl with the Golden Braids, The, 1957.
Give It All You've Got, 1958.
Give Me Love, 1955.
Give Me More, More, More of Your Kisses, 1951.
Give Myself a Party, 1958.
Give Us This Day, 1956.
Glendora, 1956.
Glow-Worm, The, 1952.
Go Away with Me, 1956.
Go Back You Fool, 1955.
Go, Boy, Go, 1953.
Go, Jimmy, Go, 1959.
Go On with the Wedding, 1956.
Go to Sleep, Go to Sleep, Go to Sleep, 1950.
God Bless Us All, 1953.
God's Country, 1950.
Goin' Home, 1952.
Goin' Steady, 1952.
Going to the River, 1957.
Gold Fever, see The Alaskans, 1959.
Gold Rush Is Over, The, 1952.
Golden Rocket, 1950.
Golden Striker, The, 1957.
Gomen-Nasai (Forgive Me), 1953.
Gone, 1952.
Gone Fishin', 1950.
Gonna Find Me a Bluebird, 1957.
Gonna Get Along without You Now, 1951.
Good Intentions, 1957.
Good Lovin', 1953.
Good Rockin' Tonight, 1956.
Goodbye Baby, 1958.
Goodbye, Jimmy, Goodbye, 1959.
Goodbye, John, 1950.
Goodbye, Old Girl, 1955.
Goodbye to Rome, see Arrivederci, Roma, 1955.
Goodnight, Irene, 1950.
Goodnight My Someone, 1957.
Goodnight, Sweetheart, Goodnight, see Goodnight, Well It's Time to Go, 1954.
Goodnight, Well It's Time To Go, 1954.
Got Her off My Hands, but Can't Get Her off My Mind, 1951.
Got You on My Mind, 1951.
Gotta Have Me Go with You, 1954.
Gotta Travel On, 1958.
Graduation Day, 1956.
Grant Avenue, 1958.
Great Balls of Fire, 1957.
Great Pretender, The, 1955.
Greatest Show on Earth, The, 1952.
Green Door, The, 1956.
Green Fields, 1956.
Green Years, 1954.
Greenbacks, 1955.
Grin and Bear It, 1959.
Guaglioni, 1956.
Guess Things Happen That Way, 1958.
Guess Who I Saw Today, 1952.
Gum Drop, 1955.
Guy Is a Guy, A, 1951.
Guy Who Invented Kissin', The, 1953.

H

Hajji Baba, 1954.
Half a Mind, 1958.
Half a Photograph, 1953.
Half As Much, 1951.
Half of My Heart, 1957.
Hallelujah I Love Her So, 1956.
Hallowe'en, 1950.
Hambone, 1952.
Hands Off, 1956.
Handy Man, 1959.
Hang Up, 1954.
Hang Up My Rock and Roll Shoes, 1958.
Hanging Tree, The, 1958.
Happiness Street (Corner Sunshine Square), 1955.
Happy Anniversary, 1959.
Happy Feet, 1950.
Happy Habit, 1954.
Happy, Happy Birthday Baby, 1957.
Happy Organ, The, 1959.
Happy To Make Your Acquaintance, 1956.
Happy Wanderer, The (Val-de Ri —Val-de Ra), 1954.
Happy Whistler, 1956.
Harbor Lights, 1950.

Hard Headed Woman, 1958.
Hard Luck Blues, 1950.
Hard To Get, 1955.
Hard Travelin', 1959.
Harry Lime Theme, The, 1950.
Have a Good Time, 1952.
Have Mercy, Baby, 1952.
Have You Heard, 1952.
Hawaiian Eye, 1959.
Hawaiian Wedding Song, The, 1958.
Hawk-Eye, 1955.
He, 1954.
He Needs Me, 1955.
Heart, 1955.
Heart of a Fool, The, 1954.
Heart of Paris, 1955.
Heart Strings, 1951.
Heartaches by the Number, 1959.
Heartbreak Hotel, 1956.
Heartbreaker, 1954.
Hearts of Stone, 1954.
Heavenly, 1959.
Heavenly Father, 1952.
He'll Have To Go, 1959.
Hello, Young Lovers, 1951.
Help Me, Somebody, 1953.
Hep Cat Baby, 1954.
Here, 1954.
Here Comes Summer, 1959.
Here Comes That Heartache Again, 1953.
Here in My Heart, 1952.
Here's That Rainy Day, 1953.
Here's to My Lady, 1951.
Hernando's Hideaway, 1954.
He's a Tramp, 1952.
He's Got the Whole World in His Hands, 1957.
He's in Love, 1953.
Hey, Doll Baby, 1955.
Hey Good Lookin', 1951.
Hey! Jealous Lover, 1956.
Hey Joe, 1953.
Hey, Little Girl, 1959.
Hey, Little Lucy! (Don' Tcha Put No Lipstick On), 1959.
Hey, Miss Fannie, 1952.
Hey, Mr. Banjo, 1955.
Hey! Mister Cotton-Picker, 1953.
Hey, Schoolgirl, 1957.
Hey There, 1954.
Hibiscus, 1958.
Hideaway, 1958.
High and the Mighty, The, 1954.
High Hopes, 1959.
High Noon, 1952.
High School Confidential, 1958.
Hi-Lili, Hi-Lo, 1952.
Hillbilly Fever, 1950.
Historia de un Amor, see The Story of Love, 1956.
Hit and Run Affair, 1954.
Hittin' on Me, 1953.
Ho Ho Song, The, 1953.
Hold 'em Joe, 1954.
Hold Everything (Till I Get Home), 1956.
Hold Me Close, see Embrasse, 1953.
Hold Me—Hold Me—Hold Me, 1951.
Hold Me in Your Arms, 1954.
Hold Me, Thrill Me, Kiss Me, 1952.
Hold My Hand, 1950.
Holiday for Love, 1957.
Home, 1959.
Home Cookin', 1950.
(There's No Place Like) Home for the Holidays, 1955.
Home is Where the Heart Is, 1954.
Home of the Blues, 1957.
Honest I Do, 1957.
Honey Hush, 1954.
Honey Love, 1954.
Honey-Babe, 1955.
Honeycomb, 1954.
Honeymoon on a Rocket Ship, 1953.
Honky Tonk, 1956.
Honky Tonk Blues, 1952.
Honky Tonk Girl, 1954.
Honky Tonk Man, 1956.
Honky Tonk Song, 1957.
Hoop-Dee-Do, 1950.
Hoping That You're Hoping, 1956.
Horse Told Me, The, 1950.
Horse with the Easter Bonnet, 1954.
Hostess with the Mostes' on the Ball, The, 1950.
Hot Diggity, 1956.
Hot Rod Race, 1950.
Hot Spell, 1958.
Hot Toddy, 1952.
Hotta Chocolotta, 1956.
Hound Dog, 1956.
Hound Dog Man, 1959.
House Is a Home, A, 1951.
House of Bamboo, 1958.
House of Flowers, 1954.
House with Love in It, A, 1956.
How Can I Replace You, 1955.

How Could You Believe Me When I Said I Love You When You Know I've Been a Liar All My Life, 1950.
How Do You Speak to an Angel?, 1952.
How D'ye Do and Shake Hands, 1951.
How Far Is Heaven, 1955.
How Green Was My Valley, 1957.
How High the Moon, 1951.
How Important Can It Be?, 1955.
How Little We Know (How Little It Matters How Little We Know), 1956.
How the Time Flies, 1958.
Howlin' at the Moon, 1951.
Huckleberry Finn, 1954.
Hula Hoop Song, The, 1958.
Hula Love, 1957.
Hummingbird, 1955.
Hundred Million Miracles, A, 1958.
Hurt, 1953.
Hurts Me to My Heart, 1954.
Hushabye, 1959.

I

"I," 1952.
I Adore You, 1958.
I Ain't Never, 1959.
I Almost Lost My Mind, 1950.
I Am in Love, 1953.
I Am Loved, 1950.
I Apologize, 1951.
I Beg of You, 1957.
I Believe, 1952.
I Believe in You, 1956.
I Believe to My Soul, 1959.
I Can Dream Can't I, 1950.
I Can See You, 1950.
I Can't Get You out of My Heart (Ti Amo—Ti Voglio Amor), 1958.
I Can't Help It (If I'm Still in Love with You), 1951.
I Can't Love You Enough, 1956.
I Can't Stop Loving You, 1958.
I Can't Tell a Waltz from a Tango, 1954.
I Could Be Happy with You, 1953.
I Could Have Danced All Night, 1956.
I Could Have Told You, 1954.
I Couldn't Keep from Crying, 1953.
I Cried, 1954.
I Cried a Tear, 1958.
I Cross My Fingers, 1950.
I Didn't Slip, I Wasn't Pushed, I Fell, 1950.
I Didn't Want To Do It, 1954.
I Don't Believe You've Met My Baby, 1955.
I Don't Care, 1955.
I Don't Hurt Anymore, 1954.
I Don't Know, 1952.
I Dreamed, 1956.
I Enjoy Being a Girl, 1958.
I Feel Like Crying, 1955.
I Feel Like I'm Gonna Live Forever, 1952.
I Feel Pretty, 1957.
I Forgot More Than You'll Ever Know, 1953.
I Forgot To Remember To Forget, 1955.
I Found My Girl in the U.S.A., 1957.
(When I Dance with You) I Get Ideas, 1951.
I Get So Lonely, see Oh, Baby Mine, 1953.
I Go Ape, 1959.
I Got a Feeling, 1958.
I Got a Wife, 1959.
I Got a Woman (I Got a Sweetie), 1954.
I Got Loaded, 1951.
I Got Stripes, 1959.
I Got Stung, 1958.
I Gotta Go Get My Baby, 1955.
I Had a Dream, 1958.
I Have Dreamed, 1951.
I Have To Tell You, 1954.
I Hear a Rhapsody, 1952.
I Hear You Knocking, 1955.
I Heard the Bluebirds Sing, 1952.
I Just Don't Know, 1957.
I Laughed at Love, 1952.
I Left My Heart in San Francisco, 1954.
I Let the Stars Get in My Eyes, 1952.
I Like It, I Like It, 1951.
I Like Myself, 1954.
I Like You, 1954.
I Like Your Kind of Love, 1957.
I Live for Only You, 1955.
I Love a New Yorker, 1950.
I Love Paris, 1953.
I Love the Girl, see I Love the Guy, 1950.
I Love the Guy, 1950.

I Love the Sunshine of Your Smile, 1951.
I Love the Way You Say Goodnight, 1951.
I Love You, 1953.
I Love You a Thousand Ways, 1951.
I Love You Because, 1950.
I Love You Madly, 1954.
I Love You, Samantha, 1956.
I Loves You Porgy, 1959.
I May Never Pass This Way Again, 1958.
I Miss You Already, 1956.
I Need You Now, 1953.
I Need You So, 1950.
I Need Your Love Tonight, 1959.
I Need Your Lovin', 1954.
I Never Felt More Like Falling in Love, 1954.
I Never Felt This Way Before, 1957.
I Never Had a Worry in the World, 1950.
I Never Has Seen Snow, 1954.
I Only Have Eyes for You, 1959.
I Quit My Pretty Mama, 1950.
I Promise To Remember, 1956.
I Ran All the Way Home, 1951.
I Really Don't Want To Know, 1953.
I Remember It Well, 1958.
I Remember When, 1952.
I Said My Pajamas, and Put on My Pray'rs, 1950.
I Saw Mommy Kissing Santa Claus, 1952.
I Say Hello, 1959.
I See the Moon, 1953.
I Speak to the Stars, 1954.
I Stayed Too Long at the Fair, 1957.
I Still Feel the Same About You, 1950.
I Still See Elisa, 1951.
I Take the Chance, 1956.
I Talk to the Trees, 1951.
I Taut I Taw a Puddy Tat, 1950.
I Thought I Saw a Pussy Cat, see I Taut I Taw a Puddy Tat, 1950.
I Thought It Was Over, 1957.
I Understand Just How You Feel, 1953.
I Waited a Little Too Long, 1951.
I Waited Too Long, 1959.
I Walk a Little Faster, 1957.
I Walk the Line, 1956.
I Wanna Be Around, 1959.
I Wanna Be Loved, 1950.
I Wanna Do More, see I Want To Do More, 1956.
I Wanna Play House with You, 1951.
I Want To Be Evil, 1952.
I Want To Be Loved (But Only by You), 1956.
I Want To Be with You Always, 1951.
I Want To Do More, 1956.
I Want To Know, 1957.
I Want To Walk You Home, 1959.
I Want You All to Myself, 1954.
I Want You, I Need You, I Love You, 1956.
I Want You To Be My Baby, 1953.
I Want You To Be My Girl, 1956.
I Was the One, 1956.
I Went to Your Wedding, 1952.
I Whistle a Happy Tune, 1951.
I Will Wait, 1950.
I Wish I Wuz (Hi Ho, Fiddle Dee Dee), 1951.
I Wish You Love, 1955.
I Wonder Why, 1958.
I Won't Be Home No More, 1952.
I Won't Be the Fool Anymore, 1957.
I Won't Cry Anymore, 1951.
I Won't Grow Up, 1954.
I'd Like To Baby You, 1951.
I'd Rather Die Young, 1953.
I'd Rather Have the Blues, see Blues from *Kiss Me Deadly*, 1955.
Idle Gossip, 1953.
If, 1950.
If Dreams Come True, 1958.
If I Give My Heart to You, 1954.
If I Had a Girl, 1959.
If I Had a Hammer, 1958.
If I Had My Druthers, 1956.
If I Knew You Were Comin' I'd've Baked a Cake, 1950.
If I May, 1955.
If I Were a Bell, 1950.
If Teardrops Were Pennies, 1951.
If You Ain't Lovin' (You Ain't Livin'), 1954.
If You Don't, Somebody Else Will, 1954.
If You Feel Like Singing, Sing, 1950.

If You Go, 1951.
If You Love Me (Really Love Me), 1953.
If You Loved Me Truly, 1953.
If You Turn Me Down (Dee-Own-Down-Down), 1951.
If You've Got the Money (I've Got the Time), 1950.
If'n, 1956.
(Day after Day) I'll Always Love You, 1950.
I'll Be Easy To Find, 1959.
I'll Be Home, 1956.
I'll Be Satisfied, 1959.
I'll Be There If You Ever Want Me, 1954.
I'll Be True to You, 1953.
I'll Buy You a Star, 1951.
I'll Cry Tomorrow, 1954.
I'll Cry Tomorrow, 1955.
I'll Drown in My Tears, 1952.
I'll Go On Alone, 1953.
I'll Know, 1950.
I'll Never Be Free, 1950.
I'll Never Get Out of This World Alive, 1952.
I'll Never Know, 1955.
I'll Never Stand in Your Way, 1953.
I'll Never Stop Loving You, 1955.
I'll Remember (In the Still of the Nite), 1956.
I'll Remember Today, 1956.
I'll Sail My Ship Alone, 1950.
I'll Wait for You, 1958.
I'll Walk with God, 1952.
I'm a Fool To Care, 1954.
I'm a Fool To Want You, 1951.
I'm a Man, 1958.
I'm a One-Woman Man, 1956.
I'm Always Hearing Wedding Bells, 1954.
I'm an Old Man (Tryin' To Live While I Can), 1952.
I'm an Ordinary Man, 1956.
I'm Available, 1956.
I'm Available, 1957.
I'm Bashful, 1950.
I'm Coming Home, 1956.
I'm Flying, 1954.
I'm Glad I'm Not Young Anymore, 1958.
I'm Gone, 1952.
I'm Gonna Be a Wheel Someday, 1957.
I'm Gonna Get Married, 1959.
I'm Gonna Laugh You out of My Life, 1955.
I'm Gonna Live Till I Die, 1950.
I'm Gonna Play the Honky Tonks, 1951.
I'm Gonna Sit Right Down and Write Myself a Letter, 1957.
I'm Gonna Walk and Talk with My Lord, 1952.
I'm Hans Christian Andersen, 1951.
I'm in Love Again, 1951.
I'm in Love Again, 1956.
I'm in Love Again, 1959.
I'm in Love with Miss Logan, 1952.
I'm in the Mood, 1951.
I'm Just a Country Boy, 1954.
I'm Just Your Fool, 1953.
I'm Late, 1951.
I'm Like a New Broom, 1951.
I'm Mad, 1953.
I'm Movin' On, 1950.
I'm Never Satisfied, 1952.
I'm Not at All in Love, 1954.
I'm on My Way, 1951.
I'm Ready, 1954.
I'm Ready, 1959.
I'm So in Love with You, 1956.
I'm Stickin' with You, 1957.
(Remember Me) I'm the One Who Loves You, 1950.
I'm Tired, 1957.
I'm Waiting Just for You, 1951.
I'm Walkin', 1957.
I'm Walking behind You, 1953.
I'm Walking the Dog, 1953.
I'm with You, 1955.
I'm Your Girl, 1953.
I'm Your Hoochie Cooche Man, 1957.
I'm Yours, 1952.
I'm Yours To Command, 1951.
Imitation of Life, 1959.
Impatient Years, The, 1955.
Impossible, 1956.
In My Own Little Corner, 1957.
In Other Words, see Fly Me to the Moon, 1954.
In Paris and in Love, 1954.
In the Chapel in the Moonlight, 1954.
In the Cool, Cool, Cool of the Evening, 1951.
In the Jailhouse Now, 1955.
In the Middle of an Island, 1957.
In the Middle of the House, 1956.

In the Mission at St. Augustine, 1953.
In Your Own Sweet Way, 1956.
Inch Worm, The, 1951.
Independent (On My Own), 1957.
India, see I Live for Only You, 1955.
Indian Love Call, 1952.
Indiscreet, 1958.
Indiscretion, 1954.
Innamorata (Sweetheart), 1955.
Inspiration, 1959.
Interlude, 1957.
Invitation, 1952.
Invitation to a Broken Heart, 1951.
Irma la Douce, 1958.
Is It Any Wonder, 1953.
Is It Wrong?, 1957.
Is Zat You, Myrtle?, 1953.
Island in the Sun, 1956.
Istanbul, not Constantinople, 1953.
It Amazes Me, 1958.
It Doesn't Matter Any More, 1958.
It Happened to Jane, 1959.
It Hurts To Be in Love, 1956.
It Is No Secret What God Can Do, 1951.
It Isn't Fair, 1950.
It Isn't Right, 1952.
It May Sound Silly, 1954.
It Only Hurts for a Little While, 1956.
It Tickles, 1954.
It Was I, 1959.
It Wasn't God Who Made Honky Tonk Angels, 1952.
Italian Theme, The, 1956.
Itchy Twitchy Feeling, 1958.
It's a Chemical Reaction, 1954.
It's a Great Life If You Don't Weaken, 1955.
It's a Lovely Day Today, 1950.
It's a Lovely, Lovely World, 1952.
It's a New World, 1954.
It's a Woman's World, 1954.
It's All in the Game, 1951.
It's All Right, 1957.
It's All Right with Me, 1953.
It's Almost Tomorrow, 1955.
It's Been So Long, 1953.
It's Beginning To Look Like Christmas, 1951.
It's Better in the Dark, 1956.
It's Good To Be Alive, 1957.
It's in the Book, 1952.
It's Just a Matter of Time, 1958.
It's Just About Time, 1958.
It's Late, 1959.
It's Love, 1953.
It's Love Baby (24 Hours a Day), 1955.
It's Not for Me To Say, 1957.
It's Only Make Believe, 1958.
It's Only the Beginning, 1958.
It's So Nice To Have a Man around the House, 1950.
It's the Going Home Together, 1954.
It's Time To Cry, 1959.
It's Too Late, 1956.
It's Too Soon To Know, 1958.
It's You, 1957.
It's You I Love, 1957.
I've Been Searching, 1955.
I've Been Thinking, 1954.
I've Changed, 1955.
I've Come of Age, 1959.
I've Got a Lot To Learn about Life, 1959.
I've Got a New Heartache, 1956.
I've Got Five Dollars and It's Saturday Night, 1950.
I've Got My Eyes on You, 1954.
I've Got To Crow, 1954.
I've Grown Accustomed to Her Face, 1956.
I've Had It, 1958.
I've Never Been in Love Before, 1950.
I've Run Out of Tomorrows, 1959.
Ivory Tower, 1956.
Ivy Rose, 1957.

J

Jailhouse Rock, 1957.
Jalousie, 1951.
Jamaica Farewell, 1955.
Jambalaya (On the Bayou), 1952.
Java, 1958.
Jenny, Jenny, 1957.
Jenny-Lee, 1958.
Jeru, 1954.
Jet, 1951.
Jezebel, 1951.
Jilted, 1954.
Jim Dandy, 1957.
Jimmie Brown, the Newsboy, 1959.
Jimmy Brown Song, The, 1959.
Jing-A-Ling, Jing-A-Ling, 1950.
Jingle-Bell Rock, 1957.
Jivin' Around, 1956.
Jo-Ann, 1957.

Joanna, 1959.
Joey, 1954.
Joey, Joey, Joey, 1956.
Joey's Song, 1957.
Joey's Theme, 1953.
Johnny B. Goode, 1958.
Johnny Concho's Theme, 1956.
Johnny Guitar, 1954.
Johnny Guitar, see My Restless Lover, 1954.
Johnny Is the Boy for Me, 1953.
Joker, The, 1957.
Jones Boy, The, 1953.
Josephine, 1954.
Jubilation T. Cornpone, 1956.
Juke, 1952.
Juke Box Baby, 1956.
Julie, 1956.
Jump Back Honey, 1952.
Junco Partner, 1952.
Just a Dream, 1958.
Just a Little Lovin' Will Go a Long Way, 1952.
Just a Little Too Much, 1959.
Just Another Polka, 1953.
Just Ask Your Heart, 1959.
Just Because, 1957.
Just Because You're You, 1952.
Just Between You and Me, 1957.
Just Born (To Be Your Baby), 1957.
Just Call Me Lonesome, 1953.
Just for Once, 1959.
Just in Time, 1956.
Just Keep It Up (And See What Happens), 1959.
Just Like a Man, 1952.
Just My Luck, 1957.
Just One More, 1957.
Just Say I Love Her, 1950.
Just Wait 'Till I Get You Alone, 1953.
Just Walking in the Rain, 1953.
Just When We're Falling in Love, 1951.
Just You Wait, 1956.
Just Young, 1958.

K

K.C. Loving, see Kansas City, 1959.
(My Heart Goes) Ka-Ding-Dong, 1956.
Kansas City, 1959.
Kathy-O, 1958.
Katsumi Love Theme, 1957.
Kaw-Liga, 1952.
Keep A-Knockin', 1957.
Keep It a Secret, 1952.
Keep It Gay, 1953.
Kentuckian Song, The, 1955.
Kentucky Waltz, 1951.
Kewpie Doll, 1958.
Kiss Me and Kill Me with Love, 1954.
Kiss Me Another, 1956.
Kiss of Fire, 1952.
Kiss That Rocked the World, The, 1957.
Kiss Them for Me, 1957.
Kiss To Build a Dream On, 1951.
Kisses Don't Lie, 1954.
Kisses Sweeter Than Wine, 1951.
Kissin' Bug Boogie, 1951.
Kissin' Time, 1959.
Knee Deep in the Blues, 1956.
Knock on Wood, 1954.
Knothole, 1953.
Ko Ko Mo, I Love You So, 1955.
Kookie, Kookie, Lend Me Your Comb, 1959.
Kookie's Love Song (While Dancing), 1959.

L

La Bamba, 1958.
La Dee Dah, 1958.
La Plume de Ma Tante, 1959.
La Ronde, 1954.
La Seine, see You Will Find Your Love in Paris, 1958; see The River Seine, 1953.
La Strada del' Amore, 1958.
La Vie en Rose, 1950.
Lady Drinks Champagne, The, 1951.
Lady Love, 1952.
Lady Loves, A, 1952.
Lady of Spain, 1952.
Lady's Man, 1952.
Land of Dreams, 1954.
Land of the Pharoahs, 1955.
Last Ride, The, 1959.
Last Waltz, The, 1952.
Lasting Love, 1957.
Late, Late Show, The, 1956.
Laugh, I Thought I'd Die, 1956.
Lavender Blue (Dilly, Dilly), 1959.
Lawdy Miss Clawdy, 1952.
Lawman, 1959.
Lay Down Your Arms, 1956.
Lazy Afternoon, 1954.
Lazy Mary, 1958.

Lazy Summer Night, 1958.
Le Gamin de Paris, 1956.
Le Grisbi, see The Touch, 1954.
Lean Baby, 1951.
Learnin' the Blues, 1955.
Left Bank, The, 1955.
Left Right out of Your Heart (Hi-Lee Hi-Lo Hi-Lup-Up-Up), 1958.
Legend of Wyatt Earp, 1955.
Let It Be Me, 1957.
Let It Ring, 1955.
Let Me Be Loved, 1957.
Let Me Be the One, 1953.
Let Me Entertain You, 1959.
Let Me Go Devil!, 1953.
Let Me Go Home Whiskey, 1952.
Let Me Go Lover!, 1954.
Let Me In, 1951.
Let Me Know, 1953.
Let Me Love You, 1954.
Let Old Mother Nature Have Her Way, 1951.
Let the Bells Keep Ringing, 1958.
Let the Good Times Roll, 1956.
Let's Go Home Whiskey, see Let Me Go Home Whiskey, 1952.
Let's Go to Church (Next Sunday Morning), 1950.
Let's Live a Little, 1951.
Let's Love, 1959.
Letters Have No Arms, 1950.
Lida Rose, 1957.
Liechtensteiner Polka, 1957.
Life Is a Beautiful Thing, 1951.
Life Is So Peculiar, 1950.
Life To Go, 1959.
Light of Love, 1958.
Lighthouse, 1953.
Lights of Paris, 1957.
Like Young, 1958.
Li'l Darlin', 1958.
Lilac Chiffon, 1957.
Lili Maebelle, 1956.
Limelight, see Eternally, 1953.
Ling Ting Tong, 1954.
Lips of Wine, 1957.
Lipstick and Candy and Rubber Sole Shoes, 1956.
Lipstick on Your Collar, 1959.
Lisa, 1954.
Lisbon Antigua, 1954.
Little Angel with a Dirty Face, 1950.
Little Biscuit, 1957.
Little Bit in Love, A, 1953.
Little Bitty Pretty One, 1957.
Little Blue Man, The, 1958.
Little Boy and the Old Man, The, 1953.
Little Child (Daddy Dear), see The Little Boy and the Old Man, 1953.
Little Darlin', 1957.
Little Dipper, 1959.
Little Drummer Boy, The, 1958.
Little Girl of Mine, 1956.
Little Lamb, 1959.
Little Love Can Go a Long, Long Way, A, 1955.
Little Mama, 1954.
Little Rosa, 1956.
Little Shoemaker, The, 1954.
Little Space Girl, 1959.
Little Star, 1958.
Little Susie, 1958.
Little Things Mean a Lot, 1954.
Little White Cloud That Cried, The, 1951.
Live and Let Live, 1953.
Live Fast, Love Hard, Die Young, 1954.
Living Doll, 1959.
Lizzie Borden, 1952.
Lollipop, 1958.
London by Night, 1950.
Lonely Blue Boy, 1958.
(I'm Just a) Lonely Boy, 1958.
Lonely for You, 1959.
Lonely Goatherd, The, 1959.
Lonely Island, 1957.
Lonely Little Robin, 1951.
Lonely Nights, 1955.
Lonely One, The, 1958.
Lonely Street, 1956.
Lonely Teardrops, 1958.
Lonely Wine, 1950.
Lonesome Polecat, 1954.
Lonesome Town, 1958.
Long Before I Knew You, 1956.
Long Black Veil, 1959.
Long Gone Lonesome Blues, 1950.
Long Hot Summer, The, 1957.
Long John, 1954.
Long Legged Ladies of Labrador, 1958.
Long Lonely Nights, 1957.
Long Tall Sally, 1956.
Longest Walk, The, 1955.
Longing for You, 1951.
Look at 'er, 1957.
Look What Thoughts Will Do, 1951.
Look Who's Dancing, 1951.

Looking Back, 1958.
Loose Talk, 1954.
Lose That Long Face, 1954.
Losing Hand, 1954.
Lost in Loveliness, 1954.
Lost Love, 1951.
Love among the Young, 1955.
Love and Learn, see Dissertation on the State of Bliss, 1954.
Love and Marriage, 1955.
Love Don't Love Nobody, 1950.
Love Eyes, 1958.
Love Has Joined Us Together, 1955.
Love Held Lightly, 1959.
Love I You (You I Love), 1954.
Love in a Home, 1956.
Love in the Afternoon, 1956.
Love Is a Golden Ring, 1957.
Love Is a Many-Splendored Thing, 1955.
Love Is a Simple Thing, 1952.
Love Is a Very Light Thing, 1954.
Love Is All We Need, 1958.
Love Is for the Very Young, see The Bad and the Beautiful, 1953.
Love Is Like Champagne, 1959.
Love Is Strange, 1957.
Love Is the Reason, 1951.
Love Letters in the Sand, 1957.
Love, Look Away, 1958.
Love, Love, Love, 1955.
Love! Love! Love!, 1956.
Love Makes the World Go 'round, see La Ronde, 1954.
Love Makes the World Go 'round (Yeah, Yeah), 1958.
Love Me, 1954.
Love Me or Leave Me, 1955.
Love Me Tender, 1956.
Love Me to Pieces, 1957.
Love Potion Number Nine, 1959.
Love Song from *Houseboat*, see Almost in Your Arms, 1958.
Love Theme from *A Farewell to Arms*, 1957.
Love Theme from *Ben Hur*, 1959.
Love Theme from *La Strada*, 1954.
Love Theme from *The Brothers Karamazov*, 1958.
Love Theme from *The Robe*, 1953.
Love Ya, 1951.
Love, You Didn't Do Right by Me, 1953.
Love You Most of All, 1958.
Lovebug Itch, The, 1950.
Loveliest Night of the Year, The, 1950.
Lovely Night, A, 1957.
Lover, 1952.
Lover's Quarrel, A, 1953.
Lover's Question, A, 1958.
Lovey Dovey, 1954.
Lovin' Spree, 1954.
Loving You, 1957.
Lucille, 1957.
Luck Be a Lady, 1950.
Lucky Ladybug, 1958.
Lucky Lips, 1957.
Lullaby in Blue, 1957.
Lullaby in Ragtime, 1958.
Lullaby of Birdland, 1952.
Luna Rossa, 1952.
Luther Played the Boogie, 1959.
Lygia, 1951.

M

M.T.A., The, 1956.
Ma Says, Pa Says, 1952.
Mabelline, 1955.
Mack the Knife, 1956.
Madly in Love, 1956.
Magic Circle, 1954.
Magic Moments, 1957.
Magic Tango, The, 1954.
(You've Got) Magic Touch, The, 1956.
Main Title Theme, see The Man with the Golden Arm, 1956.
Mainliner, 1955.
Make Her Mine, 1954.
Make Love to Me, 1953.
Make the Man Love Me, 1951.
Make Yourself Comfortable, 1954.
Makin' Love, 1959.
Making Believe, 1954.
Mama (He Treats Your Daughter Mean), 1953.
Mama, Come Get Your Baby Boy, 1953.
Mama Doll Song, The, 1954.
Mama from the Train (A Kiss, a Kiss), 1956.
Mama Guitar, 1957.
Mama Look a Booboo, 1957.
Mama, Teach Me To Dance, 1956.
Mambo Baby, 1954.
Mambo Bacan, see Woman of the River, 1955.
Mambo Italiano, 1954.
Mambo Jambo, 1950.

More I Cannot Wish You, 1950.
More Love Than Your Love, 1954.
Morgen, 1959.
Moritat, see Mack the Knife, 1956.
Morning Music of Montmartre, The, 1958.
Morningside of the Mountain, The, 1951.
Most Happy Fella, The, 1956.
Most of All, 1955.
Mountains beyond the Moon, The, 1957.
M-Squad, 1959.
Mu-Cha-Cha, 1956.
Mule Train, 1950.
Music Makin' Mama from Memphis, 1951.
Music! Music! Music! (Put Another Nickel In), 1950.
Music of Home, The, 1959.
Mutual Admiration Society, 1956.
My Babe, 1955.
My Baby Left Me, 1956.
My Baby's Coming Home, 1952.
My Baby's Gone, 1958.
My Believing Heart, 1955.
My Beloved, 1951.
My Bonnie Lassie, 1953.
My Boy, Flat Top, 1955.
My Destiny, 1950.
My Dream Sonata, 1956.
My Everything (You're My Everything), 1954.
My Favorite Things, 1959.
My First and Last Love, 1951.
My Flaming Heart, 1952.
My Foolish Heart, 1950.
My Friend, 1954.
My Happiness, 1959.
My Happiness Forever, 1956.
My Heart Belongs to Only You, 1952.
My Heart Cries for You, 1950.
My Heart Is an Open Book, 1957.
My Heart Is So Full of You, 1956.
My Heart Reminds Me, 1957.
My Heart Won't Say Goodbye, 1954.
My, How the Time Goes By, 1957.
My Jealous Eyes (That Turned from Blue to Green), 1953.
My Lady Loves To Dance, 1952.
My Lips Are Sealed, 1955.
My Love and Devotion, 1951.
My Love Is a Wanderer, 1952.
My Love, My Love, 1952.
My Love's a Gentle Man, 1955.
My One and Only Heart, 1953.
My One and Only Love, 1953.
My Own True Love, 1954.
My Personal Possession, 1955.
My Prayer, 1956.
My Resistance Is Low, 1951.
My Restless Lover, 1954.
My Shoes Keep Walking Back to You, 1957.
My Son, My Son, 1954.
My Special Angel, 1957.
My Time of Day, 1950.
My True Love, 1958.
My Truly, Truly Fair, 1951.
My Wish Came True, 1957.
Mystery Street, 1953.
Mystery Train, 1953.

N

Namely You, 1956.
Napoleon, 1954.
Napoleon, 1957.
Naughty Lady of Shady Lane, The, 1954.
Near to You, 1955.
Need Your Love So Bad, 1955.
Nel Blu, Dipinto di Blu, see Volare, 1958.
Never, 1951.
Never Be Anyone Else but You, 1958.
Never Before, 1958.
Never Give Anything Away, 1953.
Never Leave Me, 1956.
Never Let Her Go, 1952.
Never Mind, 1956.
Never Till Now, 1957.
Never Will I Marry, 1959.
Never-Never Land, 1954.
Nevertheless, 1950.
New Town Is a Blue Town, A, 1954.
New-Fangled Tango, A, 1956.
Next in Line, 1957.
Next Time It Happens, The, 1955.
Next Time You See Me, 1956.
Night Lights, 1956.
Night of My Nights, 1953.
Night They Invented Champagne, The, 1958.
Night Train, 1952.
Night Watch, The, 1954.
Nina Never Knew, 1952.

Ninety-Nine Ways, 1957.
Ninety Nine Years (Dead or Alive), 1956.
No Arms Can Ever Hold You (Like These Arms of Mine), 1955.
No Chemise, Please!, 1958.
No Help Wanted, 1952.
No Love (But Your Love), 1957.
No Man Is an Island, 1950.
No Money Down, 1956.
(My Baby Don't Love Me) No More, 1954.
No More Doggin', 1952.
No, Not Much, 1956.
No One but You, 1954.
No One Ever Tells You, 1957.
No One Knows, 1958.
No Other Arms, No Other Lips, 1952.
No Other Love, 1950.
No Other Love, 1953.
No Other One, 1956.
No Two People, 1951.
Nobody but You, 1958.
Nobody's Chasing Me, 1950.
Noche de Ronda, see Be Mine Tonight, 1951.
Non Dimenticar, 1953.
Noodlin' Rag, 1952.
North Wind, 1953.
Not As a Stranger, 1955.
Not Since Nineveh, 1953.
Nothing Ever Changes My Love for You, 1955.
Nothing in Common, 1958.
Now! Baby, Now!, 1956.
Now I Lay Me Down To Sleep, 1958.
Now That I'm in Love, 1953.
Now You Has Jazz, 1956.
Nuttin' for Christmas, 1955.

O

"O," 1953.
O Cangaceiro, see The Bandit, 1954.
O Mein Papa, see Oh! My Pa-pa, 1953.
(Dance to the Music of) Ocarina, The, 1950.
Occasional Man, An, 1955.
Off Shore, 1953.
Oh Babe!, 1950.
Oh, Baby Mine (I Get So Lonely), 1953.
Oh! Carol, 1959.
Oh, Happy Day, 1952.
Oh Julie, 1957.
Oh, Lonesome Me, 1958.
Oh! My Pa-pa, 1953.
Oh, Oh, I'm Falling in Love Again, 1958.
Oh, That'll Be Joyful, 1954.
Oh What a Dream, see What a Dream, 1954.
Oh, What a Night, 1956.
Ohio, 1953.
Old Cape Cod, 1956.
Old Man and the Sea, The, 1958.
Old Master Painter, The, 1950.
Old Moon, 1959.
Old Piano Roll Blues, 1950.
Old Soldiers Never Die, 1951.
Older and Bolder, 1952.
Oldest Established, The, 1950.
On an Evening in Roma, 1959.
On London Bridge, 1956.
On My Mind Again, 1957.
On the Beach, 1959.
On the First Warm Day, 1952.
On the Outgoing Tide, 1950.
On the Street Where You Live, 1956.
On the Waterfront, 1954.
On Top of Old Smoky, 1951.
Once, 1951.
Once Knew a Fella, 1959.
Once upon a Time Today, 1950.
One by One, 1954.
One Finger Melody, 1950.
One Finger Piano, 1956.
One Hand, One Heart, 1957.
One Is a Lonely Number, 1957.
One Little Candle, 1951.
One Lonely Night, 1953.
One Mint Julep, 1952.
One More Sunrise, see Morgen, 1959.
One Night, 1957.
One Scotch, One Bourbon, One Beer, 1953.
One Summer Night, 1958.
Only Man on the Island, The, 1958.
Only the Lonely, 1958.
Only Trust Your Heart, 1957.
Only You, 1955.
Oo! What You Do to Me, 1953.
Oooh, Oooh, Oooh, 1952.

Oop Shoop, 1954.
Open Up Your Heart, 1953.
Orange Colored Sky, 1950.
Other Woman, The, 1956.
Our Anniversary, 1957.
Our Lady of Fatima, 1950.
Our Language of Love, 1958.
Out of Sight, out of Mind, 1956.
Out of the Clear Blue Sky, 1952.
Outside of Heaven, 1952.
Over the Mountain, across the Sea, 1957.

P

P.S. I Love You, 1953.
Padam . . . Padam . . . (How It Echoes the Beat of My Heart), 1952.
Padre, 1957.
Pamela Throws a Party, 1957.
Pansy, 1958.
Papa Loves Mambo, 1954.
Pa-paya Mama, 1953.
Paper of Pins, A, see The Bus Stop Song, 1956.
Paris, 1958.
Paris Canaille, 1953.
Paris Loves Lovers, 1954.
Partners, 1959.
Party Doll, 1957.
Party's Over, The, 1956.
Patricia, 1950.
Patricia (It's Patricia), 1958.
Peanuts, 1957.
Peek-a-Boo, 1958.
Peggy Sue, 1957.
Penny a Kiss, a Penny a Hug, A, 1950.
Penny Candy, 1952.
Pepito, 1958.
Pepper-Hot Baby, 1955.
Periwinkle Blue, 1958.
Pet Me, Poppa, 1955.
Pete Kelly's Blues, 1955.
Peter Cottontail, 1950.
Peter Gunn Theme, 1959.
Petite Fleur, 1952.
Petite Waltz, The, 1950.
Petticoats of Portugal, 1956.
Philadelphia, U.S.A., 1958.
Pick Me Up on Your Way Down, 1959.
Picnic Song, The, 1950.
(My Heart Goes) Piddily Patter Patter, 1955.
Piel Canela (Tú, y Tú, y Tú), 1952.
Pillow Talk, 1959.
Pink Champagne, 1950.
Pink Shoelaces, 1958.
Pink Sweater Angel, 1956.
Pittsburgh, Pennsylvania, 1952.
Place in the Sun, A, 1951.
Plain Jane, 1959.
Plantation Boogie, 1954.
Play a Simple Melody, 1950.
Play Me Hearts and Flowers (I Wanna Cry), 1955.
Plaything, 1957.
Pleadin' for Love, 1956.
Please Don't Blame Me, 1957.
Please Don't Leave Me, 1953.
Please Love Me, 1953.
Please Mr. Sun, 1951.
Please Play Our Song (Mister Record Man), 1953.
Please, Please, Please, 1956.
Please Say You Want Me, 1957.
Please Send Me Someone To Love, 1951.
Pledging My Love, 1954.
Poet's Dream, The, 1959.
Poison Ivy, 1959.
Poison Love, 1950.
Politics and Poker, 1959.
Poor Boy, 1958.
Poor Jenny, 1959.
Poor Little Fool, 1958.
Poor Man's Riches, 1956.
Poor Man's Roses, A (Or a Rich Man's Gold), 1957.
Poor Me, 1955.
Poor Old Heartsick Me, 1959.
Poor People of Paris, The, 1956.
Popo the Puppet, 1953.
Por Favor ("Please . . ."), 1955.
Port of Rico, 1952.
Port-au-Prince, 1956.
Portuguese Washerwomen, The, 1956.
Positively No Dancing, 1954.
Preacher, The, 1956.
Pretend, 1952.
Pretend You Don't See Her, 1954.
Pretty Blue Eyes, 1959.
Pretty Girls Everywhere, 1959.
Pretty To Walk With, 1957.
Pretty-Eyed Baby, 1951.
Primrose Lane, 1958.
Problems, 1958.
Prodigal, The (Love Theme), 1955.

Ruby and the Pearl, The, 1952.
Rumble, 1958.
Run Boy, 1955.
Runaround, 1954.
Running Bear, 1959.

S

Sad Hours, 1952.
Sadie Thompson's Song, 1953.
Sadie's Shawl, 1956.
Sail Along Silvery Moon, 1958.
Sail Away, 1950.
Sailor Boys Have Talk to Me in English, 1955.
St. George and the Dragonet, 1953.
St. Theresa of the Roses, 1956.
Samba de Orfeu, 1959.
Same Old Me, 1959.
Same Old Saturday Night, 1955.
Sam's Song (The Happy Tune), 1950.
San Francisco Bay Blues, 1958.
Sand and the Sea, The, 1955.
Sands of Time, 1953.
Sandy, 1959.
Santa Baby, 1953.
Santo Natale, 1955.
Satin and Silk, 1954.
Satin Doll, 1958.
Satisfaction Guaranteed, 1953.
Satisfied, 1951.
Satisfied Mind, A, 1955.
Savannah, 1957.
Saving My Love (For You), 1958.
Say, Darling, 1958.
Say It with Your Heart, 1953.
Say, Man, 1959.
Say You're Mine Again, 1952.
Sayonara, 1953.
School Day (Ring! Ring! Goes the Bell), 1957.
Sea of Love, 1959.
Sea of the Moon, The, 1950.
Search for Paradise, 1957.
Search Is Through, The, 1954.
Searchers (Ride Away), 1956.
Searchin', 1957.
Seasons of My Heart, 1955.
Second Star to the Right, The, 1953.
Secret, The, 1958.
Secret Love, 1953.
Secret of Christmas, The, 1959.
Secretly, 1958.
See You in September, 1959.
See You Later, Alligator, 1955.
See-Saw, 1956.
Send for Me, 1957.
Send Me Some Lovin', 1957.
Send My Baby Back to Me, 1953.
Señor Blues, 1958.
Sentimental Me, 1950.
Sentimental Music, 1950.
Separate Tables, 1958.
Sermonette, 1958.
Set Him Free, 1959.
Settin' the Woods on Fire, 1952.
Seven Days, 1956.
Seven Lonely Days, 1953.
Seven Long Days, 1951.
Seven Wonders of the World, The, 1951.
Seventeen, 1955.
77 Sunset Strip, 1959.
Seventy Six Trombones, 1957.
Sexy Ways, 1954.
Shadow Woman, 1954.
Shake a Hand, 1953.
Shake Me I Rattle (Squeeze Me I Cry), 1957.
Shake, Rattle, and Roll, 1954.
Shall We Dance?, 1951.
Shane, see The Call of the Far-Away Hills, 1953.
(Why Did I Tell You I Was Going to) Shanghai, 1951.
Shape of Things, The, 1956.
Sh-Boom (Life Could Be a Dream), 1954.
She Say (Oom Dooby Doom), 1959.
She Was Only Seventeen (He Was One Year More), 1958.
Shenandoah Rose, 1957.
Shifting, Whispering Sands, The, 1950.
Shimmy, Shimmy Ko-Ko Bop, 1959.
Ship on a Stormy Sea, 1959.
Shoeless Joe from Hannibal Mo., 1955.
Short Fat Fannie, 1957.
Short Shorts, 1957.
Shot-Gun Boogie, 1950.
Show Me, 1956.
Show Me the Way To Get Out of This World ('cause That's Where Everything Is), 1950.
Show Must Go On, 1956.
Shrimp Boats, 1951.
Siamese Cat Song, The, 1953.
Sick and Tired, 1957.

Sick, Sober and Sorry, 1951.
Side by Side, 1953.
Signpost, 1954.
Silhouettes, 1957.
Silk Stockings, 1954.
Silver and Gold, 1951.
Silver Bells, 1950.
Silver Threads and Golden Needles, 1956.
(It's No) Sin, 1951.
Since I Don't Have You, 1959.
Since I Made You Cry, 1959.
Since I Met You Baby, 1956.
Sincerely, 1954.
Sincerely Yours, 1955.
Sing a Rainbow, 1955.
Sing Boy, Sing, 1957.
Singing the Blues, 1954.
Sinner or Saint, 1952.
Sinner's Prayer, 1950.
Sit Down You're Rockin' the Boat, 1950.
Sittin' in the Balcony, 1957.
Sittin' on It All the Time, 1950.
Sitting in the Back Seat, 1959.
Six Boys and Seven Girls, 1959.
16 Candles, 1959.
Sixteen Going on Seventeen, 1959.
Sixteen Tons, 1955.
Sixty Minute Man, 1951.
Skinny Minnie, 1958.
Skokiaan, 1954.
Sleep Walk, 1959.
Sleepin' Bee, A, 1954.
Sleigh Ride, 1950.
Slippin' and Slidin', 1956.
Slipping Around, 1950.
Slow Poke, 1951.
Slow Walk, 1957.
Slowly, 1953.
Slowly, with Feeling, 1955.
Sluefoot, 1955.
Smack Dab in the Middle, 1955.
Small Talk, 1954.
Small World, 1959.
Smellin' of Vanilla, 1954.
Smile, 1954.
Smoke from Your Cigarette, 1955.
Smoke Gets in Your Eyes, 1958.
Smokey the Bear, 1952.
Smokie, Part II, 1959.
Smooth Sailing, 1950.
Snowflakes, 1951.
So Close, 1959.
So Doggone Lonesome, 1956.
So Fine, 1955.
So Long, 1956.
So Long (It's Been Good To Know Yuh), 1950.
So Madly in Love, 1952.
So Many Ways, 1958.
So Rare, 1957.
Sobbin' Women, 1954.
Soft, 1952.
Soft Sands, 1957.
Soft Summer Breeze, 1955.
Soldier Boy, 1955.
Solfeggio, see Song of the Nairobi Trio, 1953.
Solitaire, 1951.
Solitaire, 1955.
Some People, 1959.
Somebody Bad Stole de Wedding Bell (Who's Got de Ding Dong?), 1953.
Somebody Bigger Than You and I, 1951.
Somebody, Somewhere, 1956.
Somebody Touched Me, 1958.
Somebody Up There Likes Me, 1956.
Somebody's Back in Town, 1959.
Somebody's Been Beatin' My Time, 1951.
Somebody's Stolen My Honey, 1951.
Someone You Love, 1955.
Someone's Been Sending Me Flowers, 1955.
Something Old, Something New (Something Borrowed and Blue), 1951.
Something Wonderful, 1951.
Something's Always Happening on the River, 1958.
Something's Coming, 1957.
Something's Gotta Give, 1955.
Somewhere, 1957.
Somewhere (There Is Someone), 1953.
Somewhere along the Way, 1952.
Song and Dance Man, 1958.
Song Angels Sing, The, 1951.
Song for a Summer Night, 1956.
Song from *Désirée*, The, 1954.
Song from *Some Came Running*, 1958.
Song from The Moulin Rouge, The, 1953.
Song of Delilah, 1950.
Song of Raintree County, The, 1957.

Song of the Barefoot Contessa, 1954.
Song of the Dreamer, 1955.
Song of the Nairobi Trio, 1953.
Sorry for Myself?, 1958.
Sorry, I Ran All the Way Home, 1959.
Sorta on the Border, 1953.
Sound of Music, The, 1959.
Sound Off, 1951.
Sous les Ponts de Paris, see Under the Bridges of Paris, 1953.
Souvenir d'Italie, 1957.
Spanish Fireball, 1953.
Sparkling Brown Eyes (Sparkling Blue Eyes), 1954.
Sparrow in the Treetop, 1951.
Speak, My Love, 1956.
Speedoo, 1955.
Splish Splash, 1958.
Spring Can Really Hang You Up the Most, 1955.
Spring Has Sprung, 1952.
Spring in Maine, 1956.
Spring Spring Spring, 1954.
Stagger Lee, 1958.
Stairway of Love, 1958.
Stairway to the Sea, 1957.
Standing on the Corner, 1956.
Starbright, 1959.
Start Movin', 1957.
Stay, 1958.
Stay Here with Me, 1957.
Stay with the Happy People, 1950.
Staying Young, 1959.
Steam Heat, 1954.
Steamboat, 1955.
Still, 1956.
Stolen Moments, 1954.
Stood Up, 1957.
Stop the World (And Let Me Off), 1957.
Story of Love, The, 1956.
Story of My Life, The, 1957.
Story of My Love, The, 1959.
Story of Our Love, The, 1959.
Story Untold, A, 1955.
Straight, No Chaser, 1951.
Stranded in the Jungle, 1956.
Strange, 1953.
Strange Are the Ways of Love, 1959.
Strange Lady in Town, 1955.
Strange Little Girl, The, 1951.
Strange Sensation, 1954.
Strange Things Are Happening, 1953.
Stranger in Paradise, 1953.
Street of Love, The, see La Strada del' Amore, 1958.
String Along, 1952.
Stroll, The, 1957.
Stupid Cupid, 1958.
Such a Night, 1954.
Suddenly, 1953.
Suddenly There's a Valley, 1955.
Sue Me, 1950.
Sugar Moon, 1957.
Sugarbush, 1952.
Sugarfoot, 1958.
Sugarfoot Rag, 1950.
Sugartime, 1956.
Summer Is A-Comin' In, 1952.
Summer Love, 1957.
Summertime Blues, 1958.
Summertime in Venice, 1955.
Summertime Lies, 1958.
Summertime Love, 1959.
Summertime, Summertime, 1958.
Sunday, 1958.
Sunday in New York, 1959.
Sunshine Cake, 1950.
(We've Got) Sure Thing, A, 1950.
Surprise, 1958.
Susie Darlin, 1958.
Susie Q, 1957.
Suzanne (Ev'ry Night When the Sun Goes Down), 1952.
Suzy Snowflake, 1951.
Swamp Girl, The, 1950.
Swanee River Rock, 1957.
Sway, 1954.
Swedish Rhapsody, 1953.
Sweet and Gentle, 1955.
Sweet Dreams, 1955.
Sweet Heartaches, 1955.
Sweet Little Sixteen, 1958.
Sweet Nothin's, 1959.
Sweet Old-Fashioned Girl, A, 1956.
Sweet Sixteen, 1952.
Sweet Sixteen Bars, 1958.
Sweet Thursday, 1955.
Sweet Violets, 1951.
Sweeter Than You, 1959.
Swingin' on a Rainbow, 1959.
Swingin' Shepherd Blues, The, 1958.
Syncopated Clock, The, 1950.

T

"T" 99 Blues, 1951.
T.L.C., 1959.
Take a Message to Mary, 1959.
Take Back Your Mink, 1950.
Take It Slow, Joe, 1957.
Take Me Along, 1959.
Take Me in Your Arms and Hold Me, 1950, 1952.
Take My Love, 1954.
Take These Chains from My Heart, 1952.
Takes Two To Tango, 1952.
Tales of Wells Fargo, 1957.
Talk That Talk, 1959.
Talk to Me, 1956.
Talk to Me, Talk to Me, 1958.
Talk to Your Heart, 1952.
Talkin' 'bout You, 1959.
Tall Paul, 1958.
Tallahassee Lassie, 1959.
Tammy, 1957.
Tangled Mind, 1956.
Teach Me Tonight, 1953.
Teacher, Teacher, 1957.
Teacher's Pet, 1956.
Tear Drop, 1959.
Tear Fell, A, 1956.
Teardrops from My Eyes, 1950.
Teardrops on Your Letter, 1959.
Teardrops Will Fall, 1959.
Tears on My Pillow, 1958.
Teasin', 1950.
Teddy, 1959.
(Let Me Be Your) Teddy Bear, 1957.
Teen Age Crush, 1956.
Teen-Age Love, 1956.
Teen Age Prayer, 1955.
Teen Angel, 1959.
Teen Beat, 1959.
Teenager in Love, A, 1959.
Teenager's Romance, A, 1957.
Tell All the World about You, 1958.
Tell Him No, 1958.
Tell Me a Story, 1953.
Tell Me Why, 1951.
Tell Me You Love Me, 1951.
Tell Me You're Mine, 1953.
Tell the Lady I Said Goodbye, 1951.
Ten Thousand Drums, 1959.
Tend to Your Business, 1954.
Tender Love and Care, see T.L.C., 1959.
Tender Shepherd, 1954.
(Love Is) Tender Trap, The, 1955.
Tennessee Stud, 1958.
Tennessee Tango, 1952.
Tennessee Waltz, 1950.
Tennessee Wig-Walk, The, 1952.
Tequila, 1958.
Terry Theme, The, see Eternally, 1953.
Thank Heaven for Little Girls, 1958.
Thank You for Calling, 1954.
Thank You Pretty Baby, 1958.
Thanks a Lot, but No Thanks, 1954.
That Do Make It Nice, 1955.
That Doggie in the Window, 1952.
That Face, 1957.
That Heart Belongs to Me, 1952.
That Hound Dog in the Window, 1953.
That'll Be the Day, 1957.
That's All, 1952.
That's All I Want from You, 1954.
That's All Right, 1955.
That's All There Is to That, 1955.
That's Amoré, 1953.
('Cause I Love Ya) That's A-Why, 1952.
That's Enough, 1959.
That's Entertainment, 1953.
That's Me without You, 1952.
That's the Chance You Take, 1952.
That's What I Like, 1954.
That's What It's Like To Be Lonesome, 1958.
That's What You're Doing to Me, 1951.
That's Why, 1957.
That's Why I Was Born, 1957.
Thee I Love, see Friendly Persuasion, 1956.
Theme from *A Summer Place*, 1959.
Theme from *Auntie Mame*, 1958.
Theme from *Baby Doll*, 1956.
Theme from *East of Eden*, 1955.
Theme from *Peter Gunn*, see Peter Gunn Theme, 1959.
Theme from *Picnic*, 1955.
Theme from *Rebel without a Cause*, 1955.
Theme from *The Proud Ones*, 1956.
Theme from *The Swan*, 1956.
Theme from *The Threepenny Opera*, see Mack the Knife, 1956.
Theme from *Zorro*, 1958.
There Goes My Baby, 1959.

There Is Only Paris for That, 1958.
There Is Something on Your Mind, 1957.
There Must Be Something Better Than Love, 1950.
There Once Was a Man, 1954.
There She Goes, 1955.
There Stands the Glass, 1951.
There You Go, 1956.
There'll Be No Teardrops Tonight, 1954.
There's a Big Wheel, 1959.
There's Been a Change in Me, 1951.
There's Never Been Anyone Else but You, 1956.
There's No Tomorrow, 1950.
There's Only One of You, 1954.
These Hands, 1955.
These Things I Offer You (For a Lifetime), 1951.
They Call the Wind Maria, 1951.
They Came to Cordura, 1959.
They Were Doin' the Mambo, 1954.
Thing, The, 1950.
Things That I Used To Do, 1953.
Thinking of You, 1950.
Third Man Theme, The, 1950.
This Could Be the Start of Something, 1956.
This Earth Is Mine, 1959.
This Friendly World, 1959.
This Happy Feeling, 1958.
This I Swear, 1959.
This Is All I Ask, 1958.
This Is My Song, 1952.
This Is What I Call Love, 1956.
This Land Is Your Land, 1956.
This Little Girl of Mine, 1955.
This Little Girl's Gone Rockin', 1958.
This Old Man, see The Children's Marching Song, 1958.
This Ole House, 1954.
This Orchid Means Goodbye, 1953.
This Should Go On Forever, 1959.
Thousand Miles Ago, A, 1959.
Thousand Miles Away, A, 1956.
Three Coins in the Fountain, 1954.
Three Cornered Tune, see Fugue for Tinhorns, 1950.
Three O'Clock Blues, 1952.
Three Stars, 1959.
3:10 to Yuma, 1957.
Three Ways To Love You, 1957.
Through the Eyes of Love, 1957.
Throw Your Love My Way, 1950.
Thumbelina, 1952.
Thunder and Lightning (Lightning and Thunder), 1953.
Tiger, 1959.
Tijuana Jail, The, 1959.
'Til I Kissed You, 1959.
'Til Tomorrow, 1959.
Till, 1957.
Till I Waltz Again with You, 1952.
Till Then, 1954.
Till There Was You, 1957.
Till We Two Are One, 1953.
Time and the River, 1959.
Time for Parting, 1954.
Times Two, I Love You, 1955.
Tina Marie, 1954.
Ting A Ling, 1952.
To Be in Love!, 1957.
To Be Loved, 1958.
To Know Him Is To Love Him, 1958.
To Know You Is To Love You, 1952.
To Love Again, 1955.
To Love and Be Loved, see Song from *Some Came Running*, 1958.
To the Aisle, 1957.
To Think You've Chosen Me, 1950.
To You My Love, 1955.
Today, I Love Ev'rybody, 1953.
Together Wherever We Go, 1959.
Tom Dooley, 1958.
Tom Thumb's Tune, 1958.
Tomboy, 1958.
Tonight, 1957.
Tonight My Heart She Is (Will Be) Crying, 1957.
Tonight You Belong to Me, 1956.
Too Bad, 1954.
Too Close for Comfort, 1956.
Too Late Now, 1950.
Too Much, 1956.
Too Much Lovin' (Much Too Much), 1953.
Too Much Monkey Business, 1956.
Too Much Tequila, 1959.
Too Much, Too Soon, 1958.
Too Old To Cut the Mustard, 1951.
Too Young, 1951.
Too Young To Go Steady, 1955.
Topsy II, 1958.
Torero, 1958.
Touch, The, 1954.

Touch of Pink, A, 1959.
Toy Tiger, 1955.
Toys, 1953.
Tra La La, 1956.
Tracy's Theme, 1959.
Trade Mark, 1953.
Tragedy, 1958.
Train of Love, 1956.
Transfusion, 1956.
Travelin' Blues, 1951.
Traveling down a Lonely Road, see Love Theme from *La Strada*, 1954.
Treasure of Love, 1956.
Treat Me Nice, 1957.
Tropical Meringue, 1955.
Tropicana, 1953.
Trouble with Harry, The, 1955.
True Love, 1956.
True Love Goes On and On, 1954.
Try Me, 1958.
Try To Love Me Just As I Am, 1958.
Trying, 1952.
Tulips and Heather, 1951.
Tupelo County Jail, 1958.
Turn Back the Hands of Time, 1951.
Turn Me Loose, 1959.
Tutti Frutti, 1955.
Tweedlee Dee, 1954.
Twelfth of Never, 1956.
Twenty Feet of Muddy Water, 1956.
24 Hours a Day (365 a Year), 1955.
Twenty-Six Miles, 1958.
(I Love You) Twice As Much, 1953.
Twilight Time, 1958.
Twisted, 1953.
Twixt Twelve and Twenty, 1959.
Two Brothers, 1951.
Two Different Worlds, 1956.
Two Faces in the Dark, 1958.
Two Hearts, 1954.
Two Ladies in de Shade of de Banana Tree, 1954.
Two Lost Souls, 1955.
Two of Us, 1954.
Two Shadows on Your Window, 1957.
Typewriter, The, 1953.
Tzena, Tzena, Tzena, 1950.

U

Uh! Oh! (The Nutty Squirrels), 1959.
Unbirthday Song, The, 1951.
Unchained Melody, 1955.
Uncle Pen, 1951.
Undecided, 1951.
Under Paris Skies, 1951.
Under the Bridges of Paris, 1953.
Under Your Spell Again, 1959.
Unforgettable, 1951.
Unless, 1951.
Unsuspecting Heart, 1955.
Untouchables, The, 1959.
Unwanted Sign upon Your Heart, 1950.
Upon the Mountain, 1956.
Use Your Imagination, 1950.
Uska Dara, 1953.

V

Valentino Tango, The, 1950.
Valley of Tears, 1957.
Vanessa, 1952.
Vanity, 1951.
Vaya con Dios (May God Be with You), 1953.
Velvet Glove, The, 1953.
Venus, 1959.
Vera Cruz, 1954.
Verboten!, 1958.
Verdict, The, 1955.
Vertigo, 1958.
Very Necessary You, The, 1953.
Very Next Man, The, 1959.
Very Precious Love, A, 1958.
Very Special Day, A, 1953.
Very Special Love, A, 1957.
Village of St. Bernadette, The, 1959.
Violins from Nowhere, 1950.
Voice in My Heart, The, 1958.
Volare, 1958.

W

Wagon Train, 1957.
Waitin' in School, 1957.
Waiting Game, The, 1958.
Waiting in the Lobby of Your Heart, 1952.
Wake the Town and Tell the People, 1954.
Wake Up Irene, 1953.
Wake Up, Little Susie, 1957.
Walk Hand in Hand, 1956.
Walk Up, 1956.
Walkin' after Midnight, 1956.
Walkin' in the Rain, see Just Walking in the Rain, 1953.

Walkin' My Baby Back Home, 1952.
Walkin' to Missouri, 1952.
Walking Away Whistling, 1959.
Wallflower, The, see Dance with Me Henry, 1955.
Waltz at Maxim's, 1958.
Waltz for a Ball, 1957.
Wanderin', 1950.
Wand'rin Star, 1951.
Wanted, 1954.
War and Peace, 1956.
Warm, 1956.
Warm All Over, 1956.
Warm and Willing, 1959.
Wasted Words, 1956.
Waterloo, 1959.
Watermelon Weather, 1952.
Way Down Yonder in New Orleans, 1959.
Ways of a Woman in Love, The, 1958.
Wayward Wind, 1956.
We Got Love, 1959.
We Kiss in a Shadow, 1951.
We Meet Again, see The Song from *Désirée*, 1954.
We Never Talk Much, 1950.
Wear My Ring around Your Neck, 1958.
Weary Blues from Waitin', 1951.
Weaver of Dreams, 1951.
Wedding, The, 1955.
Wedding, The, 1958.
Wedding Bells, see I'm Always Hearing Wedding Bells, 1954.
(In the) Wee Small Hours (Of the Morning), 1955.
Weepin' and Cryin', 1951.
Welcome Home, 1954.
Well, Oh, Well, 1950.
Wendy, 1954.
We're Gonna Be in High Society, 1955.
We're Not Children, 1958.
Western Movies, 1958.
We've Gone Too Far, 1954.
Whale of a Tale, A, 1953.
What a Diff'rence a Day Makes, 1959.
What a Dream, 1954.
What Am I Living For?, 1958.
What Am I Worth, 1955.
What Do I Care?, 1958.
What Do I Care, 1959.
What Ev'ry Girl Should Know, 1954.
What Good Does It Do?, 1957.
What in the World's Come Over You, 1959.
What Is a Husband?, 1955.
What Is a Wife?, see What Is a Husband?, 1955.
What Is Love?, 1959.
What It Was, Was Football, 1954.
What Would I Do Without You, 1956.
What Would You Do (If Jesus Came to Your House), 1956.
What Would You Do (If You Were in My Place), 1952.
What'cha Gonna Do?, 1955.
What-Cha Gonna Do Now, 1954.
Whatcha' Gonna Do When Your Baby Leaves You, 1956.
What'd I Say, 1959.
Whatever Lola Wants (Lola Gets), 1955.
Whatever Will Be, Will Be, see Que Sera, Sera, 1955.
Wheel of Fortune, 1952.
When, 1958.
When Did I Fall in Love?, 1959.
When I Fall in Love, 1952.
When It's Springtime in Alaska, 1959.
When Love Goes Wrong, 1953.
When Mexican Joe Met Jole Blon, 1953.
When Sunny Gets Blue, 1956.
When the Boys Talk about the Girls, 1958.
When the Sea Is All around Us, 1955.
(Ah, the Apple Trees) When the World Was Young, 1950.
When You and I Were Young Maggie Blues, 1951.
When You Dance, 1955.
When You're in Love, 1954.
Where Can I Go without You, 1952.
Where Did the Night Go?, 1952.
Where Is That Someone for Me, 1955.
Where Is Your Heart, see The Song from the Moulin Rouge, 1953.
Where, Oh Where?, 1950.
Where Were You on Our Wedding Day, 1959.

Where Will the Dimple Be?, 1955.
Which One Is To Blame, 1959.
While You Danced, Danced, Danced, 1951.
Whiskey and Gin, 1951.
Whispering, 1951.
Whispering Bells, 1957.
Whispering Winds, 1952.
White Lightning, 1959.
White Silver Sands, 1957.
White Sport Coat, A (And a Pink Carnation), 1957.
Whither Thou Goest, 1954.
Who Cares (For Me), 1959.
Who Needs You, 1956.
Who Shot Sam, 1959.
Who Was That Lady?, 1959.
Whole Lotta Loving, 1958.
Whole Lot-ta Shakin' Goin' On, 1957.
Who's Got the Pain?, 1955.
Who's Sorry Now, 1958.
Why, Baby, Why, 1955.
Why Baby Why, 1957.
Why Can't the English, 1956.
Why Do Fools Fall in Love, 1956.
Why Do Things Happen to Me, 1950.
Why Do You Have To Go, 1957.
Why Don't They Understand, 1957.
Why Don't You Believe Me, 1952.
Why Don't You Love Me, 1950.
Why Don't You Write Me, 1955.
Why Fight the Feeling, 1950.
Why Should I Cry, 1950.
Why Should We Try Anymore, 1950.
Why Try To Change Me Now, 1952.
Why Why, 1957.
Wild Horses, 1953.
Wild Is the Wind, 1957.
Wild Side of Life, The, 1952.
Wild, Wild Young Men, 1955.
Wildwood Flower, 1955.
Wilhelmina, 1950.
Will I Ever Tell You, 1957.
Willie the Whistling Giraffe, 1951.
Willingly, 1958.
Wimoweh, 1951.
Win Your Love for Me, 1958.
Winter of My Discontent, 1955.
Winter Waltz, The, 1950.
Wish You Were Here, 1952.
Wishing for Your Love, 1958.
Wishing Ring, 1952.
Witch Doctor, 1958.
Witchcraft, 1955.
Witchcraft, 1957.
With a Little Bit of Luck, 1956.
With All My Heart, 1957.
With All My Heart and Soul, see Anema e Core, 1954.
With These Hands, 1950.
With You on My Mind, 1957.
Without Love, 1954.
Without Love (There Is Nothing), 1956.
Without You, 1956.
Woke Up This Morning, 1953.
Woman, 1953.
Woman Alone with the Blues, 1955.
Woman in Love, A, 1955.
Woman of the River, 1955.
Wonder Why, 1950.
Wonderful Copenhagen, 1951.
Wonderful! Wonderful!, 1956.
Wonderful, Wonderful Day, 1954.
Wondering, 1952.
Wondering, 1957.
Woo-Hoo, 1959.
Work with Me, Annie, 1954.
World Is Waiting for the Sunrise, The, 1951.
World Outside, The, 1958.
Worried Man, A, 1959.
Would I Love You (Love You, Love You), 1951.
Wouldn't It Be Loverly?, 1956.
Wringle Wrangle, 1956.
Written on the Wind, 1956.
Wrong Note Rag, 1953.

Y

Yakety Yak, 1958.
Y'All Come, see You All Come, 1953.
Yaller Yaller Gold, 1955.
Year after Year, 1955.
Yellow Bird, 1957.
Yellow Rose of Texas, The, 1955.
Yellow Roses, 1953.
Yes, I Know Why, 1956.
Yes Tonight, Josephine, 1957.
Yesterday and You, see Armen's Theme, 1956.
Yesterday's Girl, 1952.
Yonder Comes a Sucker, 1955.
You, 1952.
You All Come, 1953.
You Alone (Solo Tu), 1953.

You and Me, 1955.
You and You Alone, see Love Theme from *La Strada*, 1954.
You and Your Beautiful Eyes, 1950.
You Are Beautiful, 1958.
You Are My Destiny, 1958.
You Are My Love, 1955.
You Are Not My First Love, 1953.
You Are the One, 1956.
You Belong to Me, 1952.
You Better Know It, 1959.
You Better Not Do That, 1953.
You Better Watch Yourself, 1959.
You Can Fly! You Can Fly! You Can Fly!, 1951.
You Can't Have My Love, 1954.
You Can't Run Away from It, 1956.
You Cheated, 1958.
You Done Me Wrong, 1956.
You Don't Have To Go, 1954.
You Don't Know Him, 1958.
You Don't Know Me, 1955.
You Don't Owe Me a Thing, 1956.
You Don't Remind Me, 1950.
You Fascinate Me So, 1958.
You Got Me Dizzy, 1956.
You Got What It Takes, 1959.
You Gotta Be My Baby, 1956.
You Gotta Love Everybody, 1956.
You Know I Love You, 1952.
You Need Hands, 1957.
You Send Me, 1957.
You Upset Me Baby, 1954.
You Were Mine, 1959.
You Will Find Your Love in Paris, 1958.
You Will Wear Velvet, 1954.
You Wonderful You, 1950.
You You You, 1953.
You'll Never Get Away, 1952.
You'll Never Get Away from Me, 1959.
Young and Foolish, 1954.
Young and Warm and Wonderful, 1958.
Young at Heart, 1954.
Young Blood, 1957.
Young Ideas, 1955.
Young Love, 1956.
Your Cash Ain't Nothin' but Trash, 1954.
Your Cheatin' Heart, 1952.
Your Name Is Beautiful, 1958.
Your True Love, 1957.
You're All I Want for Christmas, 1950.
You're Free To Go, 1955.
You're Gonna Miss Me, 1959.
You're Just in Love, 1950.
You're Making a Fool out of Me, 1958.
You're Mine, 1956.
You're Not Mine Anymore, 1954.
You're Running Wild, 1956.
You're Sensational, 1956.
You're So Fine, 1959.
You're So Much a Part of Me, 1953.
You're So Right for Me, 1958.
You're Still Mine, 1956.
You're Still My Baby, 1954.
You're the Nearest Thing to Heaven, 1958.
You're the Reason I'm in Love, 1956.
Yours, 1952.
You've Changed, 1952.
You've Got Personality, 1959.

Z

Zambezi, 1955.
Zing a Little Zong, 1952.
Zing Zing—Zoom Zoom, 1950.
Zorro, see Theme from *Zorro*, 1958.
Zsa Zsa, 1953.

List of Publishers

A

ABC Music Corp. (ASCAP)
136 West 52nd Street
New York 19, N. Y.

A.D.T. Enterprises, Inc. (BMI)
c/o M. Warren Troob
250 West 57th Street
New York 19, New York

A.M.C., Inc. (ASCAP)
30 West 60th Street
New York 23, New York

Aberbach, Inc. (BMI)
11th Floor
1619 Broadway
New York 19, N. Y.

Ace Publishing Co., Inc. (BMI)
Suite 900, Vincent Building
203 West Capitol Street
Jackson, Mississippi

Acuff-Rose Publications (BMI)
2510 Franklin Road
Nashville 4, Tennessee

Adams-Vee & Abbott, Inc. (BMI)
216 South Wabash Avenue
Chicago 4, Illinois

Admiration Music, Inc. (BMI)
c/o Lee Silver
3432 Mentone Avenue
Los Angeles 34, California

Advanced Music Corp. (ASCAP)
488 Madison Avenue
New York 22, New York

Aida Music, Inc. (ASCAP)
11th Floor
1619 Broadway
New York 19, New York

Alamo Music, Inc. (ASCAP)
11th Floor
1619 Broadway
New York 19, N. Y.

Alaska Music Co., Inc. (ASCAP)
Revue Studios
Universal City, California

Aldon Music, Inc. (BMI)
c/o Screen Gems-Columbia Music, Inc.
711 Fifth Avenue
New York 22, New York

Alexis Music, Inc. (ASCAP)
c/o Lee Magid
408 West 57th Street
New York 19, New York

Algonquin Music, Inc. (BMI)
1650 Broadway
New York 19, N. Y.

Almanac Music, Inc. (ASCAP)
10 Columbus Circle
New York 19, New York

Almimo Music, Inc. (BMI)
Room 710
1650 Broadway
New York 19, New York

Amano Music Corp. (BMI)
c/o Farber, Cohen, and Diamond
608 Fifth Avenue
New York 20, New York

American Academy of Music, Inc. (ASCAP)
1619 Broadway
New York 19, New York

American Music, Inc. (BMI)
9109 Sunset Boulevard
Hollywood, California

Andval Music (BMI)
c/o Milt Grant
2480 16th Street, N.W.
Washington, D.C.

Angel Music, Inc. (BMI)
Apartment 4C
150 West 55th Street
New York 19, New York

Arbee Music Publishing Co., Inc. (ASCAP)
c/o Arthur Pine
475 Fifth Avenue
New York 17, New York

Arc Music Corp. (BMI)
1619 Broadway
New York 19, New York

Arch Music Co., Inc. (ASCAP)
1650 Broadway
New York 19, New York

Ardmore Music Corp. (ASCAP)
1750 North Vine Street
Hollywood 28, California

Aries Music Co. (BMI)
3747 Ruthelen Street
Los Angeles 18, California

Ark-La-Tex Publishing Co. (BMI)
11th Floor
1619 Broadway
New York 19, New York

Armo Music Corp. (BMI)
1540 Brewster Avenue
Cincinnati 7, Ohio

Artists Music, Inc. (ASCAP)
250 North Canon Drive
Beverly Hills, California

Aspen Music Corp. (ASCAP)
c/o Tommy Valando
22 West 48th Street
New York 36, New York

Associated Music Publishers, Inc. (BMI)
1 West 47th Street
New York 36, New York

Robert Astor Music Co., Inc. (BMI)
c/o Roosevelt Music Co., Inc.
Room 408
1650 Broadway
New York 19, New York

Atlantic Music Corp. (BMI)
6124 Selma Avenue
Hollywood 28, California

Frankie Avalon Music, Inc. (BMI)
11th Floor
1619 Broadway
New York 19, New York

Avas Music Publishing Co., Inc. (ASCAP)
250 West 57th Street
New York 19, New York

Avon Music, Inc. (BMI)
c/o Michael Langford
130 West 46th Street
New York 36, New York

Aztec Music, Inc. (ASCAP)
1041 North Formosa Avenue
Los Angeles 28, California

B

B. & F. Music Co., Inc. (BMI)
1323 South Michigan Avenue
Chicago 16, Illinois

B.R.S. Music Corp. (BMI)
c/o Max J. Rosenberg
Room 1016
527 Madison Avenue
New York 22, New York

Babb Music Publishers (BMI)
48th Avenue and Tennessee
Nashville, Tennessee

Balcones Publishing Co. (BMI)
Division of Southwestern Artists Association, Inc.
c/o Edmund L. Nichols
607 West 12th Street
Austin 1, Texas

Bamboo Music, Inc. (BMI)
Suite 201
6515 Sunset Boulevard
Hollywood 28, California

The Bar Music Publishing Co., Ltd. (BMI)
11314½ South Main Street
Los Angeles 61, California

Paul Barrett Music, Inc. (BMI)
709 Central Tower
San Francisco 3, California

Earl Barton Music Co. (BMI)
1121 South Glenstone
Springfield, Missouri

Barton Music Corp. (ASCAP)
Room 716
1619 Broadway
New York 19, New York

Bayes Music Corp. (BMI)
119 West 57th Street
New York 19, New York

Beacon Music Co. (ASCAP)
441 West 49th Street
New York 19, New York

Be-Are Music Publications, Inc. (BMI)
319 Seventh Avenue North
Nashville 3, Tennessee

Beaver Music Publishing Corp. (ASCAP)
1650 Broadway
New York 19, New York

Bee Gee Music Publications, Inc. (BMI)
806 16th Avenue South
Nashville, Tennessee

Beechwood Music Corp. (BMI)
1750 North Vine Street
Hollywood 28, California

Belmar Music Publishing Co. (BMI)
c/o Sophia Lent
565 West End Avenue
New York 24, New York

Benell Music Publishing Co. (BMI)
315 West 47th Street
New York 19, New York

Ben-Ghazi Enterprises, Inc. (BMI)
c/o Jack Pearl
515 Madison Avenue
New York 22, New York

Bentley Music Co. (BMI)
Box 1170
Chapel Hill, North Carolina

Berkshire Music, Inc. (BMI)
Room 501
756 Seventh Avenue
New York 19, New York

Irving Berlin Music Corp. (ASCAP)
1290 Avenue of the Americas
New York 19, New York

Bess Music Co. (BMI)
c/o Gene Autry Music Publishing, Inc.
1556 North La Brea
Hollywood 28, California

Big Bopper Music Co. (BMI)
Post Office Box 849
Beaumont, Texas

Birchwood Music Co. (ASCAP)
c/o Don Robertson Music Corp.
Room 426
1651 Cosmo Street
Hollywood 28, California

Bishop Music Co. (ASCAP)
5101 Natilija
Sherman Oaks, California

Blackstone Music, Inc. (ASCAP)
1841 Broadway
New York 23, New York

Blackwood Music, Inc. (BMI)
1650 Broadway
New York 19, New York

Ben Bloom Music Corp. (ASCAP)
1619 Broadway
New York 19, New York

Blossom Music Corp. (ASCAP)
322 West 48th Street
New York 36, New York

Blue Grass Music (BMI)
Room 100
157 West 57th Street
New York 19, New York

Blue Ridge Publishing Co. (BMI)
c/o Bernard Pearlman
1540 Brewster Avenue
Cincinnati 7, Ohio

Blue River Music, Inc. (BMI)
c/o Harry Bluestone
Suite 211
6223 Selma Avenue
Hollywood 28, California

Bluff City Music Publishing Co., Inc. (BMI)
Room 100
157 West 57th Street
New York 19, New York

Bourne, Inc. (ASCAP)
36 West 52nd Street
New York 19, New York

Bradshaw Music, Inc. (BMI)
8745 Sunset Boulevard
Hollywood 46, California

Brandom Music Co. (ASCAP)
1323 South Michigan Avenue
Chicago 5, Illinois

Brazos Valley Music, Inc. (BMI)
Post Office Box 7508
Oklahoma City 16, Oklahoma

Bregman, Vocco & Conn, Inc. (ASCAP)
1619 Broadway
New York 19, New York

Brenner Music, Inc. (BMI)
11th Floor
1619 Broadway
New York 19, New York

Brent Music Corp. (BMI)
Suite 905
2 West 45th Street
New York 36, New York

Brewster Music Publishing, Inc. (BMI)
745 Fifth Avenue
New York 22, New York

Bridgeport Music (BMI)
253 Waverly Avenue
Highland Park 3, Michigan

Brittany Music, Inc. (BMI)
11th Floor
1619 Broadway
New York 19, New York

T. Brown & Sons (BMI)
253 Merritts Avenue
Atlanta, Georgia

Bryden Music, Inc. (BMI)
157 West 57th Street
New York 19, New York

Brynor Music, Inc. (BMI)
Suite 20F
392 Central Park West
New York 25, New York

Buckeye Music, Inc. (ASCAP)
413 Race Street
Cincinnati 2, Ohio

Buckeye Publishing Co. (BMI)
204 West Eighth Street
Cincinnati 2, Ohio

Bulls-Eye Music, Inc. (ASCAP)
6526 Selma Avenue
Hollywood 28, California

Buna Music Corp. (BMI)
Murray Nash Associates, Inc.
Post Office Box 1224
1707 Division Street
Nashville, Tennessee

Burke & Van Heusen, Inc. (ASCAP)
250 West 57th Street
New York 19, New York

Burke-Van Heusen & Associates Music Corp. (ASCAP)
250 West 57th Street
New York 19, New York

Burlington Music Corp. (ASCAP)
539 West 25th Street
New York 10, New York

Burnt Oak Publishing Co., Inc. (BMI)
Post Office Box 24B
Mobile, Alabama

Buxton Hill Music Corp. (ASCAP)
609 Fifth Avenue
New York 17, New York

C

Cajun Publishing Co. (BMI)
Commercial Building
Post Office Box 1387
Shreveport, Louisiana

Calico Records, Inc. (ASCAP)
490 Bakewell Building
Pittsburgh, Pennsylvania

Capri Music Corp. (BMI)
145 West 45th Street
New York 36, New York

Carlot Music, Inc. (BMI)
c/o Fred Raphael
6758 Colgate Avenue
Los Angeles 48, California

Carlyle Music Publishing Corp. (ASCAP)
1650 Broadway
New York 19, New York

Carmichael Music Publications, Inc. (ASCAP)
119 West 57th Street
New York 19, New York

Carnegie Music Corp. (BMI)
c/o Massey Music Co., Inc.
c/o Braunstein & Chernin
270 Madison Avenue
New York 16, New York

Carney Music, Inc. (BMI)
2203 Spruce Street
Philadelphia 3, Pennsylvania

Carrie Music Co., Inc. (ASCAP)
1841 Broadway
New York 23, New York

Case Music Corp. (ASCAP)
c/o Paul J. Case
11th Floor
1619 Broadway
New York 19, New York

Johnny Cash Music, Inc. (BMI)
11th Floor
1619 Broadway
New York 19, New York

Cash Songs (BMI)
c/o J. Dolphin, Jr.
1252 South Berendo
Los Angeles, California

Cathryl Music Corp. (ASCAP)
608 Fifth Avenue
New York 20, New York

Cavalcade Music Corp. (ASCAP)
136 East 57th Street
New York 22, New York

Cedarwood Publishing Co., Inc. (BMI)
815 16th Avenue South
Nashville 4, Tennessee

Central Songs, Inc. (BMI)
1483 North Vine Street
Hollywood 28, California

Century Songs, Inc. (BMI)
1483 North Vine Street
Hollywood 28, California

Champion Music Corp. (BMI)
c/o Bill Downer
445 Park Avenue
New York 22, New York

Chantez Music, Inc. (BMI)
Suite 2160
10 Columbus Circle
New York 19, New York

Chappell & Co., Inc. (ASCAP)
609 Fifth Avenue
New York 17, New York

Cherio Music Publishers, Inc. (BMI)
c/o Lee V. Eastman
39 West 54th Street
New York 19, New York

Choice Music, Inc. (ASCAP)
9109 Sunset Boulevard
Hollywood 46, California

Claiborne Music (BMI)
Manor Club
4000 Montpelier
Rockville, Maryland

Clara Music Publishing Corp. (ASCAP)
c/o Belafonte Enterprises
157 West 57th Street
New York 19, New York

Jack Clement Music, Inc. (BMI)
639 Madison Avenue
Memphis, Tennessee

Clockus Music, Inc. (BMI)
c/o Ed Marmor
4644 Arriba Drive
Tarzana, California

Cole and Gale Music Distributors, Inc. (BMI)
Suite 1220
250 West 57th Street
New York 19, New York

Coliseum Music, Inc. (BMI)
c/o Regent Music Corp.
Suite 507
1619 Broadway
New York 19, New York

Columbia Pictures Music Corp. (ASCAP)
666 Fifth Avenue
New York 19, New York

Command Music Co., Inc. (BMI)
Room 908
36 West 44th Street
New York 36, New York

Commander Publications (ASCAP)
1610 North Argyle
Hollywood, California

Congressional Music Publications (ASCAP)
1224 Koko Head Avenue
Honolulu 16, Hawaii

Conley Music, Inc. (ASCAP)
222 Rittenhouse Square
Philadelphia 3, Pennsylvania

Reg Connelly Music, Inc. (ASCAP)
11th Floor
1619 Broadway
New York 19, New York

Conrad Publishing Co., Inc. (BMI)
1449 South Michigan Avenue
Chicago 5, Illinois

Consolidated Music Publishers, Inc. (ASCAP)
240 West 55th Street
New York 19, New York

Cool Music Co. (BMI)
c/o Frederick Music Co.
1323 South Michigan Avenue
Chicago 5, Illinois

Copar-Forrest Music Corp. (BMI)
11th Floor
1619 Broadway
New York 19, New York

Cordial Music Co. (BMI)
1926 North St. Andrews Place
Hollywood 28, California

Cornell-Kingsway Music Corp. (ASCAP)
11th Floor
1619 Broadway
New York 19, New York

Cornerstone Publishing Co. (BMI)
c/o Liberty Records, Inc.
6920 Sunset Boulevard
Los Angeles 28, California

Coronation Music, Inc. (BMI)
c/o George Paxton, Inc.
1619 Broadway
New York 19, New York

Cosmopolitan Music Publishers (ASCAP)
Room 812
545 Fifth Avenue
New York 17, New York

Cranford Music Corp. (BMI)
c/o P. Landwehr
356 West 40th Street
New York 18, New York

Crescent Music Co. (ASCAP)
1650 Broadway
New York 19, New York

Crestview Music Corp. (ASCAP)
c/o Jack Gale
Comet Music Corp.
101 West 55th Street
New York 19, New York

Criterion Music Corp. (ASCAP)
1491 North Vine Street
Hollywood 28, California

Cromwell Music, Inc. (ASCAP)
Suite 2160
10 Columbus Circle
New York 19, New York

Crystal Music Publishers, Inc. (ASCAP)
6253 Hollywood Boulevard
Hollywood 28, California

D

Dallas Music Co., Inc. (BMI)
c/o A. Soldi
530 East Main Street
El Cajon, California

Dandelion Music Co. (BMI)
1330 West Girard Avenue
Philadelphia 23, Pennsylvania

Charles N. Daniels, Inc. (ASCAP)
11th Floor
1619 Broadway
New York 19, New York

Dara Music Corp. (BMI)
Suite 510
1619 Broadway
New York 19, New York

Dare Music Co. (BMI)
66 Forsythia Lane
Jericho, New York

Dart Music Co. (BMI)
c/o Goddard Music Co.
1453 North Vine Street
Hollywood 28, California

Dartmouth Music, Inc. (ASCAP)
Suite 2160
10 Columbus Circle
New York 19, New York

Daywin Music, Inc. (BMI)
250 North Canon Drive
Beverly Hills, California

Debmar Publishing Co., Inc. (ASCAP)
1320 Vine Street
Philadelphia 7, Pennsylvania

Dee Dee (BMI)
318 West 78th Street
New York 24, New York

Delaware Music Corp. (ASCAP)
1674 Broadway
New York 19, New York

Delmore Music Co. (ASCAP)
550 Fifth Avenue
New York 36, New York

Dena Music, Inc. (ASCAP)
6087 Sunset Boulevard
Hollywood 28, California

Dennis Music Co., Inc. (BMI)
c/o David Blum
2435 South Reese Street
Philadelphia 48, Pennsylvania

Denny Music, Inc. (ASCAP)
146 Seventh Avenue
Nashville, Tennessee

Derry Music Co. (BMI)
240 Stockton Street
San Francisco 8, California

Desert Palms Publishing Co. (BMI)
3703 North Seventh Street
Phoenix, Arizona

Desiard Music Co., Inc. (BMI)
Room 2219
250 West 57th Street
New York 19, New York

Desilu Music Corp. (ASCAP)
119 West 57th Street
New York 19, New York

Devon Music, Inc. (BMI)
Suite 2160
10 Columbus Circle
New York 19, New York

Walt Disney Music Co. (ASCAP)
500 South Buena Vista
Burbank, California

Donna Music Publishing Co. (BMI)
6 Carter Place
Woburn, Massachusetts

Dorothy Music (BMI)
c/o Consolidated Music Sales, Inc.
240 West 55th Street
New York 19, New York

Drive-In Music Co., Inc. (BMI)
7120 Sunset Boulevard
Hollywood 46, California

Duchess Music Corp. (BMI)
322 West 48th Street
New York 36, New York

E

E & M Publishing Co. (BMI)
2674 Steele Street
Memphis 7, Tennessee

Eastwick Music Co. (BMI)
1332 Philadelphia-National Bank Building
Philadelphia 7, Pennsylvania

Ecaroh Music, Inc. (ASCAP)
Suite 14L
400 Central Park West
New York 25, New York

Eden Music, Inc. (BMI)
c/o Clyde Otis
345 West 58th Street
New York 19, New York

Efsee Music, Inc. (BMI)
11th Floor
1619 Broadway
New York 19, New York

Egap Music, Inc. (BMI)
1270 Avenue of the Americas
New York 20, New York

Eldorado Music Co. (BMI)
1717 North Vine Street
Hollywood 28, California

Elizabeth Music (BMI)
c/o Script & Quill, Inc.
Suite 202
8831 Sunset Boulevard
Los Angeles 69, California

Emerald Music Publishing Co. (BMI)
c/o Ann La Vere
5425 West Division Street
Chicago 51, Illinois

Emkay Music (BMI)
c/o Milton Kellem
Wildcat Music, Inc.
Room 603A
1619 Broadway
New York 19, New York

Empress Music, Inc. (ASCAP)
119 West 57th Street
New York 19, New York

Eric Music, Inc. (BMI)
6425 Hollywood Boulevard
Hollywood 28, California

Erosa Music Publishing Corp. (ASCAP)
333 South Windsor Boulevard
Los Angeles 5, California

Erwin-Howard Music Corp. (ASCAP)
c/o Mel Howard
Room 1108
501 Madison Avenue
New York 22, New York

Essex Music, Inc. (ASCAP)
Suite 2160
10 Columbus Circle
New York 19, New York

Estella Music Corp. (BMI)
235 West 46th Street
New York 36, New York

Redd Evans Music Co. (ASCAP)
1619 Broadway
New York 19, New York

Excellorec Music Co. (BMI)
177 Third Avenue North
Nashville, Tennessee

F

Fabulous Music, Inc. (BMI)
11th Floor
1619 Broadway
New York 19, New York

Famous Music Corp. (ASCAP)
1501 Broadway
New York 36, New York

Favorite Music, Inc. (ASCAP)
c/o Patricia Music Publishing Corp.
1631 Broadway
New York 19, New York

Fee Bee Music (BMI)
4517 Wainwright Avenue
Pittsburgh, Pennsylvania

Leo Feist, Inc. (ASCAP)
1540 Broadway
New York 36, New York

Fern Music, Inc. (BMI)
1650 Broadway
New York 19, New York

Figure Music, Inc. (BMI)
c/o Jack Hooke
1631 Broadway
New York 19, New York

Fred Fisher Music Co., Inc. (ASCAP)
1619 Broadway
New York 19, New York

Flair Publishing Co. (BMI)
9317 West Washington Boulevard
Culver City, California

Florence Music Co., Inc. (ASCAP)
609 Fifth Avenue
New York 17, New York

Folkways Music Publishers, Inc. (BMI)
Suite 2160
10 Columbus Circle
New York 19, New York

Forrest Music Corp. (BMI)
c/o Copar-Forrest Music Corp.
11th Floor
1619 Broadway
New York 19, New York

Four Jays Music Co. (ASCAP)
9425 Sunset Boulevard
Beverly Hills, California

Four Star Sales Co. (BMI)
1313 North Vine Street
Hollywood 28, California

Sam Fox Publishing Co., Inc. (ASCAP)
1841 Broadway
New York 23, New York

France Music Co. (BMI)
c/o Éditions Raoul Breton
3 Rue Rossini
Paris 9e, France

Frank Music Corp. (ASCAP)
119 West 57th Street
New York 19, New York

Frederick Music Co. (BMI)
1323 South Michigan Avenue
Chicago 5, Illinois

G

G & H Music Publishing House, Inc. (BMI)
1510 Fairmount Avenue
Philadelphia 30, Pennsylvania

Gale & Gayles, Inc. (BMI)
Suite 1220
250 West 57th Street
New York 19, New York

Gallatin Music Corp. (BMI)
9033 Wilshire Boulevard
Beverly Hills, California

Al Gallico Music Co., Inc. (ASCAP)
c/o Temple Music, Inc.
101 West 55th Street
New York 19, New York

Garland Music, Inc. (ASCAP)
136 East 57th Street
New York 22, New York

Garrawak Music Co. (BMI)
761 Elton Avenue
Bronx 51, New York

General Music Publishing Co., Inc. (ASCAP)
15 East 54th Street
New York 22, New York

Gil Music Corp. (BMI)
c/o George Pincus
1650 Broadway
New York 19, New York

Glad Music Co. (BMI)
314 East 11th Street
Houston, Texas

Gladstone Music, Inc. (ASCAP)
1449 South Michigan Avenue
Chicago, Illinois

Gladys Music, Inc. (ASCAP)
11th Floor
1619 Broadway
New York 19, New York

Jack Gold Music Co. (ASCAP)
1619 Broadway
New York 19, New York

Golden State Songs (BMI)
Box 115
Madison, Tennessee

Golden West Melodies, Inc. (BMI)
1313 North Vine Street
Hollywood 28, California

Granson Music Co. (BMI)
Apartment 7M
345 West 58th Street
New York 19, New York

Gregmark Music Co. (BMI)
1610 North Argyle Avenue
Hollywood 28, California

Greta Music Corp. (BMI)
1619 Broadway
New York 19, New York

H

H & L Music Corp. (BMI)
c/o Patricia Music Publishing Corp.
1631 Broadway
New York 19, New York

Hamblen Music Co., Inc. (BMI)
7740 Mulholland Drive
Los Angeles 46, California

Hanover Music Corp. (ASCAP)
545 Muskingum Place
Pacific Palisades, California

Harman Music, Inc. (ASCAP)
1619 Broadway
New York 19, New York

Harms, Inc. (ASCAP)
488 Madison Avenue
New York 22, New York

Harvard Music, Inc. (BMI)
Room 804
1619 Broadway
New York 19, New York

Harwin Music Corp. (ASCAP)
31 West 54th Street
New York 19, New York

Hastings Music Corp. (BMI)
1540 Broadway
New York 36, New York

Hawthorne Music Corp. (ASCAP)
c/o Joy Music, Inc.
1790 Broadway
New York 19, New York

Hecht & Buzzell, Inc. (ASCAP)
119 West 57th Street
New York 19, New York

Neal Hefti Music, Inc. (ASCAP)
c/o International Korwin Corp.
57 West 56th Street
New York 19, New York

Helayne Music Publishing Co., Inc. (ASCAP)
475 Fifth Avenue
New York 17, New York

Hermosa Music Corp. (BMI)
8715 West Third Street
Los Angeles 48, California

High Society Music Publishers (BMI)
3006 Halldale
Los Angeles 18, California

Higuera Publishing Co. (BMI)
8479 Higuera Road
Culver City, California

Hill and Range Songs, Inc. (BMI)
11th Floor
1619 Broadway
New York 19, New York

Hillary Music, Inc. (BMI)
1481 North Vine Street
Hollywood 28, California

Hilliard Music Co. (BMI)
c/o Maury Foladare
1717 North Highland Avenue
Hollywood 28, California

Hi-Lo Music, Inc. (BMI)
639 Madison Avenue
Memphis, Tennessee

Hollis Music, Inc. (BMI)
Suite 2160
10 Columbus Circle
New York 19, New York

Home Folks Music, Inc. (BMI)
11th Floor
1619 Broadway
New York 19, New York

The Hub Music Co. (ASCAP)
c/o Edward Traubner
132 South Rodeo Drive
Beverly Hills, California

Hubert Music Corp. (ASCAP)
322 West 48th Street
New York 36, New York

I

Iris-Trojan Music Corp. (BMI)
37 West 57th Street
New York 19, New York

Island Music Publishing Co. (BMI)
15609 Damon Avenue
Cleveland 10, Ohio

Islip Music Publishing Co. (BMI)
c/o Bill Doggett
120 West Bayberry Road
Islip, Long Island, New York

J

Jaglea Music Co. (BMI)
Room 1203
1650 Broadway
New York 19, New York

Jamie Music Publishing Co. (BMI)
1330 West Girard Avenue
Philadelphia 23, Pennsylvania

Jamil Music (BMI)
c/o J. D. Miller
118 North Parkerson Avenue
Crowley, Louisiana

The Janfra Music Publishing Co. (ASCAP)
162-01 Powell's Cove Boulevard
Beechhurst, New York

January Music Corp. (BMI)
1650 Broadway
New York 19, New York

Jason Music, Inc. (BMI)
Suite 404
157 West 57th Street
New York 19, New York

Jat Music, Inc. (BMI)
c/o Golden West Melodies, Inc.
1313 North Vine Street
Hollywood 28, California

Jatap Publishing Co., Inc. (BMI)
451 North Canon Drive
Beverly Hills, California

Jay & Cee Music Corp. (BMI)
c/o Lois Publishing Co.
1540 Brewster Avenue
Cincinnati 7, Ohio

Jaymar Music Publishing Co., Inc. (ASCAP)
c/o Martin Mills Enterprises, Inc.
1619 Broadway
New York 19, New York

Jec Publishing Corp. (BMI)
c/o J. Cuoghi
308 Poplar Avenue
Memphis, Tennessee

Jefferson Music Co., Inc. (ASCAP)
1619 Broadway
New York 19, New York

Jimskip Music, Inc. (BMI)
Ninth Floor
136 West 52nd Street
New York 19, New York

Jobete Music Co., Inc. (BMI)
c/o Berry Gordy, Jr.
2648 West Grand Boulevard
Detroit, Michigan

Johnstone-Montei, Inc. (BMI)
6087 Sunset Boulevard
Hollywood 28, California

David Jones, Inc. (BMI)
c/o Carlton Record Corp.
345 West 58th Street
New York 19, New York

Jonware Music Corp. (BMI)
c/o Jack Pearl
515 Madison Avenue
New York 22, New York

Jot Music Co. (BMI)
2203 Spruce Street
Philadelphia 3, Pennsylvania

Joy Music, Inc. (ASCAP)
1790 Broadway
New York 19, New York

Jubilee Music (ASCAP)
609 Fifth Avenue
New York 17, New York

Ross Jungnickel, Inc. (ASCAP)
11th Floor
1619 Broadway
New York 19, New York

K

Kags Music (BMI)
c/o Allen Klein & Co.
1271 Avenue of the Americas
New York 19, New York

Kalmann Music, Inc. (ASCAP)
300 Farwood Road
Philadelphia 51, Pennsylvania

Kamar Publishing Co. (BMI)
Box 115
Madison, Tennessee

Edward Kassner Music Co., Inc. (ASCAP)
756 Seventh Avenue
New York 19, New York

Kavelin Music (BMI)
7250 Beverly Boulevard
Los Angeles 36, California

Keel Music Co. (BMI)
1595 Broadway
New York 36, New York

Kemo Music Co. (BMI)
Room 205
6087 Sunset Boulevard
Hollywood 28, California

Kentucky Music, Inc. (BMI)
11th Floor
1619 Broadway
New York 19, New York

Kingsway Music Corp. (ASCAP)
11th Floor
1619 Broadway
New York 19, New York

Knickerbocker Music Co., Inc. (ASCAP)
453 McLean Avenue
Yonkers, New York

Knollwood Music Corp. (ASCAP)
1619 Broadway
New York 19, New York

Knox Music, Inc. (BMI)
639 Madison Avenue
Memphis, Tennessee

Korwin Music, Inc. (ASCAP)
57 West 56th Street
New York 19, New York

L

La Salle Music Publishers, Inc. (ASCAP)
1619 Broadway
New York 19, New York

Lakeview Music Corp. (BMI)
1631 Broadway
New York 19, New York

Lancaster Music Publications, Inc. (BMI)
806 16th Avenue South
Nashville, Tennessee

Lansdale Music Corp. (BMI)
c/o Nicholas A. Busillo
1023 North 67th Street
Philadelphia 31, Pennsylvania

Laurel Music Corp. (ASCAP)
22 West 48th Street
New York 36, New York

Lear Music, Inc. (ASCAP)
1270 Avenue of the Americas
New York 20, New York

Leeds Music Corp. (ASCAP)
322 West 48th Street
New York 36, New York

Limax Music, Inc. (BMI)
618 South Ridgeley Drive
Los Angeles 36, California

Lion Music Corp. (ASCAP)
1540 Broadway
New York 36, New York

Lion Publishing Co., Inc. (BMI)
c/o Don Robey
2809 Erastus Street
Houston, Texas

Livingston & Evans, Inc. (ASCAP)
156 East 62nd Street
New York 21, New York

Livingston & Evans Music Co. (ASCAP)
1003 Sunset-Vine Tower Building
Hollywood 28, California

Liza Music Corp. (ASCAP)
1700 Broadway
New York 19, New York

Llee Corp. (BMI)
c/o Lee V. Eastman
39 West 54th Street
New York 19, New York

Lloyd and Logan, Inc. (BMI)
c/o Andrew J. Feinman
608 Fifth Avenue
New York 20, New York

Lois Publishing Co. (BMI)
1540 Brewster Avenue
Cincinnati 7, Ohio

Lombardo Music, Inc. (ASCAP)
1619 Broadway
New York 19, New York

Longhorn Music Co. (BMI)
1902 Leeland Street
Houston 3, Texas

Lowe Music Corp. (ASCAP)
1721 East Tulpehocken Street
Philadelphia, Pennsylvania

Lowery Music Co. (BMI)
c/o Bill Lowery
Post Office Box 9687
North Atlanta, Georgia

Ludlow Music, Inc. (BMI)
Suite 2160
10 Columbus Circle
New York 19, New York

M

M & M Music Co. (BMI)
c/o Monument Music
Attention: Larry Uttal
141 East 88th Street
New York 28, New York

M.J.Q. Music, Inc. (BMI)
Suite 4C
881 Tenth Avenue
New York 19, New York

MRC Music, Inc. (BMI)
35 East Wacker Drive
Chicago 1, Illinois

McGraw Music Co. (ASCAP)
111 Main Street
Salem, Virginia

Jimmy McHugh Music, Inc. (ASCAP)
6381 Hollywood Boulevard
Hollywood 28, California

Maggie Music Co., Inc. (BMI)
Room 715
1650 Broadway
New York 19, New York

Magnolia Publishing Co. (BMI)
14155 Magnolia Boulevard
Van Nuys, California

Malapi Music (BMI)
c/o Loy M. Clingman
4625 North 50th Drive
Glendale, Arizona

Mallory Music Publications (BMI)
c/o Woodhaven Farms
Little New York Road
Route 1
Alexander City, Alabama

Mansion Music Corp. (ASCAP)
136 West 52nd Street
New York 19, New York

Maple Leaf Music Publishing Co., Inc. (BMI)
1650 Broadway
New York 19, New York

Mara-Lane Music Corp. (ASCAP)
609 Fifth Avenue
New York 17, New York

Maravilla Music, Inc. (BMI)
6277 Selma Avenue
Hollywood 28, California

Maraville Music Corp. (ASCAP)
Room 716
1619 Broadway
New York 19, New York

Marielle Music Publishing Corp. (BMI)
119 West 57th Street
New York 19, New York

Mark VII Music (ASCAP)
4024 Radford
North Hollywood, California

Edward B. Marks Music Corp. (BMI)
136 West 52nd Street
New York 19, New York

Marlen Music Co. (ASCAP)
408 North Rodeo Drive
Beverly Hills, California

Marlong Music Corp. (ASCAP)
1650 Broadway
New York 19, New York

Kenny Marlow (BMI)
c/o Grille Music
617 Exchange Building
Nashville, Tennessee

Mack Martin Music Co. (BMI)
c/o Mack Martin
Brevoort Hotel
6326 Lexington
Hollywood 38, California

Marty's Music Corp. (BMI)
713 18th Avenue
South Nashville, Tennessee

Marvin Music Co. (ASCAP)
1619 Broadway
New York 19, New York

Massey Music Co., Inc. (ASCAP)
c/o Braunstein & Chernin
270 Madison Avenue
New York 16, New York

Johnny Mathis Music, Inc. (ASCAP)
11th Floor
1619 Broadway
New York 19, New York

Maureen Music, Inc. (BMI)
c/o Old Town Record Corp.
1697 Broadway
New York 19, New York

The Peter Maurice Music Co., Ltd. (ASCAP)
1619 Broadway
New York 19, New York

Maxwell Music Corp. (ASCAP)
1 Washington Square
Larchmont, New York

Ray Maxwell Music Publishing Co. (BMI)
Suite 300A
1800 North Argyle Avenue
Hollywood 28, California

May Music, Inc. (ASCAP)
11th Floor
1619 Broadway
New York 19, New York

Mayfair Music Corp. (ASCAP)
31 West 54th Street
New York 19, New York

Maypole Music, Inc. (ASCAP)
200 West 57th Street
New York 19, New York

Robert Mellin, Inc. (BMI)
1650 Broadway
New York 19, New York

Mellin Music, Inc. (BMI)
1650 Broadway
New York 19, New York

Mellow Music Publishing Co. (BMI)
Suite 305
1650 Broadway
New York 19, New York

Melody Lane Publications, Inc. (BMI)
1619 Broadway
New York 19, New York

Melody Trails, Inc. (BMI)
Suite 2160
10 Columbus Circle
New York 19, New York

Melrose Music Corp. (ASCAP)
31 West 54th Street
New York 19, New York

Mercedes Music Co. (BMI)
c/o Hunter Hancock
1554 North Gower Street
Hollywood 28, California

Merrimac Music Corp. (BMI)
1619 Broadway
New York 19, New York

Metric Music Co. (BMI)
6920 Sunset Boulevard
Hollywood 28, California

Michele Publishing Co. (BMI)
6724 Allott Avenue
Van Nuys, California

Midway Music Co. (ASCAP)
157 West 57th Street
New York 19, New York

Milber Enterprises Corp.
Address unknown

Milene Music (ASCAP)
2510 Franklin Road
Nashville 4, Tennessee

The Military Service Publishing Co.
Harrisburg, Pennsylvania

Bob Miller, Inc. (ASCAP)
c/o Leeds Music Corp.
322 West 48th Street
New York 36, New York

Miller Music Corp. (ASCAP)
1540 Broadway
New York 36, New York

Mills Music, Inc. (ASCAP)
1619 Broadway
New York 19, New York

Modern Music Publishing Co. (BMI)
9317 West Washington Boulevard
Culver City, California

Ivan Mogull Music Corp. (ASCAP)
1619 Broadway
New York 19, New York

Monarch Music Corp. (ASCAP)
Penthouse Suite
465 South Beverly Drive
Beverly Hills, California

Montauk Music, Inc. (BMI)
c/o Belle Nardone
1650 Broadway
New York 19, New York

Montclare Music Corp. (BMI)
Suite 407
1800 North Argyle Avenue
Hollywood 28, California

Monument Music, Inc. (BMI)
c/o Larry Uttal
141 East 88th Street
New York 28, New York

Moonlight Music, Inc. (BMI)
9155 Sunset Boulevard
Hollywood 46, California

Moorpark Music Corp. (ASCAP)
c/o Marielle Music Publishing Corp.
119 West 57th Street
New York 19, New York

Edwin H. Morris & Co., Inc. (ASCAP)
31 West 54th Street
New York 19, New York

Muirfield Music Corp. (ASCAP)
Suite 1220
250 West 57th Street
New York 19, New York

Munson Music Co. (BMI)
c/o Brent Music Corp.
Suite 905
2 West 45th Street
New York 36, New York

Music World Corp. (BMI)
Suite 409
6087 Sunset Boulevard
Hollywood 28, California

Myers Music (ASCAP)
1920 Chestnut Street
Philadelphia, Pennsylvania

Myra Music Co. (BMI)
c/o Paul Landersman
416 Butternut Court
Orange, Connecticut

N

Neil Music, Inc. (BMI)
8566 Sunset Boulevard
Hollywood 46, California

Ninny Publishing Co. (BMI)
c/o Paul Winley
205 West 84th Street
New York 24, New York

Nom Music, Inc. (BMI)
c/o Patricia Music Publishing Corp.
1631 Broadway
New York 19, New York

Noma Music, Inc. (BMI)
11th Floor
1619 Broadway
New York 19, New York

Nor Va Jak Music, Inc. (BMI)
1313 West Seventh Street
Clovis, New Mexico

Norbay Music, Inc. (BMI)
185 North Wabash Avenue
Chicago 1, Illinois

Northern Music Corp. (ASCAP)
445 Park Avenue
New York 22, New York

Northridge Music, Inc. (ASCAP)
11567 Sunshine Terrace
Studio City, California

O

Obie Music, Inc. (BMI)
c/o Roosevelt Music Co., Inc.
Room 408
1650 Broadway
New York 19, New York

Octave Music Publishing Corp. (ASCAP)
520 Fifth Avenue
New York 36, New York

Odette Music Corp. (ASCAP)
c/o Gelene Blum
3900 Greystone Avenue
Riverdale 63, New York

Sy Oliver Music Corp. (BMI)
c/o Lee V. Eastman
39 West 54th Street
New York 19, New York

Open Road Music, Inc. (BMI)
Post Office Box 128
Madison, Tennessee

Oriole Music Corp. (ASCAP)
9157 Sunset Boulevard
Hollywood 46, California

Orten Music Co. (ASCAP)
c/o N. O. Wells
634 Elmgate Drive
Glenview, Illinois

Oval Music Co. (BMI)
c/o Murray Wizzell
15 Central Park West
New York 23, New York

P

Palm Springs Music Co. (ASCAP)
1601 North Gower Street
Hollywood 28, California

Palmina Music (BMI)
Division of Request Music, Inc.
c/o Anthony S. Mammarella
1703 Jackson Street
Philadelphia 45, Pennsylvania

Pambill Music, Inc. (ASCAP)
345 West 58th Street
New York 19, New York

Pamco Music, Inc. (BMI)
c/o Irwin Garr
Room 1401
1501 Broadway
New York 36, New York

Pamper Music, Inc. (BMI)
119 Two Mile Pike
Post Office Box 96
Goodletsville, Tennessee

Panther Music Corp. (ASCAP)
1619 Broadway
New York 19, New York

Paramount Music Corp. (ASCAP)
1619 Broadway
New York 19, New York

Paramount-Roy Rogers Music Co., Inc. (ASCAP)
1619 Broadway
New York 19, New York

Parkwood Music Co. (BMI)
25615 Parkwood Drive
Huntington Woods, Michigan

Patricia Music Publishing Corp. (BMI)
1631 Broadway
New York 19, New York

Patsy Ann Music (BMI)
Suite 411
Forrest Hotel
224 West 49th Street
New York 19, Ne wYork

George Paxton, Inc. (ASCAP)
1619 Broadway
New York 19, New York

Paxton Music, Inc. (ASCAP)
1619 Broadway
New York 19, New York

Paxwin Music Corp. (BMI)
1619 Broadway
New York 19, New York

Pearl Music Co., Inc. (BMI)
Suite 1012
1619 Broadway
New York 19, New York

Peer International Corp. (BMI)
1619 Broadway
New York 19, New York

Pemora Music Co., Inc. (BMI)
1619 Broadway
New York 19, New York

Penron Music Publications (BMI)
c/o Ronald J. Hargrove
1923 Foothill Drive
Glendale 1, California

Pickwick Music Corp. (ASCAP)
322 West 48th Street
New York 36, New York

George Pincus Music Corp. (ASCAP)
1650 Broadway
New York 19, New York

Pinelawn Music Publishing Co., Inc. (BMI)
Room 501
756 Seventh Avenue
New York 19, New York

Pioneer Publishing Co. (BMI)
8665 Wilshire Boulevard
Beverly Hills, California

Planemar Music Co. (BMI)
56 Ferry Street
Newark, New Jersey

Planetary Music Publishing Corp. (ASCAP)
1631 Broadway
New York 19, New York

Play Music, Inc. (BMI)
c/o Clyde Otis
345 West 58th Street
New York 19, New York

Plymouth Music Co., Inc. (ASCAP)
1841 Broadway
New York 23, New York

Pontra Music Corp. (BMI)
3703 North Seventh Street
Phoenix, Arizona

Porgie Music Corp. (BMI)
1619 Broadway
New York 19, New York

Post Music, Inc. (ASCAP)
6425 Hollywood Boulevard
Hollywood 28, California

Elvis Presley Music, Inc. (BMI)
11th Floor
1619 Broadway
New York 19, New York

Theodore Presser Co. (ASCAP)
Presser Place
Bryn Mawr, Pennsylvania

Prestige Music Co., Inc. (BMI)
203 South Washington Avenue
Bergenfield, New Jersey

Prigan Music Corp. (BMI)
c/o Andrew J. Feinman
608 Fifth Avenue
New York 20, New York

Prince Music (BMI)
c/o Robert Prince
111-35 76th Avenue
Forest Hills, New York

Princess Music Publishing Corp. (ASCAP)
1650 Broadway
New York 19, New York

Progressive Music Publishing Co., Inc. (BMI)
11th Floor
1619 Broadway
New York 19, New York

Putnam Music, Inc. (ASCAP)
609 Fifth Avenue
New York 17, New York

Q

Quintet Music, Inc. (BMI)
11th Floor
1619 Broadway
New York 19, New York

R

R.F.D. Music Publishing Co. (ASCAP)
1619 Broadway
New York 19, New York

R-T Publishing Co. (BMI)
c/o Lois Publishing Co.
1540 Brewster Avenue
Cincinnati 7, Ohio

Ragtime Music Corp. (ASCAP)
c/o Al Greiner
1697 Broadway
New York 19, New York

Raleigh Music, Inc. (BMI)
c/o Dave Dreyer
345 West 58th Street
New York 19, New York

Rambed Publishing Co., Inc. (BMI)
1320 Vine Street
Philadelphia 7, Pennsylvania

Randy-Smith Music Corp. (ASCAP)
3941 Woodlawn Drive
Nashville, Tennessee

Fred Raphael Music, Inc. (ASCAP)
6758 Colgate Avenue
Los Angeles, California

Rayven Music Co., Inc. (BMI)
c/o Duke Niles
Room 1115
1650 Broadway
New York 19, New York

Recordo Music Publishers (BMI)
c/o Leon René
6359 Selma Avenue
Hollywood 28. California

Red River Songs, Inc. (BMI)
1001 North Lincoln Street
Burbank, California

Regent Music Corp. (BMI)
1619 Broadway
New York 19, New York

Reliance Music Corp. (ASCAP)
1619 Broadway
New York 19, New York

Remick Music Corp. (ASCAP)
488 Madison Avenue
New York 22, New York

Renda Music Publishers (BMI)
3703 North Seventh Street
Phoenix, Arizona

Leon René Publications (ASCAP)
6359 Selma Avenue
Hollywood 28, California

Republic Music Corp. (BMI)
1619 Broadway
New York 19, New York

Rice Mill Publishing Co., Inc. (BMI)
1405 Locust Street
Philadelphia, Pennsylvania

Ridgeway Music (BMI)
6087 Sunset Boulevard
Hollywood 28, California

Rio Grande Music, Inc. (BMI)
11th Floor
1619 Broadway
New York 19, New York

Tex Ritter Music Publications, Inc. (ASCAP)
1491 North Vine Street
Hollywood 28, California

J. J. Robbins, Inc. (ASCAP)
240 West 55th Street
New York 19, New York

Robbins Music Corp. (ASCAP)
1540 Broadway
New York 36, New York

Robert Music Corp. (ASCAP)
1650 Broadway
New York 19, New York

Robin-Styne Music Corp. (ASCAP)
c/o Katz, Moselle, and Schier
608 Fifth Avenue
New York 20, New York

Rockaway Music Corp. (BMI)
c/o Jack Hooke
1631 Broadway
New York 19, New York

Rockland Music Corp. (BMI)
Suite 905
2 West 45th Street
New York 36, New York

Roger Music, Inc. (ASCAP)
1790 Broadway
New York 19, New York

Roncom Music Co. (ASCAP)
405 Park Avenue
New York 22, New York

Rondo Music (BMI)
Post Office Box 2367
Hollywood 28, California

Mickey Rooney Publishing Co. (ASCAP)
c/o Spina Music
2232 Vista Del Mar Place
Hollywood 28, California

Roosevelt Music Co., Inc. (BMI)
Room 408
1650 Broadway
New York 19, New York

Rosarita Music, Inc. (ASCAP)
11th Floor
1619 Broadway
New York 19, New York

Fred Rose Music, Inc. (BMI)
2510 Franklin Road
Nashville, Tennessee

Rosemeadow Publishing Corp. (ASCAP)
1619 Broadway
New York 19, New York

Roxbury Music Co. (ASCAP)
58 Cheney Street
Roxbury, Massachusetts

Rugby Music Corp.
31 West 54th Street
New York 19, New York

Rumbalero Music, Inc. (BMI)
11th Floor
1619 Broadway
New York 19, New York

Rush Music Corp. (BMI)
Room 501
756 Seventh Avenue
New York 19, New York

Rylan Music Corp. (ASCAP)
c/o Philip Becker
545 Fifth Avenue
New York 17, New York

S

St. Louis Music Corp. (BMI)
11th Floor
1619 Broadway
New York 19, New York

Sanga Music, Inc. (BMI)
Room 901
200 West 57th Street
New York 19, New York

Saturn Music, Inc. (BMI)
Suite 1405
1650 Broadway
New York 19, New York

Saunders Publications, Inc. (ASCAP)
119 West 57th Street
New York 19, New York

Savoy Music Co. (BMI)
56 Ferry Street
Newark, New Jersey

G. Schirmer, Inc. (ASCAP)
609 Fifth Avenue
New York 17, New York

Schwartz Music Co., Inc. (ASCAP)
34 West 45th Street
New York 36, New York

Screen Gems-Columbia Music, Inc. (BMI)
711 Fifth Avenue
New York 22, New York

Sea-Lark Enterprises, Inc. (BMI)
1650 Broadway
New York 19, New York

Selma Music Corp. (BMI)
Box 461
150 Hunting Lodge Drive
Miami Springs, Florida

Shag Publications (BMI)
1861 West Adams Boulevard
Los Angeles, California

Shapiro, Bernstein & Co., Inc. (ASCAP)
666 Fifth Avenue
New York 19, New York

Shari Music Publishing Corp. (ASCAP)
c/o Belafonte Enterprises
157 West 57th Street
New York 19, New York

Sharina Music Co. (BMI)
654-660 Chelsea
Memphis, Tennessee

Shawnee Press, Inc. (ASCAP)
Delaware Water Gap
Pennsylvania

Sherwin Music, Inc. (ASCAP)
1650 Broadway
New York 19, New York

Sigma Music, Inc. (ASCAP)
11th Floor
1619 Broadway
New York 19, New York

Signet Music Co. (BMI)
1674 Broadway
New York 19, New York

Silhouette Music Corp. (ASCAP)
1842 West Avenue
Miami Beach, Florida

Silver Star Music Publishing Co. (BMI)
810 Church Street
Nashville 3, Tennessee

George Simon, Inc. (ASCAP)
1619 Broadway
New York 19, New York

Simon House, Inc. (BMI)
1619 Broadway
New York 19, New York

Singing River Publishing Co., Inc. (BMI)
c/o Marion Carpenter
210 Thomas Street
Biloxi, Mississippi

Singleton Music, Inc. (BMI)
c/o Roosevelt Music Co., Inc.
Room 408
1650 Broadway
New York 19, New York

Singular Music Publishing Co., Inc. (BMI)
Room 201, Schubert Building
250 South Broad Street
Philadelphia 2, Pennsylvania

Skidmore Music Co., Inc. (ASCAP)
666 Fifth Avenue
New York 19, New York

Snapper Music, Inc. (BMI)
1631 Broadway
New York 19, New York

Snyder Music Corp. (ASCAP)
6308 Sunset Boulevard
Hollywood, California

Sophisticate Music, Inc. (BMI)
1619 Broadway
New York 19, New York

Sounds Music Co. (ASCAP)
301 East 47th Street
New York 17, New York

Southern Belle Music Publishers (BMI)
3324 West End Avenue
Nashville, Tennessee

Southern Music Publishing Co., Inc. (ASCAP)
1619 Broadway
New York 19, New York

Spanka Music Corp. (BMI)
c/o William Lazarow
119 West 57th Street
New York 19, New York

Larry Spier, Inc. (ASCAP)
1650 Broadway
New York 19, New York

Spina Music (ASCAP)
2232 Vista Del Mar Place
Hollywood 28, California

Spinning Wheel Music Corp. (BMI)
c/o Milton Somerfield
511 Fifth Avenue
New York 17, New York

Spoone Music Corp. (ASCAP)
1271 Avenue of the Americas
New York 19, New York

Starday Music (BMI)
c/o Don Pierce
Box 115
Madison, Tennessee

Starfire Music Corp. (BMI)
c/o Milton Somerfield
511 Fifth Avenue
New York 17, New York

Starrite Publishing Co. (BMI)
311 East 11th Street
Houston, Texas

Starstan Music Corp. (BMI)
Suite 1150
742 South Hill Street
Los Angeles 14, California

Stratford Music Corp. (ASCAP)
609 Fifth Avenue
New York 17, New York

Studio Music Co. (BMI)
c/o Levington Music Co.
157 West 57th Street
New York 19, New York

Suffolk Music, Inc. (BMI)
Suite 2160
10 Columbus Circle
New York 19, New York

Summit Music Corp. (ASCAP)
1619 Broadway
New York 19, New York

Sunbeam Music Corp.. (BMI)
22 West 48th Street
New York 36, New York

Sundown Music Co. (BMI)
2437 West 34th Place
Chicago 8, Illinois

Sure-Fire Music Co., Inc. (BMI)
801 16th Avenue South
Nashville, Tennessee

Sweco Music Corp. (BMI)
250 West 57th Street
New York 19, New York

Sylvia Music Publishing Co., Inc. (BMI)
Room 510
1650 Broadway
New York 19, New York

Symphony House Music Publishers Corp. (ASCAP)
c/o Paul Siegel Productions
Tauentzien Strasse 16
Berlin W.30, West Germany

T

T.M. Music, Inc. (BMI)
Suite 906
1619 Broadway
New York 19, New York

TNT Music, Inc. (BMI)
1422 West Poplar Street
San Antonio 9, Texas

Tannen Music, Inc. (BMI)
Suite 7A
850 Seventh Avenue
New York 19, New York

Tee Pee Music Co., Inc. (ASCAP)
1650 Broadway
New York 19, New York

Temple Music, Inc. (ASCAP)
101 West 55th Street
New York 19, New York

Tempo Music, Inc. (ASCAP)
52 West 58th Street
New York 19, New York

Texoma Music Corp. (ASCAP)
Box 74A
Route 1
Park Hill, Oklahoma

Thelonious Music (BMI)
69-45 108th Street
Forest Hills 75, New York

Kay Thompson Music, Inc. (ASCAP)
c/o Frank L. Ippolito
152 West 42nd Street
New York 36, New York

Thunderbird Music, Inc. (ASCAP)
6515 Sunset Boulevard
Hollywood, California

Tideland Music Publishing Corp. (BMI)
Room 501
756 Seventh Avenue
New York 19, New York

Tiger Music, Inc. (BMI)
11th Floor
1619 Broadway
New York 19, New York

Time Music Co., Inc. (BMI)
Room 810
1790 Broadway
New York 19, New York

Top Notch Music Corp. (ASCAP)
1619 Broadway
New York 19, New York

Town and Country Music, Inc. (BMI)
756 Seventh Avenue
New York 19, New York

Travis Music Co. (BMI)
c/o Imperial Records, Inc.
6425 Hollywood Boulevard
Hollywood 28, California

Tray Music Corp. (ASCAP)
756 Seventh Avenue
New York 19, New York

Tredlew Music, Inc. (BMI)
200 West 57th Street
New York 19, New York

Tree Publishing Co., Inc. (BMI)
905 16th Avenue South
Nashville, Tennessee

Tricky Music, Inc. (ASCAP)
1631 Broadway
New York 19, New York

Ernest Tubb Music, Inc. (BMI)
11th Floor
1619 Broadway
New York 19, New York

Tweed Music Co. (ASCAP)
Apartment 8D
10 West 74th Street
New York 23, New York

Tylerson Music Co. (ASCAP)
1270 Avenue of the Americas
New York 20, New York

U

Ultra Music (BMI)
8268 Sunset Boulevard
Los Angeles 46, California

United Music Corp. (ASCAP)
101 West 55th Street
New York 19, New York

V

Valando Music Corp. (ASCAP)
22 West 48th Street
New York 36, New York

Valley Brook Publications, Inc. (ASCAP)
2733 Kensington Avenue
Philadelphia 34, Pennsylvania

Valley Entertainment Enterprises, Inc. (ASCAP)
2357 Edelweiss Drive
Beverly Hills, California

Valley Publishers, Inc. (BMI)
11th Floor
1619 Broadway
New York 19, New York

Valleydale Music, Inc. (BMI)
1619 Broadway
New York 19, New York

Valyr Music Corp. (ASCAP)
c/o Philip Becker
545 Fifth Avenue
New York 17, New York

Vanderbuilt Music Corp. (ASCAP)
c/o Al Lewis
2 Horatio Street
New York 14, New York

Vanguard Songs (BMI)
6087 Sunset Boulevard
Hollywood 28, California

Venice Music, Inc. (BMI)
8300 Santa Monica Boulevard
Hollywood 69, California

Vernon Music Corp. (ASCAP)
1619 Broadway
New York 19, New York

Vicki Music, Inc. (BMI)
20 West Alexandrine
Detroit 1, Michigan

Victory Music Co. (BMI)
Room 604
1674 Broadway
New York 19, New York

Village Music Co. (BMI)
c/o Sid Prosen
37-11 87th Street
Jackson Heights, New York

Vincent Music Co., Inc. (BMI)
1323 South Michigan Avenue
Chicago 5, Illinois

Vogue Music, Inc. (BMI)
2444 Wilshire Boulevard
Santa Monica, California

Volkwein Brothers, Inc. (ASCAP)
632-634 Liberty Avenue
Pittsburgh 22, Pennsylvania

W

W & K Publishing Corp. (BMI)
77-08 Broadway
Elmhurst 73, New York

Walden Music Corp. (ASCAP)
1841 Broadway
New York 23, New York

Walton Music Corp. (ASCAP)
12069 Ventura Place
North Hollywood, California

Billy Ward Music Co. (BMI)
1111 South Robertson Boulevard
Los Angeles 35, California

Warden Music Co., Inc. (BMI)
Box 8061
Nashville 7, Tennessee

Warock Music, Inc. (ASCAP)
400 Madison Avenue
New York 17, New York

Harry Warren Music, Inc. (ASCAP)
c/o Four Jays Music Co.
9425 Sunset Boulevard
Beverly Hills, California

Wayne Music Publishing Co. (BMI)
c/o Arnett Cobb
292 Washington Place
Englewood, New Jersey

We Three Music, Inc. (BMI)
1650 Broadway
New York 19, New York

Weiss & Barry, Inc. (BMI)
1556 North La Brea
Hollywood, California

Sam Weiss Music, Inc. (ASCAP)
6087 Sunset Boulevard
Hollywood 28, California

Wemar Music Corp. (BMI)
1619 Broadway
New York 19, New York

West-Higgins Publishing Co. (BMI)
c/o Robert West
2930 Boston Boulevard
Detroit 6, Michigan

Whitney-Kramer-Zaret Music Co. (ASCAP)
1650 Broadway
New York 19, New York

Wildcat Music, Inc. (BMI)
c/o Milton Kellem
1619 Broadway
New York 19, New York

Wildwood Music, Inc. (BMI)
c/o Personality Productions, Inc.
30 West 60th Street
New York 23, New York

Slim Willet Songs (BMI)
9109 Sunset Boulevard
Hollywood 46, California

Dootsie Williams, Inc. (BMI)
9512 South Central Avenue
Los Angeles 2, California

Kae Williams Music, Inc. (BMI)
3214 West York Street
Philadelphia 32, Pennsylvania

Williamson Music, Inc. (ASCAP)
609 Fifth Avenue
New York 17, New York

Bob Wills Music, Inc. (BMI)
11th Floor
1619 Broadway
New York 19, New York

Wintergreen Music, Inc. (ASCAP)
162 East 55th Street
New York 22, New York

M. Witmark & Sons (ASCAP)
488 Madison Avenue
New York 22, New York

Wizell & Day Music Corp. (ASCAP)
c/o Robert Day
6 North View Place
White Plains, New York

Wolf-Mills Music, Inc. (ASCAP)
Suite 109
6223 Selma Avenue
Hollywood 28, California

Wonder Music Co., Inc. (BMI)
Post Office Box 9687
Atlanta 19, Georgia

Wonderland Music Co. (BMI)
c/o James A. Johnson
500 South Buena Vista Street
Burbank, California

The B. F. Wood Music Co., Inc. (ASCAP)
1619 Broadway
New York 19, New York

World Music, Inc. (ASCAP)
1619 Broadway
New York 19, New York

Y

Victor Young Publications, Inc. (ASCAP)
c/o Chappell & Co., Inc.
609 Fifth Avenue
New York 17, New York

Z

Zodiac Music Corp. (BMI)
1733 Broadway
New York 19, New York

About the Editor

Nat Shapiro is co-editor of two standard jazz works, *Hear Me Talkin' to Ya* and *The Jazz Makers;* a frequent contributor to music periodicals in the United States and abroad; and a prolific annotator of record albums. For nearly two decades, he has been active in the creation, promotion, and production of popular music as press agent, editor, music publisher, and artists and repertoire man. As Director of International Recording and Music Publishing Operations for Columbia Records, Inc., he has produced and co-produced recordings in the United States, France, England, Holland, Germany, Italy, Spain, Argentina, Brazil, and Mexico with such artists as Lotte Lenya, Marlene Dietrich, Yves Montand, Mahalia Jackson, Michel Legrand, Miles Davis, and Jacqueline Francois, as well as original-cast albums of *The Importance of Being Oscar,* with Micheál MacLiammóir, and the Spanish-language production of *My Fair Lady*. He is currently working on a new book, *Dear, They're Playing Our Song,* a "nostalgic history" of American popular music.